New
Venture
Strategies
Revised Edition

Karl H. Vesper

University of Washington

PRENTICE HALL, Englewood

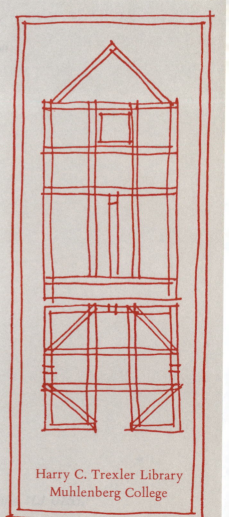

Library of Congress Cataloging-in-Publication Data

Vesper, Karl H.
New venture strategies / Karl H. Vesper.—Rev. ed.
    p.   cm.
Bibliography: p.
Includes index.
ISBN 0-13-615907-9
1. New business enterprises. 2. Entrepreneurship. I. Title.
HD62.5.V47 1990
658.1'1—dc19   88-36900
                                            CIP

Interior Design: Pam Wilder
Editorial/production supervision: Nancy Farrell
Cover design: Wanda Lubelska
Manufacturing buyer: Ed O'Dougherty

©1990, 1980 by Prentice-Hall, Inc.,
A Division of Simon & Schuster
Englewood Cliffs, New Jersey 07632

Printed in the United States of America

10 9 8 7 6 5 4 3

ISBN   0-13-615907-9

PRENTICE-HALL INTERNATIONAL, INC., *London*
PRENTICE-HALL OF AUSTRALIA, PTY. LIMITED, *Sidney*
PRENTICE-HALL OF CANADA LTD., *Toronto*
PRENTICE-HALL OF INDIA PRIVATE LIMITED, *New Delhi*
PRENTICE-HALL OF JAPAN, INC., *Tokyo*
PRENTICE-HALL OF SOUTHEAST ASIA PTE. LTD., *Singapore*
WHITEHALL BOOKS LIMITED, *Wellington, New Zealand*

To
Karl C. Vesper,
my father and
favorite entrepreneur

Contents

PREFACE   viii

1   PERSPECTIVES ON ENTREPRENEURSHIP   1

Types of Entrepreneurs   2
Individuals and Teams, 8

Entrepreneurship Versus Fraud   8

Areas of Study   9
The Entrepreneur, 9
Venture Types, 14
Entrepreneurship and the Environment, 16

Entrepreneurial Work   17
Advisability, 19

Happenstance Versus Planning   22

Advance Study   25

Summary   28

2   SUCCESS AND FAILURE FACTORS   29

Measuring Success   31
Influence of Industry, 32
Industry-Strategy Interaction, 34
Strategic Position, 35
Strategic Factors in Startup, 36
Failure Correlates, 37

Education and Experience   39

How Experience Works, 43

Collaboration   46

Prior Choices—Employer and Geographical Location   50

Starting Capital   52

Management Practices   55

Individual Makeup   58

Hard-to-Arrange Events   59

Summary   62

3 CAREER DEPARTURE POINTS   64

Occupational Starting Points   65

School to Venture   66

Job to Venture   75

Unemployment to Venture   80

Home to Venture   86
Family Ventures, 88

Sequential Entrepreneurship   89
Side-Street Effects, 91

Summary   95

4 SEQUENCES IN STARTUP   96

Milestones in Venture Creation   96
Foreseeing the Venture, 98

Quest for a General Model   98
Sequences in Conventional Manufacturing, 102
Sequences in High-Technology Manufacturing, 105
Sequences in Other Fields, 106

Five Key Ingredients for Startup   109
Contacts and Networking, 110
Sequence Variety, 112
Starting with Combinations, 117

Time Required to Start   118

Three Main Hurdles to Entrepreneural Entry   119
High-Margin Venture Idea, 120
Effective Sales Generation Scheme, 122
Operational Financing, 124

Summary   126

5 SOURCES OF VENTURE IDEAS   127

Invitation as a Venture Idea Source   127

Venture Ideas From Prior Employment   129

Legal Constraints, 132

Obtaining Rights   136
Teaming with Inventors, 138
Self-Employment as Idea Sources   140
Venture Ideas from Hobbies   143
Venture Ideas from Social Encounters   145
Pedestrian Observations   146
Deliberate Search   147
Alternative Personal Tactics, 151
Gap Analysis, 152
Strategies for Deck Stacking, 156
Summary   158

6 EVALUATING VENTURE IDEAS   159
Selection Factors   159
Preliminary Screening Questions   162
More Detailed Checkout   165
Market Analysis   167
Financial Analysis   168
Longer-Term Prospects of the Venture   171
Stably Small Firms   173
Low-pay Small Firms, 176
Strategies of Size   176
High-Pay Stably Small Firms   179
High-Growth Ventures,   183
Competitive Shield,   185
Economically Ideal Venture Types   188
Trial and Error   189
Summary   191

7 MAIN COMPETITIVE ENTRY WEDGES   192
Entry Barriers   194
Customer Characteristics: Why Should People Buy
from a New Company? 194
Competitor Employee Capabilities: What can the
Startup do better than they can?, 195
Competitor Company Assets: How Can the Startup
Acquire What Would Be Needed to Contend With
Them?, 196
New Product   197

Unsuccessful New Products, 200
Importance of Degree of Advantage, 201

New Services   203

Product-Service Sequences   205

Parallel Competition   207
Parallel Services, 209
Parallel Products, 213

Product Service Combinations   216

Franchising   217
High-profit Franchisee Strategies, 220
Becoming a Franchisor, 221

Summary   224

8   OTHER ENTRY WAGES   **225**

Taking Advantage of Partial Momentum   225
Geographic Transfer, 226
Supply Shortage, 229
Tapping Unutilized Resources, 232

Customer-sponsored Strategies   234
Customer Contract, 234
Second Sourcing, 237

Parent Company Sponsership   239
Joint Ventures, 240
Manufacture Licensing, 241
Market Relinquishment, 244
Selloff of a Division, 245

Governmental Sponsership   249
Favored Purchasing, 249
Rule Changes, 250

Combinations of Wedges   251

Application   251

Development Downstream   252

Summary   255

9   ACQUISITION FINDING   **257**

Acquisition Opportunity Situations   261

Acquisition Strategies   265

Locating Leads   269

Preliminary Screening   278

Trap Situations   283

Detailed Checkout   286

Summary   290

10 ACQUISITION DEALING   291

What is Bought   291

Determining Price   294

Terms of the Deal   302
Leveraged Buyouts, 306
Dealing with Financing Sources, 309

Tax Considerations   310

Legal Aspects   312

Negotiation   316

Bankruptcy Takeover   319

Summary   322

APPENDICES   324

A CORPORATE VENTURES   324

Venture Forms, 325
Venturing Variables, 325
Individual Perspective, 327
Corporate versus Independent Venturing, 328
Corporate Perspective, 329

B CHEMISTRY AND CULTIVATION OF ENTREPRENEURSHIP   332

Reasons for Interest,   332

Industrialized Economies, 332
Underdeveloped Economies, 333
Communist Economies, 334
Requisites for Entrepreneurship, 334
Opportunity, 334
Competence, 335
Initiative, 336
Pushes, 336
Pulls, 338
Barriers and Helps, 339

BIBLIOGRAPHY   342

SUBJECT INDEX   351

ENTREPRENEUR AND VENTURE INDEX   354

Preface

Since the first edition of this book a wealth of new research literature on entrepreneurship has emerged in the academic world. In addition new magazines, plus many more books and articles on entrepreneurs in established publications of the popular business press have appeared. Some have emphasised functional specialties such as business plans, while others have told stories about how ventures come about, particularly spectacular stories in such industries as microcomputer hardware and software. These works surround but still do not fully cover the earlier need to display the array of strategic options, both personal and commercial, open to a would-be entrepreneur. Hence, this edition still retains that objective from the first.

In addition, the many new publications have accentuated the need for frameworks to keep track and make sense of the greatly extended information available about entrepreneurship and entrepreneurs. Consequently, this revision has attempted not only to incorporate updated research information and entrepreneurial examples, but also to introduce additional conceptual schemes to facilitate display and analysis of them.

K. H. V.

Perspectives on Entrepreneurship

Independent business is an attractive occupation not only to many engaged in it but also to many who are employees managed by others and would rather direct themselves. To implement an idea for a new product or service may be one person's objective, while for another it may be to gain more independence or make more money. Other objectives may include replacing a job that has been lost, obtaining an alternative route for advancement from a dead-end job, experiencing the adventure of a startup, proving that one can accomplish a startup, adding supplementary income through moonlighting activity, joining a team of entrepreneurs for the fun of working with them, or trying self-employment simply to see what it is like.

Still others may want to learn about entrepreneurship because they think entrepreneurial skills will help in a job or because they expect to work with entrepreneurs in some capacity and therefore want to understand how they operate. With the shrinkage of large companies in recent years through job layoffs, some have turned to venturing as a path to greater employment security. According to David Birch, who has studied the subject, job security in a startup currently appears to be about as great as that in working for a *Fortune* 500 company.[1]

To pursue any of these goals, it can be helpful to study how others "played their cards" and, to varying degrees, succeeded. The variety of possible ways of working at entrepreneurship is enormous, but as examples in following chapters will show, some patterns offer more promise than others. There are facts of entrepreneurial life and technical knowledge that it can be helpful to learn, and some skills whose cultivation can raise the odds of venturing happily. Even

---

[1] David Birch, comments at the ICSB conference, Colorado Springs, June 1988.

more helpful can be an awareness of alternative strategies that have been experimentally tested by entrepreneurs who have gone before, sometimes with spectacular success. Each entrepreneurial situation is unique and the future always differs from the past, but some tricks repeat well. Knowledge of precedents can expand virtuosity in a would-be entrepreneur for creating effective approaches in new situations.

Knowledge about entrepreneurship has become more widespread in recent years, particularly from media attention given to spectacular success stories, although as Wortman has observed, "little of the *research* on entrepreneurship has been disseminated to entrepreneurs."[2] The following pages will present concepts for organizing these as well as less-familiar entrepreneurial examples in ways designed to reveal patterns that will help would-be entrepreneurs see options that may be open to them. Data concerning both successes and nonsuccesses will be drawn from existing works on entrepreneurship, including recent research studies plus numerous examples not published elsewhere. Conceptual schemes for analyzing and for developing entrepreneurial action will be introduced. It is presumed that the goal of many readers will be not only to learn what entrepreneurial work is like but also to get on with it.

TYPES OF ENTREPRENEURS

Get on with what? The entrepreneur's role can be drawn in many forms and tends to appear different from different perspectives. To an economist, an entrepreneur is one who brings resources, labor, materials, and other assets into combinations that make their value greater than before, and also one who introduces changes, innovations, and new order. To a psychologist, such a person is typically one driven by certain forces—needs to obtain or attain something, to experiment, to accomplish, or perhaps to escape authority of others. The unfavorably inclined politician may see an entrepreneur as one who is devious and hard to control, whereas a favorably inclined politician sees the same person as one who finds effective ways to get things done. To one businessperson, the entrepreneur appears as a threat, an aggressive competitor, whereas to another businessperson, the same entrepreneur may be an ally, a source of supply, a customer, or someone good to invest in. To a Communist philosopher, the entrepreneur may be a predator, one who usurps resources and exploits the labor of others. The same person is seen by a capitalist philosopher as one who creates wealth for others as well, who finds better ways to utilize resources and reduce waste, and who produces jobs others are glad to get.

Although many publications refer to "the" entrepreneur as if there were only one type, a closer look quickly reveals many. Webster's definition refers to "one who organizes, manages and assumes the risks of a business or enterprise." Schumpeter added the notion of innovator and former of new combi-

---

[2] Max Wortman, "Entrepreneurship: An Integrating Typology and Evaluation of Empirical Work in the Field," *Journal of Management*, Vol. 13, No. 2 (Summer 1987), 259.

nations.[3] Observing that "dictionary definitions are not very good," Shallenberger associates entrepreneurs with a host of synonyms ("bold, venturesome, risk-take, doer") versus antonyms ("conforming, conservative, routine").[4] Leavitt has offered another distinction by observing, "what we really need is the white-hatted entrepreneur; the innovator and relater, the developer; not the shady, expedient, unethical, black-hatted fellow."[5]

Stevenson has suggested that the distinguishing feature of entrepreneurship is business action that is "opportunity driven," as opposed to being either resource driven or resource limited.[6] Livesay's way of putting it is "an entrepreneur perceives a market opportunity and assembles the assets necessary to exploit it."[7] Lipper observes that "entrepreneurs accept risk to organize resources, especially those that create benefit and wealth."[8] In a 1969 discussion of alternative definitions, Komives suggested that an entrepreneur is simply one who starts a business, Cole added that self-employed individuals, such as independent insurance agents, should be included, Bostrom argued to include one who assumes the financial risks, and Collins distinguished between independent versus internal or "administrative" entrepreneurs.[9] Pinchot coined a new term, "intrapreneur," a contraction of intracorporate entrepreneur, to refer to those administrative entrepreneurs whose accomplishment is to create new ventures inside established firms rather than as independent enterprises outside.[10] Kanter includes as entrepreneurs "those inside large organizations who in effect bet their jobs on the outcome of an innovation."[11]

The value of exploring some definitions is that they may suggest ideas for alternative ways of operating for the would-be entrepreneur. Most would agree that entrepreneurs tend to be independent operators, though they sometimes work in teams, and that they take initiative to profit on business opportunities. But there is still room within these qualifications for a considerable variety of different entrepreneurial types, including the following. In reading through this list, a prospective entrepreneur may find it worthwhile to keep asking such questions as Which of these types could I be and how? Which of these types might I most prefer to be and why?

1 *Solo Self-employed Individuals* Readily found in the Yellow Pages of any telephone book, these include Mom 'n Pop operators, tradespeople such as agents, repairmen, and brokers, plus high-hourly-rate professionals, such as

---

[3] Joseph A. Schumpeter, *The Theory of Economic Development* (Cambridge, Mass.: Harvard University Press, 1934).
[4] Frank Shallenberger, "Notes on Entrepreneurship," *New Enterprises Course Syllabus* (Stanford, Calif.: Stanford Business School, 1968).
[5] Harold J. Leavitt, "Entrepreneurs, Mark II," address to the 22nd Conference on Higher Education, N.E.A., Chicago, March 6, 1967.
[6] Colloquium on Entrepreneurship and the Future of the Harvard Business School, Boston, 1983.
[7] Harold Livesay, "Entrepreneurial History," in Calvin A. Kent, Donald L. Sexton, and Karl H. Vesper, *Encyclopedia of Entrepreneurship* (Englewood Cliff, N.J.: Prentice-Hall, 1982), p. 12.
[8] Arthur Lipper III, "Chairman's Comment," *Venture*, March 1985, p. 4.
[9] *Proceedings of the First Karl A. Bostrom Seminar in the Study of Enterprise* (Milwaukee: Center for Venture Management, April 25, 1969).
[10] Gifford Pinchot III, "Intrapreneurship, Holding onto People with Ideas." *International Management,* March 1982; also *Intrapreneuring* (New York: Harper & Row, 1985).
[11] Rosabeth Moss Kanter, *The Change Masters* (New York: Simon & Schuster, 1983), p. 395.

accountants and physicians, who operate alone or with only a few employees and perform work personally, not mainly through others. Gartner notes several archetypes that may fall into this category:[12]

—Consumer sales—Often pursued to escape other jobs, begun part time, location important.

—Real estate—May rent, buy, and sell; may develop and sell. Debt a major factor. May borrow on one to buy another and thereby extend leverage.

—Novelty product—Idea creation and sales through trade shows, wholesalers, fairs, and retailers are the entrepreneur's functions. Manufacturing is farmed out.

—Professional service—Often built on customer contacts from prior employment in the field. Sometimes licensed (CPA, lawyer, doctor, engineer, architect), sometimes not (consultant). Other similar archetypes are what Gartner refers to as "the expert" and "the aggressive service firm." These may grow larger, possibly in the form of partnerships.

   2   Deal-to-Dealers   Many small businessowners have had more than one enterprise, frequently in different lines of work. For instance, Bob Thorssen started an enterprise to manufacture silk flowers and retail them through his own store as a subsidiary activity of his machine tool supply company in Calgary. Before that, his other enterprises—some successful and some not—included establishing a mail delivery service during a postal strike, selling mutual funds, selling condos and villas in Spain, publishing directories for oil companies, investing in real estate, mining diamonds in Australia, hand-logging in Indonesia, logging with tractors in Borneo, building by hand and operating a bar in Borneo, and logging in Sumatra.[13] From a study of ninety-five ex-entrepreneurs, Ronstadt found that about half had performed multiple ventures, that those multiple ventures tended to have started venturing earlier in life, and that their ventures typically tended to be lower in technology.[14]

   3   Team Builders   Those who go on to build larger companies using hiring and delegation can be regarded as another category. Traditional examples of such entrepreneurs include the skilled machinist who, after his apprenticeship, opens his own small shop and then gradually expands his work force as sales rise. Other examples include the janitor who breaks off on his own, bids on bigger jobs, and builds a janitorial service firm; the insurance salesman who starts his own agency, builds it up, and eventually starts his own life insurance company; and the physicist or engineer who, like Ramo and Wooldridge or TRW, recruits other skilled technologists to land large government contracts and creates a major "think tank."

   Many of the country's largest companies began as "one-man shows" and then found it possible to expand rapidly because of one or more advantages that arose. John Deere's tiny blacksmith shop shifted to rapid growth when he

[12] William B. Gartner, "Problems in Business Startups," in John A. Hornaday, Fred Tarpley, Jr., Jeffry A. Timmons, and Karl H. Vesper, Frontiers of Entrepreneurship Research, 1984 (Wellesley, Mass.: Babson Center for Entrepreneurial Studies, 1984), p. 498.

[13] Allan Gould, The New Entrepreneurs (Toronto: Seal Books, 1986), p. 148.

[14] Robert Ronstadt, "Every Entrepreneur's Nightmare: The Decision to Become an Ex-entrepreneur and Work for Someone Else," in John A. Hornaday, Edward B Shils, Jeffry A. Timmons, and Karl H. Vesper, Frontiers of Entrepreneurship Research, 1985 (Wellesley, Mass.: Babson Center for Entrepreneurial Studies, 1985).

invented a plow that would self-clean in the Midwest sod, which clung to earlier designs. Richard Crane's one-man foundry was able to expand thanks to market demand for conventional casting work in the Chicago area where he set it up, using a conveniently available corner of his uncle's lumber yard in 1885. Coca-Cola, Dr. Pepper, and Hires Root Beer all sprang from one-man drugstores. In more recent years H&R Block began as a small bookkeeping operation, Pizza Hut began as a student venture to earn college money, and Masco (Delta faucets) began as a machine shop. Thus the entrepreneurial potential of even very modest types of businesses can be great.

Any number of subclassifications might be noted within the work-force builder category. Smith, for example, has postulated an archetype based on case studies which he calls the "craftsman entrepreneur."[15] Typically, Smith says, this type has relatively little formal schooling, excels at his job as a crafts-man, rebels at subordinate employment, and finally is precipitated into starting a company when either he is fired or an opportunity to do so appears. He emphasizes personal relationships with employees and customers, believes in honest hard work, and sees expansion as a zero-sum game played against competitors.

Recognizing that there may be many other types in between, Smith puts at the other end of the spectrum what he calls the "opportunistic entrepreneur." Typically this type has a more formal and well-rounded education, progresses through much broader variety in his work career, gains exposure to high-level executives from whom he learns, and starts his company as fulfillment of long-term dreams and plans. He is less personal with employees but more willing to share company control and sees his market as controllable and allowing open-ended growth. Which entrepreneurs would fit on Smith's spectrum and where could be a subject for individual inquiry. Henry Ford, for instance, started out by joining forces with a group of investors to set up shop and start making cars. Smith concludes by noting that there may be other types, one suggested by his data, for instance, being what he calls the "inventor entrepreneur."

4 Independent Innovators Traditional inventors, like Bell, Edison, and Kettering, who hit upon ideas for better products and then create companies to develop, produce, and sell them, have been numerous, some of them well known and others not. Rapid scientific progress, particularly in electronics since the 1950s, has provided the base for many new products that have been used for "high-technology entrepreneurs" to start many highly successful new com-panies, particularly in the areas of Boston and San Francisco. Forerunners of these companies were the Hewlett-Packard Company, started from a student engineering project by two recent electrical engineering graduates of Stanford in the 1940s; Tektronix, started by an electronics repairman with a better os-cilloscope idea; Ampex Corporations, begun by immigrant Alexander M. Pon-iatoff, building upon magnetic recording technology from wartime Germany,

---

[15] Norman R. Smith, *The Entrepreneur and His Firm* (East Lansing: Bureau of Business and Economic Research, Michigan State University, 1967). Also see Norman R. Smith and Rein Peterson, "Entrepreneurship: A Culturally Appropriate Combination of Craft and Opportunity," in Robert Ronstadt, John A. Hornaday, Rein Peterson, and Karl H. Vesper, *Frontiers of Entrepre-neurship Research, 1986* (Wellesley, Mass.: Babson Center for Entrepreneurial Studies, 1986), p. 498.

and Polaroid Corporation, whose founder, Edwin Land, was a self-educated physicist whose little girl stumped him by asking why she couldn't see camera photos right after they were taken.[16]

By the early 1980s the principal field of entrepreneurial innovation appeared to be microcomputers. Over two hundred new microcomputers plus numerous peripheral products had been introduced to the market, most of them by startup companies. Over five thousand companies had sprung up within two or three years offering software products to go with them.[17] Behind them came companies in biotechnology and genetic engineering. For the future some expect yet more independent innovators to emerge with electrical devices made possible by new discoveries in superconductivity. Clearly, innovators need not necessarily be in high-technology industries only, as such startups as Federal Express with 1987 sales of $3.2 billion and Liz Claiborne with 1987 sales of $41 billion illustrate.

5 *Pattern Multipliers* These are entrepreneurs who spot an effective business pattern, quite possibly originated by someone else, and multiply it to realize profits on additional such ventures. Two classic examples are the patterns created by Colonel Sanders and by McDonald's drive-in restaurants, both of which were noticed, acquired, and capitalized on through franchise expansion by other entrepreneurs. One who started his own rather than acquiring others is William Millard, whose microcomputer manufacturing company failed, but not before he had opened a retail store, Computerland, which began franchising in 1977 and grew to sales of $1.4 billion by 1984.[18]

Becoming a franchisor is one way of multiplying effective business patterns for a profit, one that took on boom dimensions in recent decades, followed by a substantial "shakeout." The other pattern multiplication approach, chain expansion, became famous earlier through exploits of entrepreneurs like J. C. Penney, Sebastian Kresge, and others but has continued with such more recent firms as Denny's restaurants.

6 *Economy-of-Scale Exploiters* The fact that unit costs tend to shrink as volume expands has been exploited particularly by entrepreneurs in the discount merchandising business. By locating in lower rent and tax areas, and by reducing services, they are able to reduce prices, which has given them increased volume, enabling them to reduce prices still further and make it difficult for competitors to enter.

Discount stores provide numerous illustrations. Sol Price, a lawyer for seventeen years who founded Fed-Mart stores in California, sold them to a West German firm only to be fired and then see the stores fail. He began again by founding a members-only warehouse retailing firm. By 1987 the Price Company was operating thirty-nine stores with sales of $3.3 billion.[19]

Yet a different way of capitalizing on scale is to introduce new infrastructure enterprises such as supply or wholesale distribution channels as the number of enterprises in an industry expands. For example, Blueberry Woolens of An-

[16] Gene Bylinsky, *The Innovation Millionaires* (New York: Scribner's 1976).
[17] John Levine, "5,000 Entrepreneurs and Counting," *Venture,* January 1982, p. 75.
[18] Robert Levering, Michael Katz, and Milton Moskowitz, *The Computer Entrepreneurs* (New York: New American Library, 1984).
[19] Joe Mullich, "Club Mania," *California Business,* May 1988, p. 34.

ston, Maine, was started by Carol Carter when she decided to knit and sell sweaters as a way of marketing the wool from her sheep. As her sales expanded, she bought sweaters from other home-knitters, thereby expanding and multiplying their enterprises as well.[20] As microcomputer software producers began to proliferate in the early 1980s, publishing firms, such as Personal Software, sprang up to merchandise their products, thereby creating channels to support the further multiplication for software startups.[21] Trade shows, such as Comdex, and trade associations also sprang up, each in itself being a new venture.

7 **Capital Aggregators** By pulling together a substantial financial stake, ranging from roughly fifty thousand to a million dollars, either from one well-endowed source or several sources combined, it is possible to initiate such ventures as banks, savings and loan institutions, insurance companies, and mutual funds, which cannot be started without large "front end" capital. Particularly during the stock market boom and consequent high-wealth levels of the 1960s, many financial entrepreneurs began this way. Even in the low market of 1974, some proved that this technique could be used by starting mutual funds to make available to small investors the high interest rates that had become available through large-denomination notes.

One late-1970s insurance company startup was described by Bekey as follows:

◆   Neither Douglas Helm nor James Little intended to start an insurance company when they resigned within two days of each other from Employee Benefits Insurance, Inc. in the spring of 1979. Each had watched the San Jose, California workers' compensation carrier they had helped found in 1970 go public and saw their roles change from entrepreneurs to bureaucrats. But when they plotted their new venture from an ocean-view library in Malibu, their plan was far from modest: $3 million for a startup specializing in workers' compensation to be operational in less than a year. (They actually raised $4.5 million.) One reason entrepreneurs shy away from insurance is heavy regulation. State laws mandate minimum startup capital averaging $1 million, although a company planning to write only specialized coverage, such as plate glass insurance, might be started for less.[22]

8 **Acquirers** There are two ways to enter independent business—start a new one or acquire a going concern. Those who acquire have a variety of styles. Some are regarded as *turnaround artists* because they take over troubled firms and straighten them out. *Buy-sell artists* seek their profit through selling off their acquisitions, sometimes after "dressing them up" to increase their value. For instance, getting creditors to accept long-term notes in place of bills owed them can improve a company's current ratio and make it look more solid and valuable even though it is not fundamentally changed.

Speculators invest in things they typically do not operate, such as shares or ownership of such assets as real estate. *Corporate raiders* seek to acquire control of companies that can be broken up and sold in pieces for sale at a higher price than the combined pieces were worth. *Conglomerators,* are illustrated by James Ling, are no longer as fashionable as when they began in the

---

[20] *In Business,* January–February 1984, p. 48.
[21] Gary Slutsker, "The New Publishers in Computer Software," *Venture,* September 1980, p. 79.
[22] Michelle Bekey, "The Big Bucks Insurance Game," *Venture,* September 1980, p. 94.

sixties. They built corporate empires by using the stock of one company to buy another, then the stock of the combined two to buy yet another, and so forth.

When we discuss the subject of acquisition in the final two chapters of this book, our emphasis will mainly be on acquisition as a mode of entry into longer-term management of an active business where the entrepreneur clearly adds value.

Individuals and Teams

The same entrepreneur may operate in different styles for different ventures. For example, Reid Anderson acquired an extensive technical background working for Bell Laboratories, NCR, and the Stanford Research Institute and then developed an electronic metronome as an independent innovator. He sold this product from his home until the market was saturated. Then he joined forces with a partner, Ray Jacobson, to start another company with a product licensed from SRI. The partners split up in this venture, and Anderson went on to team build another company, Verbatim, which manufactures floppy disks under license from IBM and other magnetic-recording products.

This teaming activity, which we will examine later, points up a crucial aspect of entrepreneurship, which is that the entrepreneur does not venture alone. Customers, suppliers, employees, and even outside financiers are often involved. Also often involved are direct partners. Thus the term *entrepreneur* can be misleading if it is taken to refer only to the activity of a sole individual. Sometimes there are partners working in parallel, often on different parts of the startup process, and sometimes there are prime moving individuals who work in series on the startup of a venture. It can even be confusing in some cases to try discerning who the main prime mover or entrepreneur was. Most entrepreneurial episodes are described with a single apparent entrepreneur. But it should be kept in mind that other episodes also important to formation of the same venture may involve other prime movers in the startup as well.

ENTREPRENEURSHIP VERSUS FRAUD

It is in this last category of entrepreneurship, apparent value manipulation, where abuse most often occurs, producing not entrepreneurship but fraud. The two often have some common features: clever market perception, creativity, and selling competence. But whereas entrepreneurs, as that term will be used here, create real value for those with whom they do business, swindlers do not but only claim to provide value that actually does not exist. The following example illustrates fraud.

♦ Elliott Scott was convicted of fraud for persuading ladies to buy wigs they didn't get. For a while he sold through advertisements placed, but often not paid for, in newspapers across the country. Then he shifted to mailing announcements telling each recipient she was the winner of a "free" wig; all she had to pay were shipping and styling charges totaling around ten dollars. The wigs cost Scott forty-five cents, came in only one color in contrast to several colors offered, and typically fell apart. After two years of amassing evidence on Scott and his thirty-three business aliases, the U.S. Attorney's Office finally brought him to trial in 1968, having marshaled an army of four hundred women to testify how he had cheated them. An all-woman jury found him guilty.

Some ventures are legally frauds, whereas others may be more morally than prosecutably fraudulent. In the first category would be, for instance, phony insurance companies that sell coverage to high-risk clients and then are not around when the claims arrive. In the latter would be many quack schemes, such as a company that might sell prescriptions for selecting the sex of unborn children. Bottles of pink-colored water would be offered as elixir to produce girls and blue-colored water to produce boys. There would be a money-back guarantee of satisfaction. Then, so long as the seller priced the water at double its cost, profits would be assured, since on the average half of the customers would be bound to get the results they wanted.

Government agencies, including those in consumer protection, securities, and taxes, are continually mounting campaigns to snuff out fraudulent ventures. The following discussion of entrepreneurship will avoid them in favor of entrepreneurs who seek to provide what clients think they are paying for and are legally entitled to. As the examples will show, there is abundant room for creativity and shrewd competitive action within the generally accepted rules of honest business.

AREAS OF STUDY

Within the category of legitimate entrepreneurs this discussion will focus on those who build productive organizations, as opposed to those who merely buy and rent or sell for profit. Excluded, for instance, would be business brokers and real estate operators who only buy, contract any development work to others, and then rent or sell the property. Included will be those who start companies either as artisan/professionals or around new products and services, or who acquire and transform existing firms.

There still remains a variety of alternative perspectives from which the entrepreneur's job can be viewed. The point in considering them is to alert the prospective entrepreneur to some of the ways of looking at the subject in addition to the ones emphasized in this book, ways that may give additional insights regarding opportunities, how to find them, and how to make the most of them. In reviewing briefly this list of different ways of viewing entrepreneurship, the reader may find it useful to keep considering such questions as Which of these subject areas might I enjoy learning more about? Which of them might spark me to fresh ways of considering the subject? How might some of them help me find better ways of venturing for myself?

Research on entrepreneurship in recent years has proliferated into an increasing number of subareas and topics. Here they will be grouped under three broad categories: the entrepreneur, the venture, and the environment.

The Entrepreneur

1 *Tycoon History* Some tycoon stories, like that of Ford, who went from machinist to electric utility engineer to race car builder and driver before, at age thirty, forming his auto company, are common knowledge. Others, like

that of Ransome Olds, who built his first car in 1894, two years before Ford, and developed two auto companies, the Olds Motor Vehicle Company, which was sold to GM, and the Reo Motor Car Company, are less well known, but practically all are interesting and instructive.

For instance, being a good inventor is neither necessary nor sufficient for success. Oliver Winchester started out in the men's shirt business, saved enough to buy a gun company, and bought repeater design rights from other inventors to become wealthy and famous from the "gun that won the West." Another who did his own inventing thirty years earlier was Samuel Colt. The company he set up to make his patented revolver failed and was later resurrected by government contract to supply arms for the Mexican War. Forty-two years earlier than that, in 1794, Eli Whitney had patented his cotton gin, which was a success. The partnership he formed to make it failed. Turning to the gun-making business, he too was brought through by government contract. When Isaac Singer was sued for infringing the patents of others with his sewing machine, he lost. But his company was by then too strong and survived with great prosperity as it bought up and absorbed competitors.

Perhaps one of the most successful failures, though, was Milton Hershey, who bounced through seven schools in eight years and never got past the fourth grade. Entering the candy business, he failed, first in Philadelphia, then in Chicago, then in New York, where he went bankrupt in 1886, before he succeeded with the Lancaster (Pa.) Caramel Company, which he sold for $1 million in 1900. The chocolate company that he subsequently formed became worth $60 million by 1909 and world famous.

Astor, Vanderbilt, Carnegie, Chrysler, Stanford, Du Pont, Heinz, Gillette—the stories are as fascinating as the list is long. Every town has had a tycoon, every city has had many, and every tycoon's experience has had lessons for others, which makes tycoon history a worthy subject to study, though not a main focus of this book. Two aspects worth noting for would-be entrepreneurs, however, may be first the methods used by those historical figures—the strategies, tactics, and tricks they employed to succeed—which may bear repeating, and second the kind of circumstances that allowed or facilitated succeeding with those methods. Some of the techniques they used may work as well or even better today, whereas others may be entirely ineffective or even illegal.

2 *Psychology of Entrepreneurs* Some people are more likely to become successful entrepreneurs because of their mental attitudes, according to researchers who have studied them. Intensive desire for independence, or its converse, high dissatisfaction with operating under the direction of others, is one suggested explanation for entrepreneurial behavior. Collins and Moore conclude that such an urge frequently derives from an authoritarian father, whom the entrepreneur struggles to dominate and surpass.[23] An irony they point out is that when an entrepreneur finally achieves establishment of an independent firm, the sought-for autonomy may turn out to be a mirage because the company is still subjected to whims of customers, employees, governmental agencies, financial backers, and others who can "boss around" the entrepreneur anyway.

---

[23] Orvis Collins and David G. Moore, *The Organization Makers* (New York: Appleton-Century-Crofts, 1970).

Other drives proposed to explain entrepreneurial behavior include an urge for power, the will to conquer, and the joy of creating. Most commonly accepted as dominant, however, is McClelland's "need for achievement."[24] Symptoms of this need are (1) desire to take personal responsibility for decisions, (2) preference for decisions involving risk that is neither very high nor very low, but rather moderate, and (3) interest in concrete results from their decisions. To these Palmer adds (4) tendency to work harder at tasks requiring mental manipulation, (5) not working harder because of financial incentive, (6) tending to think ahead, and (7) preferring to work with experts rather than personal friends.[25]

Beyond these alleged needs other mental traits have been suggested. Shapero sees a correlation between entrepreneurial tendencies and the sum of two factors: (1) the extent to which one has accepted other entrepreneurs as "role models," such as an entrepreneurial father, other relative, or people in the local community, plus (2) the extent to which an individual believes in self-determination of his or her own destiny, as opposed to determination of economic success by factors outside the individual.[26] Thus one who would blame individual problems on "the system" would be exhibiting low entrepreneurial promise.

Swayne and Tucker suggest ego drive and empathy as key personality traits and then go on to speculate about where an entrepreneur's way of thought should fit on several managerial psychology dimensions.[27] On Maslow's hierarchy of need, they say, the entrepreneur tends to be relatively low on physiological, safety, and love needs and very high on need for self-esteem—i.e., the entrepreneur must prove himself. Among the traditional five managerial functions, planning, organizing, staffing, directing, and controlling, the entrepreneur will be strongest, they claim, on planning, selecting people, motivating and rewarding them, but weaker on other skills of formal organization. Along McGregor's dichotomy he will be either strong "theory X" or strong "theory Y," not a moderate. On Blake and Mouton's grid he will be "9, 1," placing heavy emphasis on concern for production, as opposed to concern for people. Between Hertzberg's "motivators" and "dissatisfiers" it is the former that strongly dominates, with achievement or ego drive being the main key, whereas dissatisfiers such as status, working conditions, and even money are of much less importance.

Some of the psychological theories have been systematically tested, but others have not. Support for both the achievement need and locus of control differences was found, for instance, in a study by Begley and Boyd, which applied psychological tests to the founding managers of small firms and contrasted them with the nonfounding managers of small firms.[28] Founders also displayed higher tolerance for ambiguity and propensity for risk taking than nonfounders.

[24] David McClelland, The Achieving Society (Princeton, N.J.: Van Nostrand, 1961).
[25] Michael Palmer, "The Application of Psychological Testing to Entrepreneurial Potential," California Management Review, Vol. 13, No.3, p. 32.
[26] Albert Shapero, personal conversation, 1974.
[27] Charles Swayne and William Tucker, The Effective Entrepreneur (Morristown, N.J.: General Learning Press, 1973).
[28] Thomas M. Begley, and David P. Boyd, "Psychological Characteristics Associated with Entrepreneurial Performance," Journal of Business Venturing, Vol. 2, No. 1 (Winter 1987), 79.

However, these characteristics were not significantly related to performance of the ventures.

In assessing the significance of such findings, the question is whether the differences between founders and nonfounders were a cause of the founders' entrepreneurial initiative or an effect of it. Whether the differences between the two groups existed before the founders started their firms cannot be determined.

Some support for parallels between prefounding and postfounding differences was discerned in a study by Sexton and Bowman, which reported that entrepreneurship students and business students differed in the same ways that entrepreneurs and managers differed on a list of psychological characteristics.[29] In brief, they found that entrepreneurs and entrepreneurial students scored higher on energy level, willingness to take risks, persuasiveness, desire for autonomy and freedom, dislike of routine, and acceptance of change. They scored lower on emotional responsiveness, compassion, preference for personal relationships, avoidance of danger and desire for support, sympathy, advice, reassurance, and love.

For the would-be entrepreneur interested in learning how he or she fits the profile presumed best for entrepreneurship by psychologists and others who have delved into the subject, a number of self-evaluation questionnaires are available. Some are more heavily psychological,[30] whereas others tend to be more pragmatic,[31] and still others attempt to combine both.[32] The pragmatic checklists may be helpful in provoking ideas about the best ways an entrepreneur can prepare for entering a business, possibly by teaming up with someone whose psychological profile is complementary. So far, however, the findings are open to dispute on at least four grounds: First, as noted earlier, the entrepreneurs may have had a different cast of mind before accomplishing a startup, and therefore testing them after startup may have no implications for those who have not performed startups. Second, the differences that are found to be significant statistically may not be different practically (e.g., if all the tires on one car are inflated one percent less than all the tires on a second car, then the two sets of tires have significantly different pressures on the average—but this may have no implications whatever for driving, particularly if the two cars operate in different applications). Third, the pencil-and-paper tests may not say much about how entrepreneurs operate in practice. Fourth, the findings that are assessed in terms of differences in averages between entrepreneurs and nonentrepreneurs may have no applicability whatever for any particular individual. Hence the response of a given would-be entrepreneur to a psychologically developed profile that he or she does not happen to fit may be, So what?

[29] Donald L. Sexton, and Nancy B, Bowman, "Validation of a Personality Index," in Ronstadt, et al., *Frontiers of Entrepreneurship Research, 1986,* p. 40.

[30] Marlys Harris, "Testing the Entrepreneurial You," *Money,* Vol. 7, No. 3 (March 1978), 52; John Komives, "Entrepreneurial Self Assessment Quiz" (Milwaukee: Center for Venture Management, 1973); Joseph R. Mancuso, "The Entrepreneur's Quiz," *Executive,* Vol. 4, No. 1, p. 12.

[31] Richard H. Buskirk and Percy J. Vaughn, Jr., *Managing New Enterprises* (St. Paul, Minn.: West Publishing, 1976), p. vi; *Checklist for Going Into Business,* Small Marketers Aids Number 71, Small Business Administration (Washington, D.C.: Government Printing Office 1961); Donald M. Dible, *Up Your Own Organization* (Santa Clara, Calif.: Entrepreneur Press, 1971), Appendix 4.

[32] Jeffry A. Timmons, Leonard E. Smollen, and Alexander L. M. Dingee, Jr., *New Venture Creation* (Homewood, Ill.: Irwin, 1977), Chaps.1–7.

3 *Sociology of Entrepreneurship*   Closely related to the question of what psychological programming entrepreneurs possess is the question of how they got that way, a subject pursued by sociologists. Best known are perhaps the views of Max Weber, who postulated that religious beliefs foster in some groups dedication to hard work, saving, and striving toward material accomplishment as a basis for entrepreneurship.[33] Social and religious mores, according to sociologists, explain why in some groups of people there are economic systems and psychological attitudes that foster greater productivity and wealth than in other groups. In Colombia, for example, the city of Medellín is noted for greater industry than Bogotá, the capital, even though it has no apparent geographical advantages to favor it. In Mexico it is Monterrey, and in Brazil, São Paulo, which carry similar industrial excellence, and sociologists like to explore why. Similarly, Jews in western industrial countries, Chinese in the Pacific Islands, and Ibos in Nigeria have been peoples noted for exceptional entrepreneurial performance.

Important variables from a sociological viewpoint include such things as role expectations of children and parents, impact of warfare, invasions, and migration on certain groups versus others, attitudes toward such things as innovation, wealth, and working with hands and tools as opposed to bureaucratic employment or membership in aristocracies that "don't stoop to that sort of thing." Outcast groups, for example, may have entrepreneurial advantages because they lack reverence for the established ways of doing things and are consequently more free to move ahead with better approaches. Other effects are simply mysteries. Why, for instance, should the sons of second polygamous marriages in Mormon families be disproportionately successful in business, as reported by Arrington?[34]

Possible advantages of studying works on this subject for a given would-be entrepreneur may include insights into (1) kinds of cultural blocks that may unknowingly be retarding entrepreneurial performance and whose recognition can lead to better performance and (2) information about how different groups operate, which may give clues about more effective ways of working in entrepreneurship—i.e., learning from the winners.[35]

4 *Minority Enterprise*   In recent years increasing attention to the lower economic status of certain minorities, including black, Hispanic, and native Americans, has inspired programs to promote advancement through entrepreneurship. Training programs to raise achievement motivation have been conducted, assistance in the form of counseling and guidance has been tried, and financial injections through such vehicles as minority enterprise small business investment companies (MESBICS) have been applied and to varying degrees studied. These investigations may be of particular interest to minority group members, although there are many minority groups to which they may not apply.

Three groups not much studied, for instance, whose exploits may be particularly interesting to follow, are the Cubans who fled to Florida, the Asians

---

[33] H. H. Gerth and C. Wright Mills, *From Max Weber: Essays in Sociology* (Oxford, England: Oxford University Press, 1946).

[34] Leonard Arrington, *Great Basin Kingdom: An Economic History of the Latter Day Saints* (Cambridge, Mass.: Harvard University, 1958).

[35] James L. Adams, *Conceptual Blockbusting* (San Francisco: Freeman Publishing, 1974).

who fled to the United States from Southeast Asia, and the Africans of Indian descent who were driven from Uganda and have settled in parts of the British Commonwealth. Their experience may offer valuable lessons for other entrepreneurs who find themselves at the bottom and must begin with no external resources. However, the main value of learning about minority entrepreneurship for those who would start companies has so far proved to be (1) for minority persons in learning about special advantages available so as to take advantage of them, or (2) for nonminority entrepreneurs who want to sell something to governmental agencies for helping minorities.

   5 *Female Entrepreneurship*   According to the U.S. Bureau of the Census, female-owned firms accounted for less than 5 percent of all U.S. firms in 1972 but were growing rapidly. By mid-1988 the House Small Business Subcommittee characterized the increase in the number of firms owned by women as perhaps "the most significant economic development of recent years."[36] During the seventies the growth rate of self-employment for women was roughly three times that for men in both the U.S. and Canada. In roughly fifteen years, the percentage of sole proprietorships owned by women had risen from less than 5 percent to over 25 percent in the U.S., and the government estimated that it would grow to 50 percent by the year 2000. Most of the startups appeared to have been in retailing and services—the percentage in Canada, for instance, having been 80.4 percent in these two fields, with another 12.6 percent occurring in "craft and cottage" industries and only 6.9 percent occurring in manufacturing.[37] Another study found that 90 percent of female-started businesses were in services.[38]

   One study found that in the United States, female-initiated ventures were less likely than male-initiated ventures;[39] but another study found that in Canada, female entrepreneurs had a higher success rate than male entrepreneurs.[40] It appeared to correlate with (1) taking longer to research and prepare for startup, (2) making use of professional advisers in the startup process, (3) having a background in business-related courses, (4) starting with more modest sales expectations, and (5) having a lower initial debt/equity ratio.

Venture Types

   6 *Independent Ventures*   The main focus of this book, independent ventures, will be elaborated throughout the following chapters. However, it can be noted here that they can be classified in many ways and have been for different research studies. In addition to the types noted earlier, they can be classified according to

---

[36] Committee on Small Business, House of Representatives, *New Economic Realities: The Rise of Women Entrepreneurs,* Report 100-736, Union Calendar No. 448, Washington, D.C., June 28, 1988, p. 1.
[37] Jerry White, "The Rise of Female Capitalism—Women as Entrepreneurs," *Business Quarterly,* Spring 1984, p. 133.
[38] Robert D. Hisrich, and Candida Brush, "Women and Minority Entrepreneurs: A Comparative Analysis," In Hornaday et al., *Frontiers of Entrepreneurship Research, 1985,* p. 566.
[39] Arnold C. Cooper, William C. Dunkelberg, and Carolyn Y. Woo, "Survival and Failure: A Longitudinal Study," Babson Entrepreneurship Research Conference, Calgary, 1988.
[40] White, "Rise of Female Capitalism," p. 134.

—*Growth level*. Studies of company growth consistently find that most startups never become large.[41] Birch has noted that most startups level off after employing less than a half dozen people (60 percent have four or less by the time they are ten years old), while a much smaller percentage go on to grow substantially.[42]

—*Capitalization level*. Startups with initial capitalization levels in the hundreds of thousands or millions are of particular interest in studies of venture capital and studies of economic development.

—*Industrial sector*. Retail, construction, manufacturing, mining, professional, financial, wholesale, service, and agricultural were the categories used by one study.[43] It found, for instance, that manufacturing founders were more likely to have come from large companies and to have started with partners, whereas service founders were more likely to have come from small companies and retail founders were the most likely to have come from an unrelated field.

—*Technological type*. "Hi tech" is an area of entrepreneurship that has become particularly fascinating because of spectacular successes in such fields as electronics, computers, and biotechnology. In studies, therefore, it is often singled out for special treatment. It has also been noted, however, that there are spectacular non-hi-tech startups and that the high-technology sector is extremely small, despite the attention it receives.

—*Degree of innovation*. Innovation occurs through other routes in addition to high technologies. Sometimes it simply involves the use of products, such as microcomputers, that come from high technologies—for instance, they make production of a more prosaic product or service more efficient. Other times it may simply involve new advertising ideas or ways of rendering service. There has been relatively little systematic study of the role of innovations in startups.

7 Corporate Ventures A line of argument suggested occasionally is that a would-be entrepreneur may be able to gain at least some of the advantages of venturing, such as being able to implement an idea and to create an enterprise through development of the venture inside his or her employer's organization. Several books and some research articles have been published on that subject, and a summary of the topic is included in Appendix A.

8 Small Business Management Two distinctions will be made between entrepreneurship as it will be discussed here and the topic of small business management as it is commonly viewed. First, the focus here will be on getting into independent business, whether by startup or acquisition, rather than on how to manage a small business once it is under way and operating. Second, attention will be concentrated on companies with higher profit potential, as opposed to small companies in general, most of which do not make

[41] Sue Birley, "New Ventures and Employment Growth," *Journal of Business Venturing*, Vol. 2, No. 2 (Spring 1987), 155. Also Paul D. Reynolds, "New Firms: Societal Contribution versus Potential," *Journal of Business Venturing*, Vol. 2, No. 3 (Summer 1987), 231.

[42] David L. Birch, "Live Fast, Die Young," *Inc.*, August 1988, p. 23.

[43] Arnold C. Cooper, and William C. Dunkelberg, "A New Look at Business Entry," in Karl H. Vesper *Frontiers of Entrepreneurship Research, 1981* (Wellesley, Mass.: Babson Center for Entrepreneurial Studies, 1981), p. 1.

substantial profits and never will. Sometimes, as noted above, prosaic enterprises grow into large ones. Other times seemingly ordinary businesses, job machine shops for instance, generate very high profits even though most in those lines of work do not. Moreover, sometimes very small ventures, even losers, can provide valuable learning exercises for entrepreneurs whose eventual aims are higher. Consequently, a few examples from lines of work in which high profits are the exception will be included. But for the most part small service firms, retailers, and eating establishments will be left out of this discussion. There are numerous books on small business management available in libraries. Publications on specific types—dry cleaners, automatic laundries, grocery stores, and so forth—are available from the Small Business Administration.

   9   Ambitious New Venture Entry   Two general routes for venture entry are startup of a new company or acquisition of a going concern. Either usually involves getting into a company that is small, at least initially. Of main interest here, however, will be those small companies that either have the potential to grow substantially larger, possibly through fine tuning and franchising of an ordinary type of business, or have the potential to earn high profits for the entrepreneur, either through operations or through resale of the business, though it may remain small. It will be presumed that the would-be entrepreneur has higher aims for the business than simply surviving with a job, aims such as creating jobs for others and achieving substantial wealth and other fringe benefits possible in successful business development.

Entrepreneurship and the Environment

   10   Economics of Entrepreneurship   What kinds of effects ventures have on the economy and what effects the environment has on ventures are topics around which economists have spun many theoretical arguments. In these the entrepreneur is viewed with considerable impersonality and usually in an aggregate as a risk-taker, innovator, combiner of resources, manager, or mixture of these and is discussed in terms of market structure and opportunities, investment climate, governmental restrictions or encouragements, and technological change. Underlying these arguments there often appears to be an implicit assumption that the occurrence of latent entrepreneurs is a rather random occurrence and that whether they act out this inclination is governed by the economic environment at hand.

   One aspect of possible interest to would-be entrepreneurs in these academic excursions may be speculation about what circumstances are most likely to be supportive of which kinds of entrepreneuring. One line of economic reasoning, for instance, claims that inflationary settings hold less promise for manufacturing startups, as opposed to real estate or other asset speculations. Another points out that shifts in governmental trade restrictions and tariffs may create shelters for new types of startups or trade opportunities for import-export ventures.

   A second aspect of economic theorizing that may contain useful ideas for entrepreneurs concerns the kinds of functions they may perform. Joseph Schumpeter suggested five categories (1) introduction of new goods, (2) introduction of new methods of production, (3) opening of new markets, (4) opening of new sources of supply, and (5) industrial reorganization.[44]

11 Fostering Entrepreneurship In recent years the contributions of entrepreneurs in economic development have increasingly been appreciated by governments in both developed and underdeveloped countries and by those of not only capitalist but also Socialist and Communist persuasions. This has led to governmental actions aimed at entrepreneurial encouragement. To the extent that these are successful, they may add to both the incentives and the assistance available to entrepreneurs in the future. In the meantime, some entrepreneurs may find opportunities to sell entrepreneurial assistance programs to governments, as in the development of incubator facilities, for example. Appendix B contains a brief overview of the chemistry of entrepreneurship as a basis for considering possible policies for fostering it. Possible policies based on this chemistry have been proposed elsewhere but are beyond the scope of this book.[45]

It can, however, be noted that programs aimed at fostering entrepreneurship through education, infrastructure, and governmentally sponsored venture capital are currently under way in a number of countries, particularly Canada, the United Kingdom, Sweden, and France. How these programs fare in attempting to cultivate entrepreneurship deliberately should be an interesting question to examine as the programs progress.

ENTREPRENEURIAL WORK

The path to venture entry usually includes surprises for the entrepreneur. Key events may begin occurring well before it is apparent that they are leading toward a venture. The entrepreneur may be taking actions crucial to the venture before realizing that they are part of venturing: establishment of vital contacts, or learning about availability of resources or market needs. It may be a happy occurrence, such as having a promising idea for the venture concept, that reveals the opportunity. Or the sequence may begin with a less happy event, such as being fired from a job without the prospect of any particular venture in view. The venture may emerge from a series of small decisions, none very dramatic in itself, possibly beginning with a suggestion by someone else that the to-be entrepreneur pursue a line of action not foreseen as a venture but turning into one. Or there may be a deliberate search for a suitable venture; possibly to find an existing company to buy, or to find a promising product or service to begin with. Such a search sequence is typically a discouraging process for the most part, as one idea after another is uncovered, only to reveal itself as a "dud" upon closer scrutiny.

Even if the idea holds up with examination, finding support for it will typically be difficult as the entrepreneur enters into a phase of checking it out,

---

[44] Joseph A. Schumpeter, *The Theory of Economic Development* (Cambridge, Mass.: Harvard University Press, 1934).

[45] Karl H. Vesper, *Entrepreneurship and National Policy* (Chicago: Heller Institute for Small Business, Walter E. Heller International Corporation, 1983).

working out plans for getting it into action, and trying to recruit a work force, money, and other resources. With whom should the entrepreneur discuss it? What if somebody else decides to take off with the idea? If assistance of some kind is needed from the other person, how should that person be paid? Should he or she be given a slice of ownership, and if so, how much? How should new people be checked out in advance to ascertain whether they can produce what is desired from them and whether they will follow through on any commitments? How can those who don't produce, or don't fit in, or whose services are not needed after all be phased out?

There will be factual questions. What licenses are required? What products or services like this are available already? Who would be likely customers for the new enterprise? How much will incorporation cost, or would some sort of partnership be preferable? At what point could somebody file a lawsuit? Who in the bank handles loans for ventures of this sort? What kind of terms will suppliers give the new firm? How much will advertising cost, or salespeople, or floor space? When do taxes have to be paid, and what kinds? What red tape will apply if someone is hired? If someone lends the company money, what form should the note take? And whose lawyer should look at it, the company's or the entrepreneur's, or both? What will that cost?

There will be questions of opinion. Who is the appropriate lawyer to consult in the first stages of the venture? At what point should an accountant be called in, and how much should his or her first consultation cost? Should the same lawyer be used for drafting up or checking out contracts as the one who helps with incorporation? How big should the sales forecast be? To what extent should the product or service be tested on a small scale before being offered openly on the market? Will the company's resources last that long? What things can cause delays, and will the money run out before sales start bringing more in? What amounts of supplies should be ordered to begin with, under what terms? If suppliers will not extend credit, then what?

Some answers can come from books. Most will come from either simply "asking around" or the course of events, which many times present few choices. Some will be disappointing. In testing out the idea for the new product or service, for instance, people will frequently express enthusiasm—"That sounds like a great idea"—provided that they are not asked to make any commitments— "No, I'm not really in a position to put any money into something of that sort right now. My savings are tied up in certificates of deposit, and if I pull it out there will be a big interest loss." Worse yet will be instances where a pledge made early is later withdrawn—"I thought we could start with a purchase order for your new company, but my partners said it would be better to begin with an order on consignment to see how the customers like it first. Frankly, we are afraid of getting stuck with your stuff if it doesn't sell."

The founding president will be working in all functional areas, finance, sales, production, accounting, engineering, and so forth from before the enterprise is formed up through its early existence. With no staff of specialists, the starting individual or team will have to worry about real estate, advertising, sales commissions, purchasing, what to do with unhappy customers, how to handle charitable contributions, safety regulations, employee parking, stationery letter heads, zoning laws, consumer protection, bad checks, slow-paying customers, withholding taxes, janitorial maintenance, typewriter repairs, and changing locks on the doors. Selling will have to be handled, personally, not only to potential customers and repeat customers but also to suppliers, the banker, and employees. There will be no maintenance department to take care of breakdown in a complicated machine or even a leak in the roof.

In early stages most companies go through a survival period that becomes desperate at times. When things go awry there will be a drain on cash, and the entrepreneur(s) will have to persuade sources of capital to provide more. It will be hard to press customers for faster payment; many of them will take advantage of the new company's weakness to drag payments out and thereby make their own working capital go further. At the same time, suppliers will be reluctant to extend credit to the new firm because of its insecure future and consequently questionable ability to repay. Even if things go well there will be cash problems, because then the new company will need more working capital to support increased sales. Hence, either way there are likely to be persistent worries about the bank balance as payrolls have to be met, bills have to be paid, and the company moves from one squeeze to another.

Time will also be chronically short. There will be deadlines on deliveries, and in new products or services there are likely as well to be unanticipated "bugs" that cause delays. The only expediter available will be the entrepreneur, who may have to cajole suppliers to hurry up please, help employees learn about and solve problems of the new product or service, pacify customers who are intolerant of delays, and afterward deal with their dissatisfactions as they find things wrong with what they finally received. Although no studies have reported typical numbers of hours worked per week during the various stages of venture creation, it appears that typically both long hours and intense dedication are likely to be needed, as suggested by Morrison:

◆   The new owner-manager has just one job to do, the most immediate and important job in his life: to get his business operating successfully. He is likely to pursue that goal with a singleness of purpose that shuts out all extraneous activities, all diversions, and all social and civic involvements, that might in any way interfere with his getting his company into a sound, profitable condition. This channeling of his attention may be hard on his family and friends and even on his community but failure would be much harder on everyone concerned. Singleness of purpose include concentrating on one product, process, or market until the company succeeds in it.[46]

After the business is up and running, the time requirements continue to be high in many cases. In a 1985 study of 150 founders, Cooper et al. learned that the average number of hours worked per week was more than 60 hours for 24 percent and less than 40 hours for only 11 percent.[47]

Advisability

Even these exertions may not be enough to pull the company through, and for any of a variety of reasons it may fail, as suggested by Collins and Moore:

[46] Robert S. Morrison, *Handbook for Manufacturing Entrepreneurs* (Cleveland: Western Reserve Press, 1973), p. 26. Used with permission.
[47] Arnold C. Cooper, William C. Dunkelberg, and R. Stanley Furuta, "Incubator Organization Background and Founding Characteristics," in Hornaday et al., *Frontiers of Entrepreneurship Research, 1985,* p. 78.

◆   The machinery which he went into debt to buy may prove inadequate, the customer he counted on may be lost, or the item he was going to make may not be salable. He may find that the infant firm is feeding too many mouths, that he cannot wait until receipts start coming in, or that he has the wrong skills for the field he has entered. He may lose his plant space, or he may find that short-term loans will not be extended. He may find that supplies cannot be obtained, or he may get embroiled with tax or labor trouble. Finally, the long hours and anxiety may take such a toll that he cannot continue.[48]

In a 1985 study of eleven ex-entrepreneurs, Brockhaus identified the following reason for discontinuance:[49]

* Hours too long
* Disappointing growth potential
* Low sales volume
* Inadequate financing
* Business burned
* Interest rates too high
* New and stronger competition

He also found differences between expectations and experience: dealing with the public was disappointing, timed demands of the work were high, and profits were low. A majority of the ex-entrepreneurs indicated that they would not start a business again, but nearly all said they were glad they had started one.

On the other hand, there are abundant success stories to be seen in magazines and books, illustrating both that success is highly possible and that its rewards can be great.[50] The entrepreneur who succeeds can enjoy vastly greater independence and freedom than his or her employed counterpart. There is no need for the entrepreneur to ask "the boss" for permission to try a new approach or to buy an attractive new piece of equipment or to extend a vacation from one week into six. There is no need to look far for new challenges and opportunities, because once an entrepreneur is successful and that word gets around, others will continually bring in new ideas seeking support, and many times those who bring the ideas will themselves be exciting prospective entrepreneurs. The successful entrepreneur will find himself or herself encountering other successful people not only at business meetings and conferences but also in community activities and groups such as Rotary and Young Presidents Organization; these can be great sources of stimulation and inspiration as well as of information regarding further opportunities. To take care of "grunt work" such as tax forms, routine property repairs, and domestic chores, others can readily be hired. Company resources can provide paid vacations virtually anywhere—sometimes tax-free—leased cars, and sometimes private aircraft and

---

[48] Collins and Moore, *The Organization Makers*, p. 159.
[49] In Hornaday et al., *Frontiers of Entrepreneurship Research, 1985*, p. 468.
[50] For example, see *The Innovation Millionaires*, op. cit. Also see Lawrence Armour, *The Young Millionaires* (Chicago: Playboy Press, 1973); Peter Weaver, *You, Inc.* (Garden City, N.Y.: Doubleday, 1973); David L. Goodrich, *Horatio Alger Is Alive and Well and Living in America* (New York: Cowles, 1971); Harry Miller, *The Way of Enterprise* (London: Deutsch, 1963).

even pleasure autos. Moreover, the company need not necessarily be large to provide such things. All these were enjoyed, for example, by the owner of a ten-man shop that ground automotive racing cams.

Freedom and independence tend to be the most cherished advantages of self-employment by those who have achieved it. One entrepreneur made a typical comment:

♦   I don't mind working hard, but I don't like anybody else to be able to tell me what to do or when or how. When I fell like taking a day off or coming in late or working late or fooling around with a new idea I enjoy doing it without having to ask somebody else for permission.

Any number of other advantages can be noted. There is no mandatory retirement age for an entrepreneur. It is sometimes possible through a company to buy things at discount, like tools, supplies; one small businessowner noted he was even able to get original equipment manufacturers' discounts on things like motorcycles. Another said his business gave him opportunities to barter. This man, whose small company manufactured hi-fi speakers, pointed with pleasure to a fancy watch on his wrist. "I got that from a friend of mine in exchange for two speakers," he said. "He is a dentist, and it was given to him in exchange for some dental work by a computer salesman who received it as an award from his company for breaking a sales record."

Some people embark on new ventures simply because they are unemployed and don't know what else to do. When Walter Meyer was laid off as a Boeing engineer at age sixty, he felt there were not many options open to him. "It isn't too easy to find another job as an unemployed aerospace engineer these days," he said, "especially for an older person." Consequently, he pursued an idea he had for a fireplace heat exchanger that would both provide room heat and serve as an alternative cooking range for emergencies. Using his own savings, he created a new company to manufacture the product.

Many others start companies out of dissatisfaction with jobs. One entrepreneur recalled his line of reasoning in this regard as follows:

♦   Why should I work my heart out for some nameless, faceless stockholders, and let them make big profits off of my ideas and sweat when I can be taking home those profits myself. Some people may like the security and fringe benefits of a big corporation, but I find them dull and deadening. To me a life that has excitement and adventure in it is well worth the insecurity I pay for it.

Another entrepreneur with a small manufacturing company employing a half-dozen people also stressed the value of independence and added his pleasure with the freedom "to be able to tell anybody to go to hell."

♦   I thought one of the big local department stores might find our product of interest, so I called up and made an appointment with one of the buyers for the next Tuesday at 10 A.M. I got to his office a few minutes early and waited. But he was not there when 10 o'clock arrived. I waited another ten minutes and then I left.

I guess he'd seen the product showing up some other places around town, though, because he called me up and asked what had happened to me. I told him that I'd waited ten minutes and then had to move on to other activities.

He offered another appointment and I said OK. Again it was for 10 A.M. Again I got there on time. Again he was late. And again I waited ten minutes and left. A few days later he called again and we went through the same conversation and he said let's set up another appointment. I said, OK, but this time it has to be in my office. He agreed, and we had our little meeting, and I got a nice purchase order from him. If I had been working as a salesman for somebody else I never could have gotten away with playing it like that.

Other reasons for entering independent business have been advanced by various authors.[51] It is a myth that all the good opportunities are gone or that small new companies cannot compete with big established ones. This is perhaps easiest to see in the continuing proliferation of new companies in the electronics and computer industries, but it can be seen in others as well. It is not so hard to enter business as many imagine. Sources of all sorts of help, both technical and administrative, are available and can often be bought either with money, which is also available for the entrepreneur with a good idea and the initiative to pursue it, or with a share of the business. The sacrifices commonly associated with taking on a new business are often in fact not really made. As will be seen in examples of later chapters, there are entrepreneurs who started with no money of their own, entrepreneurs who took little or no drop in life-style to get into business, even entrepreneurs who were able to enter business without devoting great amounts of time to it. Moreover, although it is true that most small businesses are low-paying and high in risk and time demand, there are always some that are highly prosperous, as some mentioned above and many to be described later will illustrate.

The risk of failure is much less than popularly imagined in ventures chosen with care. Although roughly half of new businesses fail within the first five years overall, in some industries the prospects are completely the reverse. With high-technology startups, roughly four out of five succeed.[52] In economic downturn, moreover, the risk is also relatively low. During the great depression, for instance, around 40 percent of people who worked for others lost their jobs, yet less than 2 percent of businesses failed. Regardless of the business outcome, there is certain to be a high profit in terms of both learning and adventure for the entrepreneur who gives it a try. Win or lose, new venturing tends for most to be an exhilarating experience. "Finally," Baty has pointed out, "we reach the consideration that is probably more significant than the rest together: Starting a new business is more fun than almost anything else."

HAPPENSTANCE VERSUS PLANNING

Whether entrepreneurs are born or made should be irrelevant to one who wants to begin a business venture. History contains success examples of such a variety that it would be hard to rule anyone out, although there does tend to be a

---

[51] For example, see Gordon B. Baty, *Entrepreneurship for the Eighties* (Reston, Va.: Reston Publishing, 1981).

[52] "New High Technology Firms Post 80% Success Record," *Industrial Research*, November 1970, p. 26.

positive correlation between possession of both experience and education with success. Credit in many cases must go to either circumstance or personal will or both. Many times the emergence of an entrepreneurial career will be unforeseen, or even surprising. The 1985 study by Cooper et al. found that one-third entered entrepreneurship following termination of their prior employment and slightly less than one-half (47%) quit their prior jobs with plans for their startup.[53] The remainder either quit with no plans (14%) or had no prior job (3%).

One wealthy businessman commented upon being told that a former classmate had recently been appointed dean of an engineering school:

◆　　　It's funny. This man who became dean and his brother started out on exactly opposite paths from each other. His brother was going to become a physics professor, and the future dean was determined to build his own company. As it turned out they both did well in school and decided to stick to academics. Then the physicist in his research hit on the basis for a valuable product. He got a government contract to develop it on his own, found it necessary to hire some help, then found more work to keep them on when the contract ran out, and wound up with his own company while his brother continued in academics and has now become a dean.

My own career also turned out differently than I had expected. I was planning to be an engineering professor. During World War II the Navy pulled me out of my college and set me to counting inventory. That was driving me up the wall and I managed to get transferred to work on jet engine research. When the war ended I went to work for a large aircraft company that needed to diversify out of war work and wanted me to set up a laboratory to develop products for them. One idea from the lab which enthused me was the design for a new antitank missile. The company bureaucracy wouldn't buy it, though. This exasperated me so much that I asked permission to quit and develop it on my own, which they said was all right with them. Some friends and I teamed up, with one doing the aerodynamics and body, a second designing the guidance system, and I working up the rocket motor. We sold it to the Defense Department and each of us wound up with his own company as a result. A few years later we had all sold out and were financially well off. Two of us are now back in academics, but I've been getting progressively more involved in some real estate.

I don't plan to build another company, though. It's too much of a strain. I'm glad I did it and wound up as I did, though I probably wouldn't try it again.

Was this entrepreneur's progress into an entrepreneurial path and along it to success mainly happenstance? His words made it seem that he thought so, although by curious coincidence his two brothers also developed their own successful independent ventures, one in real estate and the other in meteorological services. This offers at least some grounds for speculation that factors beyond chance events were at work in their careers. A clearer case of one who developed his own company by deliberate intentional design was that of another engineer:

◆　　　He had been brought from Germany following World War II as one of many

---

53 Cooper, Dunkelberg, and Furuta, "Incubator Organization Background and Founding Characteristics," in Hornaday et al., *Frontiers of Entrepreneurship Research, 1985*, p. 75.

scientists "imported" by the U.S. government. When interviewed in 1958 he was working at the Defense Department's Aeromedical Laboratory in Dayton. "I picked this job rather than something that would pay me a lot more at a private company in the missile industry for two reasons," he said. "First, this laboratory does not develop weapons, and they are something I want nothing more to do with. Second, the government policies under which this laboratory operates will permit me to keep rights to the patents which I develop. I plan to create products that I can use to build my own company so I can become independent as I was in Germany before the war."

When the laboratory he was working for decided to cut back on some of the prosthetics projects he was working on, he solicited support from another government agency to take them over on his own. He installed some machine tools in his basement and carried on the work, first as an after-hours, part-time venture. Soon there were some other people employed in the basement as his little company began to sell innovatively designed hydraulic knees for artificial legs, and then a machine that would read books aloud to blind people. Government contracts for further research and product development followed as the engineer quit his job, opened up a shop on new premises, and carried out his plan to build and operate his own business.

An even more spectacular startup that appears to have come from an orchestrated process was that of Tandem Computer by James Treybig under the sponsorship of Thomas Perkins, a San Francisco peninsula venture capitalist. Silver describes it as follows:

◆   "Treybig earned a bachelor's degree in electrical engineering and an MBA from Stanford University before going to Hewlett-Packard Company as a marketing manager for five years. Perkins got wind of this bright, energetic young man and asked him to come to Kleiner & Perkins and read business plans and listen to the proposals of other entrepreneurs for a year, then write down his own business plan. . . .

"When his incubation period was over . . . Treybig had formulated one of the largest problem areas of the day: the need for a double fail safe computer." Starting in 1974 he built the company from sales of zero to over $1 billion in ten years.[54]

Studies of many startups show that so far this sort of systematic identification of opportunity and development of a venture is the exception. As Shapero has observed:

◆   In the many studies of technical company formations, seldom is a case found in which a gradual, phased, carefully planned succession of actions and discussions leads to a company formation. The situation is better described as one in which the individual or group is subjected to a constantly interacting and dynamic field of forces that pushed him in all directions. These forces include both internal and external components and the individual is often balanced between internal pushes and external constraints, or vice versa. Usually the forces counterbalance each other so that there is some stability and continuity in an individual's occupational movements. When the forces are out of balance, the

---

[54] A. David Silver, *Entrepreneurial Megabucks* (New York: Wiley, 1985), p. 430.

individual is "pushed" to act; if he is a potential entrepreneur, the act may be a company formation.[55]

For a given would-be entrepreneur the important fact is not that cases of deliberate rather than accidental entry are rare, but rather that they do occur and consequently have been proven possible. The question then becomes how best to prepare for such entry and arrange it.

ADVANCE STUDY

Three kinds of mental programming seem to go into venture creation. First is the basic mental programming of the individual. This appears to be a combination of innate programming or talent or ability, together with general life experience, that makes the person's mind what it is.

Second is what might be regarded as venture specific programming or learning that pertains to the particular enterprise. This may include professional training, such as that received by an accountant, a barber, or a physician. And it will likely include experience relevant to the venture which most often comes through work or sometimes comes through hobby activity.

Third is what might be termed general entrepreneurial learning. It includes the kind of knowhow that would apply across many ventures. Part of it is the learning about business that would apply to any business, whether startup or ongoing. This is the learning that business schools seek to impart to all their students. The other part of it is learning about business that would apply to startups in particular and is the subject of entrepreneurship courses and this book.

Such entrepreneurial learning can in turn be subdivided into strategic and mechanical types. Strategic information concerns how entrepreneurs can play their cards to discover and enter new ventures and how those new ventures can play their cards to prevail against entry barriers in the world of commerce. The mechanical information concerns nuts-and-bolts information about how to write a business plan, how to raise capital, how to set up sales channels, and so forth. This book focuses on the first of these two topics. It touches on mechanics in many of the examples and some of the discussions, but it does not attempt to treat mechanics as exhaustively as other books that concentrate on such topics as legal aspects, venture capital, and plan writing.

Most entrepreneurs learn how to start a venture simply by doing it, the same way the first engineers and doctors must have learned their professions, except that the lore of business is more common knowledge and is more widely disseminated by modern media. There are academicians who argue that entrepreneurship cannot be taught,[56] and many others teaching courses in it who

---

[55] Albert Shapero, "The Process of Technical Company Formation in a Local Area," *Technical Entrepreneurship*, eds, Arnold C. Cooper and John L. Komives (Milwaukee: Center for Venture Management, 1972), p. 79.

[56] Jim Roscoe, "Can Entrepreneurship Be Taught?" *MBA Magazine* (June–July, 1973), p. 12.

argue that it can.[57] There is research that indicates that entrepreneurs do learn from entrepreneurial experience and also from formal education, as well as research indicating that the probability of succeeding is highest for entrepreneurs who have both experience and education.[58]

Probably the best way to learn about entrepreneurship is, as in many fields, to plunge in and become involved in it. Two key words in this process are "action" and "exposure" on the part of the would-be entrepreneur. Each action taken in the way of pursuing a venture—talking to someone such as a potential partner, financial backer, or customer, or attempting some sort of venture, even as humble as deliberately buying a used car with the aim of reselling it at a profit—constitutes an experiment whose outcome will have some instructive value. Exposure, particularly in the way of developing new personal contacts who can be helpful in getting into a venture, can multiply the odds that more and better opportunities will be encountered. The more people who know that the would-be entrepreneur is seeking a venture, the greater the likelihood that someone may be put in touch who has a venture to offer, or part of a venture, or who needs some sort of help, or who can in some way collaborate for mutual benefit.

Reading information about venturing such as that presented in this book may also be helpful. It represents a distillation of experience from hundreds of ventures lived by others, and these can have instructive value to others in addition to those who lived them. By examining what those experiences were like, a person considering entrepreneurship as a career option may get useful ideas about whether venturing is for him or her, and if so what kind of venturing has most appeal. If the decision is to pursue venturing, then this distillation of prior experience can show what kinds of approaches have worked for others and may be workable again by new entrepreneurs. Thus the reading can become a helpful adjunct and guide to the kinds of action and exposure that can lead to success.

This book is broadly divided into two sections, strategies of individuals and strategies of companies. The first centers on the entrepreneurs, how they start out, links between their personal lives and the ventures they undertake, how they find their venture ideas, and through what sequences of events they marshal the key ingredients used to initiate their ventures.

Chapter 2 presents findings from the literature about factors that seem to account for the successfulness of some entrepreneurs versus others. Based on research studies of many different ventures, an exploration is made of the causes of success and failure, leading to suggested conclusions about how individual entrepreneurs can improve their chances.

Chapter 3 identifies different points in life from which individuals embark on ventures, career positions ranging from school through employment, un-

---

[57] Karl H. Vesper, *Entrepreneurship Education, 1985* (Wellesley, Mass.: Babson Center for Entrepreneurial Studies, 1985); and H. E. Kierulff, "Can Entrepreneurs Be Developed?" working paper, University of Southern California, 1973.

[58]. Lawrence Lamont, "What Entrepreneurs Learn from Experience," Douglas E. Durand, "Training and Development of Entrepreneurs," *Journal of Small Business Management,* Vol. 12, No. 4 (October 1974), 23; William P. Hoad and Peter Rosko, *Management Factors Contributing to the Success and Failure of New Small Manufacturers* (Ann Arbor: University of Michigan, 1964), p. 11.

employment, home, and retirement. A given reader will tend to identify most closely with one of these career points and less with others, and may choose to be selective in deciding where to begin this chapter.

Chapter 4 describes sequences, whatever the career starting points, that lead to ventures and by which ventures are created. It is shown that many sequences are possible but that generally five key ingredients must be recruited by the entrepreneur, either intentionally or otherwise, before the venture can be brought into being. Three major hurdles to be overcome in creating a company are identified, the most important one of which is generally the finding of a venture idea with sufficient margin potential.

Where such venture ideas come from is taken up in Chapter 5. Examples illustrate that most often they arise out of prior employment but that several other sources can also serve. It will also be seen that most often the ideas are not deliberately and methodically sought out, contrary to exhortations of much of the literature, but that methodical planning may be able to help. Suggestions are offered as to how the odds of discovering a viable venture idea through methodical efforts may be increased. The chapter concludes the first section with discussion of how a personal venture development strategy can be pursued.

The second section shifts attention to the enterprises themselves and strategies new companies can employ to break into the stream of ongoing economic competition. First, the range of choice in terms of different types of companies and lines of business is described in Chapter 6, together with the kinds of factors that lead entrepreneurs to choose some ventures rather than others. Although personal and venture strategies are to some extent segregated in the chapters of this book, it will be seen particularly in Chapter 6 that the two are often immediately interrelated, particularly as regards the influence of prior employment in choosing a particular type of company to develop, a theme that crops up repeatedly throughout the book.

Chapters 7 and 8 describe kinds of special advantages new ventures use to get started. Three main economic entry wedges, introduction of a new product or service, parallel competition not involving anything really new but employing lesser differentiation, and franchise entry are presented in Chapter 7. Another dozen competitive strategies less frequently used but equally powerful as entry wedges are presented in Chapter 8.

Chapters 9 and 10 take up a quite different but equally important strategy for business entry, which is to buy a going concern rather than starting a new one. The first of these two chapters describes methods for finding prospective acquisitions and checking them out. Chapter 10 then gives methods for determining price, describes different kinds of deals, and illustrates how they can be put together.

For those who may have an interest in new venture creation within large corporations, this subject is summarized in Appendix A. The chemistry of entrepreneurship from a policy-making perspective is discussed in Appendix B.

This book does not offer a unified formula for entrepreneurial planning. Rather, it attempts to increase the reader's capability for such planning by illustrating the great variety of strategic approaches that have proved to work for others. If there is any central theme it is that a large number of effective strategies are possible. The aim here is to acquaint the reader not with a comprehensive theory but rather with a spectrum of possibilities illustrated by real-life experiences. What the reader should get is the distillation of a great amount of entrepreneurial experience that can be absorbed on a collapsed time scale. The reader should become sensitized to a variety of types of opportunities and thereby more likely to recognize any that may come his or her way and to be able to act on them before someone else does. The beginnings of a "bag of tricks" for taking such action effectively should also be acquired by learning from the entrepreneurs in the examples.

Real-life examples are used throughout the book both to illustrate points and present them. Conceptual frameworks are used to organize the main points and to structure the arrangement of examples for more convenient reference, but many times the examples make points that speak well for themselves and need not be elaborated in the discussion. They also tend many times to confirm or reillustrate points made in other sections in a somewhat different way. The examples are not intended only as something to be skimmed while the text is carefully read but rather should themselves be read with care for the experience they contain. They may seem to be much to digest, and they are. The collective experimentation and experience they represent for the entrepreneurs who lived them represent an enormous investment of living, doing, and learning that the reader may share.

SUMMARY

Although the concept of entrepreneurship, as being associated with starting new businesses, may seem simple at first, there are in fact a great number of facets to this subject. This chapter pointed out eight different types of entrepreneurs, each of which could be subdivided into any number of types. It was noted that eleven different fields of entrepreneurial study can be identified within the existing literature, and here again much more subdivision would be possible. The aim of this book is not to attempt coverage of all of them but rather to concentrate mainly on entry, whether by startup or acquisition. Strategies for entry will be presented principally through examples, from which the reader may draw his or her own conclusions about whether entrepreneurship should be pursued as a career path and, if so, how.

chapter 2

Success and Failure Factors

Every entrepreneur, whether successful or not, has opinions based on prior experience about "rules" in entrepreneuring that tend to promote success. Most are willing to comment on the subject and will go on to indicate how they use such rules as guides to effective action. It has been observed that entrepreneurs become "better" with practice in starting companies,[1] and it can be inferred that improvement is in part attributable to refinement of individual operating rules. Collins and Moore have characterized this learning of effective rules as a sort of matriculation and advancement through a "school of experience," which includes such courses, for instance, as "basic dealing," in which entrepreneurs learn effective rules for striking bargains and interpersonal contracts.[2]

The kinds of rules entrepreneurs feel they learn are propounded in numerous books and articles that entrepreneurs themselves have written. Thus Baty tells the reader, "Remember, your banker is the fellow who's going to rent you working capital that you'd otherwise have to buy with undervalued stock."[3] Dible warns, ". . . if they are true entrepreneurs, their eyes will be bloodshot, and large black rings will have taken up residence just underneath."[4] Mancuso advises, "Think of failure as a resting place, and you're in the proper frame of mind to start a business."[5] Morrison suggests, ". . . it is essential to concentrate

[1] Lawrence M. Lamont, "What Enterpreneurs Learn from Experience," *Journal of Small Business,* Summer, 1972.
[2] Orvis Collins and David G. Moore, *The Organization Makers* (New York: Appleton-Century-Crofts, 1970), Chaps. 5 and 6.
[3] Gordon B. Baty, *Entrepreneurship—Playing to Win* (Reston, VA.: Reston Publishing, 1974), p. 163.
[4] Donald M. Dible, *Up Your Own Organization* (Santa Clara, Calif.: Entrepreneur Press, 1971), p. 46.
[5] Joseph Mancuso, *Fun & Guts, The Entrepreneur's Philosophy* (Reading, Mass.: Addison-Wesley, 1973), p. 41.

on one product until it is in profitable production."[6] Weaver cautions, "... remember, before you make any long-term commitments leasing an office or hiring a full-time employee, let your lawyer and accountant know about it."[7] Ablah offers twelve guidelines, including "identify the mutual benefit in all transactions," "measure the upside and downside," and "sales come first."[8] Brandt, among his "ten commandments," intones "define the enterprise in terms of what is to be bought, precisely by whom and why" and "project, monitor and conserve cash and credit capability."[9]

The basis for advice from experienced entrepreneurs is usually anecdotal. Sometimes it will have been a personal catastrophe that has impressed a lesson—e.g., "I will never take in a partner again"—that may be less than universally applicable. Other times it will be shared experience that the entrepreneur has gained: "My father said there was a name for anyone who would countersign a bank note. Do you know what it was? Fool." Typically, the basis for such remarks will be based on a sample of experience which, although it may be extensive for the particular entrepreneur, is nevertheless confined to a small number of people and ventures.

Methodical studies of broader samples have been made by a number of researchers exploring correlates of venture performance. Although they are often academically oriented toward discovery of correlations largely for the sake of simply explaining and understanding them, there are at least three reasons why a would-be entrepreneur might want to get acquainted with them. First, the studies do sometimes uncover generalizations which, although they do not apply 100 percent of the time, do nonetheless indicate how the odds run between particular lines of action and success. Second, consideration of things that tend to correlate with success and failure can be another way for an entrepreneur to take a fresh look at ways of operating based on the experience of many rather than only one individual. Third, in negotiation for support from others to get a venture started, perhaps to raise capital or to recruit key employees, customers, or suppliers, it may be helpful to display awareness of a broad perspective about what tends to work and not to work in entrepreneuring.

There are also good reasons for being chary of "guidelines" that might be inferred from such studies. The experiences of every entrepreneur are unique and therefore may be different from all findings of such studies. Such studies in pursuit of generalizations tend to look for consensus and to ignore many exceptions that might be closer to the case of a given entrepreneur. Entrepreneurs almost by definition are people who win by finding new breaks in patterns. Thus it may be almost the reverse of the pattern, something never stressed by its author, which the entrepreneur should contemplate rather than the pattern of any particular study or set of studies.

The entrepreneur is ultimately the one who determines whether the venture goes or not and who sets it up for failure or success through myriad other choices—hence the venture capitalist's dictum that "it is better to bet on a grade

---

[6] Robert S. Morrison, *Handbook for Manufacturing Entrepreneurs* (Cleveland: Western Reserve Press, 1973), p. 28.
[7] Peter Weaver, *You Inc.* (Garden City, N.Y.: Doubleday, 1973), p. 236.
[8] *Venture*, May 1987, p. 6.
[9] Steven Brandt, *Entrepreneuring* (New York: New American Library, 1982).

"A" person with a grade "B" idea than a grade "B" person with a grade "A" idea. Some of these choices may begin well before the venture idea occurs, and others as it progresses, as we will see shortly. Elements of the individual that are influential, for instance, emerged in a 1988 study by Cooper, Dunkelberg, and Woo.[10] They found that of 2,994 startups among National Federation of Independent Business members, surviving firms were more likely to have been started by full-time college-graduate entrepreneurs who had prior closely related work experience in the same industry but not necessarily in management and who were accompanied by full-time partners.

MEASURING SUCCESS

Venture success can have many different definitions. They can depend on the stakeholder: founder, investor, supplier, customer, employee, or lender. They can depend on the time frame: short versus long term, and when in the venture's life they are measured. They can vary in dimension: profit, return on investment, sales growth, number employed, happiness, reputation, and so on. Survival, growth, and profitability are alternative dimensions on which firms can differ markedly, as illustrated by the following findings of Birch from a study of data on over a half million firms started between 1978 and 1982.[11]

Most Likely Survival	Most Likely Growth	Most Likely Started
Veterinarians	Savings Banks	Business Services
Mortuaries	Electrical Parts Mfg.	Eateries, Pubs
Dental Offices	Cardboard Box Mfg.	Miscellaneous Shopping Goods
Savings Banks	Computer Mfg.	Auto Repair
Hotels, Motels	Paper Products Mfg.	Home Construction
Camps, Trailer Parks	Plastic Products Mfg.	Machinery, Wholesale
Doctors Offices	Basic Steel Mfg.	Real Estate Operators
Barbershops	Pharmaceutical Mfg.	Miscellaneous Retail Stores
Bowling, Billiards	Commercial Equipment Mfg.	Furniture Stores
Cash Grain Crops	Office Fixture Mfg.	Computer Services

---

[10] Arnold C. Cooper, William C. Dunkelberg, and Carolyn Y. Woo, "Survival and Failure: A Longitudinal Study," *Babson Entrepreneurship Research Conference*, Calgary, 1988.
[11] David L. Birch, "The Truth about Startups," *Inc.*, January 1988, p. 14.

There was little correlation, moreover, between these three dimensions. Thus while miscellaneous business services were most frequently started, their growth rank was 103 and their survival rank was 132. And while commercial savings banks were most likely to grow significantly and also had a survival rank of 4, their startup rank was only 93. Difficulty of entry, and just what it requires, can be an interesting dimension to trace through these lists.

Profitability can be yet another contrasting dimension. For example, among the manufacturers studied by Hoad and Rosko, the five-year survival rate was higher among process firms such as heat treating (92%) than among the makers of products (72%).[12] But the percentage of firms making a "healthy profit" was much lower for process firms than for product firms (15% versus 35%). More of the process firms appeared to be marginally surviving (38% versus 17%) rather than even paying their entrepreneurs a "moderate wage" (5% versus 9% for product companies).

Influence of Industry

The importance of industry choice was also observed in a study of one hundred startups by Murphy, who commented:

◆   In both my surveys, the conclusion remained the same. The man who chose the promising field did better than the man who elected to slug it out in one already crowded. Or, when the same man tried both, he often failed in the highly competitive business and went on to success in the growing one.[13]

Testament to the importance of line of work in achieving startup success is the great number of companies that violate rules of effective management and yet thrive. A fairly common recollection of many founders of companies that became successful is, "When we were starting we broke just about every rule in the book." An officer of one struggling small New England company observed: "If your company is headed in the right general direction, you can make an awful lot of managerial mistakes and still pile up profits."

Survival rates appear to have varied not only by industry but also by time period and geographical area, as shown in Table 2–1. Overall, a study of the six-year survival rates of startups among 3.6 million firms by Phillips and Kirchhoff found that "two out of five new firms survive at least six years, and over half of the survivors grow."[14] But the survival rate in manufacturing was a third higher than that in construction, for instance.

Table 2–1 also shows that survival rates continue to vary as categories are broken into smaller categories. Thus Draheim found that within high-technology manufacturing, medical device firms had considerably lower survival rates in the fifties than did other instruments and controls. Within manufacturing,

---

[12] William M. Hoad and Peter Rosko, *Management Factors Contributing to the Success and Failure of New Small Manufacturers* (Ann Arbor: Bureau of Business Research, University of Michigan, 1964).

[13] Thomas P. Murphy, *A Business of Your Own* (New York: McGraw-Hill, 1956). Used with permission.

[14] Bruce D. Phillips and Bruce A. Kirchhoff, "An Analysis of New Firm Survival and Growth," Babson Entrepreneurship Research Conference, Calgary, 1988.

TABLE 2-1 SURVIVAL AS A FUNCTION OF INDUSTRY

Study	Types of Companies (number)	Period (years)	Survival (percentage)
Birch, 1988*	Overall (1.1 million)	4	75
Phillips and Kirchhoff,	Overall (3.6 million)	6	40
1988†	Manufacturing		47
	Wholesale		44
	Agriculture, Forestry, Fishing		43
	Services		41
	Transport, Communications, Utilities		40
	Mining		39
	Finance, Insurance, Real Estate		39
	Retail		38
	Construction		35
Reynolds, 1986	Consumer Service (24)	1	96
(Minnesota)‡	Construction (107)		94
	Producer Service (102)		94
	Manufacturing (105)		93
	Distribution Service (123)		88
	Retail (84)		83
Bruno, Leidecker, and Harder, 1986§	Hi Tech, Silicon Valley (250)	15	62
Roberts, 1970‖	Hi Tech, Boston (250)	5	80
Hoad and Rosko, 1964	Small Manufacturing (95)	5	62
(Detroit area)#	Industrial Processing (13)		92
	Industrial Products (46)		72
	Consumer Nondurables (10)		40
	Consumer Durables (26)		38
Draheim, 1950–1961,	Hi Tech, Overall (111)	11	76
(Twin Cities)**	Supporting Firms (21)		95
	Controls, Instruments (17)		82
	Computer Gear (11)		82
	Electrical, Electronic (44)		73
	Medical Devices (43)		43
	Other (4)		100
Mayer and Goldstein, 1961 (Providence)††	Local Service Firms	2	51
McGarry, 1930‡‡	Druggists	1	73
	Hardware Stores		66
	Shoe Stores		56
	Grocery Stores		40

*David L. Birch, "Live Fast, Die Young," *Inc.*, May 1988.
†Bruce D. Phillips and Bruce A. Kirchhoff, "An Analysis of New Firm Survival and Growth," Babson Entrepreneurship Research Conference, Calgary, 1988.
‡Paul D. Reynolds, "Predicting Contributions and Survival," in Ronstadt et al., *Frontiers of Entrepreneurship Research, 1986*, p. 594.
§Albert V. Bruno, Joel K. Leidecker, and Joseph W. Harder, "Patterns of Failure among Silicon Valley High Technology Firms," in Ronstadt et al., *Frontiers of Entrepreneurship Research, 1986*, p. 677.
‖Edward Roberts, in Arnold C. Cooper and John L. Komives, *Technical Entrepreneurship* (Milwaukee: Center for Venture Management, 1972), p. 139.
#William M. Hoad and Peter Rosko, *Management Factors Contributing to the Success and Failure of New Small Manufacturers* (Ann Arbor: Bureau of Business Research, University of Michigan, 1964).
**Kirk Draheim, "Factors Influencing the Rate of Formation of Technical Companies," in *Technical Entrepreneurship*, a Symposium (Milwaukee: Center for Venture Management, 1972), p. 8.
††Kurt Mayer and Sidney Goldstein, *The First Two Years: Problems of Small Firm Growth and Survival* (Washington, D.C.: Small Business Administration, 1961), p. 80.
‡‡Edmund D. McGarry, "Mortality in Retail Trade," as reported in Godfrey M. Lebhar, *Chain Stores in America: 1959–1962* (New York: Chain Store Publishing, 1963), p. 97.

Roberts found a great difference between commercial and a small number of consumer products startups, which he recalled as follows:

◆ We expected about a two-thirds failure rate, but we found a 91 percent failure of consumer-oriented manufacturers. I think this must be a little worse than the general situation. It's harder to produce a consumer-oriented product and stay alive; it's easier to run a drug store or a grocery store. This was the most frustrating study we did. The research assistant who was working on this used to come crying to me each week and telling me how miserable things were. One of the interesting things was that he located one of the entrepreneurs in an insane asylum.[15]

The reasons for correlation between choice of industry and performance are not hard to discern. When the Arab oil embargo hit, it was bad to have entered the filling station business or to be making motor homes. When housing starts are up, it is good to be in the construction business.

Just as a company with a good strategic position can be hard to kill, one with a poor position can be virtually impossible to save, as illustrated by the following case of a fifty-seven-year old jewelry manufacturing company supervisor who wanted to escape the tensions of his job, found a cookie store for sale from the newspaper classified ads, and used up his savings to purchase and keep it open for a year before shutting down. The location, according to Mayer and Goldstein, who studied the case, was simply wrong:

◆ The failure of the business cannot be attributed to a lack of effort or motivation on Gould's part. He very much wanted the business to succeed and worked very hard. When he took over, he expanded the stock of cookies and put in a sideline of such items as candies and potato chips; he hoped that the greater variety would stimulate an increase in business. In general, he engaged in sound business practices. He determined his markup by the prices charged by the larger chain stores who were his main competitors. His practice of buying loose cookies in bulk and his relatively low overhead enabled him to undersell the chain stores and still realize a good profit. Yet, despite attractive prices and good quality, there was simply not enough demand to increase his volume sufficiently. He advertised extensively and ran special weekly sales attempting to attract more customers, but, on the whole, these efforts proved fruitless.[16]

Industry-Strategy Interaction

There appears to be a typical pattern of industry rise and decline where many new firms enter at the outset and then, as the industry matures, most of the entrants are killed off. Illustrations offered by Knight et al. have included the automobile, vacuum tube, semiconductor, and airline industries.[17] In a *Venture* magazine report on the largest founder-managed companies in 1976–86, com-

---

[15] Edward Roberts in Arnold C. Cooper and John L. Komives, *Technical Entrepreneurship, A Symposium (Milwaukee: Center for Venture Management, 1972), p. 139.*
[16] Kurt Mayer and Sidney Goldstein, *The First Two Years, Problems of Small Firm Growth and Survival* (Washington, D.C.: Small Business Administration, 1961), p. 80.
[17] "Venture Survivability," in Neil C. Churchill, John A. Hornaday, Bruce A. Kirchhoff, O. J. Krasner and Karl H. Vesper, *Frontiers of Entrepreneurship Research, 1987* (Wellesley, Mass.: Babson Center for Entrepreneurial Studies, 1987), p. 138.

puter and computer-related companies accounted for almost half of the top one hundred, with companies offering health-care-related products and services next. As a reminder that a single company is individual, not statistical, however, it may be noted that the top company on the list was Home Shopping Network, a video-shopping company founded in 1977 by Roy Speer, whose personal net worth by 1988 had reached $600 million.

The competitive patterns in an industry typically seen to vary with both the nature and the age of the industry. Aspects of the industry considered significant by Sandberg and Hofer included (1) structure in terms of monopoly versus competition; (2) stage of maturity, growth versus decline; (3) degree of equilibrium in terms of price consistency; (4) barriers to entry; and (5) industrial sector. Venture strategies analyzed across these included such dimensions as price, quality, innovation, and other aspects of differentiation. Seventeen ventures were classified on these variables, and their performance was judged by venture capitalists. There appeared to be some correlations, although the sample size was small. For instance, focus on a narrow market segment seemed to work better for startups in more mature markets than in newer markets.

A subsequent study by McDougall and Robinson explored the effect on market share and return on investment of the interaction between industry structure and strategy in 247 new ventures.[18] *Industry structure* was defined mainly in terms of entry barriers and *strategy* in terms of an assortment of variables statistically grouped through cluster analysis. Their finding was that both strategy and industry structure, measured as statistical composites, had significant effects on performance, but that interactions between the two produced the strongest effects. Both these researchers and Sandberg and Hofer also considered some variables associated with the individual entrepreneurs themselves but did not find links between those and venture performance.

Strategic Position

In the short run, the strategic position of a startup firm typically benefits from offering something ahead of competitors and therefore essentially having little or no competition. If the product or service is one the market really wants, then competition will enter, as the following entrepreneur learned.

♦   We were one of the first companies to start making this product (a gas heater for recreational vehicles), and for about five years we made a lot of money on it. But then more competitors started making it, and some of them began to grow a lot bigger than we were. Now I claim the distinction of being the only entrepreneur in this kind of business whose company hasn't made him a millionaire. We're on our last production run now and the auction of our plant equipment is scheduled for next month.

In the longer term beyond startup, profitability in terms of return on investment *on the average* (an important distinction in all statistical generaliza-

---

[18] Patricia P. McDougall and Richard B. Robinson, "New Venture Performance: Patterns of Strategic Behavior in Different Industries," presented at the Babson Entrepreneurship Research Conference, Calgary, 1988.

tions) appears to be determined by the firm's strategic position. According to Strategic Planning Institute data on over 2,500 strategic business units of large firms, the four key factors correlating with profitability are (1) low capital intensity, (2) high market share relative to competitors, (3) having a differentiated, rather than commodity, product, and (4) being in a growing market.[19]

Strategic Factors in Startup

In new ventures of large companies, success tends to go with (1) entering a growing market, (2) with few dominant rather than many fragmented competitors, (3) selling to relatively few customers, (4) a product or service that is not a major purchase for them, (5) putting the venture's emphasis higher on gaining market share in a narrow segment rather than initial profitability, and (6) being initially bold in terms of high quality, high production capacity, strong marketing push, and strong R&D effort. The extent to which these historical findings would apply to independent startups is not known, and if it were, the applicability to the prospects of a particular new venture would still, of course, be a matter of judgment.

For high-technology independent startups, Stuart and Abetti reported on results from twenty-four new ventures proximate to a university incubator which highlighted the importance of both the entrepreneur and the management.[20] Statistically significant relationships to success were found to be associated with the following, regardless of the apparent initial market attractiveness:

a Start with a good entrepreneur.

b Work in an area where the team has market and technical expertise.

c Work in a market not changing chaotically.

d Do not overemphasize research and technology.

e Run a tight ship.

f Ensure a normal balance in such areas as strategy and organization.

A clue that timing of the venture is an important variable can be observed from the fact that no new scheduled airlines existed in the five years preceding deregulation, whereas twenty-two started in the five years following it.[21] The interplay between timing, line of business, and the particular product or service concept is illustrated by Ted Harwood's experience:

◆　　　In the fall of 1976 Ted Harwood had succeeded in licensing a pocket calculator game to Texas Instruments for a handsome advance and had then gone on to develop a new game. He persuaded another young entrepreneur to

---

[19] Robert D. Buzzell and Bradley T. Gale, *The Pims Principles* (New York: Free Press, 1987).

[20] Robert Stuart and Pier A. Abetti, "Field Study of Start-up Ventures," in Robert Ronstadt, John A. Hornaday, Rein Peterson, and Karl H. Vesper, *Frontiers of Entrepreneurship Research, 1986* (Wellesley, Mass.: Babson Center for Entrepreneurial Studies, 1986), p. 21.

[21] *Inc.,* February 1984, p. 33.

make the plastic injection molds in return for 25 percent of the stock. Taking a prototype of the new game to Dallas, he managed to get a buyer at Horchow's mail-order house to play a round (which she won) and place a verbal order for seven hundred units, contingent on presentation of an acceptable final production version of the game and on ability to deliver. Another store, Neiman-Marcus, said "Maybe," which to Ted sounded very promising. At this point he began investing money to get production going, considerably more money than he had expected and with the emergence of more problems than he had anticipated.

Sales also proved disappointing. The first one to Horchow's went all right, but others turned out to be miniscule, far short of hopes and of what was needed to cover Ted's higher than anticipated costs. Ultimately, he folded the enterprise with a substantial loss and the following observation: "It might have been the right product two years earlier when pocket calculator sales were peaking and only I knew how to best fabricate and market it. It was the wrong product by 1977–1978. The correct line of innovation was not a game to be played with a calculator but games with electronics built into them, which have done astoundingly well the past several years."[22]

Failure Correlates

In their examination of failures in eleven high-technology companies, Bruno et al. identified the following ten causes, half of which centered on the fit between the company, its product, and the market connection: (1) product timing, (2) product design, (3) inappropriate selling/distributing strategy, (4) unclear business definition, (5) overreliance on one customer, (6) initial undercapitalization, (7) debt instrument too early, (8) venture capital relationship, (9) team formation, and (10) human failings.[23] Second to the nature of what the business was trying to do seemed to be problems in the area of finance, followed by "people" problems.

Some specific things that can go wrong in a high-technology manufacturing startup are listed in Table 2–2.

In a study of venture capitalists' views on why ventures fail to meet expectations, Gorman and Sahlman found that the most frequently mentioned problems—after those of the clearly dominant category, "ineffective management"—were delayed or unsuccessful product development followed by failure of the end-user market to develop as expected, problems with sales channels, problems with competition, and poor product/market fit, in that order.[24] The problem areas ranked not most frequent but most severe when they did occur were inadequate quality control followed by poor product performance. In a study by Neiswander and Drollinger, the opinions of entrepreneurs in successful growth firms of Northeast Ohio as to what was most important were found to

[22] See Ted Harwood, "A Venture Is Not a Game," *In Business,* November–December 1980, p. 42.
[23] Albert V. Bruno, Joel K. Leidecker, and Joseph W. Harder, "Patterns of Failure among Silicon Valley High Technology Firms," in Ronstadt et al., *Frontiers of Entrepreneurship Research, 1986,* p. 677.
[24] Michael Gorman and William A. Sahlman, "What Do Venture Capitalists Do?" in Ronstadt et al., *Frontiers of Entrepreneurship Research, 1986,* p. 429.

TABLE 2–2 Some Failure Causes in High-Technology Startups

A. Product Choice
   1. We did not pick what the market wanted (e.g., competitors came out with something better).
   2. We did not design what the market wanted most (e.g., we went for low price and cheap quality when the market wanted high quality).
B. Product Development
   1. It was beyond our technical capabilities (e.g., we could not get the product up to target specs).
   2. The development was too slow and costly (e.g., we ran out of money before it was done).
   3. There were too many bugs (e.g., we started selling it while there were still too many uncorrected imperfections).
   4. Our competitors leapfrogged us (e.g., the first generation we introduced was superseded before we could match it).
C. Sales
   1. We couldn't connect with the target segment (e.g., they might have wanted the product, but we couldn't reach them without advertising effectively enough).
   2. We were too dependent on one customer who didn't reorder enough.
   3. Our volume was too low to cover costs (e.g., maybe we didn't or couldn't price high enough).
   4. We chose weak dealers or couldn't recruit strong ones.
   5. We set up inadequate servicing (e.g., we tried to save money by hiring cheaper but inexperienced field reps).
D. Production
   1. New and inexperienced employees failed to produce adequate quality.
   2. Our suppliers didn't provide what we needed (e.g., our specs were wrong, or they couldn't do it, or our incoming inspection was remiss).
   3. Supplies did not arrive on time (e.g., suppliers delayed our job to work on a bigger one for someone else).
   4. Our design was not sufficiently developed to accommodate effective and efficient production.
E. Cost Control
   1. Sales costs were too high (e.g., we underestimated the advertising expenses or salespeople's salaries).
   2. Returns were too high (e.g., more problems than expected with the product).
   3. Interest was more than expected (e.g., receivables got out of hand because people didn't pay when they said they would).
   4. Service costs were too high (e.g., we expanded production too fast and costs got out of control).
   5. Manufacturing costs were too high (e.g., too much rework, or training needs exceeded expectations, or volume was too low to be efficient).
   6. Insufficient internal controls (e.g., we were preoccupied with some other problems and paid more than we had to on ordering materials, buying things, and making use of labor).
F. Finance
   1. We didn't have enough financing (e.g., lack of capital forced us to cut corners that hurt in other ways).
   2. It was too hard to get capital (e.g., we had to spend too much time seeking it, and this interfered with getting work done).
   3. Money cost us too much and ate away our profits.

be quality and ability to deliver on time, whereas industry contacts, appreciation of customer needs, innovativeness, patent protection, long-term contracts, and location were deemed less important.[25]

EDUCATION AND EXPERIENCE

Prior mental programming in the form of both formal education and experience in the particular line of work of the new venture repeatedly crops up as correlated in generally positive ways with odds of success in studies of startups. In a study of 120 successful small metalworking plants in Ohio, a Case Western Reserve University researcher found success both in entering and in surviving depended heavily on operating competence derived from prior experience.[26] Main conclusions of the study were as follows:

1 Characteristics of the industry, current product needs, location and timing for entry are important. Most industries, however, include *enough weaker operators* whose low quality, high prices, and/or poor service *allow entry.*

2 Most successful entrepreneurs had prior experience in the line of work and were recognized specialists in some mechanical, fabricating, or technical art. They also were either competent in a variety of business functions or sought complementary assistance. Most had earlier been successful but unhappy working for others.

3 In operation they tended to know what was going on at all times throughout the firm, who was doing what, how, and how well. They were effective also in getting information out where needed.

4 They were not oriented toward substantial further growth, but rather cherished their firms as they were.

The second of these four findings, which particularly emphasizes prior experience and competence, parallels in that respect the profile of the typical successful high-technology entrepreneur, although in other respects the two categories display contrasts. Entry in the high-technology firms is facilitated more by new product developments than by weaknesses in competitors, technical education is more highly emphasized, and for the most part such firms are not content to remain small but seek to grow as rapidly and large as possible. In reviewing eight separate studies of high-technology startups in different parts of the country, Shapero describes the typical founder as follows:

♦   He is approximately thirty-five years old at the time of founding his company. He is highly educated as compared to the general population. The majority have

---

[25] See D. Kirk Neiswander and John M. Drollinger, "Origins of Successful Start-up Ventures," in Ronstadt et al., *Frontiers of Entrepreneurship Research, 1986*, p. 335.
[26] Kenneth Lawyer et al., *Small Business Success: Operating Executive Characteristics* (Cleveland: Bureau of Business Research, Case Western Reserve University, 1963).

TABLE 2–3 SIGNIFICANCE OF EXPERIENCE VERSUS EDUCATION

	Sample Size	Total	Profit	Moderate Wage	Marginal Survival	Failure or Dormant
Experienced						
Educated	13	100%	61%	8%	8%	23%
Uneducated	4	100	25	9	14	52
Inexperienced						
Educated	24	100	25	12	17	46
Uneducated	37	100	8	24	38	30
	78					

a college degree, a percentage have graduate degrees. He is primarily educated in physics and engineering (this conclusion is biased by the fact that there have been no studies of the company formation process in the chemical, petroleum, pharmaceutical, and software industries). His work experience is fairly varied and extensive, the great majority having worked for two or more employers in their professional careers even though they are relatively youthful. The previous occupational experience was varied in marketing, finance, production management, and research and development. He is personally secure in that he feels no doubt in his ability to obtain work if his business fails. . . .[27]

As regards education, this finding about high-technology entrepreneurs is in some contrast with the findings of Collins and Moore's "low-technology" entrepreneurs, who tended not to be particularly highly educated, but it is in line with the finding of Hoad and Rosko, who also studied low-technology startups and found that the highest correlation with success occurred with possession of both experience and education (taken to mean one or more years of college). From their results, which are summarized in Table 2–3, it appears that the most likely combination to fail turns out to be experience without education, while second most likely to fail is education without experience. Conversely, most likely to be profitable is experience plus education and second most likely is a tie between having one of these two ingredients but not the other. Thus the safest strategy would seem to be betting on both.

An important factor appeared to be the amount and variety the work experience contained. From Table 2–4 it can be seen that either selling or finance plus three other skills had substantially higher correlation with success and less correlation with failure than having had experience in fewer skills. This too is a parallel with findings about high-technology entrepreneurs.

Stuart and Abetti studied fifty-two technical ventures and found that senior managerial experience in prior venture startups was the single greatest influence

---

[27] Albert Shapero, "The Process of Technical Company Formation in a Local Area," *Technical Entrepreneurship,* eds. Arnold C. Cooper and John L. Komives (Milwaukee: Center for Venture Management, 1972), p. 79. Used with permission.

TABLE 2–4 SIGNIFICANCE OF EXPERIENCE VARIETY

Types of Experience	Sample Size	Profit	Moderate Wage	Marginal Survival	Failed or Dormant
			Fraction of Sample		
Selling only, or fewer than three other skills	19	5%	10%	32%	53%
Selling plus three or more other skills	37	38	19	16	27
Finance plus three or more other skills	27	41	15	15	29
	83				

on performance.[28] This appeared to be further qualified in a study of one hundred "automation alley" startups by Chambers, Hart, and Denison, who found that startup experience was more associated with higher performance only when *some* of the founding team members had it.[29] From a study of 237 software firms, Tarpley[30] found positive correlation with success and (1) team size and (2) prior employment in mid-management as opposed to lower or higher. But the strongest correlate was (3) prior experience in the software business.

Yet another study with similar results was that of Woodworth et al.[31] These researchers sought factors that appeared to account for some firms being more successful while others were simply "typical," and they took a different approach in gathering data. Rather than judging the firms themselves they solicited views from professional advisers: sixty-one bankers, eighty-four lawyers, and eighty-one accountants. Such advisers have the advantage of seeing firms through life cycles of many years as opposed to studies that view them only at one point or over periods of only a few years at most. Entrepreneurs of more versus less successful firms were generally found to differ in the following ways:

[28] Robert W. Stuart and Pier A. Abetti, "Field of Study of Technical Ventures—Part III: The Impact of Entrepreneurial and Management Experience on Early Performance," presented at the Babson Entrepreneurship Research Conference, Calgary, 1988.

[29] Brian R. Chambers, Stuart L. Hart, and Daniel R. Denison, "Founding Team Experience and New Firm Performance," Babson Entrepreneurship Research Conference, Calgary, 1988.

[30] Actually, I guess the reference should be to Teach, et al. the article is: Teach, Richard D., Tarpley, Fred A., Jr. and Schwartz, Robert G., "Software Venture Teams," in Ronstadt, Robert, Hornaday, John A., Peterson, Rein and Vesper, Karl H., *Frontiers of Entrepreneurship Research, 1986,* Wellesley, MA, Babson Center for Entrepreneurial Studies, p. 546.

[31] Robert T. Woodworth et al., "The Entrepreneurial Process and the Role of Accountants, Bankers, and Lawyers," unpublished paper (Seattle: Graduate School of Business, University of Washington, 1969).

Typical Entrepreneur	More Successful Entrepreneur
First-time startup	Had prior startup experience
Sought professional help in response to problems	Sought professional help in anticipation of problems
Did not know what advice he needed about problem	Knew which specific advice he needed from professional
Felt competent in all areas	Felt weaknesses in certain areas
Not sure where to go for advice	Knew where to seek what advice
Lacked the most key skills of the line of work, although having other important but less key skills	Either had or acquired key skills of the particular line of work
Operations oriented; emphasized quality of output	Total business and profits oriented; concerned with operations only as part of whole
Fairly well educated	Slightly better educated.

Here, in addition to Hoad and Rosko's finding that variety of experience pays, there is also the implication that prior experience in startup is particularly valuable. Reinforcement for this view can be seen in the Lamont study mentioned earlier and the study of Collins and Moore, who observed that many of their successful entrepreneurs had gone through several startups, many of them failures, prior to creating a "winner."

People without advanced education and without experience can become successful entrepreneurs. This is implicit in the statistics, wherein all rules show exceptions. It appears, though, that to play with the odds a would-be entrepreneur might do well to give favorable consideration to the following possible preparatory actions:

1 Seek higher education
2 Seek work experience in several functional areas, preferably including marketing and finance as well as line work
3 Take advantage of opportunities to participate in initiation of new ventures as educational trials in preparation for the "main event"

The "course of study" most emphasized by Collins and Moore is what they call "basic dealing." As they see it, this "course" is implicit in experiences wherein the future entrepreneur practices making "deals" that bring ideas, people, and resources together to make profits. Many of these experiences will have intensely uncomfortable aspects, such as being disdained by acquaintances as a hustler, having to solicit funds and being turned down, being squeezed out of deals by associates so they need share less, learning that what looked like the long end of a bargain was in fact the short end, and being accused of double dealing by associates who believe they got the short end. Obviously, these are not experiences to be sought directly. But they may be consequences of experiences in arranging deals that do exercise and develop entrepreneurial ability.

How Experience Works

The kinds of lessons experience teaches about entrepreneuring are illustrated by some of the exhortations of authors like Baty, Mancuso, and Morrison mentioned earlier. But reading such "rules for success" is usually not enough. Morrison makes this point, illustrating it with the example of a would-be entrepreneur who, upon asking about the rules for success, is advised by a successful businessman to "plead poverty and cheat everyone you can." Proof that the imprint of such verbal lessons can be shallow appears some time later when the younger man enters into a deal with the same man who advised him and is cheated.

A more penetrating learning which can be harder to describe in a few words is that which provides automatic reflexes, almost instincts. Moreover, these can be shaped not only in favor of successful entrepreneurship by some types of experiences, such as practice entrepreneuring, but also against it by contra-entrepreneurial experiences. Such contra-training may have been picked up by two civil service employees who had become skilled in "empire building" in a government agency before they teamed up with an independent entrepreneurial venture.

♦ Having built a successful consulting trade, an entrepreneur began branching into development of measuring instruments used for his research. Because it appeared to him that substantial governmental markets were likely to open for use of the instruments, he recruited two research administrators from a nearby governmental laboratory who had reputations for having built the laboratory to considerable size and reputation. His intent was that these two would guide his small ten-man company on a similar path of growth and prosperity through their intimate knowledge of governmental personnel in the growing field.

Upon joining the company, the two former "bureaucrats" immediately hired some additional people and set the company to work building apparatus with which to demonstrate new systems that they believed would identify the company with frontier capability in the state of the art and thereby help it win contracts. Soon a lot was "going on." The company was bustling and growing in personnel.

The added personnel and materials purchased to build the new systems put heavy loads on the company's finances. When "bugs" developed in the new designs, the limits of money resources in the company were reached. The contracts did not materialize, and to keep from going under the entrepreneur was forced to sell out on terms less favorable than he might have wished. The bureaucrats went back to the government.

Another type of experience is simply knowhow in a particular line of work. Venture capitalists are expressing concern for this factor when they ask for information about the "track record" of founders who want capital for a new company. What they hope to see is that among the founders is included a history of unique achievement in the particular field to be entered, evidence that the founders have the special expertise that shows that they can do a better job in the particular field they plan to enter than anyone else already there. This field may be extremely narrow—a special price range where no competitors are now operating, performance specifications such as extreme accuracy in a particular type of product which no other firms can presently offer, or close familiarity with the needs of certain important customers which other firms have not been able to acquire.

Questions that a would-be entrepreneur may use to test for existence of this special expertise are: What can I (or my founding team) do better than anyone else? What do we know more about than anyone else? What do we have more working experience in than anyone else? If the answer turns out to be some phase of steel plant operation, or university management, or governmental lobbying, wherein it is extraordinarily difficult to build a business, then the entrepreneur's only entry choice may be some type of consulting. If the answer is, "Nothing; there are many like us," the problem is much worse. But if it concerns some new product or service with an expanding market, or if there is a way to develop expertise in such a direction from the point where the entrepreneur now stands, then the chances are favorable.

One way of going into business, for example, can be to buy the assets of a bankrupt company at auction. Anyone unfamiliar with the line of business using this method to get started would in some respects be in the position of one who was not at all acquainted with autos trying to buy a used car, only worse, because auction buying is an art based on experience in its own right. How would the newcomer know that the other bidders, who if they are experienced are likely to know each other, have not agreed secretly in advance how far they will go, a practice known in the trade as a "kipper"? Or how will the newcomer know whether they may not be signaling to each other as one scratches his nose and another absentedmindedly flicks his cigarette lighter?

In fact, if he doesn't take care the newcomer may himself accidentally make some signal that awards him the purchase of something he had no intention of buying. He may fall victim to any number of other "insider" tactics: the auctioneer who has worked out a deal in advance, perhaps for a price, to sell to a certain bidder; or merchandise disguised to look as if it is worth less than it is by someone who then bids higher than the others to get it; perhaps a bolt of cloth mismarked to contain more than it does. Or merchandise disguised to look better than it is, a barrel with good items on top and junk at the bottom. In auctions there are no warranties, and when experienced operators are knocking down 100 lots per hour or one every thirty-six seconds, the newcomer has to make his permanent decisions very fast. How can an entrepreneur not experienced in the line of business he is buying for compete with an experienced auctioneer who in describing his art observes, "Look into a man's eyes and you can tell if he really wants a particular item"?

Even a modicum of "peripheral" experience related to the area of the business, although tremendously helpful, may not be sufficient to ward off serious problems that call for sustained working experience, as illustrated by the following episode.

♦ In July 1961 a young man working on the docks in Alaska, who had been giving serious thought to the possibility of opening a fish smoking house as soon as he and his wife had saved some money, suddenly learned that his father had died. As a result he was faced with a decision about whether to take over a small fish brokerage business that his father had developed, largely as a hobby, after selling off a cannery some years earlier and retiring. Although the young man had worked in his father's cannery during his school years and also on fishing boats, his father had never invited him to participate in the brokerage, because as he put it, the young man "didn't pack the equipment" at the time.

The brokerage business involved buying fish from other brokers and from fish processors and arranging for sale to other brokers and distributors in distant localities, such as New York and abroad. The current volume in the company, whose only tangible assets were a desk and a $28,000 bank account, was $125,000 gross sales per year, on which it did slightly better than break even for the owner.

The young man took the business on, agreeing to pay his mother the $28,000 as soon as the company could spare it, and drawing a salary of $250 per month for himself. A secretary-bookkeeper was also retained part time for $250 per month who let him use her kitchen table for a desk. The company's sole customer was a broker in New York, who promised to continue buying what the company could provide. The main supplier, however, would not guarantee anything.

Attempting to buy fish proved to be a serious problem. It was several months before the young entrepreneur found out that the "old hands" he was buying from were charging him higher than usual prices while at the same time misrepresenting quality in the fish he bought. A supplier might say a load of salmon were caught by trolling when actually they had been gill netted, making them worth twenty cents per pound less. The young man knew how to tell the difference visually, but most orders were processed remotely, and when the fish arrived at the buyer, the young man would have to pay the difference. It seemed to him that his suppliers would not take him seriously, as they had his father, in business deals. At the end of the first year his new company showed a loss of $3,000 on sales of $100,000 and and things were not improving.

This example of problems with inexperience concerned the area of purchasing. Others can be found in any other functional area. In the next example, for instance, they occurred in sales.

◆   The restaurant equipment business looked attractive to one would-be entrepreneur, who was thinking of acquiring a small manufacturer of such products. These products were sold to restaurants and hotel supply houses, which in turn sold them to the trade. He noticed that in the showrooms these products were offered at list prices suggested by the manufacturers, and the manufacturer he was considering acquiring informed him that the standard discount to such supply houses was 50 percent off list. These figures made the business appear to be an attractive proposition, and he was puzzled that it was not making money.

He was saved from his illusion by an experienced salesman, who let him in on the fact that there were other factors at work in the sales picture. Competitors of the small firm offered wider lines of products, and were able to offer rebates on purchases, which could be larger because more different items were included. They were also able to spread advertising costs thinner across the wider lines. In making shipments to the supply houses, they were able to offer freight discounts by packing different kinds of products together and thereby shipping optimally loaded containers to take advantage of certain levels in the standard freight rate schedules. In all, he found that the small company was at a substantial sales disadvantage not easily evident to the eye of a newcomer.

In the operations area, an entrepreneur who founded a company making artificial limbs learned, from experience, some of the ways his employees could "take" him if precautions were not applied. One many working in assembly would, when anyone was around, work very energetically assembling wrist units. Some of them he would later hide under his bench, and these he would use at later times as evidence of his output following sessions in which he "goofed off," working on personal projects of his own at company expense. Also it was learned that the janitor, whom the entrepreneur had been trying in spare moments to upgrade by teaching him machine operations, had been carrying off small tools of the company and selling them to a nearby hock shop.

There are also numerous examples of entrepreneurs who started successfully without advanced education and/or without prior experience in either entrepreneuring or the particular line of work. Some of these can be seen among the illustrations presented in the preceding pages, and others will be seen later. They tend, however, to be the exception, with the rule rather being that entrepreneurs most often start in lines of work where they have had some degree of prior experience. The exception frequently occurs when the entrepreneur enters the venture through acquisition of a going concern rather than startup, as will be further discussed in later chapters.

COLLABORATION

Before it goes very far, any venture has to involve collaboration between the entrepreneur and others, and the effectiveness of this collaboration can be crucial to success. For convenience, collaboration can be considered in three categories:

1 *Internal team.* Members who may participate in the founding of the firm.
2 *External team.* Advisers and other outsiders who actively work for the venture.
3 *Connections.* Individuals who, although they are not directly hired for services, nevertheless interact with and affect the company's progress.

For many entrepreneurs, the instinct in forming a new venture is to "go solo." Often the reasons for choosing to start a company in the first place are part of a quest for greater personal freedom and liberation from authority of others. If the entrepreneur can manage to retain all ownership in the new company, there should be no disputes about who has control or how things should be done, and less time will be wasted informing people and coordinating to get action. Moreover, retention of ownership can mean not having to share the spoils of success, if they come, with partners. Finally, a decision to go solo can represent a rejection of weakness, an overcoming of the fear of taking chances alone, as Weaver recalls of his own venture:

♦   Your insecurity tends to push you toward the comforting image of a partnership. "We can do it together," you say. You won't have to face all those decisions alone. I know, I was looking around for a partner in the early stages of my breakout. I must have looked pathetic, like a dog searching for a friend, or a child hunting for a security blanket.[32]

[32] Weaver, *You, Inc.,* p. 201.

There are also, however, some strong reasons to favor the use of an *internal team* in founding a venture, including that (1) teams make available larger labor effort, and (2) teams can provide a more complete balance of skills and other resources with which to start. With a team, (3) the departure of any given member is less likely to be disastrous for the venture than with a lone entrepreneur. (4) With a team, the venture should be able to grow further before having to expand valuable management effort in seeking out and recruiting additional key talent. (5) A willingness and ability on the part of the initial entrepreneur to assemble and work with a team can be symptomatic of ability to attract and manage people, whereas inability or disinclination to work with a team may signal, particularly to potential investors, a lack of managerial capacity for growth. Finally, (6) the attempt to recruit team members can be a preliminary stage of checkout of the venture idea. Their willingness to join can be indicative of its merit as well as the founder's.

Venture capitalists clearly favor team-initiated ventures for all these reasons, based on their observations of many startups and the problems they have lived with. Buchele notes that a long-time recipe for startup disaster has been that of the star salesman who, acutely aware of the importance of sales to any firm, particularly the one he works for, decides to start his own company and thereby realize more fully the fruits of his great ability.

◆   Why, indeed, shouldn't he start his own company instead of having other persons riding along on his genius? So he starts a company, sometimes in partnership with a man who has production experience, but they fail because of unwise financial commitments, or because of neglect to secure and use accounting data, or because of some other error.

In more recent years, with the increased emphasis on technological advance, a common pattern is for engineers or scientists to go down a similar path to failure. Their reasoning starts with, "After all, in this age of technology, design ability is the critical factor..."[33]

Findings of studies as to the relationship between solo versus team ventures are somewhat mixed. Collins and Moore were not explicit on this point, but it appears that most of their success stories were solo rather than team.[34] Miller indicated that among his twenty success stories "more than half of the businesses started on one man's initiative, the rest on the cooperation of two or three partners."[35] Baty, however, fairly summarizes much of the literature on the high-technology startups by saying that "both academic studies and venture capitalists' experiences seem to confirm that a team effort is more likely to succeed than is the individual effort."[36] Bruno and Cooper, for instance, studied San Francisco peninsula high-technology startups and reported that the main correlates of success were (1) multiple founders, (2) coming from prior employment with large organizations, or incubators, as will be discussed shortly,

[33] Robert B. Buchele, *Business Policy in Growing Firms* (San Francisco: Chandler, 1967), p. 18.
[34] Collins and Moore, *Organization Makers*.
[35] Miller, *The Way of Enterprise*, p. 124.
[36] Baty, *Entrepreneurship—Playing to Win*, p. 51; also Susbauer in Cooper and Komives, *Technical Entrepreneurship*, p. 45.

(3) in a related product area.[37] Teach, Tarpley, and Schwartz found that in computer software startups, greater success tended to accompany larger teams whose members had worked in middle management and who had previous software industry experience.[38] For fourteen educational software startups supported by corporate sponsors in particular, Van de Ven, Hudson, and Schroeder reported that on a composite success measure the correlates were education, experience, internal locus of control, number of ways of minimizing risk, a broad view of the business idea, and personal investment by the entrepreneurs.[39]

Four general conclusions regarding internal teams suggested by the literature are as follows:

1 Advisability of teaming depends on the nature of the venture. A venture that must begin on a larger scale typically needs a team more than one that can begin very small. Artisan ventures often can start solo. High-technology ventures more often call for teams.[40] Ventures requiring more startup capital more likely will have to start as teams.

2 Advisability of teaming depends on the entrepreneur. One who in prior work has been highly specialized more likely needs complementary partners. One who prefers to deal with only certain types of problems— technical, or sales, or wheeling and dealing, or some other particular area—or one who wants to operate only part time rather than plunging fully into the new venture to the exclusion of all other activities more likely should have partners.

3 From the above it follows that generally partners (or other shareholders) should have things to contribute to the venture that are complementary to each other, and between them they should provide a fully rounded managerial capability in sales, production, technology, finance, accounting, and so forth. A weak link can kill the venture.

4 The advantages of going solo stated earlier suggest that generally the smaller the team that can provide the needed rounding of management, the better. In Baty's words, "the burden of proof is definitely on the larger team."

External teaming, as with bankers, lawyers, accountants, and consultants, is highly important in the opinion of some entrepreneurship authorities (particularly those who sell consulting services). Swayne and Tucker, for example,

---

[37] Arnold C. Cooper and Albert V. Bruno, "Success among High Technology Firms," *Business Horizons,* Vol. 20 (April 1977), 16.

[38] Richard D. Teach, Fred A. Tarpley, and Robert S. Schwartz, "Software Development Teams," in Ronstadt et al., *Frontiers of Entrepreneurship Research, 1986,* p. 546.

[39] Andrew H. Van de Ven, Roger Hudson, and Dean M. Schroeder, "Designing New Business Startups," *Journal of Management,* Vol. 10 (1984), 87.

[40] Shapero (in Cooper and Komives, *Technical Entrepreneurship,* p. 70) notes, "One study of 955 prospectuses for company offerings shows that 59 percent of the technical companies were formed by groups, as compared to 27 percent of the nontechnical companies. A study of company formation processes in Austin, Texas (Susbauer, 1969) shows that approximately half of the formations studied (11 out of 23) were group formations."

TABLE 2–5 ADVISERS SOUGHT PRIOR TO ESTABLISHING BUSINESS

Type of Adviser	Fraction of Successful Firms	Fraction of Marginal Firms	Fraction of Failures
Lawyer	67.6%	40.9%	58.3%
Banker	48.6	31.8	52.8
Accountant	51.3	40.9	36.1
Future customers	43.2	36.4	30.5
Consultants	8.1	4.5	13.9
Wife	62.1	68.2	61.1
Friends	43.2	45.4	38.9

suggest identification of outside-help needs as the third out of fifty-seven steps to go through in starting any enterprise.[41] Mancuso stresses importance of lawyers, bankers, accountants, insurance agents, advertising agencies, and man-ufacturers' representatives.[42] Weaver indicates that "skillful use of these professional helpers can make it easier to get along with fewer full-time, paid experts in your own company. You buy consulting help only when you need it. Having a full-time partner to fill an expertise void in your business can be much more costly."[43]

Among entrepreneurs, those who pay the bills of such assistance, the exhortation to engage such outside team members is less unanimous. Studies of correlation between use of this assistance and success offer mixed results. Clearly, for some tasks such external advisers are essential, particularly after the firm gets going, but also in some of the setup steps. Most needed, perhaps, is the lawyer who helps with drafting of partnership or corporate papers, checks contracts, and so forth. Yet some entrepreneurs handle even these matters themselves, sometimes getting into trouble and sometimes not. Hoad and Rosko found, for example, that only 67 percent of the successful companies, as compared with 58 percent of the failures, consulted lawyers before establishing their businesses, and only 8 percent of the successes versus 14 percent of the failures engaged consultants prior to startup.[44] These results appear in Table 2–5.

More important than whether such external team members were used, perhaps, is how they were used. The study by Woodworth et al., for instance, found that both typical and more successful engineers utilized outside advisers, but that more successful entrepreneurs exhibited more specific knowledge of what advice was needed and why. This may suggest that a would-be entrepre-

[41] Charles Swayne and William Tucker, The Effective Entrepreneur (Morristown, N.J.: General Learning Press, 1973), p. 104.
[42] Mancuso, Fun & Guts, pp. 57–69.
[43] Weaver, You, Inc., p. 223.
[44] Hoad and Rosko, Management Factors, p. 68.

neur should obtain some education about each of these specialties in advance of engaging the specialists so as to use them most effectively.

Personal contacts or connections who are not formally paid by the venture include some of the advisers mentioned above and also others who can be extremely helpful at times. Examination of the history of startups reveals that the idea to form a particular type of venture in the first place often comes from some sort of contact: conversation with an acquaintance, former employer, customer, or other business associate who never becomes hired by the firm. In order to start, the entrepreneur will have to form numerous external connections, with governmental agencies, suppliers, sales channels, a landlord, sometimes even with competitors. Some connections will be easy to form and utilize. Others, as illustrated by the example of the young man entering the fish brokerage business, may be difficult.

It is desirable, insofar as possible, to line up in advance of forming the new company as many of the needed team members and connections as possible, so that excessive effort in the crucial startup phase will not have to be diverted to that activity. "People aspects" are likely to become critical before long, as underscored by a study of some 757 small firms in Georgia, which concluded:

◆   Regardless of the number of workers employed, the most prevalent problems that small manufacturers encounter in developing and managing their businesses are again confirmed to be those relating to the procurement, development, and utilization of manpower.[45]

PRIOR CHOICES—EMPLOYER
AND GEOGRAPHICAL LOCATION

Any of the success-related factors mentioned so far may be heavily influenced by the would-be entrepreneur's choice of employer(s) prior to startup. For instance, Feesser and Willard compared computer equipment companies, thirty-nine of them high growth from the *Inc. 100* list and thirty-nine low growth from Dun and Bradstreet data, and found that high-growth founders tended to come from larger and publicly held organizations competing in technologies and markets similar to those of the ventures.[46] It is, therefore, not surprising to find among studies of success that some employers, sometimes referred to as "incubator firms," tend much more than others to breed new independent ventures. Illustration can be seen in the fact that in 85 percent of the startups studied by Cooper the technology of the new venture was similar to that of the incubator, and 64 percent displayed similarity of markets.[47] Similar relationships

---

[45] Jerry L. Lewis, *Identification and Evaluation of Problems and Needs of Small Manufacturing Management* (Engineering Experiment Station, Georgia Institute of Techology, July, 1973), p. 17.

[46] Henry R. Feesser and Gary E. Wilard, "Incubators and Performance: A Comparison of High and Low Growth in High Tech Firms," Babson Entrepreneurship Research Conference, Calgary, 1988.

[47] Arnold C. Cooper, *The Founding of Technologically-based Firms* (Milwaukee: Center for Venture Management, 1971).

are depicted in "begat charts" of studies from other geographical areas. Sus-bauer, for example, traces some twenty startups to three initial incubators in the Austin, Texas, area,[48] and Draheim traces numerous "begats" from such companies as Univac Division of Sperry-Rand and Bell Laboratories.[49] A begat chart example for Fairchild Semiconductor is shown in Figure 2-1. One thing that can be traced through such charts is the proliferation of a technology. Or put another way, the choice of employer may represent the choice of a tech-nology that is suitable for startup companies. The August 1984 issue of *Venture,* for example, listed sixteen companies founded by people who had left Memorex in the early 1970s and whose sales by 1984 amounted to over $750 million.[50] All of them appeared to be either directly or very closely related to magnetic recording, the focus coincidentally of Memorex, which itself came from Ampex, also a magnetic recording products company. In summary of the type of firm most likely to serve as an effective incubator, Cooper offered the following list.[51]

More Likely Incubator	*Less Likely Incubator*
High-growth industry	Slow growth industry
Rapid technological change	Slow technological change
Low capital investment required	Heavy capital investment required
Minor economies of scale	Substantial economies of scale
Small number of employees	Large number of employees
Product-decentralized organization	Functionally specialized organization
Recruit capable, ambitious people	Recruit average technical people
Afflicted with periodic crises	Relatively well managed
Region of high startup rate	Located where few startups occur

It can be noted from the last item on this list that the choice of geographical area can influence entrepreneurship. For startups in general, Dennis observed that some states have much higher rates than others (in the 1976–78 period, Nevada had 4.63 startups per thousand people and Florida 4.22 versus Penn-sylvania 1.87 and West Virginia 1.66), which seemed to be associated with the population's level of mobility (even after being corrected for size).[52]

For high-technology industries in particular (e.g., electronics, computers, biotechnology) as opposed to startups in general, such areas as Boston, Palo Alto, and Los Angeles have been unusually prolific. In those areas there appear to be a number of reinforcing factors for new industry (not to be confused with branch plants) particularly including skilled venture capitalists, and other entre-preneurs from whose experiences helpful lessons and counsel can be mined. One study found marked contrasts in the behavior of bankers in regions of

[48] Jeffrey C. Susbauer, "The Technical Entrepreneurship Process in Austin, Texas," in Cooper and Komives, *Technical Entrepreneurship,* p. 33.
[49] Draheim, in Cooper and Komives, *Technical Entrepreneurship,* p. 28.
[50] Sabin Russell, "Life After Memorex," *Venture,* August 1984, p. 44.
[51] Cooper, *Technologically-Based Firms,* p. 58.
[52] Shapero et al., *The Role of the Financial Community in the Formation, Growth, and Effec-tiveness of Technical Companies* (Austin, Tex.: Multidisciplinary Research, 1969).

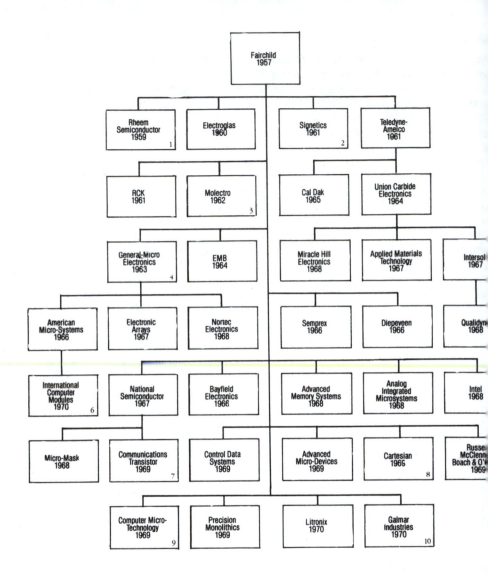

NOTES:
1. Acquired by Raytheon in 1961.
2. Two founders were from Semiconductor Corp.
3. Assets of Molectro acquired in reorganization of National, which moved from Connecticut to California.
4. Acquired by Ford-Philco in 1966.
5. Other founders were from Circuit Engineering & Design, Fairchild, GE, and Union Carbide
6. Three founders from AMI and three from Hewlett-Packard.
7. Two founders from Fairchild.
8. One founder from Philco-Ford Microelectronics.
9. Four founders from Fairchild and one from ITT Semiconductor.
10 Two founders from Fairchild, and one from Semimetals Inc. and one from Peripheral Systems Corp.

FIGURE 2-1 FAIRCHILD BEGAT TREE (1957-70).

Source: Draheim, Kirk P., "Factors Influencing the Formation of Technical Companies," in Cooper, Arnold, and Komiles, John, *Entrepreneurship: A Technical Symposium,* Milwaukee, Center for Venture Management, 1972.

high startup rates as opposed to regions where few startups occurred.[53] The former displayed skills much more likely to be of help to new firms (i.e., requiring a well-balanced board of directors in the new company and maintenance of key ratios as the basis for sustaining a loan rather than requiring collateral). Similarly, it might be expected that attorneys, accountants, and tradesmen in areas of high startup rates help make those regions more conducive to startups, if for no other reason than that they have had more practice at it.

Past experience indicates that entrepreneurs typically do not move to new areas to start firms, but rather start them where they happen to live. However, there are exceptions to this rule just as there are numerous examples of highly successful companies that located in unlikely places. Tektronix, the leading maker of oscilloscopes, started in Portland, Oregon, where most of the high-technology location factors mentioned above did not exist. K-2, the nation's leading ski maker, grew up in an almost totally nonindustrial area, a rural island in the middle of Puget Sound. The reasons are that those places were where the founders lived. In the following case, however, the entrepreneur did move to start a business:

♦ "The reason Bruce Burdick (who was living in Sioux City, Iowa) started his chain of retail computer stores in Kansas City has little to do with geography and everything to do with the difference between luck and Burdick's keen eye. At 39 he was operating a greenhouse and raising worms with his stepfather in Sioux City. In 1978, on his way home from a worm-ranchers' convention in Dallas, an article on computers caught his attention, and within a few months he had moved his wife and four children to Kansas City, where a Computerland franchise was available. Last year Burdick's Computer Store's six Kansas City retail outlets generated sales just shy of $10 million. Two new stores opened this fall. 'My mother says I was lucky,' Burdick remarks, 'that I was in the right place at the right time. I tell her, no, I was in Sioux City, which was the wrong place. I had to move. There were millions of people in Kansas City who could have taken advantage of that opportunity, but I recognized it and they didn't. It's not just luck.' "[54]

STARTING CAPITAL

An interesting counterpoint can be found in studies that looked at relationships between capitalization and success. Roberts found that "...the larger the amount of initial capitalization and the larger the number of initial founders, the greater the likelihood of the company's later success."[55] A similar correlation between starting capital and successfulness was found in another study of startups by Lamont.[56] These findings seem appropriately in line with the fact that when a company fails it is always out of money. A larger initial capitalization can in effect give the company a longer period in which to work out its problems and survive. The founder of one company that ran short of capital and failed recalls:

[3] William J. Dennis, Jr., "Explained and Unexplained Differences in Comparative State Business Starts and Start Rates," in Ronstadt et al., *Frontiers of Entrepreneurship Research, 1986*, p. 313.
[4] Tom Richman, "Going Their Way," *Inc., December 1983*, p. 70.
[5] Edward B. Roberts, "How to Succeed in a New Technology Enterprise," *Technology Review*, Vol. 73, No. 2 (December 1970), 25.

♦ We had made one big delivery on which the customer was slow in paying, and that started our problems. Then we ran into some "bugs" in production that slowed our shipments, which meant we couldn't bill some other customers as soon as we had planned. Because this cash was not coming in, we started getting behind on paying our own suppliers, and as soon as we started getting a little over ninety days behind on payables, a couple of them put us onto COD. They essentially wouldn't let us have anything else until we paid. I had to break off from trying to make a couple of sales in order to bring in more cash. The bank wouldn't load against the big receivable we were having trouble collecting, and they also wouldn't loan anything on inventory, which was the only other collateral we had, since our plant and much of the equipment were leased. I was spending more and more of my time trying to wheedle supplies for production here and there, and trying to talk the stockholders into putting up some more capital to tide us over. I couldn't work on the production bugs, as a result, nor on getting new orders, which then slowed way down. This decreased sales volume pushed us farther into the red, and when finally one of our suppliers decided to sue us for payment, the game was over.

A correlation between startup capital and survival was also found in a 1988 study of 2,994 firms by Cooper et al.[57] However, what is needed can obviously vary with many factors, including the degree of industry maturity. In the fresh-squeezed orange juice industry, for instance, Duchesneau and Gartner found that while unsuccessful firms had low capitalization, successful firms also did when the industry was new. It was only when the industry matured that higher capitalization became important.[58]

Studies of failures, on the other hand, do not point to inadequate capitalization as the most frequent cause. Dun and Bradstreet data, for instance, indicate the array of causes shown in Table 2–6.[59]

Although these figures are based largely on retailing concerns, similar conclusions as regards the noncrucial nature of initial financing in manufacturing companies are supported by other studies. For instance, in their study of successes and failures among Pennsylvania manufacturers, Woodruff and Alexander do not note initial capitalization, as can be seen from the list of causes in Table 2–7.[60] Often many apply, unfortunately. In a survey of venture capitalists' opinions, Goslin and Barge observed that "the quality of a management team is of primary importance" and found that the elements of this factor in order of importance were management experience, marketing experience and balance on the team, followed by a proven track record, finance experience, and realism about the venture's shortcomings.[61]

In each of the failures additional capital could presumably have extended

[56] Lawrence M. Lamont, *Technology Transfer, Innovation and Marketing in Science Oriented Spinoff Firms* (PhD Dissertation, Ann Arbor, University of Michigan, 1969).
[57] Cooper, Dunkelberg, and Woo, "Survival and Failure: A Longitudinal Study."
[58] Donald A. Duchesneau and William B. Gartner, "A Profile of New Venture Success and Failure in an Emerging Industry," Calgary, Babson Entrepreneurship Research Conference, 1988.
[59] *The Failure Record Through 1969* (New York: Dun and Bradstreet, 1970). Used with permission (These figures total more than 100 percent due to some listings of multiple causes.)
[60] Reprinted from *Success and Failure in Small Manufacturing* by A. M. Woodruff and T. G. Alexander by permission of the University of Pittsburgh Press. © 1958 by the University of Pittsburgh Press.
[61] L. N. Goslin, and B. Barge, "Entrepreneurial Qualities Considered in Venture Capital Support," in Ronstadt et al., *Frontiers of Entrepreneurship Research, 1986*, p. 366.

survival, but never was it clear that more capital would have allowed success. There is probably truth in the claim that "if a company is promising enough, the capital for it can be found." At the same time, it is also clear that companies have been retarded substantially in formation due to lack of capital

TABLE 2–6 CAUSES OF BUSINESS FAILURE

Deficiency	Percentage of Failures
Inadequate sales	39.0%
Competitive weakness	21.2
Excessive operating expenses	11.2
Receivables collection difficulties	9.3
Inventory difficulties	4.2
Excessive fixed assets	3.6
Neglect	2.8
Poor location	2.6
Disaster	1.4
Fraud	1.2
Other	1.4
Reason unknown	2.1

Xerox for example), while others have failed from a number of causes, one of which was lack of capital, provoking such moves as premature marketing of products whose further development could not be afforded with the existing take.

It is also important to keep in mind the obvious fact that larger capitalization, although possibly correlated with success, does not necessarily drive it. More money available can simply mean more to be lost and wasted.

TABLE 2-7   A LIST OF FAILURE CAUSES AMONG TEN SMALL MANUFACTURERS

One-man management	Too much machinery
Lack of internal communication	Overloaded payrolls
Lack of technical knowhow by management	Tooling up without study
	Inadequate dealer representation
Squabbles among top executives	Sales to insolvent customers
Nepotism	Ineffective bidding
Absentee management	Poor market research and sales records
Uncertainty of objectives	
Lack of diversification	Poorly managed subcontracting
Unwise product planning	Neglected tax liability
Inadequate records	Dissipation of assets
Elaborate but unusable records	Unrecognized expansion cost
	Excessive borrowing

MANAGEMENT PRACTICES

In the above lists of failure causes it is apparent that management practices figure heavily, at least downstream from startup. Most often it appears that when a business fails, many things can be found to be weak in the way of management practices. The extent to which they are "causes" versus "symptoms" of failure is often less clear. Most often mentioned, for example, is failure of the company to keep good records. Possibly there were no good records because the company was failing and other activities deemed more likely to extend survival, such as cutting overhead and emphasizing delivery, tended to get higher priority. Such interaction of cause and symptom may lie behind other apparent symptoms of failure, but weaknesses in management practices may nonetheless be important to long-term survival. Woodruff and Alexander summarized differences in such practices between the successful and unsuccessful firms they studied as follows:[62]

1 None of the unsuccessful firms had good financial records, but all of the successful companies did have complete records and made full use of them.

2 Every one of the unsuccessful firms regarded selling as a nuisance, whereas all of the successful ones emphasized it. In nine out of ten successful firms top executives actively participated in selling.

3 Few of the unsuccessful firms consciously worked on research and development. Nine out of ten successful ones did.

4 All unsuccessful firms exhibited "inept" administration. The successful ones, while not "textbook managed," had clear lines of authority and made decisions "without fuss."

How neglect of important management areas can come about is not hard to imagine, particularly in companies with solo founders as opposed to founding teams. Such founders are typically either former production personnel (who are most aware that to do anything else a company must produce), or sales people (who realize that sales are the key to all company action), or engineers (who know that no other intellectual tasks in the company are more demanding or important than good design). Intensity of experience in one area may lead to lack of appreciation for the importance of others, as was typified by one scientist-turned-entrepreneur:

◆   One scientist built a profitable consulting practice while keeping accounting records in his checkbook. When he decided to expand his activities to include manufacture of instruments, he believed he could continue that way. For a while his bank account grew as he subcontracted manufacturing and became a middleman for sales of the instruments, which were essentially custom made.
     As the market for this equipment grew, however, he found a number of other firms beginning to compete with him, driving prices down. At the same time the fact that the instruments were starting to be bought in larger batches made it attractive to establish his own production capability. He consequently began to invest in more equipment and inventory, which caused his bank account to shrink. Determined to keep "unnecessary overhead" down, however, he avoided hiring

[62] Woodruff and Alexander, *Success and Failure,* p. 119.

any managers, or setting up any formal systems. He continued to keep track of income and expenses with his checkbook, regarding accounting as a waste of time. "It doesn't solve technical problems, which are the heart of this business, it doesn't design instruments or make them, and it certainly doesn't make any sales."

When the increases in business had drained off his entire bank account for new equipment, inventory, and financing of customer purchases, he set out looking for venture capital. When asked how the business was doing, he confidently whipped out a list of prominent customers and amounts sold to them, pointing to the rising quantity of sales income. How about profits? "Well they are there, but invested in inventory and equipment." How much of each? Well, that was hard to say. It depended on how things were valued. No books were available to establish how accruals had changed. No managers were even on hand to say what was going on and how things were kept under control. The venture capitalists were not impressed.

Only by expenditure of a great amount of money on a "rush" accounting job by professionals was the entrepreneur able to get out some statements and save his company. The venture capital deal he obtained on the somewhat dubious records thus generated likely also cost him more of his stock than he would have paid with good records.

Planning is a particular management practice whose influence on success, although management pundits might prefer it otherwise, has historically been less than clear. Teach et al. reported that software startups that did formal planning grew larger on the average than those that did not.[63] But this report is rare in that it bases its findings on that subject on systematic studies of statistical data. If the new company needs a large amount of external capital, there is generally no choice but to develop detailed lists of steps that will be taken and forecasts of what events will follow in development of the company. Most entrepreneurs who are not required by such exigencies to develop plans simply start doing things required to get the company into action and gradually expand to larger levels of activity, doing forecasting and planning only as needed from step to step. As Miller observes from his twenty success stories:

◆   Few of the businesses were precisely planned or proceeded according to plan. A business is an organism and not a mechanism, liable to get somewhat out of hand, finding its own direction or level, and carrying the management with it.[64]

Hoad and Rosko found that the typical time lapse between thinking of starting a company and when it was established ranged from zero to over twenty-four months, with no particular correlation to successfulness. More important appeared to be taking action of some sort, as opposed to more theoretical and experimental anticipation of the venture, as illustrated in Table 2–8.[65]

The study also found a positive correlation between successfulness and knowledge of competition, but not a strong one. As regards knowledge of markets, the results appear to be clearer. In the Hoad and Rosko study, less

[63] Richard D. Teach, Fred A. Tarpley, Jr., Robert G. Schwartz, and Dorothy E. Brawley, "Maturation in the Microcomputer Software Industry: Venture Teams and Their Firms," in Churchill et al., *Frontiers of Entrepreneurship Research, 1987,* (Wellesley, Mass.: Babson Center for Entrepreneurial Studies, 1987), p. 464.
[64] Miller, *The Way of Enterprise,* p. 121.
[65] Hoad and Rosko, *Management Factors,* p. 65.

TABLE 2-8 Activity During Planning Period

	Successes	Marginals	Failures	Total
		Fraction of All Firms (n = 92)		
Action-raised funds, obtained assets, sought location	11.9%	1.1%	4.3%	17.3
Worked in same business	7.6	5.4	2.2	15.2
Thinking, study, experimentation	7.6	5.4	15.3	28.3
Other	5.4	3.3	3.3	12.0
None	7.6	8.7	10.9	27.2
	40.1	23.9	36.0	100.0

than 10 percent of the firms were started with what the researchers considered as a "good" prior market investigation, but of those none failed and few were marginal, 89 percent being characterized as successes. Susbauer found that "most" of his successful high-technology startups "began with a guaranteed first customer."[66]

Thus, although there tends to be a generally positive correlation between "good" management practices and successfulness, the place where their role is strongest appears to be more downstream of startup than prior to or during startup, a possible exception being the importance of market research. Mayer and Goldstein place somewhat more emphasis on managerial "competence" rather than managerial practices, but go on to add that from their studies it must be complemented by other factors of personality to promote success:

◆　　Although adequate capital and managerial competence are indispensable for survival, they are rarely sufficient in themselves to insure it. They must be supplemented by other factors, such as motivation, hard work, persistence, and flexibility.[67]

INDIVIDUAL MAKEUP

It seems hard to deny that some individuals are simply born with a proclivity toward entrepreneurship. Collins and Moore estimate that out of the hundred entrepreneurs they studied, *no more than six* had this characteristic, commenting, ". . . if one reads back through the life histories of these men, there seems to have been no time when they were not living and breathing business enterprise."[68] Consider the following example:

♦   Two high school boys in southern California in the late nineteen-forties were at the beach when one hit upon a way to obtain lunch money. "We'll charge to park cars," he said. Walking to the entrance of the free public parking lot, they began to stop cars with "twenty-five cents to park you car, sir." Soon they had collected enough for hamburgers, and movies later on as well.

Later the same one with the parking lot idea suggested they spend a week of vacation in the mountain resort area at Lake Arrowhead. "We'll take along some palm fronds like we use for weaving hats at the beach and sell them to the rich tourists." After visiting the Santa Monica public parks, they soon had a trunkful of fronds, which turned out to be worth a dollar apiece after a few minutes' processing on the Lake Arrowhead shorefront.

Enjoying some prosperity from these hat sales, the boys one evening approached a pay phone to call some girls, to whom they had sold hats, to ask for dates. Lifting the receiver off its hook, they found someone had ripped its cord entirely loose from the phone box. Both laughed, and then the one who had suggested the parking lot and hat sales ideas said, "I'm going to sell it." Entering the nearby drugstore he held up the receiver with its dangling cord to the proprietor and asked, "Here's a new novelty you could have some fun with. How would you like to buy it?" For fifty cents the druggist did.

Twenty years later this boy had become a successful dentist. With the healthy income from that profession he had entered a number of other successful enterprises, which were multiplying his wealth rapidly.

It would be hard to discern a formula for this instinct. It is clear that only one of the two boys (and interestingly enough, not the one of the two whose father was an entrepreneur, but rather the one whose father was a part-time actor and full-time piano tuner for a large store) was the "idea man" in each of these instances. In each event he somehow saw a way of transforming something that was available for free into a sale for profit. Both had the same opportunities, but only one saw them and acted.

As noted in Chapter 1, academicians have tried to discover psychological characteristics that discriminate between entrepreneurs and nonentrepreneurs, but the findings have been relatively mixed. Some characteristics may be inborn and uncontrollable. Others may be subject to cultivation, such as the following:

Personality Characteristics	*Possible Development Tactics*
1. Achievement motivation	1. Imitate successful symptoms— follow rules of Ben Franklin, Dale Carnegie, and other how-to-be-a-success books.
2. Role models	2. Cultivate acquaintances with successful entrepreneurs. Study how they work and try to work with and learn from them.
3. Self-determinism (nonfatalism)	3. Similar to (1) above. Possibly experiment with techniques for altering your self-concept to greater "success affirmation."

[68] Collins and Moore, *The Organization Makers*, p. 110.

HARD-TO-ARRANGE EVENTS

History clearly shows that some times are more favorable than others for starting new ventures. In the late 1950s to mid-1960s were new enterprise boom times, especially in semiconductors, electronic instrumentation, and computer industries. Many companies raised starting capital before even developing prototypes and some went public on the same basis. On the stock exchanges, companies with histories of nothing but losses were in some instances selling at high prices based on vast expenditures in R&D expected to yield wondrous new products in the future.

This period was followed, however, by one in which funding for new ventures, quite beyond the control of entrepreneurs themselves, became much harder to obtain, in some fields virtually impossible.

♦   Three engineers, dissatisfied with various aspects of their current jobs and noting the spectacular success records of men from similar circumstances who had started high-technology new companies, decided in late 1968 to embark on a similar direction. Because they had seen several successful startups in the computer peripheral equipment business which led to enormously profitable sell-outs for founders, and because their current technical expertise lent itself to development of such equipment (though none of their employers made such products), they decided to design a portable computer terminal.

Examining existing products, they developed design goals well in advance of what presently existed—greater speed, more flexible graphic as well as alphanumeric capability, lower cost—and began work in evenings and on weekends, using personal savings for seed money. As design work progressed and showed promise, one of the three quit his job to work full time on the new product and on organization of the venture. He developed a full list of venture capital sources in the local area as well as leads in other cities such as San Francisco and Boston, where many established sources existed. Patents were applied for on some facets of the design which were particularly novel.

When the prototype was ready and worked well, the patent search had shown high likelihood of producing strong coverage and a business plan had been worked out in detail, as recommended by experts on venture capital, the entrepreneurs began looking for capital among organized venture divisions. A nationwide search produced consistently negative answers. "If you had been looking a year ago, you'd have had it made. But now computer peripherals are a drug on the market. Your product looks good, but not overwhelmingly good enough to gamble against the tide. Sorry." During the year since design had begun the economic scene had wiped out chances for this company. And it died.

The would-be entrepreneurs cannot control tides like this. They can only try to be sensitive to them and exploit those that run their way. In doing so they, like investors in the stock market, inevitably play in some degree a game of chance.

Obviously, tides can run in both directions and entrepreneurs who succeed often find themselves to be those who happened to be in fortuitous and unforeseen circumstances. Those in the high-technology business who went after capital a couple of years earlier than the entrepreneurs have often found it easy to obtain, even before they had products developed. Colonel Sanders could not have foreseen that one day a young man would come with a scheme for promoting his Kentucky Fried Chicken worldwide to make him a multimillionaire. William G. McGowan could not have foreseen that he would be contacted by a man who was ready to give up on seeking Federal Communications Commission permission to build a microwave link between Chicago and St. Louis for his mobile radio business MCI. Buying the company for $50,000, McGowan continued the fight, obtained the permission one year later, and within four years had raised another $100 million to establish a nationwide long-distance phone company. The following entrepreneurs had no way of controlling the end of a war that made surplus available at profitable prices, nor could they foresee that high profits would come from starting with a venture concept that initially was unworkable.

♦   When the end of World War II made vast quantities of surplus materials available, two ex-army officers, Carl Kessler and Hugh Wolfe, thought they would take advantage of it, although they were not sure how. Without knowing what they would do with them, each put $4,500 into surplus aluminum flanged U-beams, which they figured they could use somehow. The idea they came up with was to sell them as fence posts. But it failed. So they looked for other ideas, and hit upon the notion of making them into farm gates. They developed a design, which they were able to patent, and in the fall of 1946 began selling the gates, first through a paid advertisement (costing $90) in *The Cattleman,* and then from a livestock exposition booth, where they promptly liquidated their stock.

When development of hard-to-control events creates a "right time and place," it often seems to happen that one or another entrepreneur is in it. These two men managed to move quickly from a wrong one, fence posts, to a right one, gates. This too is often characteristic of entrepreneurs, and many times it is hard to determine to what extent entrepreneurial success was created by circumstance versus being the cause of the circumstance. Like campus fads, the basic mechanism seems often to contain a persistent ingredient of mystery that cannot be fully extracted. A would-be entrepreneur can note, however, that hard-to-control events often play an important role in sorting success from failure, and that success and failure can occur in any sequence, with the long-run odds, if brought into play by entrepreneurial persistence, favoring success.

After a review of expert statements, statistics, and anecdotes about what works best in startups, there remains the fact that, as Low and MacMillan observed from their review of the research literature, "each venture will have its own success factors, any one of which will be sufficient to kill it if overlooked."[69] Typically, some of the generalities will apply and others will not, as illustrated by perhaps the most exceptional startup to occur in recent years or arguably recent decades, Apple Computer.

♦   In 1974 the MITS company introduced the first microcomputer kit, the Altair (named after the spaceship in Startrek). MITS had made the right *choice of business.* Its founder, Ed Roberts, expected to sell about eight hundred kits in 1975. A cover story in the January 1975 issue of *Popular Science* imparted an

---

[69] Murray Low and Ian MacMillan, "Entrepreneurship: Past Research and Future Challenges," *Journal of Management,* Vol. 14, No. 2 (June 1988), 139.

unexpected impulse, not only to MITS but to other subsequent microcomputer startups as well. MITS sold two thousand Altairs in 1975 and was itself sold in 1977 for $6 million; it was a very successful startup, even though it did not survive its early takeover.

Steve Jobs and Steve Wozniak wanted an Altair kit but could not afford the $400 cost. Consequently, they "liberated parts" from their *employers*, as Steve Jobs put it, and made their own. At that time Jobs was working for Atari designing video games, and Wozniak was working for Hewlett-Packard concentrating on pocket calculators. The two had been boyhood friends and had earlier obtained *experience* in electronic circuit design when they *teamed up* to build some "blue boxes" (illegal devices for making long-distance calls without getting charged) after reading an *Esquire* article about them.

The two took their first computer creation, the Apple 1, to the Home Brew Computer Club, a hobbyist organization that was popular in the San Francisco *geographical area,* where it immediately drew interest and requests from friends for copies. Jobs recalls: "So we were spending all of our time helping them build their computers. It was taking up our weekends, our nights, everything. So I sold my Volkswagen. Woz sold his calculator, and we got 1,300 bucks together. We paid a friend of mine to lay out a printed circuit board."

Having recognized that there was a promising market, they had suggested to their employers that here was a good new product opportunity. Jobs recalled that Nolan Bushnell, the founder and CEO of Atari, had said his company's resources were already fully committed and that Hewlett-Packard had said something like "Why you guys don't even have MBA's . . . we'll do it ourselves." So the two Steves decided to move ahead with it on their own.

Their first concept for the business was to sell kits, and they sought an order from The Byte Shop, a local microcomputer hobbyist store. They figured that since the parts would cost $25 per computer, they would try to sell them for $50 to gain a $25 profit. The Byte Shop agreed to buy fifty, but only if they were assembled and ready to run, observing that "we already have kits and don't need another one." The store also agreed to pay cash on delivery if the computers worked.

Now Jobs approached parts suppliers and persuaded them to sell him one hundred computers' worth of parts on the same terms as they sold to other manufacturers, thirty days net. Jobs recalled: "We took all those boxes of parts home. We built one hundred boards, and we took fifty down to The Byte Shop and we were paid cash. We paid the suppliers in twenty-nine days." And they still had fifty computers' worth of parts left for the next order. Thus, in effect, they started with virtually no *starting capital.*

Soon, however, it became apparent that outside capital would be needed. Don Valentine, a local venture capitalist who had been recommended by Nolan Bushnell, declined to invest but recommended that they contact another venture capitalist, Mark Markkula. When Markkula found that Jobs and Wozniak had no business plan and didn't even know what one was, he offered to spend a week helping them write one. Then, he said, he would decide whether to invest. If he did, they had capital. If he didn't, at least they would have a plan they could use to approach other sources.

"After that week together," Jobs recalled, "we agreed to two things. One was that the three of us wanted to keep working together on this. The other was that none of us was qualified to run the company." Consequently, they recruited Michael Scott, director of manufacturing at National Semiconductor, to become president. Jobs became chairman, Wozniak vice-president for R&D, and Valentine chairman. Valentine invested $91,000 and helped get another $250,000 line of credit from the Bank of America. The company had sales of $700,000 its first year, 1977. By 1984 sales were $1.5 billion and the company had entered the *Fortune* 500 faster than any other company in history. What were the key factors in Apple's success? Some of these, including the presence of a *management team* from the outset, can be identified above. But scores of other microcomputer companies had started at almost the same time. By 1980 there were all sorts of guesses about which, including Apple, would survive. When IBM introduced its PC in 1981, there were predictions that Apple would surely be eclipsed. Yet it continued to prosper.

Some claim that a key factor was the *unanticipated event* of introduction by a Harvard Business School student, Dan Bricklin of Visicalc, the first spreadsheet program, which was highly successful and written for Apple. Another factor was Apple's cultivation of software development by independent entrepreneurs, in contrast to other microcomputer companies that tried to write all their own and keep control of it. By 1983 there were fifteen thousand programs available for Apple, 95 percent of them created by independents. Still later the introduction of the Macintosh, a highly user-friendly machine in contrast to those of the main competitors, IBM and Radio Shack, kept the company's fortunes advancing. Steve Jobs, although replaced as head of the company by John Scully, a successful big-company leader, had headed the team that developed the product.

Thus, in hindsight, it appears that Apple not only was first in key innovations but also applied effective *management practices* relative to its competitors. Initiative from bright and creative founding entrepreneurs was a necessary ingredient, but not the only one.

SUMMARY

Both success and failure can take different forms. Success can mean survival, growth, profitability or satisfaction for the owner. Failure can mean less of such things than one might prefer, which can be different than what another might prefer. Regardless the measures used, however, performance depends upon a complex of factors. "Being in the right business at the right time and place," whether a cliché or not, is clearly very important. Both education and experience also tend to be important, particularly in ventures requiring high skill levels or esoteric knowledge. Coupling with partners appears to raise odds of success, not only by adding needed expertise but also by adding, through appropriate selection, balance to a startup team. Starting with a larger capitalization also, on the average, tends to correlate with higher odds of success. Applying better management practices may not turn a losing company into a winner but it can make it more likely that a startup will succeed. Inevitably, however, elements of coincidence and luck can be seen in hindsight to play important parts in the outcome of many ventures. Perhaps for that reason it has been said that Napoleon preferred lucky generals.

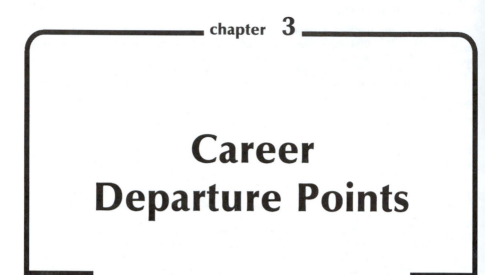

chapter 3

Career
Departure Points

Most of the individuals who eventually become entrepreneurs did not foresee their entrepreneurial career, as illustrated by Ronstadt's finding that among business graduates of Babson College, less than 20 percent either pursued entrepreneurship as a first career or chose other jobs with the aim of preparing themselves for pursuing entrepreneurship.[1] Is there a "best" stage in life for beginning a venture? Various "authoritative" opinions have been offered. "As soon as you have come into possession of a good idea and a million dollars to finance it" was the suggestion of one businessman with a sardonically conservative turn of mind. A professor at Harvard used to advise entrepreneurially inclined students first to work for a large company, the bigger the better, achieve at least two significant promotions, and only then consider going independent, not before. Others have emphasized accumulation of personal savings in preparation for entry. One author, for instance, says he would advise someone who had accumulated around $20,000 in net personal assets plus a 50 percent home equity to continue working a few more years and cut down drastically on personal expenses to get more cash for entry, since a bank would be unlikely to extend enough against such a present stake, particularly to an inexperienced entrepreneur.[2]

Discovery of opportunity, such as encountering a significant invention and/or clear indication of customer desires, should set the timing, according to one other school of thought. It argues that successful entry is mainly a product of circumstantial factors largely beyond control of the entrepreneur, who should wait and watch for opportunity, and if it does not by chance happen to appear,

---

[1] Robert Ronstadt, "Does Entrepreneurial Career Path Really Matter?" in Karl H. Vesper, *Frontiers of Entrepreneurship Research, 1982* (Wellesley, Mass.: Babson College, 1982), p. 540.
[2] Robert S. Morrison, *Handbook for Manufacturing Entrepreneurs* (Cleveland: Western Reserve Press, 1973), p. 53.

should keep his or her job. In contrast, however, advocates of careful scheming argue that *any* position can be used to start planning and working toward a venture, first perhaps on a part-time basis and then on a gradually larger scale.[3] The important thing, they claim, is a state of mind dedicated to achieving self-employment. The real key, says yet another author, is independent of age, position, sex, and even physical handicaps, and is embodied in the six-word injunction "Find a need and fill it."[4]

So much for claims about where an entrepreneur should start. What does the record show happens? By exploring the spectrum of starting points that have worked for others, a would-be entrepreneur may be better able to chart a course and choose an effective sequence for entrepreneurial entry. In examining the series of examples to be presented here, it may be useful for the reader to keep reconsidering what factors were important in determining each starting point and what other starting points could also have worked, both for the particular individuals in the examples and for the types of ventures involved.

The examples to follow will be grouped first according to occupations from which the entrepreneurs proceeded to enter ventures: school, the student's occupation; employment in firms of others, unemployment, and finally the home. It will be seen that entrepreneurship can occur in all different life stages— early, middle, and retirement years. Then entrepreneurship itself will be considered as a starting point for venturing, which thereby leads to ventures in sequence, rather than as "one-shot only" departures from earlier patterns. From this array it will be seen that many entry points are possible, and for someone who does not see a good way to embark on entrepreneurship immediately, there can still be many further chances at other points ahead.

OCCUPATIONAL STARTING POINTS

Excuses can be found to reject most career situations for launching ventures. School can be seen as poor, because students typically have little or no money or experience, both of great value in new ventures. Moreover, even their education, by definition of the circumstances, is incomplete. Those holding jobs, on the other hand, face other obstacles. They must work every day, and therefore may have a hard time working on other ventures, particularly since it is during working hours when many key personal contacts, such as bankers, suppliers, and customers, are uniquely accessible. Moreover, someone who already has a job is less in need of a venture for income, and so might have lower inspiration to stride into the unknown of a new company attempt.

Unemployment might impress higher motivation to use entrepreneurship for creating a source of income, but it also suffers some handicaps as a launching position. It emphasizes the need to husband with care whatever financial resources are available, since there will be no job income to fall back on if the venture fails. Time must also be used with care, since it will be needed to find another job if venturing does not succeed, and it may be difficult to be sure how long that will take. The more prudent course may appear to be using time immediately to find a job, to get that task out of the way before squandering

---

[3] Peter Weaver, *You, Inc.* (Garden City, N.Y.: Doubleday, 1973).
[4] Marvin Small, *How to Make More Money* (New York: Pocket Books, 1953).

any of it on some risky entrepreneurial notions. Unemployment is not typically a time of high confidence and willingness to experiment.

Nor is the home the sort of place many would view as ideal for business development. A household tends to be cut off from many connections of commerce that can be important in forming a company—jobber and wholesaler connections, commercial bankers, attorneys, and shop and research facilities.

Regardless of which starting point may apply to a given reader at the moment, there may be value in reading about other starting points as well for three reasons. First, the venture approaches that work for one type of starting point may be applicable to others as well, and may also trigger additional ideas that apply to other starting points. Second, the reader may shift positions either voluntarily or otherwise, so that other starting points become appropriate. Third, by learning about how individuals begin ventures from other starting points, it may more readily be found possible to join forces with a person in that other position to initiate ventures. Some readers, however, may prefer to skip ahead in this chapter and begin with those career points most similar to their own.

SCHOOL TO VENTURE

Because it offers so much freedom the academic world is in some ways well suited to venturing, from either a position as an employee or as a student. A 1982 survey of Canadian university engineering and science department chairmen by Doutrioux and Peterman turned up 109 spinoff ventures, of which 28.5 percent were started by students either during or immediately following school and the remainder by faculty and staff.[5] A limitation of school is that it tends to focus on technology rather than customers, and not surprisingly, particularly considering the departments from which leads came, respondents attributed their success predominantly to technical expertise and product uniqueness rather than marketing effectiveness.

At least seven ways of launching ventures directly from or following after school can be identified, and these will be illustrated in the following order:

1 *On-campus sidelines.* Ventures operated from campus to serve the school market.

2 *Off-campus sidelines.* Operated from campus but serving markets beyond school.

3 *Curricular startups.* Ventures started as part of for-credit course work.

4 *Curricular followons.* Design of the venture is done as course work leading to a venture started later.

5 *Extracurricular followons.* Ventures organized on the side during school but begun following graduation.

6 *Dropout ventures.* Pregraduation withdrawal from school followed by venture development.

---

[5] Jerome Doutrioux and Branko M. Peterman, "Technology Transfer and Academic Entrepreneurship," in Vesper, *Frontiers of Entrepreneurship Research, 1982,* p. 430.

TABLE 3–1 SPECTRUM OF STUDENT ENTREPRENEURIAL VENTURES*

Selling food door to door
Food stands
Food and drink delivery
Food for spectators
Selling mail-order birthday cakes to students' parents
Selling mementos—mugs, clothing, jewelry, souvenirs, buttons, stationery
Selling luxuries—hi-fis, magazines, gifts, firewood, flowers, furniture
Services—laundry, linen, typing, copying, tutoring, book exchange, haircuts, ticket
    procurement, vending machines, insurance, transportation, rentals, parking, catering,
    booking, furniture exchange, hauling, storage, advertising, answering service,
    babysitting, housework, yardwork, odd jobs agency, curb numbering, advertising,
    information research, janitor service, modeling, watchman, artistic entertainment as
    performer or as agent, publications, writing, printing, film making, computer
    programming

*This list, although it can illustrate the spectrum, does not indicate the many variations possible and details involved in such ventures. Readers seriously interested in small student ventures such as these should read the Sandman and Goldenson reference mentioned earlier, from which this list was abstracted.

7 *Direct postgraduate startups.* Wherein the graduate starts a company rather than working for another following graduation.

Although quantitative data on such startups have never been compiled, they would probably show that the first of these types accounts for the largest number of school to startup ventures, the second accounts for the second largest number of ventures but generally has larger and more profitable ventures than the first, and the last three probably include on the average still larger and more profitable, although less numerous, ventures.

Over three hundred ways to make money in college ventures were identified in a 1967 survey of schools by Sandman and Goldenson.[6] From a summary list, which appears in Table 3–1, it can be seen that most of these ventures are operated as *on-campus sidelines* serving other students. Some students manage enterprises that acquire high-quality lecture notes and sell them. Others buy and sell various appliances that are uneconomical for prior users to take with them, such as iceboxes. One became a dealer in paperbacks when the campus bookstore refused to carry them. (The bookstore later changed its policy and bought him out.) The variety of examples is endless and new ventures are constantly appearing. Most of these ventures stay small and have low earnings power—typically less than $2,500 profit per year—occasionally changing hands for a price when their founders graduate, and sometimes dying out. The chief reason they do not amount to more is that they are local services aimed at small markets and have little transferability to larger markets.

Sometimes, however, something larger develops. *The Student Entrepre-*

[6] Peterman Sandman and Dan Goldenson, *How to Succeed in Business Before Graduating* (New York: Collier Books, 1968). Used with permission. © 1968 by Peter M. Sandman and Daniel Goldenson, Macmillan/Collier Books.

neur's Guide, for instance, describes several ventures, including "Crowd Caps."[7] Started by a Harvard freshman who had been selling T-shirts at ball games, it introduced housepainters' hats emblazoned with designs of interest to college students. Within three years, by 1981, the hat venture was grossing over a half million dollars per year. Sandman and Goldenson reported that the following five out of all student ventures they found yielded the highest dollar payoffs for their founders.

1 Business forms By the time he was a senior, an Amherst student was flying weekly to his home in Philadelphia to oversee a company he had started as a freshman in 1963, Titan Business Systems. At school he worked between classes on design and promotion to businessmen of such forms as sales books, ledger sheets, invoices, and multiple carbon forms to allow writing a check, stub, and tax journal entry without repeating words.

2 Charter flights A University of Texas student built within four years of school a charter flight service, serving all sixty-three Texas colleges and universities, with sales of $350,000 per year. His strategy involved obtaining student representatives at many schools, which enabled him to operate at lower costs per flight than smaller localized campus charter flight groups. He also emphasized advertising and direct mail brochures to publicize his low rates. A half-dozen employees were helping with the work while he was finishing law school.

3 Entertainment booking Started by a Brigham Young University junior in 1966, SAK United Entertainment by mid-1967 had arranged more than fifty concerts and dances in five states and taken over management of four recreational sites in Utah. The organization's main function was providing band entertainment for student groups, a special service being that of transporting bands to different schools. SAK's founder commented, "College talent which is of no great interest on its home campus can be a real marquee-value attraction 100 miles away." Services offered to any group, such as a high school prom or a party, included publicity materials prepared by SAK, help in planning the function and selecting appropriate entertainment, and sending along a personal representative to each function to make sure things worked out right, as well as the standard booking service associated with lining up entertainers for a fee.

4 Discount cards In 1964 a Trinity College student started Varsity International Sales Association (VISA) to sell (1) cards to students (at $1.50 each) identifying them as eligible for VISA discounts, (2) listings to merchants in the VISA directory which informed students of discounts available to them as VISA members, from those listed merchants (average listing fee, $25), and (3) additional advertising space in the catalog to those merchants wishing to buy it (full page, $2,500). Within three years the company, working through local student representatives, was publishing directories in eleven states and had sold 100,000 cards.

5 Computer date matching Two Harvard students in early 1965 hit on the idea of having students who wanted blind dates give information on themselves which would then be fed to a computer. The computer would give back

---

[7] Brett Kingstone, *The Student Entrepreneur's Guide* (Berkeley, Calif.: Ten Speed Press, 1981).

a list of names for each student selected to meet the student's individual profile and desires. Investing $1,250 for computer usage and 10,000 questionnaires, the two entrepreneurs started the service in Boston at $3 per listing. Within three months 7,800 students from 100 New England colleges were listed. A year later the number was up to 100,000 and the enterprise was going nationwide, although dozens of competitors were entering. Plans were under way for parlaying the venture through magazines and other products into a major company.

A sixth example worth noting is that of hi-fi sales:

◆   While attending M.I.T. in the mid-sixties, Sand Ruby began assembling and selling hi-fi component kits on campus. Hi-fi was catching on with students at the time, and he was soon grossing as much as $1,000 per week from his room where other students dropped in to buy. He and a partner were impelled to open a storefront in 1967 when told they could no longer put components in their dormitory's janitor closet. The first store was successful and led to others, and by 1973 there were sixteen with total sales of $12 million.[8]

One characteristic that sets these larger-scale student ventures apart from those in Table 3–1 is that they all sell to markets far beyond the campuses where they started. Another pointed out by authors Sandman and Goldenson is that they are highly unusual. These, they emphasize, were the only ventures they found earning each of their founders over $10,000 per year. If we look further, however, it can be seen that in fact there have been many other substantial ventures arising out of school. One example, was that of Goldenson himself, who, besides writing the book with Sandman, went on to start his own company, Resource Publications, which operated as follows:

◆   The company invited employers who wanted to recruit engineering graduates each to write a one-page profile of job opportunities it had. This was to be submitted in a specified format that could be printed directly and to be accompanied by a $150 fee. The magazine was then distributed to students free by Goldenson's company. By 1968, less than two years after his graduation, Goldenson was publishing 1,500 such profiles in twenty-two regional issues. He sold the company to a conglomerate, Gulf and Western, for stock then valued (it subsequently fell) at around $1 million.

There have been other campus enterprises that have made high profits, such as a travel book by Harvard students, *Let's Go, The Student Guide to Europe,* and another, *Class, The Student Guide,* which was still selling well in campus bookstores over a decade later.

Two frozen yogurt shops that were losing money in 1978 became the business entry point for a Southern Methodist University junior. He offered to run one shop for six months and pay for the losses if he could also pocket the profits. Hiring new employees, tightening cost controls, and mounting a marketing campaign, he turned the stores around. Then with $30,000 in savings he bought out both stores and started adding others in partnership with his

---

[8] Jeffrey Tarter, "Can He Keep His Customers Tuned In?" *Inc.,* November 1980, p. 73.

sister, also an SMU student. By 1984 the two had a chain of twenty-three stores and were still expanding.[9]

◆ Mark Vittert, a speech major at DePauw University, began selling by direct mail to parents of students a campus "survival kit" for their children who were away at school, consisting of a package of fruit, peanut butter, and candy for $5 to help them through final examinations. As soon as he graduated, he went to nearby Indianapolis, where he persuaded a group headed by an alumnus of the university whom he had never met to invest $150,000 in his College Marketing and Research Corporation. He then hired a staff of five and traveled around the country on cut-rate "youth fare" tickets attempting to recruit clients.

When his attempts to sell to middle managers failed, he began telephoning top executives at home and got results. An oil company hired his firm to sell students over twenty-one on using its credit cards, and then other companies took on the same service. For other companies his firm performed market research polls and designed advertising campaigns. Profits the first year were $105,000 after taxes on sales of $896,000. Only eighteen months after graduation he sold his enterprise to Playboy Enterprises for $1.5 million in cash and stock, plus a contract that left him in charge of the operation as division president.

Another venture above that stands out as a somewhat different type was the business forms company, in that although begun and operated by a student its market was off campus. It can be regarded as an *off-campus sideline,* which is a category of student-initiated ventures also containing varied sequences and degrees of success.

Reaching for an off-campus market can have the advantage of greater freedom of action. There are fewer campus rules to content with, the venture can operate in areas where there are no campuses, and people in the off-campus population are both vastly more numerous and, in spite of the affluence of a few students, in better positions to spend money. At the same time, for a student to develop access to off-campus markets presents a greater challenge, because those markets are less familiar.

Despite conventional wisdom, which argues that students are not yet ready to run businesses, many students have done so successfully, and in fact a careful look at school circumstances reveals a number of advantages as a launching site. Schools are a relatively "low risk" environment where some ventures can be operated on a small scale and others, of larger proportions, can be tried first on paper. Many schools offer courses focused directly on startup of new ventures in which venture designs can be developed and given critical feedback without financial risk. A fraction of these turn into actual ventures, which could in a sense be regarded as *curricular startups,* since they are done for course credit. Bob Howard, a University of Washington MBA, recalled how his company, Fireside Lodge Corp., had begun in a course three years earlier:

◆ "So there I was with a class assignment to start a business, any business, operate it, analyze it and turn in a report on it by the end of the quarter only ten weeks away.

[9] "I Can't Believe It's Yogurt," *Entrepreneur,* July 1984, p. 24.

"With no idea of what to do about it I wandered down to the student lounge, sat down on the couch by another student whom I didn't know and said, 'Boy, have I got a problem. I have to start a business for one of my classes.' He said, 'That's interesting; I have an idea for a product. I don't know if you've ever tasted hot spiced wine like they drink in the ski lodges, but it turns out there's no easy way to make it. You have to get a recipe, buy all the ingredients separately and mix them yourself. So why not start producing a ready-to-use hot spiced wine mix and sell it through grocery stores?'"

Howard agreed it was a promising idea, the two students joined forces, and by three years later their company was selling mix at a rate of $400,000 per year.

Inquiries about the impact of school ventures on the grades of their founder/operators have produced mixed results. A study by Van Slooten et al. found that among ninety-three student entrepreneurs, 51.7 percent felt their grades had been unaffected by venturing, 30.0 percent felt their grades had been negatively affected, and 18.3 percent felt their grades had improved.[10]

For graduating students there may be a choice of starting a venture directly following school or later. A 1986 study by Shuman et al. found that a remarkably high percentage of the business school alumni of Bentley College (which has a heavy orientation toward the accounting profession), 65 percent, had started a business at some point after college, but less than 13 percent had ventured directly following college.[11] The 46 percent of alumni still running ventures as opposed to 19 percent who had attempted but dropped ventures in favor of working for others had started earlier in considering venturing, and more of them had chosen their prior careers with an objective of venturing and saw their prior work as relevant to the ventures. Thus it appears that although only a minority enter venturing with deliberate career objectives of doing so, those who do endeavor to shape their careers toward venturing seem more often to end up with ventures that last rather than ventures that are less attractive than working for others.

If startup is an objective following school, there will probably be opportunity to work at preparation during school, so it becomes a *curricular followon*. Courses, term papers, and thesis work may all be able to contribute. One spectacular success that began as a student paper was Federal Express. Another was the following:

♦ As an MBA student at Stanford, Philip Knight developed a term paper on the market for high-quality athletic shoes, which he suspected could be imported from Asia at a lower cost than domestic lines. Upon graduating he took a job with Coopers and Lybrand, the accounting firm, but on the side contacted his former track coach at the University of Oregon, Bill Bowerman, about forming an import company. On weekends and evenings he began selling Japanese track shoes to school athletic teams.

---

[10] John D. Van Slooten, Robert Layne Hild, and H. Keith Hunt, "Characteristics of Collegiate Entrepreneurs and Their Ventures," in Robert Ronstadt, John A. Hornaday, Rein Peterson, and Karl H. Vesper, *Frontiers of Entrepreneurship Research, 1986,* (Wellesley, Mass.: Babson College, 1986), p. 52.

[11] Jeffrey C. Shuman, John A. Seeger, Judith B. Kamm, and Nicholas C. Teebagy, "An Empirical Test of Ten Entrepreneurial Propositions," in Ronstadt et al., *Frontiers of Entrepreneurship Research, 1986,* p. 187.

Bowerman, meanwhile, began experimenting with new shoe ideas, including waffle-patterned soles that he made with his wife's waffle iron. When th ? Japanese supplier, Tiger, demanded a 51 percent ownership share of Knight and Bowerman's company, they refused and instead sought a manufacturer to produce the new designs they had developed. An employee suggested the name Nike, and a new brand was born. As serious athletes began to appreciate the superior product it represented, the name Nike became a dominant leader in athletic shoes and by 1984 sales of the company had passed $1 billion.

By working on ventures while still attending school, it is possible for entrepreneurs to draw on resources inaccessible to others outside school, including not only library materials but also companies that will provide information and sometimes even direct assistance in the form of parts and other materials without charge. Most professionals in the industrial community are glad to show students how they operate and help them learn. Professors in such subjects as law, engineering, and business are available and can sometimes be very helpful, as was Professor Frederick Terman of Stanford when he suggested to William Hewlett and David Packard that a certain engineering student design project might yield a product they could use to start their company. Their holdings in the Hewlett-Packard company rose in value past a half billion dollars apiece. Less exceptional than that spectacular success was the experience of two Portland State University students:

◆   Early in the last year of their MBA studies the two discovered in conversation that they both preferred the idea of becoming self-employed rather than going to work for another company after graduation. So they decided to team up and start looking for possible ventures. Among many ideas they uncovered was one suggested by a marketing professor whom they consulted for advice. He indicated that there might be room for a company that specialized in gathering information for clients, including market and other data research. He also told them about a potential client presently in need of such service, and put them in contact with both a lawyer and an accountant to advise them on setting up their business.
        By January 1971, four months after the first venture discussions, the two had chosen their line of work, had had a 50/50 partnership agreement drafted and notarized, had worked out financial forecasts with the accountant which showed a breakeven within nine months, and had signed a contract to perform market research for a local inventor on his new product. Each had paid in $750 total, and $300 had been spent on legal services, the remainder going for expenses on the first job. At graduation time in June they rented a small office and used receipts from the first billing to buy used furniture and to underwrite selling expenses as they went after additional clients door to door. A month later their second job came in, and then others rapidly began to follow as their reputation grew. By October they had been evicted for bringing too much traffic to the building their office was in and had moved to larger quarters as sales and profits continued to grow.

Not the least of resources on campus is the student body itself, from which an entrepreneur, whether personally a student or not, may be able to recruit in forming a company. There may be considerable variety of talent among students, including some with industrial experience and, depending on the school, possibly different professions, such as business, engineering, and law, who can contribute in their areas of specialty. One problem to be resolved by the entrepreneur must be to find eligible partners, and a second, obviously, is to select among them. Then come issues of how to work with, manage, and compensate them. One who made use of academic resources in forming a venture was a student at the University of Washington, whose venture also serves to illustrate the *extracurricular followon,* an enterprise organized during school, outside class, to be pursued full time following graduation:

◆   After six years as a navy pilot, he had enrolled in oceanography graduate school to complement his undergraduate studies in chemical engineering and equip himself to land a "job as an engineer, probably with some big company." Although he had not been particularly interested in biological aspects of ocean-ography, one day he went to watch salmon return to experimental rearing pens at the university. Suddenly he was struck by the contrast between abundance in the returning horde of fish and his recollection of seeing starving people during service tours. "I had heard the state had recently passed regulations allowing private rearing of salmon, and it hit me that this could be a business with real potential," he recalled.

In the weeks that followed, he began talking to other students, particularly in marine biology and fisheries, to learn what might be required for a salmon farm. Eggs, he learned, could be bought from the state, but trays with circulat-ing water were needed to hatch them. Then a freshwater pond would be re-quired for early rearing on feed pellets, after which they would be transferred to saltwater pens for growth to one pound, at which size they could be harvested and sold.

With a fisheries student he began working up a feasibility study for the enterprise and recruiting other partners. "I figured we should have maybe twenty-five people all working part time, but six other people already working on it voted me down, so we went with seven. I had talked to maybe two hundred people, most of whom had come to me when they heard what was afoot. I'd never ask them for anything, but every so often one would say, 'Hey, let's do something about this,' and then I'd figure I had a live one. All the people we chose had working wives or other sources of income and were willing to take some risk."

The first three partners paid in $5,000 each to form a corporation in which each held 500 shares out of a total issuance of 1,500 shares. The corporation then agreed to pay the others three and one-half shares per hour of work. "That gave us a real problem on taxes," he observed. "If our lawyer had just said he didn't know how to handle it, we might have been all right. But they never do that. Professionals seem to think they have to act like they know everything. But he didn't know the answer, and IRS couldn't tell us, and we're still living with the problem."

During summer break the group scouted for real estate. They found that asking people was better than looking at maps or other references, and that by making the visits in pairs one could keep notes while the other asked questions and negotiated. Numerous required permits were obtained from government agencies, a site was obtained, and construction of facilities began in July 1972, eight months after the venture idea had first occurred. Eggs were obtained in January 1973, and a few weeks later the company began its first sales of fingerlings to Indian tribes who would rear them further while the company retained part of the crop for further rearing itself.

This particular venture, however, did not work out well. Caught between the cost of feed for the fish, the attrition due to disease, and the market price of pan salmon as a relatively new product, the enterprise, like others that started in the same line of business at the time, failed to profit.

School dropout ventures are relatively easy to find among young entrepreneurs. A venture begun in school may become so successful that it overwhelms studies. For instance, a Stanford engineering student in the mid-1960s became interested in a current fad, go-cart racing. Dissatisfied with the crude wheels available for these vehicles, he developed a pattern for his own. Others expressed interest in his wheels, so he began selling them. Soon his sales were taking so much time that his studies were suffering, and he dropped out of school to work full time on his company, which then began making first other go-cart accessories and then other lines of products.

Probably the grandest dropout venture of all in recent years, however, is that of Microsoft:

◆   Bill Gates, who characterized himself as a "hard-core technoid," began working with computers in seventh grade when the Mothers' Club of his private school donated time on mainframes for the students. One summer he earned $4,200 doing class schedules for the school.

At age fifteen Gates teamed up with Paul Allen, a schoolmate two years further along, to form a company called Traf-O-Data, which earned a revenue of $20,000 for analyzing Seattle auto traffic patterns with a computer using the just-introduced Intel 8008 microprocessor chip. At age seventeen Gates went on leave from high school to work as a programmer with Allen for TRW, reportedly for a salary of $30,000.[12] The 1975 Popular Electronics cover story on the Altair microcomputer kit introduced by MITS in Albuquerque gave impetus to many computer pioneers, including not only the founders of Apple but also Paul Allen, who was by then working for Honeywell in Massachusetts, and Bill Gates, who had become a prelaw freshman at Harvard. Allen persuaded Gates to take time from his studies to work with him in adapting BASIC software from mainframe computers to run on the MITS Altair machine.

This adaptation was not actually developed on the Altair but rather on a mainframe simulator of the Intel 8080 chip that the Altair used. The two agreed to take a paper tape of their new program to Albuquerque and demonstrate it for MITS. "Everyone," Gates recalled, "including ourselves, was amazed when this BASIC worked the first time. Many MITS employees who couldn't comprehend what to do with an Altair saw the value of the computer for the first time. Paul and I were ecstatic that all our work had paid off."

The two dropped their Massachusetts occupations and moved to Albuquerque, Allen to work as director of software development for MITS and Gates to work in a hotel across the street, adapting BASIC for other computers. A year later Allen left MITS to join Gates. MITS was sold in 1977 and Gates, now twenty-one, and Allen, twenty-three, both returned home to the Seattle area where they continued Microsoft. Gates owned 60 percent of the stock, Allen 40 percent. By 1979 MITS had vanished completely. By 1986 Microsoft had gone public and the value of Gate's shares had reached $350 million.[13]

A second dropout pattern begins with a student first dropping out of school because of a feeling that students are insufficiently challenging and not leading anywhere, and then starts a venture.

[12] Robert Levering, Michael Katz, and Milton Moskowitz, The Computer Entrepreneurs (New York: New American Library, 1984), p. 158.
[13] Bro Uttal, "Inside the Deal That Made Bill Gates $350,000,000," Fortune, July 21, 1986, p. 23.

◆   Stan Buchtal, who had dropped out of Boston University, was working in
New York's garment district and in his spare time designing "mod" clothes. His
former college roommate, Robert Margolis, was working in a Madison Avenue
advertising agency and "dreaming of moneymaking schemes." Conversations
started them thinking about making low-priced clothes for young people and with
$10,000 pooled savings they started making some in a rented townhouse. Their
designs, beginning with denim "baggies," caught on in high schools and colleges,
and in 1974, two years after starting, their firm employed 150 people (average
age, twenty-seven) and was selling over $12 million worth of clothes per year.
Both founders were by this time twenty-six years old.

Direct postgraduate startups, in which students graduate and then start
a new company rather than going to work for one already established, are
typically hard to separate from ventures that are first conceived in school and
then started following graduation. It appears that unless a student has already
worked out an idea for venturing during school, either as part of course work
or on the side, the temptation to take a job with a company, rather than drift
in search of a startup following graduation, will be too great. If a venture then
ensues, it will be after work in another company first.

JOB TO VENTURE

Most companies are started by people who leave jobs with other firms to pursue
entrepreneurship, as opposed to people who are students, homemakers, or
unemployed.[14] Four ways in which such direct transitions from job to startup
occur will be examined in this section:

1 *Direct job outgrowth.* In which activities of the prior job itself directly point
   the way to the new venture.

2 *Tangential opportunities.* Startups that arise from outside events having
   nothing particular to do with the prior job.

3 *Sideline startups.* Ventures started on a "moonlight" basis after hours and
   on weekends during other employment, which grow into full-time businesses.

4 *Planned direct post-job startups.* Which involve planned venture design
   during employment in preparation for resignation and startup thereafter.

Depending on how distinctions between these categories are drawn, the
fraction of startups accounted for by each historically has probably occurred

---

[14] Detailed quantification of this observation would require careful definition and population sampling, which has not been done. Clues, however, to the orders of magnitude can be gleaned
from Sandman, who found only six substantial student-entrepreneur-started ventures among
some 500 colleges and universities. Other researchers (Myles S. Delano, Dudley W. Johnson,
and Robert T. Woodworth, *The Entrepreneurial Process,* University of Washington, 1966) found
that out of 384 entrepreneurs sampled, only 125 could be classified as "Employment Seeking
and By-Chance" (32.5 percent). The fraction who go from home to startup (homemakers and
family ventures) is clearly small, as evidenced by their relative absence in all the references so
far mentioned.

roughly in order as above, starting from most frequent down to least. As far as interest to would-be entrepreneurs is concerned, the order may be somewhat the reverse, because while the last two types above can be willfully controlled to a considerable degree by the entrepreneur, the first two tend more often to result from unforeseen events.

There are many ways in which entrepreneurial opportunity can emerge as a *direct job outgrowth* during employment with others. One pattern involves acquisition. The employer of the entrepreneur may decide, because of desire to move into other activities, or to retire, or for any number of other reasons, to sell out to the entrepreneur. Or the employer may relinquish a product, as in the following case.

◆   An aerodynamicist with the Hamilton Division of United Aircraft in Hartford, Connecticut, Charles Kaman, conceived during World War II a way of controlling helicopter rotors by using servo flaps to make the craft much more stable and maneuverable. Because the company was not interested in pursuing the idea, he was able to get permission to use it himself. With $4,000 he set up his own corporation in 1945 and continued experiments in his mother's basement. Using an old auto chassis, he built a test rig and applied for patents. Friends from his former employer helped out evenings and weekends in return for stock. In 1946 he was able to obtain a navy contract for $15,000 to build a rotor for NACA to test. As he needed additional capital, he sold stock to friends and acquaintances around Hartford. After his first machine flew in January 1947, he gave demonstrations at a nearby airport and sold more stock to spectators. By 1949 eight of his helicopters were making money for him crop dusting in the summers, although the company was still not profitable. The machine had proven itself, however, leading to military contracts. The first profits, $27,000 on sales of $4.8 million, finally came in 1951.

This particular opportunity would have been hard to anticipate. However, noting that such opportunities can arise out of work, a would-be entrepreneur may be better able to choose an employer and position within the firm where entrepreneurial opportunities are more likely to occur. Questions to consider with regard to positions may include the extent to which new technologies or new ground rules for operating are occurring, whether other employees have found entrepreneurial opportunities in those positions, and what attitude the company exhibits toward permitting or even encouraging employees to start their own firms. The Hewlett-Packard company, for example, once advertised itself as a good place to learn for employees who might want to start their own companies, and it has pursued deliberate policies of encouraging employees to develop their own companies as suppliers of Hewlett-Packard. Reflection on such questions may suggest to a would-be entrepreneur ideas for changing positions within his or her employer's firm or even changing firms to reach a spot where startup opportunities are more likely to occur.

Usually it is not necessary to ask a former employer for permission because the new venture, although it may draw upon skills and contacts from the entrepreneur's prior job, will not be using anything on which the former employer can make a proprietary claim. Quite possibly it will represent an opportunity the employer could have taken advantage of, but one the employer considers insufficiently related to its main line of business; one it is neither interested in nor well positioned to exploit, as in the following example:

◆   John H. Johnson sought a career in publishing because of his high school experience managing the school newspaper and serving as business editor of the school yearbook. One of his interviews for the school paper was with the president of a black insurance company. The president offered his young interviewer a job that included, among other duties, publishing a newsletter for the company. This brought Johnson into contact with leaders in Chicago's black community and gave him the idea for starting a magazine of his own directed to blacks. From *Reader's Digest* he decided to call it the *Negro Digest.* This he launched in 1942 with $500 borrowed against his mother's furniture. As his *Digest* began to prosper he thought of imitating another magazine, *Life,* and in 1945 launched his own picture magazine, *Ebony.* Then he started still other magazines, *Tan* and *Jet,* as well as book publishing, radio, television, and cosmetics businesses.

Failing to find such opportunities on the job does not rule out the possibility that *tangential opportunities* entirely unrelated to the job may occur, allowing the entrepreneur to move out of the job directly into self-employment. By definition, these will be opportunities that occur during free time, possibly in connection with social activities, hobbies, or simply in the course of living, and be quite independent of the job or company worked for.

◆   Masayoshi Ikeda's job was washing dishes and sweeping floors for a restaurant in New York City, where he had arrived from Japan in 1962 with no friends, no money, and slight knowledge of English. To save transportation money he walked a lot and indulged in one of the few hobbies he could afford, window shopping. One day some Japanese tourists stopped him on the sidewalk and asked for help in buying diamonds. He guided them to a jewelry store and served as interpreter. After the sale, the jeweler paid him $10 and promised 10 percent on any other sales he brought in. (It might be asked who was more the entrepreneur in this situation.)

Diamonds at the time were cheaper in New York than in Japan. Ikeda began cultivating other customers, and shortly entered the diamond business for himself. By 1968 at age thirty-two he was out of the dishwashing job with his enterprise paying him $50,000 a year. He branched into other gems, and at the Olympic games in Mexico made $1 million in twelve days by selling $100,000 worth of Mexican opals he had bought to visiting Japanese tourists. By 1972 his business had grown in sales to over $7 million per year.

Somewhat less "out of the blue" can be a venture begun after working hours as a *sideline startup.* Here, by definition, the enterprise begins as a part-time activity only possibly later growing into a full-time occupation. In the following case, two brothers began a sideline by bidding for a subcontract from a larger company.

◆   A journeyman machinist who enjoyed working on cars as a hobby was occasionally asked by acquaintances to do repairs on fiberglass Corvette bodies. Through several discussions he and his younger brother, who was manager in a firm distributing pipe fittings and valves, decided to try bidding on a job to fabricate a prototype fiberglass waste container for Boeing. They won the contract, and during evenings and weekends did the work. In the process, they also developed sources of supply for quantity discounts on fiberglass raw materials and learned techniques for using the materials from suppliers, one of whom sent a salesman to work with them for three days on development of molds.

The two men bought a fiberglass dune buggy body to go on a Volkswagen chassis and began using their skills in plastic to modify it. Someone offered to buy it, and other acquaintances began to ask for copies. This prompted them to make a mold, and soon they were turning out car bodies in a volume that strained their capital. They had used $10,000 of their original $30,000 equity investment for equipment, and the remaining $20,000 of working capital was being stretched too thin. For half the equity they obtained another $30,000 from a venture capital firm, and quit their jobs to work full time on the new company. By 1972, four years after it began, the company had diversified into other fiberglass products and sales were up to $600,000 per year.

The many virtues of starting small with a sideline venture both as a way of learning how to start and run a business and as a way of creating a base on which to build one that can eventually become full time are extensively discussed by Peter Weaver.[15] While working full time as a magazine writer, he began in his free time a small venture on the side which consisted of reports on Latin America to be sold to U.S. newspapers. This venture did not succeed, but Weaver started another similar one and gradually built it up to a syndicated column in newspapers, followed by syndicated tapes for a radio show, a magazine column, and personal lectures. When he felt the sideline was sufficient to support him, he quit his regular job and went full time at his company, in which his book, *You, Inc.*, became one project.

The next example of moving from employment to a sideline startup followed a different pattern, in that the entrepreneurs formed their company before they had any idea what line of work it would pursue. As will be seen later, they eventually built it into a multimillion-dollar enterprise supplying animals and equipment for research laboratories from the following beginnings:

♦   Kirby Cramer and Wally Opdyke were investment analysts for a mutual fund owned by Safeco Insurance. With Larry Wells, a vice-president of the fund, they began having after-hours discussions about possible ways of forming a company. After six months of these talks Cramer over a beer one evening said, "I've got the name. Seadyne." "That's it," Opdyke and Wells agreed. "We weren't sure what we would have, but that was the name," Cramer later recalled.

The conversation continued: "Let's incorporate. We need a lawyer. I'm familiar with equity. Wally, you know bonds, and Larry, you're a CPA. We need someone in policy and administration." The three agreed to think about who might fill that gap. Cramer talked to a business policy professor he had studied under as an MBA student (as an undergraduate, Cramer had majored in art history), who in turn referred them to an attorney. These five (Cramer later observed that they began with no experience whatever in either production or sales) donated a total of $900, and the Seadyne corporation was formed. Tentatively, they planned to find a company that they could buy well below book value on borrowed down payment and then resell for a profit. Attempts to purchase a flour mill whose $48 book value stock was being traded at $15 per share failed, and Cramer turned to trading with the paid-in capital in high-technology stocks.

What if a suitable line of business for the sideline is not found, or is not possible because the regular full-time employer does not permit part-time work,

---

[15] Weaver, *You, Inc.* (Garden City, N.Y.: Doubleday, 1973).

or is such that it cannot be done with the scale of effort that is possible part time? If no tangential opportunity happens to present itself, should it not be possible to perform the design and preparation of a venture so that it will be ready to proceed with as a *planned direct post-job startup* immediately following resignation? Desire to do so was apparent in the following financial section advertisement in a March 1969 issue of the *Palo Alto Times:*

◆ PLEASE READ THIS—We are four able executive engineers who are tired of working fourteen hours a day for an ungrateful employer. We have developed many new processes and products which have enriched everybody but us. We want to form a company to produce electronic devices for which there is a world-wide market. We know we can do this, because we already did—for someone else. We need some investors to put up a half-million dollars: business men, doctors, widows, or misers; anybody with some vision. The money is for equipment and machinery and will be fully secured. We can sell three million dollars worth of our products the first year.
Won't you at least talk to us?"

Whether they received the money was not reported, but it seems unlikely. The advertisement may, however, have been inspired by other electronic "spin-off" company formations by dissatisfied employees who managed to raise capital more conventionally and resign to start their own enterprises. From his examination of some 250 high-technology company startups in the San Francisco area, Cooper described a "typical" story as follows:

◆ The marketing manager of a rapidly growing electronics firm in Palo Alto had, for several years, considered taking the step of starting his own firm. He had previously worked in engineering for two different firms in the East and then had worked in positions of increasing responsibility in sales for a West Coast firm which grew fifty-fold during his time with it. He then became head of marketing for a Palo Alto firm, and helped that company grow approximately forty-fold during the next few years.
While with the Palo Alto firm, he began to disagree with certain important decisions in regard to product development and the selection of key personnel. He said, "I saw myself on a collision path with the president, and knew that I would not stay with the company." In addition to his increasing dissatisfaction with his future in this firm, he had increasingly thought about taking the entrepreneurial step himself. In his own words, "I had finally gotten the bug. I thought I'd like to try it myself . . . to try to create something out of nothing . . . to try to make a company important in its field." *In the past, he had considered with certain friends and colleagues a number of product-market opportunities which might be the basis for a new company; however, nothing had quite jelled. Finally, a specific opportunity came into focus,* relating to the development of a particular component with technical capabilities exceeding anything then on the market.
In the fall of 1965, he and three other engineers from the same firm left the parent company and started on their own. They estimated that their own savings, including stock ownership, were sufficient to support the company for six to nine months. They believed that they easily could raise additional funds from five different men they knew, all of whom were technical executives who had invested in other new, technologically-based firms in the past. *When they started, they had no product developed and had not specifically talked to any cus-*

tomers, yet . . . "We were tremendously confident . . . Even if we had to work twenty-four hours a day, we were determined to meet our goals."[16]

Such a pattern of startup is closely similar to the direct job outgrowths mentioned earlier, except that the new company's product or service was not itself developed at the former employer; it was just in the same category of technology. When the technology of the new company is different, it is harder to find examples that involve preparation to start performed during employment but no actual start on some sort of sideline small-scale basis before departure.[17] Examples do, however, occur, as illustrated by the following:

♦ An atomic energy scientist who had a high salary but was unhappy with his company's management and disappointed at not being promoted into management began looking for ventures in business opportunities classified advertisements of newspapers. In his search he looked at farms, ranches, motels, resorts, and several industrial firms, on some of which he made offers, but without success. In early 1972 a second scientist who had some money to invest expressed interest in collaborating. The two became interested in a hydroponic greenhouse for sale, and after visiting a number of other such firms they decided to buy it.

The partners sold their homes, invested $100,000 of their own money, and bought the enterprise. The first entrepreneur immediately quit his job to work full time on the venture, assisted by other members of both families. The second kept his job and contributed half his salary to the first for income while the business was getting underway. A year later this arrangement still continued, although the firm was now succeeding according to plan with surprisingly few problems. The entrepreneur who had gone full time into the venture commented that his only regret was that they had waited fifteen years before starting.

This startup differs from the one preceding in that the scientists' new company was not at all in the same line of work as that of their former employer. Such departures in line of work for the new venture on the part of would-be entrepreneurs who are currently employed are much more likely to occur as either tangential startups, where the new venture opportunity comes as a surprise, or as sideline ventures in which the ground can be tested on a small scale before the leap from employment is taken. The other type of circumstance that occurs in a healthy fraction of cases is among those whose starting point for entrepreneurship is unemployment.

UNEMPLOYMENT TO VENTURE

People can become unemployed in a variety of ways, which will here be described in four categories (not counting refugees, as noted in Chapter 1 under "minority enterprise"):

[16] Arnold C. Cooper, *The Founding of Technologically-Based Firms* (Milwaukee: Center for Venture Management, 1971), p. 9 (Italics added.) Used with permission.
[17] Cooper does not sort the firms he studied as to starting point, and hence all types are lumped together. He found that among the high-technology startups 63.7 percent had markets similar to those of the parent firms, while 85 percent had technology similar to the parent firm.

1 *Intentional resignation.* Wherein the employee deliberately quits, typically out of dissatisfaction.

2 *Layoff.* The employee's job is lost because his or her employer is forced by economic developments to cut back.

3 *Discharge.* The employer fires the employee, typically because of some dissatisfaction on the part of the employer.

4 *Retirement.* In which the employee is let go because of age under company regulations or chooses to quit to be eligible for Social Security income.

Unemployment from all four of these causes has provided starting points for entrepreneurs who succeeded. Probably the order of frequency is the same as the list above, with the largest fraction of successful ventures beginning from the first of these starting points and the smallest from the last (except in periods just after wars, when laid-off ex-servicemen have started many companies). Cooper, for example, found that over twice as many startups (30 percent of his sample) followed from entrepreneurs who quit as from those who were forced to leave their previous positions (13 percent).[18]

He goes on to illustrate the typical *intentional resignation* startup, which began as follows:

♦   A typical situation involved an engineer in charge of one product line in a small firm. He had grown increasingly disturbed over his relationship with his superior, whom he believed lacking in competence; he also thought that he was being inadequately paid, considering the long hours he was working. When a proposal he had developed to expand his product line was rejected, he quit. Later that day, he asked himself, "What am I going to do now?"[19]

At another point Cooper, again stressing with regard to the entrepreneur that "he had not planned to quit; he had not planned to become an entrepreneur," tells how such a typical story continued:

♦   He made the decision to start a company specializing in the same kind of instruments he had been responsible for in his previous job. He tried to raise capital from a number of sources, but was successful only in raising a small amount of money from previous colleagues who planned to join him after the company got going. He bid on and succeeded in getting an order to deliver some technically advanced instruments. Subsequently, he discovered that he had inadequate funds to carry through on the order. Because of financial problems, he changed the strategy of the business and became a subcontractor, primarily designing and producing particular components for one large local firm.[20]

It can be noted that a number of factors favored these startups, particularly with regard to the lines of work they pursued—electronics—and the geographical area of the San Francisco peninsula, which, like a few other areas, such as Boston and Los Angeles, is known for many startups. The products can often be developed and produced with low investment in plant and equipment. They

---

[18] Cooper, *Technologically-Based Firms,* p. 24.
[19] Ibid., p. 23.
[20] Ibid., p. 10.

are often small enough that a team of less than five people can develop and produce them. The area abounds in knowhow about startups because of others that have occurred and is a good recruiting ground for both talent and venture capital as a result.

But what if the prior line of work is one, such as building nuclear submarines, that cannot be started on a small scale, and what if the geographical area is not one conducive to entrepreneurship in terms of supportive connections available or in terms of where the entrepreneur might prefer to live? One predictable result would be that fewer startups would occur in such a geographical area and fewer would grow directly out of such lines of work. Most areas of the country and most lines of work in fact bear out this conclusion, having few startups, except localized, stable, small service, or "Mom 'n Pop"-type firms.

The would-be entrepreneur in such a situation then faces more severe obstacles to ambitious venturing. Intentional resignation and departure for another geographical area is still one alternative, and although there are indications that few choose it, certainly some do, as illustrated by the following case.[21]

♦   An engineer at one of the "big three" Detroit automakers had risen rapidly with the company and at age thirty-five was in charge of engineering for a major auto division. He chafed, however, at subordination and at what appeared to him as a disparity between his relative pay versus contributions to profits and his relative compensation for those contributions, and he believed that he could do better on his own. He announced his intention to resign, and in spite of pleas from his superiors to remain ("Some of them confidentially said they wished they had the nerve to quit too," he recalled, "but they were afraid they had too much to lose."), he bought a trailer, packed in the family belongings, and with his wife and four young children drove to the coast of southern California, which appealed to him for living, although it had never been his home before.

While his family "camped" in a trailer court, he began looking for a company in which to acquire an interest. Through friends in Detroit he acquired connections in the Los Angeles business community, and after several months of search met a man with a small job machine shop who was willing to take on a partner. Over several years the engineer saved and bought out the original owner's interest. Then he began developing products of his own. A pogo stick he designed for the toy market caught on well and gave the tiny firm a boost, then a line of tubular-framed products, such as hat racks and bussing carts for commercial kitchens and other institutional use, proved successful. Another very high profit item, though for a limited time, was an instrumented test stand console for rocket engines, which the entrepreneur designed and produced on competitive bid for a local aircraft company. A few of his colleagues who remained with the auto company eventually became wealthier than the entrepreneur, though his company made him quite prosperous (annual profits ranged upwards of $125,000 in his solely owned firm), but he observed that none had enjoyed the freedom of living and expression that he had.

For a would-be entrepreneur to opt for resignation as a starting point to

[21] In Cooper's sample, for instance, 97.5 percent of the companies had at least one founder who had previously worked in the same geographical area where the company started, and 92.2 percent had founders all of whom had worked in the area (Cooper, *Technologically-Based Firms*, p. 18).

develop a new venture, rather than at least developing plans for it during employment so as to use the job as a starting point, generally requires either a very high sense of self-confidence, particularly regarding ability to obtain another job, or most intense discomfort in the present job, or both. However, it is not necessary to resign in order to become unemployed. The next examples will illustrate how some ventures have begun starting from *layoff.*

After every war, thousands of men are laid off by the armed forces, as well as from defense industries, and at the same time there tend to be both pent-up demands for goods that were made scarce by wartime exigencies and shifts in both consumer and industrial needs as the economy readjusts and as a result of new technologies developed by war research which may have peacetime applications. James Ling became one of the more famous ex-G.I. entrepreneurs by parlaying his army experience as an electrician into an enormous empire:

◆   Following discharge, Ling sold his house, paid off some debts, and with $2,000 remaining bought some surplus electrical equipment and a used truck to become an electrical contractor. He started on such jobs as doorbell and lighting fixture installations, grossing $70,000 the first year with negligible profit. Before long, however, he had shifted away from residential wiring and was selling his services to construction firms that did industrial and government installations. Volume in his second year, 1948, rose to $200,000, this time with a good profit, and then doubled again in 1949. By 1954, at age thirty-two, he had a contracting firm doing one million dollars' worth of business per year. It was then that he decided to go public, distributing prospectuses from a booth at the county fair, and then began acquiring other companies with various mixtures of stock and cash to build the conglomerate empire that made him famous, though it ultimately came near total collapse in the late 1960s.

Ling's experience was an exception in terms of fame, but the basic pattern, of being unemployed from armed forces cutback and consequently going into business, has been repeated innumerable times. Another such startup that rose more slowly but to a more sustained success was that of William Kirschner:

◆   A mining engineering graduate from the University of Washington, he had worked for a while after graduation in 1939 for the Tacoma Copper Smelter and had then gone into mining in Idaho. When the war came in 1941, he was classified as an essential worker ineligible for the service and, because there were no ships bringing in ore to process, spent much of the war playing cribbage. When the Battle of the Bulge began there was a call for more men, and Kirschner left his job for the service.

While out of a job and waiting to be processed for active duty, he began making surgical splints in his parents' basement. Both his brother and his father were at the time selling surgical and orthopedic supplies and sold these splints along with their other lines. Kirschner recalled, "It didn't take any money to get into making these things, and we had none."

His father began to point out needs for other items, such as splints for animals that could not be chewed off before healing had occurred, and better animal cages that had no seams and rounded corners for better sanitation. Bill Kirschner worked on design and manufacturing of these products while his father and brother sold them, and a little company, Kirschner Manufacturing, gradually took shape from a rather unlikely setting for industry, their home on Vashon Island, a pleasant rural and recreational setting in the middle of Puget Sound.

An interesting aspect of these opportunities arising out of layoffs is that the particular ventures could as well have been started by any number of others had they chosen to resign their jobs and do so. The same is true of the following enterprise, which was stimulated not by a layoff from the service but rather from industry:

♦   In the spring of 1969 a manufacturing engineer was laid off at a major aerospace firm due to industry cutbacks. At age fifty-seven he was a graduate engineer with degrees in both mechanical and industrial engineering, had risen to chief of manufacturing engineering in six years with one company and to production manager in two years with a second company, and had then spent fourteen years with the aerospace firm, where he was a specialty tool designer. Realizing it would be hard to obtain another position at his age, he started a venture to mix and sell a chemical vegetation killer with another laid-off aerospace worker.

By summer of the following year, 1970, the chemical enterprise was not earning enough combined with his wife's job to provide living expenses when his unemployment compensation ran out in the coming winter. But no other sources of income were turning up.

More months rolled by, and then at a Christmas party a friend reminded him about twenty pairs of snowshoes he had designed and built for his son's Boy Scout troop. They had worked well for the scouts and the engineer had also made himself a pair that he used on winter backpacking trips. Why, the friend wondered, didn't he make some for sale?

He made and sold to friends sixteen pairs, which were well received. Encouraged, he made improvements in the design and between February and September of 1971 sold another ten pairs. He also sent a product information letter to the U.S. General Services Administration, the Forest and Park Services in all western states, and to western dealers in recreational equipment. Because his product was new, he priced it in the midrange of those already on the market, quoting typical industry discounts. Meanwhile, he utilized all the funds he could spare to build a seventeen-pair inventory, and at the suggestion of two friends who had bought shoes the previous winter, began designing a shoe harness to solve some problems with existing standard designs.

Orders for samples started coming in the fall of 1971, and the engineer filled them with shoes incorporating the new harness, with the result that two weeks after shipment one dealer ordered thirty pairs of harnesses, but no shoes. This made a patent search seem worthwhile, so he engaged an attorney to initiate one.

During the winter of 1972 sales were running between twenty and thirty pairs per month, the entrepreneur was working seven days a week to turn them out, and the enterprise was generating a worthwhile income. Sales slowly increased each year thereafter as he added additional variations and products to the line. With development of the North Slope activity a steeper increase began, and by early 1975 the company had received a $50,000 loan for expansion from the bank under an SBA guarantee and the entrepreneur was looking for more factory space in which to expand.

It should be noted that this venturing was not typical of laid-off aerospace personnel. Although many tens of thousands were laid off in the Seattle area in the early 1970s, almost none of them were successful in starting companies. Few even tried. Moreover, it is hard to see any appreciable way that the large-company employment helped this entrepreneur get started. Army experience was much more helpful to Ling. And it was the Boy Scout work that helped with this project. One moral this might suggest for would-be entrepreneurs may be to avoid working for large organizations in which they will be highly specialized and not thrown into contact with small business opportunities or other people who could help them. Another moral might be to follow Weaver's advice and work on sideline ventures to develop entrepreneurial capacity, regardless of what sort of full-time employer is selected.

The following entrepreneur worked for a smaller enterprise, and when he became unemployed found himself able to land on his feet by moving into a similar enterprise of his own. His route to unemployment was also different, because he was not laid off as a result of a company cutback. The starting point for him was one of *discharge*.

◆ He had started as a gas station attendant, then worked in the shop of an auto dealer, then finally in a tire store, where he rose to the position of manager. He had thought from time to time about possibly opening his own store, but by the time his age had reached forty-one he had decided he was too old to take such risks and too well established in the company to quit. Then suddenly to his surprise, he was fired and found himself out on the street with no job and no plans.

He visited other tire stores and wholesalers looking for work, but without success. When one of the men in another shop asked why, with his experience, he didn't open a tire store of his own, he began to think about the possibility. Then in his job search he ran into a shop for sale. Talking with other dealers, his banker, his lawyer, and an accountant, he collected advice about what to look for in buying such a company and how to work out terms for price and purchase.

He bought the business, and using tricks he had learned from his own work experience plus ideas he had picked up from other firms in his job search, he soon had it growing in sales and profits. "I found myself working about three times as hard as I had for the other company, but really enjoying the work for a change, and making a heck of a lot more money," he recalled. He expanded to other outlets and a dozen years later sold a part interest in the chain, mostly to his own employees, for a half-million dollars. "Tell your boss you want to buy him out after you've worked for him a while and done a good job," he suggested, "The fact is, it can be hard for him to find someone reliable to take over and let him cash in his investment on a sound basis. So you can do him a favor and become your own boss at the same time."

The final route to unemployment for most people is *retirement*. For some this is a welcome change, but for others it is not. Some have a choice in the matter, particularly those who are self-employed, and also many who work for smaller firms where rules about such things are not rigid. Employees in larger and more bureaucratic organizations, however, generally have no choice. At General Motors and many other giants, even the president is automatically removed from his position when he turns sixty-five. He at least will have no income problems, but many other retired people do. It has been estimated that only 15 percent of retired people receive pension benefits in addition to Social Security. So unless a person has accumulated substantial savings, retirement can mean poverty. Worse for some people may simply be the fact of being put out of action with no essential service to perform.

At least five remedies for this are possible, of which three require entrepreneuring. First would be to save enough money to have greater freedom of action in retirement. Second would be to be self-employed in a venture that can be carried on as long as desired. Third would be to select an employer who does not force retirement at a fixed age. Fourth is Weaver's approach of developing a sideline venture for supplemental income that will carry on during retirement. Fifth would be to start a venture after retiring. This last is, like startups among laid-off employees of big companies, a rare occurrence. The following, however, illustrates how it can happen.

◆   A man who retired from construction work in the late 1960s thought he would develop a hobby of making things out of old bottles. He wanted to cut off the necks to use the lower parts in making vases and drinking glasses but could not find anyone who could tell him how to do it. He began struggling with the problem himself and wound up inventing a fixture by which an ordinary glass cutter could be mounted and rotated smoothly around the bottle to sever the neck. Since he knew of no other such device, he decided to apply for a patent and offer it for sale by mail order.

When his cutter received a recommendation in the *Whole Earth Catalog*, sales took a large leap upward. Within two years, the retiree was employing two hundred people on three shifts, turning out 10,000 to 14,000 cutters per day, and consuming more 1/8-by3/4-inch aluminum strip, from which the cutter holding fixture was constructed, than any other user in the country. He was selling the products, which cost him $2.00 to make, for $3.08 each, and reflecting about what to do for an encore as more competitors began copying his design and the market saturated.

HOME TO VENTURE

The home can be regarded as another starting point for entrepreneurial ventures, although to some extent it will be found to overlap with other starting points. For instance, Kirschner Manufacturing, which was mentioned earlier as an unemployment-initiated venture, could also be regarded as one that started out of the home, as did the snowshoe venture of the aerospace engineer. Two subcategories that will serve to distinguish other home starts from these two and will be illustrated here are as follows:

1 *Homemaker-started ventures.* Enterprises begun typically by women starting from a home base.
2 *Family ventures.* Wherein husband and wife, and sometimes also children of the family, join in developing the enterprise.

Occasionally, and perhaps with increasing frequency as "women's lib" advances, women begin enterprises from career-starting points similar to those of the men mentioned so far in this chapter. Historically, enterprises begun by women have been few compared with those begun by men, and most have begun out of homes rather than out of careers. Also, most of them have tended to be of the stably small venture variety, as opposed to ambitiously growth-oriented. For instance, two housewives bought combs and decorated them by hand for sale through costume jewelry counters; many others have developed various types of handicrafts, operated small retail outlets, such as boutiques, antique shops, hobby stores, and millinery stores. There have been numerous small local publications started by homemakers, an example being a Washington, D.C., weekly newsletter telling other housewives about comparative grocery store prices and where the best bargains are.

Many of these *homemaker-started ventures* remain part-time activities while others evolve into full-time activities, possibly through a path of evolution such as the following:

◆   Patricia Gofette became a general contractor. With a degree in finance and accounting, she had worked for eighteen years for construction-related firms. "In my last job," she recalled, "working for a homebuilder, I ran a one-girl office. I did everything from answering the phone to all the bookwork and taxes, except for the corporate income tax. I picked out all the siding and the colors and decorated the insides of the houses."

She also sold her sports car and did some investing in the stock market, which produced starting capital. Then she began buying and selling land, gradually learning what to watch out for, and then she started building houses on the land. "At first I built one house at a time, and later I started two. I'd get one half-finished and start the second. Right now I have five going and will probably be starting another one in a few weeks. So that's six houses plus a remodeling at a main shopping center."[22]

More rare are *homemaker-started ventures* that grow into major corporations. But they have been happening occasionally for many years and continue to happen currently, as illustrated by the following two enterprises in very different lines of business:

◆   Margaret Rudkin's son had trouble with asthma, and the doctor suggested it might be due to chemical additives in his food which caused an allergic reaction. This prompted her to seek a natural diet for him, and she began baking bread from an old recipe of her grandmother's, which included home grinding of whole wheat flour. It worked. The doctor tasted her bread, then asked if she would bake some for him, and then asked if she would bake some more for some of his patients. She tried the bread on friends, who also liked it and asked for loaves. Then she tried selling some through a local market, and the market started ordering more. Her husband, a New York stockbroker who commuted from their Connecticut home, took some into the city to try it on some department stores, and soon he was carrying all he could handle every trip. Within a year she was selling 4,000 loaves per week, and soon after that as many loaves per day. Her company, Pepperidge Farm, eventually grew large and in the early 1960s was sold to a still larger company, Campbell's Soup, to make her a millionairess.

◆   Sandra L. Kurtzig had worked in computer systems marketing for General Electric but quit in 1972 to start a family. As a sideline she invested $2,000 of her savings to start a contract-programming business out of her apartment. Her first job, a program for newspapers to keep track of carriers, led to others, and she

²² Terri P. Tepper, and Nona Dawe Tepper, *The New Entrepreneurs: Women Working from Home* (New York: Universe Books, 1980), p. 36.

began adding other programmers. By 1978 with the help of a Hewlett-Packard computer that a nearby company allowed her to use at night, her company had developed a proprietary program for inventory control. By 1980 sales had reached $1.9 million, and in 1984 sales were $65 million with a profit of $6.1 million.

Family Ventures

The term "Mom 'n Pop" is generally taken to mean something stably small at best in the way of a venture, possibly only marginally surviving, or maybe earning a modest income, but not certainly on the way to great growth and financial success. These inferences fairly well characterize most startups that are *family ventures* from the outset. There are numerous firms, like Mattel Toy Company, in which husband-wife teams have played an important role *after* startup, but it is hard to find dramatic success stories initiated by family teams. Without data regarding final outcomes of such ventures, the following may illustrate how family startup can work:

◆   In 1971 R. D. Benson, a systems analyst in Arizona, began discussing with his family the possibility of starting a business. His son, Bruce—soon to graduate in electrical engineering—his wife, and his daughter—about to start college—were interested in the idea. To find venture ideas they began looking at franchises but disliked the fees, royalties, and management constraints imposed by the franchisors. Mrs. Benson, who did a great deal of sewing for the family, called their attention to mill-end fabric shops that had started selling cloth scraps by the pound in Phoenix and appeared to be thriving. On a vacation trip to the Northwest they noticed there was no such store in Seattle. They searched for a building to lease, but when a cash-flow analysis showed ownership was cheaper, they bought a building instead. In January 1973 the store opened with Bruce working full time, his mother and sister working part time, and his father retaining his analyst job for financial backup.[23]

With the long American tradition of family farms, companies whose last word(s) in the name is "brothers" or "and son," and numerous "Mom 'n Pop" enterprises, it seems rather surprising that more of the companies that rise on substantial growth trajectories were not initiated by family teams. Certainly many of them involved supporting spouses who provided sustaining income while the ventures were getting started. And the number of companies, both large and small, that have been continued as family enterprises after one member of the family started them is legion. Advantages of cooperating as family founding teams can clearly be present, as seen in the above case. Yet few growth companies appear to start this way, and the reasons have yet to be unraveled.

A venture that came close to providing an exception was that of Vector Graphic, which quickly went from nothing to growth and fame, only to collapse:

[23] By mid-1979 the business was still going strong with Bruce working full time and his mother working part time. His sister had now become a nurse, but his father, while still an analyst, participated in the business after hours. The value of the company's land and business had more than tripled since the outset of the family venture. As of 1988 the store was still going strong at roughly its original size.

◆   Lore Harp had visited America from Germany just after high school, met and married Bob Harp, an electrical engineering PhD student, obtained a BA in anthropology herself, and gone on to law school. She dropped out of school to care for their young children, but then got tired of hanging around the house. With Bob and with her friend, Carol Ely, she discussed the possibility of starting a business. Bob, who had now become a senior staff scientist at Hughes Aircraft, had designed a microcomputer memory board on the side and suggested the two women might try selling it.

Knowing nothing about computers, Lore and Carol visited a computer show and came away convinced that there was a market. They formed a corporation called Vector, had an accountant set up books, and created an office in the Harps' house. They also ran advertisement, attended shows, talked with dealers, and shipped products C.O.D. Eventually the company introduced its own computer, and by 1981, five years after it had been established, had sales of $30 million, after-tax profits of 10 percent, and a public stock offering on the way.[24] Bob stayed full time at Hughes and continued designing new products after hours for a 5 percent royalty on sales.

The future, however, was not as bright as it seemed. When IBM introduced its personal computer, Vector's market collapsed. The Harps got a divorce and Bob went on to form another microcomputer company, Corona, to make PC clones.[25] Lore left Vector in 1983 after trying to contend with its collapse plus a struggle with the board of directors. Then in 1986 she formed another company to produce and sell feminine hygiene products.[26]

SEQUENTIAL ENTREPRENEURSHIP

Perhaps the most fascinating and promising of all entrepreneurial starting points are those that occur in series, the multiple ventures performed by deal-to-dealers mentioned in Chapter 1. Moreover, the ventures may occur either sequentially or overlapping, and one study by Ronstadt found that either is equally likely to occur.[27] It fairly frequently happens that one entrepreneur will start a venture, possibly succeeding in it, possibly not, and regardless of whether it succeeds or not, go on to start a second new venture, a third, and so on, building an entire career of entrepreneuring. Likely there are many patterns into which such careers develop. Two will be illustrated here:

1 *Similar venture sequences.* In which the entrepreneur sticks to one field, such as electronics instruments or furniture manufacturing.

2 *Varied venture sequences.* In which the entrepreneur goes from one line of business to another in successive ventures.

The logic in the first of these two patterns is clear. An entrepreneur is able

---

[24] Susan Benner, "Next Stop Wall Street," *Inc.,* March 1981, p. 37.
[25] John W. Verity, "Startups Emulate IBM with PC's," *Venture,* June 1983, p. 86.
[26] Daniel Cohen, "Lore Harp is Back on Her Feet," *Venture,* July 1986, p. 42.
[27] Robert Ronstadt, "Every Entrepreneur's Nightmare: The Decision to Become an Ex-entrepreneur and Work for Someone Else," in John A. Hornaday, Edward B. Shils, Jeffry A. Timmons, and Karl H. Vesper, *Frontiers of Entrepreneurship Research, 1985,* (Wellesley, Mass.: Babson Center for Entrepreneurial Studies, 1985), p. 409.

to carry the knowhow of one venture on to the next, hoping to sell out each time at a profit. It has been suggested that there may be two kinds of small business operators, "starters" and "runners." The second of these types is able to change to new skills needed as the business grows and calls for different styles of management, typically progressing from less to more formal procedures with increases in size.[28] A "starter," on the other hand, excels in starting new firms, and rather than change methods as the firm grows, may sell out, then repeat what worked before to start another new firm. More often, however, it appears that sequential startups are more forced by circumstances, as in the following *similar venture sequence:*

◆   In Germany before World War II a man started a rubber company manufacturing tennis shoes. The company grew and prospered, but because he was Jewish, the Nazis ran him out. He went to Poland, and finding tennis shoes unavailable, set up another tennis shoe company, which again prospered but was cut short when the Nazis moved in and ran him out again. He moved to Cuba, and again finding no local source of tennis shoes, set up a plant to make them. Again the plant did well, but again he was run out, this time by the Communists because they considered him a capitalist. He moved to the United States and established a successful rubber products company.

In this venture it appears that the entrepreneur repeatedly succeeded by employing expert knowhow of the particular industries he was in, and it may be an open question how well he would have done had he switched industries. If he had happened to succeed as well in varied industries, then other explanations would have been needed to account for the success. Characteristics sometimes alleged to be common to many entrepreneurs—a penchant for hard work, high sales ability and empathy for customers, sensitivity to situations containing profit potential, skill in marshaling resources, connections for obtaining them, knowledge of entrepreneurial options in general, and drive toward creating and building—have all been suggested. If these are so important, then it should be possible for entrepreneurs to shift among types of enterprises. Sometimes they do, as illustrated by the following *varied venture sequence:*

◆   How William Kirschner moved from unemployment to development of a medical equipment manufacturing concern was described earlier in this chapter. Because sales of animal splints were too small to provide a living, Kirschner kept looking for other products. He found that there was need in laboratories that used animals for cages with rounded corners and no seams, and he looked into ways of making them. He found that the cost of tooling dies to deep-draw cages from metal was far more than the company could manage, and so started making them out of reinforced plastics. "A friend who worked at Boeing in fiberglass-reinforced plastics provided helpful technical advice," Kirschner recalled, "and that became a fair business. We had the only decent cage available at the time, and we had the marketing capability."

Numerous other product attempts followed: wound fiberglass-reinforced plastic missile nose cones; a lettuce wrapping machine; aircraft job shop work during the Korean war ("We lost our shirts on that," he recalled); laboratory chairs

---

[28] See, for example, Robert B. Buchele, *Business Policy in Growing Firms* (San Francisco: Chandler, 1967).

for monkeys; fiberglass boats ("Six months and $25,000 down the drain later we got out of that. Too many people were in it already. Anybody with a paint brush and bucket could enter."). Sinks, bathtubs, shower stalls of fiberglass, all were tried, but Kirschner found shipping costs and packaging to sell beyond the local area cost too much. Besides, there was considerable opposition in the family to these diversification attempts. It was felt that they wasted money and too much of his time, even though he did much of the work in evenings.

Partly to save money, partly to try another idea, and because he liked to ski, Kirschner decided to try making himself a pair of skis out of fiberglass and plastic. "Mostly what I was trying to do was avoid going out to buy a pair," he said. So in the fall of 1961 he made up a pair, tried them, and was somewhat surprised to find he liked the way they worked. Intrigued that they might be a salable product, but knowing nothing of the ski market ("Maybe there were hundreds of them on the market, for all I knew," he commented), he visited the head of a ski pole manufacturing and distributing firm, A & T Ski, in Seattle to get an informed opinion. He found that (1) there were no other fiberglass skis available—Head Ski had considered but rejected the idea—and (2) there was what he called a "market hole"—Head's metal skis sold for $115–$140 per pair, and next down were Fischer wood skis at around $50. If he could make plastic skis in the $80 price range they would offer something in the market hole.

Kirschner then began pulling together the new venture. (Family opposition to the risky idea led to its becoming a separate organization from their existing company.) Arrangements were made for A & T Ski Company to handle all marketing and also much of the financing. The prototype handmade first ski design was reworked to facilitate production; tooling was designed to produce them, and production of K-2 skis began slowly at first, then as their reputation spread and racers began using them, rapidly, eventually eclipsing the leading manufacturer, Head, to make Kirschner's company the leading ski maker in the country.

Several important links can be seen between the first Kirschner venture and the second one. Fiberglass manufacturing experience was a main one. With it came not only the ability to use the material in fabrication, but the fact that he had been seeking ways to apply it to new products gave Mr. Kirschner some virtuosity in creating skis with it. Practice with production also gave him a better basis for estimating costs than a less-experienced person would have had. Familiarity with all aspects of the business, which managers of small companies get because they lack the luxury of specialized staffs, also gave him a basis for delving into problems of sales and finance as well as production. Finally, he knew from experience how to operate on a small scale with minimal capital to get the company going.

Side-Street Effects

Most entrepreneurs find, as Kirschner did, that once they get into business many opportunities come their way to embark on new projects. When an entrepreneur is known to be successful, people will bring ideas looking for support. And as entrepreneurs operate in their particular line of business, they will discover other opportunities because of where the ventures lead them. Thus, embarking on a venture can be like starting along an avenue down whose side streets lie opportunities that could otherwise not be seen.

In his study of ex-entrepreneurs who had shifted to working for others,

Ronstadt found that 49 percent of the ninety-six respondents had operated more than one venture.[29] In a subsequent study he found that 60 percent of a sample of 1,537 entrepreneurs had started more than one venture and concluded that there was a "corridor principle" operating wherein pursuit of one venture led to discovery of another.[30] Lest the terms *corridor* and *principle* seem too directive or imply that the entrepreneur will be irresistibly channeled into good opportunities after startup, it should be noted that most startups never grow much. Phillips and Kirchhoff, for instance, reported that "few firms grow in their first four years,"[31] while Birch observed that "growth comes to few, and for those few it is almost always preceded by a long gestation period."[32] Rather, there seem in some instances to be side-street glimpses of opportunities during some ventures, a fraction of which are exploited.

In the following two cases noted in the Fucini book *Entrepreneurs,* the entrepreneurs pursued inventions, only to discover that the inventions had promise, not in the way they were intended but rather in ways that were not originally planned on.[33]

◆   Conrad Hubert, a restaurateur, bought an invention consisting of a tube with a battery and light inside. The tube was supposed to be fastened to the side of a flowerpot so the light would shine up the tube and illuminate the flowers. When it failed to sell as an "electric flowerpot," he decided to sell the light mechanism on its own, which he renamed the Eveready Flashlight.

◆   Joshua Lionel Cowen, who had invented and sold the light mechanism to Hubert, later came up with an idea for a mine detonator that he sold to the U.S. Navy. He used the money to start manufacturing portable electric fans. He tried adapting one of the fan motors to make a retail store window display consisting of a small electric locomotive that would run around a track to attract attention. The result was that store customers started buying the display for their children, and Lionel found himself manufacturing electric trains.

Usually, side-street opportunities have links to the original venture, links in manufacturing like Kirschner's or in sales channels or technical knowhow. In the following example it appears that the original venture both prompted the discovery of a new opportunity and provided the initial sales channel for it:

◆   Anna and Melville Bissell had started a shop in Grand Rapids selling crockery. The products were packed in straw to protect them during transit, but the straw produced an allergic reaction in Mel. To reduce the problem, he developed a lightweight sweeper to pick up dust from the floor. When customers of the shop saw the sweeper, they asked how they could buy one. Anna and Mel formed the Bissell Carpet Sweeper Company to produce them.

[29] Ronstadt, "Every Entrepreneur's Nightmare."
[30] Robert Ronstadt, "The Corridor Principle," *Journal of Business Venturing,* Vol. 3, No. 1 (Winter 1988), 31.
[31] Bruce D. Phillips and Bruce A. Kirchhoff, "An Analysis of New Firm Survival and Growth," Babson Entrepreneurship Research Conference, Calgary, 1988.
[32] David L. Birch, "Live Fast, Die Young," *Inc.,* May 1988.
[33] Josepy Fucini, and Suzy Fucini, *Entrepreneurs* (Boston: G. K. Hall), 1985.

It may be helpful to catalog briefly some of the general directions side streets can take:

1 *New versus Extended Venture*—The Bissells went from pottery sales to appliance manufacturing, a new venture. In contrast, the five Ball brothers, who had formed a can company, sought new ways of fastening the cans in order to pay patent royalties. Invention led them to glass and they made their fortune in fruit jars through extension of the can company.

2 *Building on Technology versus Market Links*—Technical links are apparent in the Lionel and Eveready ventures. Market links were the key for Dwight Baldwin, a music teacher, who at forty-one put his life savings into a piano store. He then took on a partner and started manufacturing pianos when an existing supplier, Steinway, terminated his dealership.

3 *Integration versus Diversification*
   a Elizabeth Arden integrated backward from sales to production. Originally named Florence Nightingale Graham, she wanted to be a nurse, like her namesake, but took a job with a cosmetic specialist in New York. Subsequently, she opened her own beauty salon and with the help of a chemist began developing her own cosmetics.
   b Milton Bradley integrated forward. Starting with a print shop, he sought to occupy idle press time by following the suggestion of a friend that he develop, print, and sell board games.
   c Thomas Armstrong diversified. He ventured into cork to take advantage of the Union army's need for medical supplies during the Civil War. When his success in bottle corks was threatened by prohibition, he branched into the manufacture of cork-based linoleum, which led to other construction products.

In some degree of contrast to the above examples where the side-street links were either technically or market based, the following illustrates a *varied venture sequence* that was based mainly on contacts and observations.

◆   After working as a barber from ages seventeen to nineteen in Texas, brief stints in premed studies, the navy, prelaw, and finally civil engineering—in which he received his bachelor's degree from Howard University in 1948—a young man accepted a $3,000-per-year job in the building department of a West Coast city. He was happy in the job and got along well but became intrigued by the adventures of an ex-carpenter from the department who had managed to raise some capital and quit to strike out on his own as a builder of apartments. The man frequently came in to obtain permits and keep his projects moving, which it turned out were doing quite well.
     Investigating further, he gathered that there was a demand among blacks for new housing which white firms were not filling, and which offered an attractive market. He also found that the FHA was sympathetic to this need and willing to help with credit. With only $500 of his own capital he was able to buy a lot, and in the process he became acquainted with a black contractor who had credit and wanted to team up on construction of a house. Finishing that job, the two went on to build another house across the street, then an apartment, then a second apartment. He was now twenty-three years old.

While this construction sideline was developing, the engineer also became impressed by the fact that the man from whom he bought insurance was making roughly four times his building department salary. This prompted him to get a license and become an insurance broker, first part time, then full time when he quit his three-year tenure in the building department. Soon he too was making four times as much on insurance commissions as he had in city employment. Then he started selling other lines, food plans, home freezers, siding, and roofing in addition to the insurance.

One day the owner of a black-audience newspaper came to solicit advertising of the siding and roofing. The two men got along well, and shortly thereafter the owner of the paper talked him into lending him some money in return for a half-interest in the paper. At a later date it was necessary for the borrower to leave town for a while, and the former engineer found himself first running the paper, then owning it when the former owner decided to relinquish his half-interest in return for cancellation of his remaining debt.

In 1953, two years after leaving city employment, the young entrepreneur decided to check on boasts by a lady in the nursing home business about how much money there was in her work. It appeared she was right, so he obtained a permit from the welfare department to provide a small nursing home facility in his apartment. After renovating the first floor, largely by himself, and acquiring a staff, he was surprised to find that in spite of the evident demand for nursing home space nobody came. Checking into the referral procedure, he found that welfare department counselors were referring to his as "the nice colored home," and most of their clients were white. He persuaded the department to stop mentioning race, and soon there were so many tenants he decided to convert the second floor as well.

By 1958 he had expanded to a second nursing home but had also become interested in building them. Consequently, he took time out for two years to obtain a degree in architecture. He then joined with another architect, obtained an FHA loan, designed and built a new $300,000 nursing home, followed by another costing $500,000 and then several apartment buildings totaling $4.5 million.

Finally, in 1971, this entrepreneur decided to cut back on some of his business activities. He canceled plans to build a 1,000-bed nursing home and decided not to start a mortgage company for which he had already arranged a $3.5 million line of credit and also not to make a public stock offering. Instead he formed a foundation to assist minority students; as the holder of mortgages on property worth $9 million and with his operations grossing about $3 million, he turned his attention toward enjoying his prosperity. His comment on entrepreneurship, "If you're going to do a project, make it a big one, because a small one is just as much work."

Patterns of sequential entrepreneurship are both fairly common and extremely varied. In their study of many startups Collins and Moore saw the sequences largely as educational processes in which entrepreneurs learned by mistakes and failures how to accomplish startups "right."[34] Sometimes the followon opportunity comes as an externally imposed event, such as a wartime need for something. Other times it may come as an observation that customers are inconvenienced by something. Still other times it can be the entrepreneur's desire to discover a "hit" through search and experimentation. It can be helpful to have an existing venture as a base from which both to discover such op-

[34] Orvis Collins and David G. Moore, *The Organization Makers* (New York: Appleton-Century-Crofts, 1970).

portunities and to proceed in exploiting them. How to develop that first venture will be the focus of the next chapter.

SUMMARY

Research studies have found that the most common age for starting new business ventures is around thirty-five years old. The explanation would seem to be that at earlier ages a person has not developed the knowhow, financial resources, or business connections to master a startup, whereas at more-advanced ages a person competent to start a venture will have progressed to income and privilege levels in his or her job at which venturing has less marginal attractiveness. Also, such a person will have more to risk in the way of position and savings and will have greater family responsibilities, and hence less freedom to pursue self-centered projects.

This chapter has shown that whatever the most common age or career starting point for venture startup, a great number of others are possible and are used. Entrepreneurs start ventures while in school, following school, during employment, during unemployment, and even out of home kitchens. This proves that it is possible to start a venture from virtually any career point (it has even been done from prison), and no person need necessarily feel cut off from entrepreneurial opportunity. The examples in this chapter illustrated ways it can be done. The next will look in more detail at the kinds of sequences that may be used.

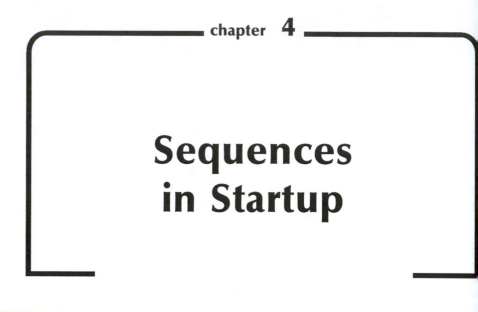

Sequences
in Startup

The preceding chapter illustrated a variety of career points at which entrepreneurs can embark on ventures. But what about the sequences through which the venture components are brought together? Are they too widely varying, or are there typical sequences? Is it possible to formulate a standard sequence that can be used for forming most ventures, or must each one be a highly special case? Can the main hurdles in forming most companies be anticipated, or is the array of possibilities so large as to be mainly unpredictable? How can a would-be entrepreneur best prepare to meet them?

This chapter will explore these and other questions associated with the paths entrepreneurs travel in pulling their ventures together. Five key ingredients will be identified as necessary and sufficient for creating a new company, and different ways in which they can be brought together will be illustrated. Three main obstacles along the path to startup will also be identified.

MILESTONES IN VENTURE CREATION

What sort of event signals the creation of a new venture? Many candidates might be nominated, such as

1 When the desire for entrepreneurship is recognized
2 When the idea for what the new venture is to be occurs
3 When the break is made with former employment

4 When contracts are made with a potential partner, lawyer, banker, accountant, or other outside adviser

5 When legal papers for partnership or incorporation or business licenses are filed

6 When the first dollars are invested in the new venture

7 When the firm becomes ready to accept orders

8 When its logo is first displayed

9 When the first order arrives

10 When the first delivery or performance is done

11 When the company first breaks even

12 When the first profitable year has been accomplished

Which of these events should be regarded as the "true" inception point can be argued without resolution. A venture typically emerges from a series of such occurrences spread over time in which its existence becomes progressively more established. At the first of the above points it would be hard to claim that a venture had been started, while at any of the last few it would be hard to argue that the firm had not become a going concern, even if it were later to vanish. Examples will show, moreover, that the order in which points in between occur differs among startups, and also that between such events as those above there can be many other dramatic moments in the startup of a venture, such as

- The day a lease is signed for space to operate. Now the company has a home. Will it someday own the real estate? How long will it be before more space is needed?
- The day a line of credit is granted by the bank. This can be a big day for the banker, too, who hopes the company will grow to become a large and profitable customer. The banker may take the occasion to introduce the entrepreneur to the president or one of the senior vice-presidents, who may ask some questions about the company's hopes and then wish it well.
- The day a first payroll is met. The entrepreneur may not be on that payroll personally yet or may be receiving a lower wage than any other employee. Payroll is one bill that has to be paid exactly on time. Meeting payrolls is to some entrepreneurs the "true" initiation rite of self-employment.
- Arrival of the first customer payment. Whether in cash or check, that currency has special meaning. A customer has now demonstrated with money that the new firm truly offers something of value. Now the entrepreneur must hope the sale will stay made and not be plagued by "bugs" that bring a demand for a refund.
- Arrival of the first *repeat* order or the first order from referral by a satisfied customer. Now sales are beginning to look more secure. Soon there should be some testimonial letters expressing satisfaction.
- The first period in which the company passes breakeven and earns a profit. In a seasonal business the period of calculation may have to be a year in order to "count." In other businesses a month in the black may

do it. In still others it may be a period of cash breakeven, when the money coming in pays for the outflow, including loan payments.

Which of such events is most significant can of course vary from one business to another. A brief reflection can also suggest ways in which the order of such events might differ from one venture to another as well, and this in turn may suggest that different ventures can have different birth sequences. But could enough commonalities be found to support a general entrepreneurial sequence for arriving at an operating new enterprise?

Foreseeing the Venture

At some point before these milestones happen, the entrepreneur may begin to foresee them and the other events needed to bring them about in what amounts to mental vision or projection of the venture. In a study of how entrepreneurs use visualization and mental imagery, Rockey found that at least some of them imagined pictures, almost like movies, of physical arrangements and events in company startup and development and that they considered these helpful and a cheap way to ward off some problems, solve others, and identify effective ways of operating.[1] Things visualized in these mental previews of future events included mental rehearsal of presentations, product selection and design, plant layout, equipment design, shop decor, organization design, types of employees, negotiations, costs, and other financial items. Some entrepreneurs set aside specific time periods for envisaging, while others imagined their scenarios during recreation—e.g., running, or during meditation, or in the course of ordinary activities such as showering.

Benefits the entrepreneurs claimed included testing the workability of plans, foreseeing pitfalls, discovering better ways to do things, identifying opportunities, increasing motivation and confidence, and gaining advance experience through a kind of mental sparring in preparation for the real-life main event so they could handle it more competently. Some said anticipating the possible moves and countermoves let them respond more quickly and effectively. Not all the outcomes were successful, although apparently all the "dreams" were. In fact, one entrepreneur said she deliberately avoided having negative visions because life tended to unfold too much as foreseen. One man's vision of selling his business turned out true to his vision except that the buyer was crooked, pillaged the firm, and left the seller with debts. But from the responses to Rockey's inquiry, it often seemed that real life followed the preconceived scenario almost like a scripted play. According to Rockey, "the greater the gap between the internal picture and the actual situation, the greater the likelihood of costly adaptation" in the venture.

To develop strength in creating more accurate venture visions, it may be helpful to practice with component steps that make up a venture formation process. Some steps will be unique to a particular business. Others may be common to many startups.

[1] Edward H. Rockey, "Envisioning the New Business," in Robert Ronstadt, John A. Hornaday, Rein Peterson, and Karl H. Vesper, *Frontiers of Entrepreneurship Research, 1986* (Wellesley, Mass. Babson Center for Entrepreneurial Studies, 1986), p. 344.

QUEST FOR A GENERAL MODEL

Several general flow charts for entrepreneurship have been proposed by different authors. Webster has postulated that an "entrepreneurially attractive" venture typically involves six stages: (1) a pre-venture stage in which the entrepreneur searches for, evaluates, and negotiates rights for a venture idea, (2) an organization stage in which the grounding colleagues energetically set up shop, (3) financial jeopardy while debugging prototypes and establishing sales channels, (4) product introduction with renewed hope despite continued cash shortages, (5) the "rapacious act" of the entrepreneur who gains control by squeezing colleagues out, and (6) an outcome stage culminating in survival or failure.[2] No detailed order is set forth within each stage, so the overall framework allows any number of subsequences. By the same token, the problem of what those specific sequences should be is left for the reader to puzzle out.

A longer sequence reaching to more maturity in the enterprise has been offered by Long and Ohtani as follows:[3]

1 Identifying realizable opportunities
2 Designing feasible products
3 Planning resource requirements
4 Negotiating resource and client contracts
5 Engineering efficient production
6 Regularizing sales revenue
7 Standardizing operating performance
8 Expanding strategically and opportunistically
9 Professionalizing middle management
10 Institutionalizing innovative capacity

In application to one venture, Tapp and McMullan found that such a sequence description was helpful in providing benchmarks, avoiding sidetracks, shifting to necessary new operating modes at different stages, and getting bogged down.[4]

Entrepreneurial tasks that are more sharply focused on startup but not necessarily in order of performance have been offered by Kilby as follows:

1 Perception of market opportunities
2 Gaining command over scarce resources
3 Purchasing inputs

[2] F. Webster, "A Model for New Venture Initiation," *Academy of Management Review*, Vol. I, No. 1 (January 1976), p. 26.
[3] Wayne A. Long and Nobuki Ohtani, "Facilitating New Venture Development through Market and Design Feasibility Study," In Ronstadt et al., *Frontiers of Entrepreneurship Research, 1986*, p. 463.
[4] John G. Tapp and W. Ed. McMullan, "Following a Theoretical Road Map as a Venture Development Strategy," in Ronstadt et al., *Frontiers of Entrepreneurship Research, 1986*, p. 227.

4 Marketing and responding to competitors
5 Dealing with the public bureaucracy
6 Managing human relations in the firm
7 Managing supplier and customer relations
8 Managing finances
9 Managing production
10 Acquiring and overseeing factory setup
11 Industrial engineering
12 Upgrading processes and product quality
13 Innovating in products and processes

Much more detailed is a prescriptive sequence billed by Swayne and Tucker as a "road map" by whose application "one should be able to start any business."[5] The authors add that because the sequence was formulated for manufacturing concerns, it includes some extra steps not needed for service firms. Three overall stages—concept, planning, and implementation—embrace a sequence of fifty-seven steps listed in Table 4–1, beginning with evaluation of personal goals by the entrepreneur (1) and proceeding through such others as locations evaluated (22) and supply needs defined (23) to conclude with first sale delivery (57). Some steps could perhaps as logically be set in different order. For example, supply sources might be selected (48) before an operating plan and budget were finalized (32), or definition of the distribution system (25) could be shifted to precede definition of manufacturing needs (19). But that does not mean that the sequence could not work in the order given. Additional steps advisable for some ventures have also been suggested, as noted by asterisks in the exhibit.

The sequence is described in terms of steps completed, which leaves it to the reader to decide when each one should be started, which could be in quite a different sequence than their completion. Thus the "road map" of Swayne and Tucker does not tell the reader in what order to undertake actions. A more serious deficiency, however, is its treatment of steps 4 and 5. The consumer need that the company is to fill and the product to be used in filling it are simply assumed to be known, with little suggestion regarding how they are to be found, although these are among the most important steps in the entire sequence. As will be shown in the next chapter, this is a shortcoming shared by most works on entrepreneurship. At least this sequence offers some sort of starting point in terms of detailed actions for creating a company.

A still more elaborate prescriptive scheme appears in a set of twelve "Entrepreneurial Flow Charts" offered by E. Joseph Cossman as a "road map to business success" with the claim that they "bring together the information necessary to create, protect, manufacture, publicize, market, and merchandise a product or service."[6] They begin with a step entitled "Adopt the Cossman

[5] Charles Swayne and William Tucker, The Effective Entrepreneur (Morristown, N.J.: General Learning Press, 1973).
[6] E. J. Cossman, Entrepreneurial Flow Charts (Palm Springs, Calif.: Cossman International, 1975)

TABLE 4–1 SWAYNE-TUCKER STARTUP "ROADMAP"*

I Concept Stage	II Planning Stage	III Implementation Stage
** Venture Idea search	** Demonstration prototype constructed	38. Incorporation completed
** Begin patent notebook	** Prototype tried on buyers	39. Whether to market test decided
1. Personal goals evaluated	17. Sales tactics defined	40. Whether to subcontract decided
2. Own strengths, weaknesses identified	18. Make or buy issues assessed	41. Market test completed
3. Outside help needs identified	19. Manufacturing needs defined	42. Capital obtained
4. Consumer needs identified	20. Engineering and design needs	43. Management people hired
5. Product identified	21. Technical people needs defined	44. Sales campaign begun
** Physical feasibility studied	22. Locations evaluated	45. Salespeople hired and trained
** Physical prototypes made	23. Supply needs defined	46. Sources of supply found
6. Market identified	24. Supply sources availability assessed	47. Make or buy decision made
7. Future market identified	25. Distribution system defined	48. Supply sources selected
8. Target market identified	26. Salesperson needs defined	49. Location selected
9. Personal investment capacity determined	27. Management information system	50. Technical people hired and trained
10. Return on investment goals defined	28. Administrative people needs	51. Management information
11. Profit goals defined	29. Management people needs defined	52. Manufacturing plant set
12. Ballpark of costs estimated	30. Outside help needs finalized	53. Administrative people hired and trained
13. Sales goals defined	31. Organization structure defined	54. Production people hired and trained
14. Timing evaluated	32. Operating plan and budget	55. Materials inventory purchased
15. Legal constraints evaluated	33. Capital needs defined	56. First product made
** Patent search	34. Capital needs for buying going concern defined (if needed)	57. First sale and delivery made
** Patent application	35. Buyout versus startup choice made	
16. Review and revision performed	36. Overall policy finalized	
	37. Review and revision performed	

*Adapted with variations from Swayne and Tucker, *Effective Entrepreneur*, pp. 100–102. By permission of Silver Burdett Company.
**Additional steps suggested by the author.

Success Formula," followed by phases of self-assessment, preparation, and learning in which the would-be entrepreneur is directed to seek "exposure" to possible venture opportunities. The introductory chart shows a sequence in which the other eleven—each of which covers a different topic, such as goal setting, utilizing government services, and marketing in foreign trade—are presented as parallel in time, so that apparently no particular order for executing one chart versus another seems to be required. Within each chart serial sequences—like those of Swayne and Tucker—and decision trees—which present a variety of alternative choices at some of the junctures—are used. Consequently, Cossman's charts present a more detailed listing of options for the entrepreneur than do the charts of Swayne and Tucker. He also gives somewhat more attention to the topic of finding the product or service, as will be further discussed in the chapter to follow. Cossman's own experience appears to have been largely in promotion and sale of novelties to the consumer market, mostly through mail order, and the focus of his charts tends to reflect that experience, dwelling less on how to develop manufacturing capacity than do Swayne and Tucker.

Other somewhat more hypothetical flow charts have been proposed. The Institute for New Enterprise Development of Belmont, Massachusetts, designed a sequence consisting of three main parts, one to select entrepreneurs in economically backward areas who would develop new companies to help their economies, a second part consisting of an "idea bank," which would be a repository of venture ideas, and a third part consisting of selection of venture ideas, analysis, evaluation, and planning of new companies to exploit them. Reflecting later on the scheme, one of the researchers involved in the project commented, "I told them the idea bank would not work, and it didn't." Many of the other ideas utilized in the program appeared in a textbook and emphasized personal self-assessment and planning as part of the venture-forming process.[7]

A scheme proposed by Osgood and Wetzel suggested replacing the individual entrepreneur by a "team of business initiation specialists" to improve upon the historic process of entrepreneurship, which the authors claim is "too random and inefficient."[8] Problems of venture initiation were, they claimed ". . . not very different from one situation to another." Consequently, a formalized procedure was proposed in which opportunities would be sought through market research and economic forecasting efforts of a project team. These would be screened on the basis of feasibility analyses, and those that passed would be presented as proposals to venture capitalists. With this capital the project team would then initiate the enterprise and begin the search for an administrator to take over as the venture stabilized, while the team would become directors of that company and go on to seek out the next venture idea around which to develop another company. Ten years after this proposition there were no reports of its having been tested.

[7] Jeffry A. Timmons, Leonard E. Smollen, and Alexander L. M. Dingee, Jr., *New Venture Creation* (Homewood, Ill.: Irwin, 1977).

[8] W. R. Osgood and W. E. Wetzel, "Systems Approach to Venture Initiation," paper presented to Academy of Management Annual Meeting, Kansas City, August 1976.

Sequences in Conventional Manufacturing

The sequences by which entrepreneurs actually arrive at ventures, in contrast to proposed models of how some people think they should, have been studied by other authors and revealed other patterns. An early landmark work in this area was that of Collins and Moore, who studied over a hundred manufacturing enterprises, predominantly in mechanical manufacturing in the Midwest, often associated with the auto industry and started mainly during the 1940s and 1950s.[9] They traced influences that led ultimately to venture creation all the way back in time to years before the entrepreneur even thought about startup. This broader view sees ventures as outgrowths of preparatory sequences measured in years and decades, sequences not necessarily begun with aims of eventual venture initiation or even sensed by the to-be entrepreneur as leading in that direction possibly even until the moment of startup itself. This way of viewing paths to startup allows different sequences for different entrepreneurs but typically includes the following general stages:

1 *Schooling* Mostly in "hard knocks" and mostly by experience, beginning with treatment as a child, often involving exposure to privations, though not always, sometimes including self-employment examples on the part of parents, and possibly some apprenticeship in family enterprises, often resulting in an intolerance of subjection to higher authority and a driving urge for independence and self-determination, coupled with belief in competence and hard work.

Following childhood comes experience in technical aspects of business performance, generally through line jobs in which the entrepreneur becomes competent, sometimes to the point of "showing up" peers and superiors and becoming contemptuous of employers who fail to recognize this competence through immediate promotion. Also often acquired through industrial experiences prior to startup are "facts of life" in the rough and tumble, often ruthless struggle of competitive independent business. The "basic course" in this educational process is what the authors refer to as "basic dealing" or how to "jell" a deal.

Lessons in these subjects, their case histories indicate, often involve series of jobs working for others plus attempts at venture startup, some successful and others not.

2 *Role deterioration* In this stage the entrepreneur becomes "fed up" with his or her prior employment. The authors note that not all startups, however, follow intense dissatisfaction with prior employment, but most do.

3 *Projecting* Projecting the enterprise (having the idea) is a key event that follows this educational process. At this point, whose importance often is clear only in hindsight, the idea for coalescing ingredients to form a venture emerges. Some entrepreneurs, these authors found, first had the idea of an invention, and then only at a later stage began creating an organization bringing together the resources to manufacture and market the invention. Others first had the idea of making an organization, then went on to the problem of what

[9] Orvis Collins and David G. Moore, *The Organization Makers* (New York: Appleton-Century-Crofts, 1970).

to produce. Still others thought they saw a spot in the economy where something was needed, went back to the organization creation stage, and finally arrived at a specific sort of product. Others were simply invited by someone else to enter into a partnership or a business relationship and subsequently took over. One or two had the beautifully direct and simple idea of earning a great deal of money. As one man said, "The idea was to make money. The product was to be money. With that idea, everything else began to take shape." (The authors do not reveal further the chemistry of this case.)

4   *Creation*   The act that translates the above "projection," or idea, into being. It begins with gathering and organizing resources, capital, personnel, plant, customers, and the formal execution of legal documents setting up the firm. But the authors point out that "the process of creation does not in reality exist in neatly separated compartments, with one phase always ending before the next begins. There is a flow of events involved."

5   *Through the knothole*   The survival stage of the business, typically a traumatic experience, as described in Chapter 1 under Entrepreneurial Work, when many things go wrong and failure often seems imminent and the entrepreneur may often have doubts about whether the whole effort was really worth it or not.

6   *Maybe recycling*   If the company in fact does not make it through the knothole, and many do not, then this experience becomes part of the schooling process in stage 1 above, leading to another try based on strengthened experience at a later date. In contrast to the examples of Chapter 2, which involved series of successful ventures, Collins and Moore found many series in which only the last venture was successful, with those created earlier being educational but unsuccessful.

7   *Taking full charge*   In the knothole stage, the entrepreneur, as Collins and Moore see it, is typically subordinate to other people—customers, partners, financiers, possibly even employees—in trying to pull the venture through. When the venture gets beyond this stage, the entrepreneur may rise above these pressures, building with his own capital, squeezing out partners, and generally taking command. (The authors appear to focus heavily on autocratically dominated "one-man shows" to the exclusion of other types of new companies, which also succeed.)

Thus to the detailed tasks that should be remembered in the Swayne-Tucker model, the Collins and Moore depiction adds for the would-be entrepreneur a reminder that startup typically has important antecedents, which implies that the planning of a startup may be approached at times more appropriately as a longer-run career goal and not simply as an abrupt turn into startup.

As to the actual sequences by which the ventures themselves were pulled together, the Collins and Moore study is somewhat incomplete. But from what it does tell, some outlines of typical sequences are not difficult to interpolate. In almost all cases the entrepreneurs appear to begin by learning the business in the shop as production workers. Presumably, they also thereby become acquainted with customers and suppliers as well as prospective partners and employees. Then they get the idea of starting a company similar to that of their employer, in several cases because the employer was failing, in other cases simply because they felt they could do as well or better on their own. Next, they obtain the assets for their own shop, possibly buying them used from savings, or by recruiting partners who put up the money. They open for business and solicit orders in the same way as their prior employers did, and the business is under way. Such a sequence often occurs in custom manufacturing businesses, job machine shops, screw machine shops, plating and heat treating companies.

Sequences in High-Technology Manufacturing

Quite different patterns seem to have led to creation of companies operating in higher technologies than those studied by Collins and Moore. Typical starting points were illustrated in Cooper's examples of the preceding chapter. In common with the entrepreneurs of Collins and Moore, it appears that job dissatisfaction usually played a key role in stimulating the entrepreneur to seek a venture startup as a way out. High competence in the technology of the enterprise was also a common feature of both entrepreneurial types, but in contrast to the production shop men of Collins and Moore, those in high technology tended to come from engineering departments. Also in contrast to many of the Collins and Moore entrepreneurs, those in high technology had received much more advanced educations, had not had such deprived childhoods, and had not come up "the hard way" or progressed through a series of preliminary ventures.

Based on their experience in the microcomputer industry, Osborne and Dvorak suggested four steps for starting a high-technology hardware company. "First, a prototype product must be designed and built. Second, venture capital must be raised. Third, personnel must be hired. Fourth, visibility must be acquired for the company and a consumer base must be developed.[10]

Typical startup sequences in some high-technology companies can be seen among the six detailed case histories of very successful enterprises plus briefer descriptions of several others published by Bylinsky.[11] A very important ingredient in most of them which set them apart from the startups of Collins and Moore was early injection of a substantial amount of venture capital from outside sources to get the company going. The following examples may illustrate:

- *High-Voltage Engineering.* Two M.I.T. scientists got the idea of building electron accelerators for use in hospitals, then went after $200,000 from a venture capital firm, which they used to start business.
- *Ionics.* At the urging of a Harvard scientist, $50,000 in venture capital was invested to set up desalting equipment using new membrane technology.
- *Intel.* Two of the eight scientists who had earlier founded Fairchild Semiconductor and made roughly a million dollars each on it saw computer memories as a new opportunity area, invested $250,000 each, and recruited another $2.5 million from a venture capitalist to start the business.
- *Alza.* A PhD chemist who had risen from director of biological research to executive vice-president of Syntex and made millions in the process invested $2 million of his own, recruited a blue-ribbon panel of directors

---

[10] Adam Osborne and John Dvorak, *Hypergrowth, The Rise and Fall of Osborne Computer Corporation* (New York: Avon Books, 1984), p. 17.
[11] Gene Bylinsky, *The Innovation Millionnaires* (New York: Scribner's, 1976).

and advisers, and then raised another $21 million through sale of stock and warrants to start a drug company. Another $29 million was raised by the company before sales of its first product began.

Not all high-technology companies followed this pattern of heavy startup capital injections. Litronix was begun by a former Monsanto engineer, who started designing products on his dining room table with $10,000 of his own seed capital. The Hewlett-Packard Corporation was begun with personal savings in a rented garage and operated on very meager capital in its early days. But most often even the small starts in high technology, if they went on to become large, did so with the benefit of large venture capital injections at some early stage before the major growth began. Each also typically began with some sort of technological breakthrough involving a very high profit margin clearly in mind from the outset and probably also reduced to written description in a formal venture plan, another contrast to the patterns encountered by Collins and Moore.

Thus there tended to be several types of clear differences between the conventional manufacturing startups of Collins and Moore and those in more recent high-technology companies. The life histories and educational levels, fields in which they gained their work experience, kinds of business strategies with which they began their companies, simply adding more manufacturing capacity versus beginning with product breakthroughs, were different. The kinds of resources with which they began, personal savings of the entrepreneurs and partners versus use of investor venture capital, were different. A common factor seems to have been that virtually all the entrepreneurs in both categories knew the business well from a technical standpoint on the basis of successful work experience in the companies of others before starting their own. In the Collins and Moore cases this technical knowhow appears to have been an ability to solve production problems and get the work out faster, better, and cheaper. In the technology startups it was in how to design a next-generation product.

Sequences in Other Fields

A sequence that can often be seen in both of the startup categories above and others as well involves first learning a line of business, then thinking of the idea of entering that line of business with some variation on the employer's strategy, next recruiting the physical wherewithal to start, which may involve either spending savings to buy assets or drawing on money from others, such as friends, relatives, partners, and/or venture capitalists. Then with the assets in hand the entrepreneur simply opens up shop and solicits business. This sequence can frequently be found in services as well as manufacturing industries. James Ling learned the electrical business in the service, and then upon discharge made a modest investment in the equipment needed to set up shop as an electrical contractor. Later he developed his conglomerating strategy and used it to transform this relatively modest and ordinary enterprise into something vastly larger and more spectacular.

This might be regarded as perhaps the most elementary startup pattern, and it is one that applies to many small businesses. At the childhood level a lemonade stand is begun simply by setting up a box, juice, and glasses from savings, painting a sign and taking the orders as they come, and then pocketing the change. A retail firm may be started in the same way: renting a store front, buying inventory and a cash register with savings, putting in some long hours to spruce the place up, and then opening the door and accepting orders. Similarly, service and even small manufacturing firms can begin with buying a few tools, putting out advertisements to attract business, and then going out and performing the work in response to customer requests. By this sequence virtually anyone can open for business, whether to offer domestic cleaning services personally, or in buying a brush and ladder to start a house-painting service. By a similar pattern many eating establishments are started: undertaking a lease on some premises, investing savings in redecorating, inventory, and printing a new menu and sign on the front, and then opening for business. Most of these establishments fail, but some go on to great things, as in the following case:

◆ Dan Lasater learned the restaurant business by working for McDonald's franchise, starting at age seventeen. By age nineteen he had helped his employer open several new outlets and had gone out of his way to learn everything he could about the business. "Sports had been my life in high school," he recalled. "McDonald's was my life when I graduated. I didn't have anything else I wanted to do and I really got into it. I liked the work and I spent just about all my time there. If I was supposed to come in at nine, I'd get there at seven-thirty to punch out and watch John do the inventory and close the store. McDonald's had a wonderful training manual, and when I was made manager it kind of became my bible."

Eventually, however, he became somewhat bored and figured he did not want to spend the rest of his life as a unit manager. "I wanted to run a restaurant," he said, "but I wanted to be involved as an owner." So he began soliciting financial support from potential backers. After four or five failures in this quest, he met a young Oldsmobile dealer who agreed to finance him in return for 75 percent of the equity, and the two built a restaurant similar to McDonald's. Sales were initially disappointing until they tried cutting prices on hamburgers and raising them on french fries. Volume doubled, then tripled, and the pair built two more stores that immediately succeeded. Later, the two developed a second chain, the Ponderosa, which by 1970 had annual sales of $60 million. At that time Lasater's net worth had reached $30 million, at age thirty and after twelve years in the business.

Here the sequence began with learning the hamburger business, and then with getting the urge to own as well as manage by starting an enterprise like the employer's. Next was the problem of recruiting the resources with which to enter business, and these were located by seeking out contacts until one was located who could provide what was needed and was willing to do so. Then the facilities were built and the business began. Later, a similar pattern was repeated again when the entrepreneur and his partner observed the establishment of another company that was succeeding with a format different from hamburgers, and the Ponderosa idea began.

In an entirely different line of business, stock brokerage, the same sequence can again be seen as used by Dan W. Lufkin:

◆   Teaming up with two partners, Bill Donaldson and Dick Jenrette, Lufkin recruited $500,000 in cash and collateral from friends and business acquaintances to buy a seat on the New York Stock Exchange and set up a small office. All three had formerly been university classmates and had then worked at New York brokerage firms. Each of the three was at a different firm, but they began having discussions about the possibility that there might be a market among institutional investors for a new brokerage firm that would specialize in providing better-quality research than was presently being provided by established houses on small, growth-oriented companies. Each of the three took charge of a particular aspect of the new business, with Jenrette heading up internal administration and investment counsel, Donaldson serving as "deal man" in charge of mergers, acquisitions, and private placements, and Lufkin coordinating research and institutional business. Initial salaries were $7,500 each per year. Office furniture included orange crates for chairs when they began in 1959, but the market for the type of companies in which they specialized, such as Xerox, boomed, and the new firm prospered accordingly. When the market in glamour issues collapsed two years later, business declined greatly, but by then the new company was firmly established. By 1971 Lufkin's personal fortune was estimated at $35 million.

The next example also begins in the brokerage business, as did that of Lufkin, Donaldson, and Jenrette, but follows quite a different strategy, ending not in a new brokerage firm but rather in a conglomerate. Another difference is that the entrepreneur and his partners never obtained full ownership of the enterprise but rather only control, with which they were able to operate it as they pleased.

◆   Meshulam Riklis, age twenty-nine, was working as a security analyst in Minneapolis when it occurred to him that he might be able to obtain control of some companies whose stocks were currently depressed and combine them into a conglomerate whose growth rate would be higher and whose stock price would consequently not be depressed. If this could be done, then the stock would enjoy a higher price/earnings ratio, which would multiply the earnings of the component companies to a higher figure and thereby make money for the shareholders. The method would be first to buy control of one company, using mostly debt to do it. Then the assets of the company would be used to pay off this debt and also to buy control of another company, and so forth. Selling his idea to contacts with money, he was able to raise $400,000, of which $25,000 came from his own savings, and to buy enough shares to take control of Rapid Electrotype, a printing equipment company with a net worth of $2.8 million and liquid assets of $1.6 million. Making himself chief executive officer, he then used the cash, assets, and credit of this first company to buy control of a second, American Colortype, which had around $2.5 million in cash. Merging these two manufacturing companies, he used the combined assets to buy a large retail chain, Butler Brothers, and so forth until he controlled a multibillion dollar empire.

From this last example several points might be noted. First, it is not necessary to own a company to be in charge and enjoy it. Control may be enough. Second, starting from a given starting point, in this case the brokerage business, there may be many entrepreneurial directions in which to go. Lufkin, for instance, took one and Riklis another. Third, it may not be necessary for the entrepreneur personally to have experience in the line of business chosen.

Riklis did not have experience with printing equipment. The company he took over, Rapid Electrotype, needed that expertise but already had it internally, so Riklis did not have to bring it with him.

FIVE KEY INGREDIENTS FOR STARTUP

Buying stock to take control of a complete company, as Riklis did, can be one way to obtain all the ingredients needed for a going concern. But what ingredients are needed to create a new company? Examination of the examples reveals that generally there are five:

1 **Technical knowhow** Someone in the business must possess the professional skill and knowledge to generate the company's product or service. If it is a plumbing company, somebody in it must know how to put pipes together. If it is a travel agency, someone must know how to deal with carriers, read schedules, and perform the other transactions needed to provide the service for customers. The entrepreneur may possess much of this technical knowhow personally, as did the manufacturing entrepreneurs, both conventional and high technology, mentioned earlier. Or the entrepreneur may be able to hire or acquire them, as Riklis did. But they have to be in the company somehow.

2 **Product or service idea** The concept for what product or service the company will offer must become clear before the venture can succeed. This does not rule out the possibility that a venture may start with one idea and then succeed not with that idea but with another.

3 **Personal contacts** Although some would-be entrepreneurs might prefer it that way, ventures are not started by people in isolation. History indicates that vital roles are typically played by connections with other people with regard to virtually all requisites of startup and operation, including getting the idea for the venture.

4 **Physical resources** Physical wherewithal must be obtained for any business. These resources, which can include various kinds of assets and capital, may have to be substantial for some types of manufacturing or can be modest for some types of services. Pulling them together is the main role of entrepreneurs as viewed by some historians and economists.

5 **Customer orders** Without orders from customers, obviously no venture can succeed. Hence, seeking these, either personally or through others, must be a vital early activity for the entrepreneur.

Evident as these five key ingredients may seem, it often happens that would-be entrepreneurs concentrate on some and ignore others, resulting in serious problems or failure for the venture. Investors—in entrepreneurs, for instance—sometimes focus on *the idea* to the exclusion of *contacts* and *orders*. Promoters may, on the other hand, emphasize obtaining *resources* with insufficient attention to *knowhow*. Sales-oriented entrepreneurs have been known to work at getting *orders* with insufficient attention paid to obtaining *resources* needed for making delivery on them. Skilled workers and technicians whose strength is in *knowhow* have sometimes "hung out a shingle" without crystallizing a clear conception of the venture *idea*.

Contacts and Networking

The first of the key ingredients for startup, *knowhow,* was discussed earlier in connection with success correlates. The second, fourth, and fifth, the *idea, resources,* and *sales orders,* will be discussed later in this chapter. The remaining element, *personal contacts,* may lead to all the others and deserves further mention at this point. It is an aspect of entrepreneurship that has only recently come under study, and despite its importance, little is known about it.

From a study of eight startups, MacMillan noted the importance of contacts for following through on ideas.[12] "In every case," he observed, "it was important for the entrepreneur to develop a contact network." Startup of the venture, he found, always drew opposition from some who would have a vested interest in its failure and required support from others. The opposition could be dealt with by (1) co-opting opposers to give them a vested interest in success, (2) bypassing them either through an "end run" to avoid them or by appealing to a higher level of support, or (3) forming an alliance to overcome the resistance.

The alliance for overcoming resistance would be brought about by the entrepreneur through other contacts. Essentially these involved finding a common ground with the contact to enlist help, or identifying problems the contacts had and then helping to solve those problems, or asking advice of the contacts to draw them into alliance, or some combination of these three approaches. Once the entrepreneur was able to establish credibility with supporters and particularly to demonstrate commitment by at least one powerful ally—such as a supplier who would lend credit, equipment, or support services, or a potential customer who would express intent to buy—the resisting forces would be overcome.

According to a study by Birley, *informal contacts* come first in the process and *formal contacts* later, particularly during capital raising.[13] The former include business contacts as well as family and personal contacts, while the latter include bankers, accountants, lawyers, government officials, realtors, and chambers of commerce. "Informal contacts," she found, "mainly business contacts, were seen overall to be the most helpful in assembling the elements of the business." Family and friends helped particularly in seeking location, employees, and, interestingly enough, sales.

Whether informal or formal, contacts as sources of information and as helpful in innovations by startups were noted in a 1983 study by Leonard-

---

[12] I. C. MacMillan, "The Politics of New Ventures," in Karl H. Vesper, *Frontiers of Entrepreneurship Research* (Wellesley, Mass.: Babson Center for Entrepreneurial Studies, 1981).

[13] Sue Birley, "The Role of Networks in the Entrepreneurial Process," in John A. Hornaday, Edward B. Shils, Jeffry A. Timmons, and Karl H. Vesper, *Frontiers of Entrepreneurship Research, 1985* (Wellesley, Mass.: Babson Center for Entrepreneurial Studies, 1985), p. 325.

Barton, which found that American entrepreneurs used them more than Swedish entrepreneurs, or at least were more willing to admit it.[14]

Another type of contact, the mentor, was identified by Carsrud et al. in a 1986 study, which somewhat surprisingly found that in a sample of 246 women entrepreneurs, the use of mentors was negatively correlated with success.[15]

Contacts that come from prior business employment are yet another type. Coining the term *extrapreneurs* as "individuals who launch ventures based on contacts gained during prior employment," Johannisson found that among Swedish entrepreneurs, those who started businesses had developed more elaborate contact networks in their jobs than those who did not start businesses.[16]

Illustrations of key contacts were described by Mitton in connection with deal making by Doug Manchester, a San Diego developer, who among other deals managed to earn "an instant $28 million equity" with no cash investment of his own.[17] Contacts identified in his case included the following:

- High school football team captain
- College—popular fraternity man
- Married to daughter of prominent local businessman
- Sold life insurance to prominent clientele
- Joined Young Presidents Organization
- Cultivated acquaintances with key San Diego county governmental decision makers
- Contributed $500,000 to San Diego University and sat on its board of trustees
- Worked one deal after another showing what he could do

When Manchester received the contract that yielded his instant $28 million, the Port Property manager explained that "Manchester's financial statement wasn't that great, but we chose him over the other bidders because of his track record."

Much remains to be learned about contacts and how they can best be cultivated and utilized by entrepreneurs. After studying patterns of networks in four Swedish communities, Johannisson suggested some guidelines for net-

---

[14] Dorothy Leonard-Barton, "Interpersonal Communication Patterns among Swedish and Boston-Area Entrepreneurs," in John A. Hornaday, Jeffry A. Timmons, and Karl H. Vesper, *Frontiers of Entrepreneurship Research, 1983* (Wellesley, Mass.: Babson Center for Entrepreneurial Studies, 1983), p. 538.

[15] Alan L. Carsrud, Connie Marie Gaglio, and Kenneth W. Olm, "Entrepreneurs—Mentors, Networks and Successful New Venture Development," in Ronstadt et al., *Frontiers of Entrepreneurship Research, 1986*, p. 229.

[16] Bengt Johannisson, "New Venture Creation—A Network Approach," in Ronstadt et al., *Frontiers of Entrepreneurship Research, 1986*, p. 236.

[17] Daryl G. Mitton, "No Money, Know How, Know Who," in John A. Hornaday, Fred Tarpley, Jr., Jeffry A. Timmons, and Karl H. Vesper, *Frontiers of Entrepreneurship Research, 1984* (Wellesley, Mass.: Babson Center for Entrepreneurial Studies, 1984), p. 414.

working.[18] They should be viewed as ways of gaining control of resources. They apply particularly where formal contracts do not operate. Other entrepreneurs can be especially helpful. Each person in a network may be a connecting point to other networks. Social as well as business contacts can help business, and so forth. But just how they work remains to be described.

Sequence Variety

In pulling together the five vital ingredients for startup, it might seem logical to expect that there would be a "best" sequence to follow—quite possibly the one illustrated in several cases above in which an entrepreneur (1) acquires technical knowhow, (2) crystallizes the venture idea for capitalizing on that knowhow, (3) proceeds to develop connections, (4) uses them both—knowhow and connections—to obtain the work force and physical resources needed to operate, and (5) obtains customer orders as the business is begun. This is in fact the most frequent sequence, and it is an option that any would-be entrepreneur can seek to pursue as a path to startup. But it will not fit every venture opportunity, and in fact any number of other sequences can and do occur. Theoretically over one hundred are possible, and most if not all have probably occurred at one time or another. Examples to follow demonstrate some of the variety possible by illustrating how each of the five key ingredients can come first.

As an example of a sequence beginning with knowhow first, the following occurred in a line of business quite unlike those illustrated above:

◆   *Knowhow.* In 1940 a young air force officer who had served three years in materiel had become aware of a number of things that would later serve him in starting a venture. He had extended his chemical engineering education in his work, learning about metal alloys, particularly magnesium, what their properties were, and how they could be worked. He had participated in decisions on buying materials, plants, and equipment and on selecting manufacturing firms to provide the government with weapons. He noted that the military tended to buy very large quantities of war materiel, stockpile it for specified periods of time, and then auction it to the highest bidder, often for a vastly lower amount than it cost.

Venture idea. His duty changed in 1943, and he found himself working with the British aircraft industry on propeller problems ranging from design to assembly on the aircraft. This activity, combined with his knowledge of military procurement procedures, gave him the idea for what he would do when released from active duty. He would buy surplus propellers from the U.S. government, service them as needed, and sell them to foreign governments and airlines. He estimated that he could sell them for 75 percent of original cost but buy them for much less.

Contacts. He began developing lists of government inventories and people with whom he could deal in buying and selling the propellers. He also made note of technicians whom he could hire to help with refurbishing.

Resources. When his release came, he started the enterprise with $3,000 of his own savings, plus a like amount borrowed from his parents, plus $5,000 borrowed from a bank against his house. From his military acquaintances he hired a chief mechanic and four technicians.

---

[18] Bengt Johannisson, "Network Strategies: Management Technology for Entrepreneurship and Change," *International Small Business Journal*, Vol. 5, No. 1 (Autumn 1986), 19.

Customer orders. His first successful bid was $4,000 for fifty P38 propellers, which after minor repairs he resold for $180 each. Within two years sales were $200,000 per year. By 1957 sales had reached $900,000 per year.

Could someone have done the same venture with a different sequence? Perhaps the idea could have come first to someone who knew little or nothing about propellers but who simply heard that there would likely be war surplus propellers available and then set about finding out whether there might be customers for them—airlines, foreign governments, or private pilots. The key resource needed, in this case $11,000 in capital, might have been in the person's possession to begin with. Thus he could have started with either the resources or the idea first. Or he could have happened to know both the buying and selling people and thereby have begun with the key contacts, possibly as a result of being in some aspect of military procurement and then having been contacted by future customers. Finally, the sequence could have begun with a customer order if, for instance, a foreigner contacted the entrepreneur, possibly as a result of a reputation the entrepreneur had as being a person who could get things done, and asked the entrepreneur to help arrange purchase of propellers after the war. Thus there was nothing necessarily preordained about the sequence by which this venture got started. It could have happened in many ways and with sequences beginning with any of the key ingredients.

The next example also begins with acquisition of startup relevant knowhow, but after that the sequence is different from the one in the preceding example. The role of unforeseen events is also apparent.

◆　　*Knowhow.* In 1975, after two and one-half years as a teacher of eighth-grade English ("the most physically and mentally taxing job I've ever had"), Lorraine Mecca moved from Arizona to Los Angeles and took up a new line of work. In an electronic components distribution company she learned the business from the bottom up, starting at four dollars per hour answering phones, making computer entries of orders, and handling receipts. She rose rapidly to operations coordinator as her understanding of electronics wholesaling improved.

Contacts. She met and married a fellow employee, who with a partner in 1977 had set up a sideline business renting and retailing microcomputers. Both soon quit the electronics distribution company, he to concentrate on the microcomputer venture full time and she to study business.

Venture idea. When she expressed a distaste for the typing required in her schoolwork, her husband suggested that she use a microcomputer for word processing. Through this she glimpsed a new potential: "I realized that if I, who was an extremely nontechnical person, could enjoy computers that much and find them so useful, than anyone in the world who wrote, or anybody working in any office would be using home computers or personal computers in the future," she recalled. Her thinking further crystalized when, sidelined by illness, she became frustrated by inactivity. Combining the observation that microcomputer storeowners like her husband found it easy to obtain computers but hard to get peripherals, with her experience in electronics wholesaling she decided to undertake the wholesaling of microcomputer peripherals.

Customer orders. Checks with her husband and other retailers readily confirmed the presence of a market.

Resources. Using $25,000 from the sale of a house from a former marriage, Lorraine Mecca incorporated Micro D, rented a building in Orange County, negotiated credit terms from vendors, and began deliveries with the assistance of a cousin who owned a van. Sales were $60,000 in the first six weeks. The company operated in the black from the beginning. By 1983 sales were $71 million. The company was owned 51 percent by Mecca, 49 percent by the public, and 0% by her husband, although he had now sold his former business and joined her company. Her share was worth $59 million.

Although most startup sequences begin with acquisition of technical knowhow about the particular kind of business, as illustrated above, the popular conception is that most of them begin with the venture idea, as suggested by the Swayne-Tucker model, for instance. In fact, they do sometimes begin that way, particularly when an invention is involved. An oculist who was hospitalized and had difficulty drinking through straws while lying down, for example, thought of making straws that incorporated a bellowslike section so they could flex. After recovery, he started a strawmaking company, something entirely new to him. Collins and Moore tell of inventors who resorted to setting up companies only because they were unsuccessful in trying to sell their inventions. In one case, they report, "Mr. Roland went on the road to try to sell his invention. When he could not find a buyer, he began projecting the notion of setting up a firm and manufacturing it himself." In another case they describe an inventor who created a toy car. "His first impulse was to sell the idea to an automobile company and let them make the cars as a promotional item. The automobile people let Victor know that they were interested only in making 'big' cars. It was only after this impasse was reached that Victor began projecting his own business."[19]

In these three cases the idea of starting a business came as something of a surprise, but it can also be something that the entrepreneur has carried around for some time, as the following example illustrates.

◆ *Idea.* Ever since childhood, a certain aerospace worker had thought from time to time about owning a movie theater. He and his neighbor, an architect, had been active in community affairs and as a result became aware of a women's club building being put up for sale. The architect was fond of the ancient building and wanted to see it preserved. When the two were discussing its possible fate at the hands of groups that were variously proposing it be replaced by a parking lot or converted to offices or a mortuary, the possibility of making it into a movie theater occurred, and they decided to make a bid.

Connections. Although neither had any prior experience in running any business or in working with films, they contacted a lawyer, had papers of partnership drawn up, and submitted a bid. The partners never learned whether theirs was the high bid, but possibly because the ladies were impressed that their club would be largely preserved if used for movies, the bid was accepted. The two now found themselves forced to make many new acquaintances. Financial arrangements had to be made. A zoning variance had to be obtained. Business contacts had to be established for obtaining movies, hiring personnel, publicizing the theater, and refurbishing it.

Knowhow. The two men learned the business as they went along, often encountering unanticipated problems, and soliciting counsel from others in the business, such as movie distributors and other theater owners as well as friends. They found that in applying for one permit, such as an amusement license, many others were needed, but the sources of each knew about the others.

---

[19] Collins and Moore, *Organization Makers,* pp. 119–120.

Resources. Of the $38,000 needed for down payment and refurbishing the building, approximately half came from friends and the other half from a banker against personal guarantees. The two had themselves put up $10,000 for projection equipment. The banker predicted that they would fail but figured that they would be able to repay him from income they obtained at their regular jobs. Friends and neighbors helped out with the work as they went to work remodeling the theater and adding new essentials such as a ticket booth, which they built themselves.

Customer orders. The two developed relationships with entertainment editors and feature writers of local and regional newspapers, explaining the idea of their theater, which they had decided would distinguish itself by having a more homelike atmosphere than typical theaters, including a large and comfortable waiting room serving cheese and crackers, a roaring fireplace in the winter, selection of lesser-known movies of high intellectual quality, and introductions to those movies provided by waiting room lectures by the partners. The two even worked up their own copy, which a number of editors considered suitable for printing as submitted, and on opening night the theater enjoyed good publicity. For the first few months, audiences were small but rose gradually as word spread. Then one movie, *The Prime of Miss Jean Brodie,* suddenly drew greatly heightened interest, and thousands of new patrons started coming. By February 1971, fourteen months after the two men decided to pursue the idea, the first was able to quit his aerospace job and join the theater full time, as opportunities for expansion to other outlets began to present themselves. Four months later, the architect also shifted full time to the new venture.

A common thread of high, and very often overlooked, importance is the crucial role played by personal and business contacts in business startups.[20] The above entrepreneur had been intrigued with theater ownership ideas since youth but got going on it only after interacting with the architect, who had not thought of it before. Thus the personal interaction was a key to the venture for both men. For one of them the idea was the first ingredient, and for the other it was the personal contact. Thus contacts too can be the first key ingredient in startup and for that reason are worth seeking deliberately. Recognizing this fact, the following entrepreneur undertook a calculated search strategy centering on contacts as a way of finding the other key ingredients.

◆ *Connections.* In 1968 an engineer told his prospective employer that it was his intention eventually to head up a company of his own. The employer said that was all right so long as his independent entrepreneuring did not conflict with his job in preliminary design and development of electronic controls. Taking the job, he began devoting his spare time, lunch hours, evenings, and weekends seeking a proprietary product that would involve high technology, serve an expanding market, and yet involve relatively small initial investment.

He made it a practice to contact an average of at least one person per day who might be able to help him in his quest, including prospective suppliers, customers, inventors, venture capitalists, and so on. He also took every opportunity to learn about entrepreneurship through reading, and attending related courses

---

[20] The role of contacts outside the firm is great in established businesses as well as startups, and it seems puzzling that it is given little or no attention in most studies of business. Virtually none of the research on business seems to deal with this subject, although the cliché that "it's not what you know but whom you know," overstated though it may be, is widely known and little disputed.

and conferences. By 1970 he had met another engineer who was interested in collaborating, and the two formed a partnership with a handshake, opened a joint bank account under a name chosen for their company, and deposited $1,500 each.

In 1972 their joint search uncovered the opportunity to perform a $15,000 design contract for a ship winch control system, so although they saw it as a diversion from the goal of a proprietary product, they rented space and took it on, performing the work in evenings, while continuing their jobs and product quest by day.

Idea. In early 1973, one of their contacts paid off by putting them in touch with a professor who had developed an electronic medical diagnostic instrument. The university held rights to the product and was willing to license it to the two men, who by now had the beginning of a performance record with their winch design job. An exclusive licensing arrangement was made for manufacture of the patented instrument.

Knowhow. With the license came full information about the technology of the product and cooperation of the university staff who had developed the prototype.

Resources. Because each unit cost $20,000, substantial capital had to be added. Based on plans developed during the checkout and negotiation stage above, the company was incorporated, venture capital was brought in, larger quarters and equipment were obtained, and additional people were added in different areas of specialties needed to work out production design of the instrument and put it on the market.

Customer order. It was not until mid-1974 that the production design of the unit was completed and sales literature prepared. At a trade show in October 1974 the first order was received from a customer. Four months later in February 1975 the first unit was shipped. Within a year sales were running at a half-million dollars per year, and the year after that they doubled to one million with the prospect of continued acceleration in the future.

This approach of beginning with contacts by deliberately seeking them out on a persistent schedule is worth nothing for a would-be entrepreneur, because it is an approach that anyone can adopt and stay with until it pays off. It will be further considered in the next chapter, which deals with the problem of finding venture ideas.

To obtain as a first step all the physical and financial resources needed to create a venture is not so easy. But that too sometimes occurs. Earlier the example of Alejandro Zaffaroni, the founder of Alza corporation, was mentioned. He was able to launch the enterprise with $2 million of his own money and then to add to it another $29 million before sales began. Although that was an extremely rare exception, it is possible to find many other resource-first startup sequences where entrepreneurs—particularly inventors and also people who enter as agents, brokers, and other types of middlemen, or as service enterprises such as management consulting and investment counsel—are able to begin with very modest savings and such physical assets as a home office or shop. The following example illustrates a startup in which physical resources became the first key ingredient acquired in the sequence.

◆   *Resources.* In early 1972 a West Coast student dropped out of undergraduate business school one term short of graduation with doubts about the value of his studies. Although he had no prior experience in photography, nor did any of his friends, he followed an impulse and bought $200 worth of developing equipment "because it looked interesting."

Technical knowhow. He taught himself how to work the equipment and began making enlargements.

Customer order. Two weeks later he showed one of his enlargements to a friend. Somewhat to his surprise, the friend offered to buy it.

Venture idea. This purchase triggered the thought that perhaps he might be able to sell enlargement services to others.

Contacts. With the help of his younger brother, he began contacting stores and soliciting orders, which he received. The business began to grow, and over the next year and a half reached ten employees. His capital shrank as receivables mounted, and he saw serious cash problems ahead. He was discussing this problem one day with a friend, who suggested that perhaps he should sell through mail order because then he would receive payment in advance and not have to finance receivables. This seemed sensible, so he tried advertising experimentally in some photographic trade journals. Suddenly in the fall of 1973 orders began to pour in for high-quality color enlargements, each enclosing cash in advance. By late 1974 he had incorporated, installed automated processing equipment in a 16,000-square-foot warehouse, and with fifty employees was handling orders at an annual rate of one million dollars and rapidly rising.

Rarest of all are ventures where the first startup ingredient to arise is a customer request or order. Why, after all, should a customer request a product or service from an entrepreneur without knowhow, resources, connections, or even the idea of offering it? Because there is no better source in view, presumably. One situation where this occurred was illustrated earlier by the experience of Mr. Ikeda, the Japanese immigrant dishwasher whose encounter with tourists got him started in the gem business. Another was the highly profitable though short-lived adventure of a man who became involved in selling pennies:

◆   *Customer order.* A young insurance salesman in Portland, Oregon, approached a potential customer who happened to be a coin dealer. As part of his sales procedure he asked the coin dealer about his business and the man mentioned a problem he had encountered. This coin dealer knew another in New York who wanted to obtain for resale some San Francisco-minted but uncirculated pennies. Obtaining the New Yorker's name, the insurance salesman checked and verified the man's desire to buy.

Connections. Another man to whom the salesman had been selling insurance was a young banker in town. Calling this client, the salesman asked if there were a way the bank could get him San Francisco mint pennies. "I don't know," the banker replied, "but I'll check with the Federal Reserve Bank."

Knowhow. The banker informed him that he could obtain up to $500 worth of pennies per day. The insurance man also found how to package and ship them by air freight to New York.

Resources. Soon the salesman was making one trip per day to the bank, where he would load $500 worth of pennies on a cart in the basement vault, lift them via the elevator, push them through the lobby ("The cart wheels would squeak and everyone in the lobby would look at me," he recalled. "It was really embarrassing."), load them into the trunk of his car, air freight them at the airport, and wait for the five cents apiece he would receive for them from the man in New York, who he later learned then sold them for a dime apiece.

More knowhow. This profitable process continued for several days until two well-dressed men stepped up to the insurance man on his squeaky passage through the lobby. One was a bank vice-president. The other asked where the coins were going. "To my car," replied the salesman. "Then where?" asked the stranger. "That's my business," was the reply. "Ours too," the man added, displaying a Treasury Department badge.

The salesman was told that his actions appeared to involve speculation in U.S. currency, a federal offense for which he could be tried and jailed. Completely surprised by this news, the salesman agreed to stop the penny business immediately, no charges were filed, and he used the profits that had already accrued to start another venture.

Starting with Combinations

It can be seen from these examples that many sequences are possible. Actually, the lines between the five key startup ingredients are also somewhat arbitrary. A close look at the examples shows that they can be highly interrelated, and it can be difficult to pinpoint where a given ingredient comes into being. Any entrepreneur is bound to have some knowhow or other that applies to his or her startup at the outset, and very likely also some connections that will prove important, as well as some resources to draw upon. Even the venture idea itself may come and go, possibly changing form with time, so it is difficult to spot a point in time when it truly emerged.

The value in viewing startup examples in terms of the key ingredients for a would-be entrepreneur should be threefold. First, they illustrate that there need not be one particular startup sequence to which the venture is constrained. Sensitivity should be developed to many possible combinations so that the number of opportunities likely to be recognized will increase and with it the chance of spotting good ones that other people might miss. Second, a recognition that these factors are *all* necessary for successful startup should make it clearer to a would-be entrepreneur what to work on in anticipation of startup. It is not sufficient only to save money so that there will be resources to work with, or only to keep looking for venture ideas hoping for a lucky thought to strike. Connections, knowhow, and customer orders should also be sought as part of a personal startup strategy. Thus a would-be entrepreneur should keep working to marshal key ingredients on any or all of five fronts, any one of which may at any time throw into motion a startup sequence. Third, when such a sequence does appear to be shaping up, the entrepreneur who is familiar with these five factors will know in advance what else needs to be worked on, because all five will be required. At the same time, if one of the factors is unduly expensive to obtain, then the venture is probably a bad bet and should be dropped in favor of continuing the search for others.

TIME REQUIRED TO START

From the preceding discussion of inception points and sequences, it can be seen that the question of how long a startup takes can be as complicated as anyone wishes to make it. Still it is possible to choose arbitrary points in the sequence and ask how long startup takes. One study of some four hundred startups checked the time elapsed between conception of the idea and execution of the first sale and found a range of from less than one month to over five years, with an average between four and seven months for mostly service firms.[21] One-third took longer than a year. When this startup period was divided into three subperiods, from idea to startup decision, decision to formation, and formation to first sale, it was found that the first took an average of three months, with 80 percent completing this stage within one year. The second stage, from startup decision to formation, took an average of less than two months, with 94 percent taking less than one year. From formation to first sale was the shortest stage, with 98 percent of the firms completing it within one year.

A more interesting question for most entrepreneurs is how long they can expect to have to subsist on financial reserves before the new company can support them. The preceding examples demonstrate that the time needed for a company to reach breakeven plus a salary for the entrepreneur can range considerably. Some services, like the pennies trader and others mentioned in earlier chapters, may reach breakeven within weeks or even days. Others, like the theater and machine shop examples, may take months to a year. A buyout may already be profitable and hence beyond breakeven right from the start. New product manufacturing companies typically take the longest. The medical instrument company mentioned above took over three years to break even, and of course some companies never reach it and consequently fail. As Morrison points out, "a new enterprise producing proprietary products is not likely to become profitable in its first year. The fact that breakeven time can range so widely depending on the particular enterprise is one of several reasons for preparing careful financial forecasts before 'plunging,' particularly into manufacturing."[22]

THREE MAIN HURDLES TO ENTREPRENEURIAL ENTRY

Why many of those who wish to enter independent business do not succeed is a question on which there has been almost no methodical research. If asked why they did not go further with their venture ambitions, the answers they give will often center on a state of mind. "I didn't really have the nerve." "The risks simply outweighed the potential benefits, so I decided not to go on." "I decided things were not really all that uncomfortable where I was, or so it seemed when I considered what a big gamble and how much strain would be involved in trying a new company." "After all, it isn't easy to get another job if you fail when you're over forty, like I am."

Although "frame of mind" and psychological factors are undoubtedly important in explaining nonstarts, there are usually good business reasons as well. The three main obstacles are as follows:

1 Failure to find a venture idea with sufficient margin potential
2 Failure to develop an effective sales generation scheme

---

[21] Robert T. Woodworth et al., *The Role of Accountants, Bankers, Lawyers and Government Agencies in the Entrepreneurial Process* (Seattle: University of Washington, 1974).
[22] Morrison, *Handbook for Manufacturing Entrepreneurs* (Cleveland: Western Reserve Press, 1973).

3 Failure to obtain operational financing

These three are probably in relative order of severity for a "typical" entrepreneur, although the order can vary and the three may obviously be interrelated. From interviewing entrepreneurs who had already dealt with the first of these, three different researchers found different ratings. In a study of Dandridge, financial and marketing problems were found to be equally severe, both trailing "learning how to run a business," according to the entrepreneurs responding.[23] A study by Hisrich and O'Cinneide comparing male versus female entrepreneurs in Ireland found that the main problems during startup typically were in getting money, whereas later on when the business had started the main problems were in getting sales.[24] Women seemed more impeded by marketing problems than men. The most serious problem area during startup was found by Gartner to vary with type of startup.[25] In some it was finance and in others marketing.

These clearly correspond to three of the five startup essentials discussed above but extend them just a bit. It is not sufficient to have a venture idea; the idea must carry an adequate profit margin. It is not sufficient to obtain initial sales orders; a scheme must be introduced that generates continuous orders and reorders. It is not sufficient to provide the seed capital needed to germinate the venture; either that capital must grow fast enough through high initial profits or it must be augmented with additional injections for longer-term survival. Each of these three main hurdles on the path to startup deserves a more careful look than the success stories mentioned above with the five key factors might imply.

High-Margin Venture Idea

It has been said that to achieve more than the barest survival at best, a venture needs the "3Ms," and that these stand for one word, margin, margin, and margin. First is *margin to make a profit.* Second is *margin to provide for unforeseen problems,* which virtually always arise in any new venture ("when you least expect them," says Baty. "You'll see.")[26] Third is *margin to keep making a profit and coping with problems after competitors have entered and attacked or counterattacked with reduced prices.* Although it varies with industry, a rough rule of thumb for any manufactured product is that it must sell to the end user for at least four to five times the direct costs—labor and materials— needed to produce it. If there are other channels downstream from the manufacturer, such as distributors, wholesalers, and retailers, this means that the manufacturer must typically charge as its own selling price at least twice its direct costs for goods picked up at the factory.

Without such a margin-generating idea at the core, the profit-making heart

[23] Thomas C. Dandridge, "Encouraging Urban Entrepreneurship," in Karl H. Vesper, *Frontiers of Entrepreneurship Research, 1982* (Wellesley, Mass.: Babson College, 1982), p. 153.

[24] Robert D. Hisrich and Barra O'Cinneide, "The Irish Entrepreneur: Characteristics, Problems and Future Success," in Hornaday et al., *Frontiers of Entrepreneurship Research, 1986,* p. 79.

[25] William B. Gartner, "Problems in Business Startups," in Hornaday et al., *Frontiers of Entrepreneurship Research, 1984,* p. 496.

[26] Baty, *Entrepreneurship—Playing to Win.*

of a venture is missing, and so is its justification for existing in the world of business. (Though it may still have a place in the world of charity, perhaps.) If the venture idea has only a low margin potential but not a high one (in total, not necessarily per unit), then it will be unlikely either to grow large or to attract outside capital or to provide much income for the entrepreneur (although there have been ventures, unsuccessful in general, that have nevertheless accomplished these things). Most "Mom 'n Pop" enterprises are in this low-total-margin category, and many fail.

How many people want to and try to start companies but fail to get started at all has never been studied. Presumably there is always some reason or combination of them that explains these "nonstarts," and probably the most common reason is failure to identify a high-margin venture idea. There would be some who, although desiring to do so, were unable to identify any venture ideas they considered worth serious effort, or who were for some reason disinclined to apply effort to test any ideas. There would be another group, probably smaller in number, who identified one or more ideas and investigated or tried them to some extent but concluded that their ideas were insufficiently promising or were too risky to carry further. And there would be still another group whose ideas were proven inadequate by full-scale implementation culminating in venture failure. One survey of would-be entrepreneurs found that less than 10 percent felt they had been able to formulate any high-margin potential venture ideas.[27] The following examples may serve to illustrate some less-than-promising venture ideas:

- A carpenter had lost his job and thought he might find work easier and more lucrative if he developed his own contracting firm. He had never worked in the "business end" of such an enterprise or had any schooling in business, and was quite unsure how to go about starting a firm.
- A recently discharged veteran thought he would start a service station with his brother. He had no background or training in operating any type of business. Eventually he dropped the venture idea in favor of selling used cars by day and pumping gas in someone else's station by night.
- A purchasing agent, discontented with his job, and believing his hobby-developed woodworking skills could be the basis of a new firm of his own, rented plant space, bought some woodworking machines, built a paint spray booth, and started manufacturing novelty items such as checker and backgammon boards, knife holders, wine racks, and game boxes. Contracts were signed with novelty distributors, and a few orders came and were filled. Prices were able to cover labor and materials, but volume was insufficient to support indirect expenses. Customers were slow in paying, and some in distant cities did not pay at all. The entrepreneur and his wife were reduced to living and paying off the company debts from her salary as a nurse.

Whether any given venture idea has high margin potential or not clearly

---

[27] Roger Harman, "Study of the Entrepreneurship Symposium Given by the University of Washington on May 22, 1971," unpublished paper, University of Washington, Seattle, 1972.

depends on the place, time, and person. Although the above carpenter, ex-GI, and ex-purchasing agent did not have high margin ideas, as it turned out, others have moved from such prior jobs to such ventures at other times and places and been very successful. It is to test the promise of such combinations of ingredients that analysis and planning with care, whether formally or not, are often advocated as important activities on the path to startup, though many entrepreneurs proceed without them, some happily and some, like those above, less than happily. More information about margin in different lines of work will be presented in Chapter 6.

Effective Sales Generation Scheme

Once the hurdle is passed of locating an idea that appears to have high margin potential, a second major obstacle is that of developing a scheme to generate orders for customers.

◆   An idea to develop and manufacture illuminated plastic road curbing for streets and driveways looked good enough to a number of serious investors that its inventor was able to raise several hundred thousand dollars through a small public stock offering to get started. Prototypes of the curbing were developed, and potential purchasers such as city, county, and state road agencies, as well as private real estate developers, were approached. But nobody would buy the product. Too much expense. Too hard to install and maintain. Probably not durable enough. The market's verdict was that the product should not be bought.
        New management was brought in, and it had another product idea, a miles-per-gallon meter for cars. The product was developed, packaged, tested, and perfected. But how was it to be sold? Mail-order advertisements sold a few, but not enough to break even. Manufacturers' representatives were contacted, but it was hard to get them to put effort on a new product when they could get more certain orders with existing lines. Similarly, retailers were reluctant to put it on the shelf, because the public was not acquainted with the product and was therefore slow to buy.
        As a variation to that product a gallons-per-hour meter for boats was developed. This was cheaper to make and yet could sell for as high a price, because margins in the boat industry are higher than those in the auto industry. But now the company needed to start over again on selling, because the channels for boats are also different from those for cars. With its initial capital all used up, the company was now looking for ways to become acquired by another company, because it could not find ways to sell the products.

        It was pointed out in a preceding section that obtaining orders is one of five key factors in getting started, but it should also be noted that one sale or even a few sales are not enough. Success requires many customers in most ventures and an automatic repeating pattern of ordering. How to achieve this is treated in texts on selling techniques and marketing and need not be repeated here. It is vital, however, that a would-be entrepreneur recognize the importance of this hurdle, not just assume it away, and develop plans for coping with it. These must include clear answers to basic questions, such as Who can be expected to want what it is the company will sell? How much will it be worth to such people and why? Where will they become aware of it and how? What difficulties may they have in recognizing its value to them, and how can the company solve these?

Failure to obtain orders can result from many causes, including the following:

1 *Basic weakness in what is offered.* Some engineers who developed a computer program for improving electronic circuit design and formed a company to sell their design-improvement service to electronics companies found that none of them would buy. The purchase decision at those companies was stymied by their own circuit design engineers who were not anxious to be supplanted by an outside contract service.

2 *Established relationships market.* It can be hard to break into markets of high volume such as detergents, cosmetics, and other products where bureaucratic buyers tend to buy from established rather than new companies. William Lear developed an automatic landing system for aircraft and tried to sell it to the government. Instead, the government gave contracts for developing such a system to some other larger and more established companies, who then reinvented Lear's system. His diagnosis was that bureaucrats were safe if the system was bought from a big, "obviously reliable" company and failed to work, but not if they bought from a small company like his.

3 *Wrong channel choice.* New manufacturing companies often sell through manufacturers' representatives to avoid the expense of setting up their own sales forces. If the choice of representatives is not right, they find that no sales result, because the representatives are pushing other products in their lines, because they get larger commissions on them, because they are better established and easier to sell, because they have so many products they cannot really bother with the new one unless they are asked for it by customers, or for some other reasons. Other companies may set up their own sales force only to find that the product volume is insufficient to support it.

4 *Long warmup markets.* When aluminum pots and pans were first introduced, nobody bought them because people were accustomed to cast iron and steel. It took years for the manufacturers to convert people to a perfectly good innovation. A similar phenomenon accompanied introduction of aluminum bearing inserts in place of babbitt for diesel engines, even though the customers for these were presumably rationally oriented decision makers.

5 *Message choice.* "Checks perspiration" was chosen as the advertising message for a new deodorant called "Perstick" which was dreamed up after a series of unsuccessful products by an innovative entrepreneur named Marvin Small.[28] The first effect of this slogan coupled with the new design was enthusiastic buying by customers. The second effect of it was a drop of the sales to zero. Why? A market researcher, engaged for $2,000,

[28] Marvin Small, *How to Make More Money* (New York: Pocket Books, 1959).

found that customers had thought from the slogan that the deodorant would stop perspiration from occurring, not just from smelling. They were disappointed to find the claim was not fulfilled.

In this case by happy coincidence a young inventor who had unsuccessfully been trying to interest companies in a new formula that did actually stop perspiration happened to call on Small's company, the last one on the list after all the others that had turned the formula down. Small accepted it, and the new cream product, Arrid, soon outsold all other brands combined.

In the earlier chapter on success factors it was observed that concern with sales was a common feature among successful companies, while inattention to it was characteristic of unsuccessful ones. The folklore that customers will seek out and buy a better mousetrap simply cannot be depended on. (In fact, the claim in a literal sense has been proven untrue. One company makes virtually all the mousetraps bought in the United States. But when it developed through research an improved design and put it on the market, the customers did not buy. Rather than spend money to push sales, the product was withdrawn.)

Operational Financing

Most would-be entrepreneurs can muster enough capital to go through many of the steps of starting a venture, often to get it actually operating on a small scale. Sources typically begin with personal savings, then pull in savings of family members, friends, and other acquaintances and those of partners. This may be enough to draw up legal papers, obtain space, perform some market research, and perhaps develop a prototype, packaging, initial advertising, some fixed assets, and inventory. If the venture is to be a small one, this seeding may be enough to make the venture permanent. If the initial profits are high enough, the venture may even be able to grow large on small initial seeding from personal assets.

If, on the other hand, there is substantial developmental expense involved in creating the product and getting it into production, or if the venture is one in which profits will come only after a period of operation and expansion, if the cost of initial inventory and setup is high, or if the personal assets of the entrepreneur and his or her associates are small, then it is typically necessary to secure additional external capital beyond personal assets before the venture can truly become operational. This is often the case with ambitiously oriented ventures, and consequently obtaining operational capital is often a critical hurdle in getting ventures started.

Having solved the hurdle of finding a good margin idea does not necessarily solve the capital problem. A classic example was the Xerox process, which knocked around, unable to obtain backing, for years before support was found. Ironically, it can happen that the higher the margin potential, the bigger the amount of capital needed and consequently the bigger the problem of obtaining financing. If the margin promises to be very high, then it can be desirable to move on a large scale fast to stay ahead of competitors, who are bound to be attracted to the high-profit line of business once the new venture exhibits the opportunity. An example was the Bowmar corporation, which was first with pocket calculators, only to be trampled in the stampede by giant competitors like Texas Instruments, which followed Bowmar into the market with drastic price slashing to grasp the largest market share.

Margin is obviously only one of the dimensions of interest to venture capitalists. Although typically about 20 to 30 percent of their deals are with startups, according to a study by Timmons, the remainder are investments in going concerns rather than startups.[29] Moreover, their industrial preferences are about 60 percent aimed toward high-technology startups, and they aim at rates of return of around 30 percent annually on investments of $250,000 on up. In total they account for only a very small fraction of startup capital.

"Informal investors," individuals who sometimes put money into ventures but not as a full-time occupation, seem to have similar preferences, according to a study by Wetzel and Wilson.[30] Hence the typical entrepreneur must plan to rely on personal savings plus those of partners, friends, and relatives. Sometimes it is possible to obtain trade credit and sometimes bank loans, although in very early stages before the company has demonstrated creditworthiness these can be difficult or impossible to obtain.

Even solving the hurdle of a clearly workable sales scheme guaranteed to produce orders does not necessarily ensure that the operational financing hurdle will also be solved, as the following experience illustrates.

◆   Some graduating MBA students who wanted their own venture hit upon the idea of manufacturing bicycles with frames made of titanium instead of conventional steel to achieve advantages over existing bicycles in terms of both weight and stiffness. They pooled $25,000 of personal savings, which they used for travel to approach needed connections, for supplies, and to hire as consultant an aerospace engineer who was expert in fabricating this hard-to-form metal.

Serious technical problems beset the development of prototypes but were solved by the consultant to produce three shiny and unique new bicycles, which were tested and performed well. The plan was to manufacture frames and assemble them with purchased components such as handlebars, seats, sprockets, and wheels, but it was found that a bicycle boom at the time had siphoned off all sources of supply for these parts, which thus became almost impossible to obtain. Consequently, the young entrepreneurs were delighted when they found a very large bicycle distributor who had access to foreign supplies of these parts and was willing to help.

This distributor gave them a letter of intent, which guaranteed not only to provide all the components they needed but also to purchase for resale all the bicycles they could produce! Beyond that, he offered personally to invest $60,000 in the venture if they could line up the remaining $200,000 startup capital. Detailed financial projections had been prepared by the MBAs showing why this amount was needed and how it would generate profits. A prospectus was carefully prepared and presented for review to a series of advisers, including one of their former professors, people of the local financial community, and other entrepreneurs. Based on comments by these reviewers, the document was modified and polished for presentation to professional venture capitalists.

---

[29] Jeffry A. Timmons, "Venture Capital Investors in the U.S.," in Vesper, *Frontiers of Entrepreneurship Research, 1981*, p. 199.
[30] William E. Wetzel and Ian G. Wilson, "Seed Capital Gaps," in Hornaday et al., *Frontiers of Entrepreneurship Research, 1985*, p. 221.

The ensuing search for capital terminated the venture. Many individuals, companies, and venture capital firms were contacted in several cities. During one visit to a San Francisco firm, a prototype was even demonstrated by riding it around the hallway of a skyscraper where the firm was located. But all to no avail. Some said the founders had too little "track record" in the bicycle business. Others pointed out that the margin on frame manufacturing would be diluted by purchasing so many parts that could not be given high markups. Still others observed that because the same distributor was supplying both parts and sales channels, he would have power over the new firm and could "squeeze it" as he chose, simply by raising parts costs or lowering sales prices or both. Finally, some predicted that the current boom in bicycles would attract so much competition that margins would soon shrink and drive newcomers out. In a short time their seed capital was depleted and the MBAs decided to discontinue the venture. They concluded that the venture had been expensive but had taught them much about entrepreneuring, convinced them that they wanted to do more of it when again they were financially able, given them a number of valued connections (some who turned them down on the bicycle deal were sufficiently impressed to offer them consulting contracts to investigate other deals), and a few extremely expensive personal titantium-framed bicycles.

Many other hurdles, of course, occur in paths to venture startup. Some ventures are stymied by technical problems, others by lack of time, competitors' actions, planning and management errors, partner disputes, caprice of government, and other causes seen in the chapter on success factors. The three main hurdles suggested here often are interrelated. Finding an idea can be the key. If its margin potential is great enough, ways can usually be found to line up the sales and financing. The chapter to follow will focus on where venture ideas come from.

SUMMARY

There have been attempts to formulate standardized sequences for creating new ventures, and to some extent these may be useful as checklists for things an entrepreneur must do or as starting points for planning. But history shows that rarely are the sequences of steps involved in creating any two ventures alike. To some extent the variety depends on field, with conventional manufacturing companies tending to show one set of typical startup patterns, high-technology manufacturing companies another, and so forth. There are always five types of key ingredients the entrepreneur must muster: the venture idea, physical resources, technical knowhow in the particular line of work, personal contacts critical to the business, and sales orders from customers. But historical examples show that many different sequences are possible in acquiring them. The three most difficult to acquire are the venture idea, the sales orders, and financing. Most important among these three in many cases is the venture idea, because when it is good the others tend to be much easier to come by.

chapter 5.

Sources of
Venture Ideas

The most precious of the five key venture ingredients described in the preceding chapter is a high-margin venture idea. Most would-be entrepreneurs have at least some of the other four ingredients all the time, and it is when the venture idea occurs that the others are brought into action. Even if all the others are missing, they can generally be obtained if the venture idea has sufficient margin promise. So it is worth looking for.

Seeking a good venture idea is almost never a straightforward task. Most who find one do so rather inadvertently, and many of those who deliberately search for them fail. Many have driven themselves partly or entirely to ruin seeking and testing venture ideas that did not work out. Even so creative a person as Mark Twain spent much of his time and fortune without success trying unworkable ideas. Hence, how good venture ideas can be found is a topic particularly worth study.

This chapter will show through examples where successful venture ideas tend to come from. From these as well as examples in other chapters, it can be seen that most emerge rather unexpectedly and are not the result of either methodical searching or brilliant discovery. A number of ways of looking for good venture ideas that have been advocated by various authors will be summarized, and suggestions about how a would-be entrepreneur may be able to increase the odds of his or her encountering promising venture ideas will be developed. Trial and error, as Timmons has observed, works.*

---

* Timmons, Jeffry A., Smollen, Leonard E. and Dinzee, Alexander L., *New Venture Creation,* Homewood, Ill., Irwin.

INVITATION AS A VENTURE IDEA SOURCE

Sometimes the idea for a particular venture comes "out of the blue" in the form of a proposal by someone else who has seen an opportunity and wants to collaborate in exploiting it. If the entrepreneur is defined as the person who carries through the actions required to start up the business, as opposed to the one who suggests the idea of doing so, then to the entrepreneur the venture idea comes in the form of an invitation, usually quite unanticipated, to take charge of the startup. In the following example from Collins and Moore the venture was offered in the form of a job, but the entrepreneur chose to make it a startup instead.[1]

◆ A young man skilled in light manufacturing was approached by a delegation of creditors of a failing business. They offered him a salary to take over the company, but after checking out the company the young man decided the firm was too far gone. Instead, he recommended forming a new firm to buy the assets and start over.

In another case that they describe, the decision had already been made by four men to create a new company.[2] They regarded it as an investment, but none of them had time to run it. Consequently, they approached an entrepreneur, curiously enough one who had already gone bankrupt in one company and had been squeezed out of another before taking a job as sales director in a large company. They asked him to take charge of the startup. He agreed to do so if he could be paid partly in stock, since he had no money to invest. This was done, and the company succeeded. In a third case that Collins and Moore tell the story of a professor who was approached by an employee of a large corporation for which he had done consulting work with the suggestion that he start a new company.[3] The authors' impression is that the professor was "dragged into entrepreneurship by his heels" in forming this company, because initially he was reluctant to do so, having already established himself solidly in an academic career. They also note that several of the large-company employees invested in the venture and that it obtained process rights from the large company "at a ridiculously low figure," an implication perhaps of skulduggery.

A similar reluctance appears in the story of a more recent startup in high technology described by Goodrich.[4] He quotes the entrepreneur, Sanford D. Greenberg, as follows:

◆ When I had been at Systems Development Corporation for six months one of the partners of White, Weld and Company, the Wall Street investment banking firm, came to me with a very attractive offer, which ultimately resulted in the founding of my company, EDP. I had met him when I was working on compressed speech. White, Weld became interested in that and wanted to back me, but I

[1] Orvis Collins and David G. Moore, *The Organization Makers* (New York: Appleton-Century-Crofts, 1970), p. 125.
[2] Ibid., p. 126.
[3] Ibid., p. 124.
[4] David L. Goodrich, *Horatio Alger Is Alive and Well and Living in America* (New York: Cowles, 1971), p. 186.

suggested that we wait and work together on something else in the future. When White, Weld approached me again they asked if I would be interested in planning, setting up, and running a computer firm. They put up some of the original investment of two million dollars; some money also came from a group headed by William Rosenwald, a New York investor. EDP was founded in early 1968, in a small office in Washington. The original staff was two people—myself and a colleague.

How does a would-be entrepreneur become "invited" to pursue a particular venture idea by someone else? Perhaps the best way to explore the question is from the viewpoint of the other person. Who would be the best person to invite? Someone who is handy? Perhaps. No searching for new acquaintances as candidate entrepreneurs was apparent on the part of those who offered the venture ideas in the preceding examples. Someone who is searching for ventures? Apparently not. None of the preceding four entrepreneurs seem to have done so, and at least two were outright reluctant. Thus it is hard to infer strategic guidelines for being invited to participate in a venture beyond cultivating contacts who might conceivably make such an invitation and seeking to perform in a way that would make them want to collaborate.

VENTURE IDEAS FROM PRIOR EMPLOYMENT

Most venture ideas come from former jobs held by the entrepreneurs. As mentioned earlier, Cooper found in 85 percent of his high-technology startups that the products of the new companies were similar to those of prior employers of the founders.[5] In a more recent study of firms not concentrated in high technology, Cooper and others again found that a majority of the founders had discovered their ideas through their prior job and also that a majority offered products or services that were the same as or similar to those of the prior employer and sold to the same or similar customers.[6] Long and McMullan also found that prior employment was the most frequently mentioned influence in their 1984 mapping of the venture opportunity identification process.[7] In all the high-technology startups reported by Bylinsky, this appears to have been the case. In about 20 percent of the startups reported by Collins and Moore it appears the entrepreneurs simply restarted companies of former employers who had run into trouble, while in most of the other startups they report— although sometimes a shortage of data makes it difficult to tell—it appears the entrepreneurs pursued lines of work very similar to prior employment.[8] In the

---

[5] Arnold C. Cooper, *The Founding of Technologically-Based Firms* (Milwaukee: Center for Venture Management, 1971).

[6] Arnold C. Cooper, William C. Dunkelberg, and R. Stanley Furuta, "Incubator Organization Background and Founding Characteristics," in John A. Hornaday, Edward B. Shils, Jeffry A. Timmons, and Karl H. Vesper, *Frontiers of Entrepreneurship Research, 1986* (Wellesley, Mass.: Babson College, 1986), p. 61.

[7] Wayne A. Long, and W. Ed. McMullan, "Mapping the New Venture Opportunity Identification Process," in John A. Hornaday, Fred Tarpley, Jr., Jeffry A. Timmons, and Karl H. Vesper, *Frontiers of Entrepreneurship Research, 1984*, p. 567.

[8] Collins and Moore, *Organization Makers.*

ventures reported by Miller it appears that around 75 percent bore close re-semblance to prior employment, while in those of Armour the figure appears to have been 66 percent and for those of Lynn around 50 percent.[9]

When the entrepreneurs in those books above did depart from prior work experience, it usually happened via one of two routes, each of which ac-counted for roughly half of those departures. One was to enter the venture by means of acquiring a going concern rather than starting a new one. The second was to start a company in a rather prosaic line of work such as rent-als, turkey raising, hamburger stand operation, travel tours, and body and fender repairs. One other route used for departure, but very infrequently among the examples of these authors, was that of teaming up with someone whose prior work was aligned with that of the new venture or bringing in such a person as partner.

In the ventures closely linked to prior work, there did not appear to have been much need for search to find the venture idea. Dan Lasater, after learning the hamburger business as a McDonald's employee as described in the pre-ceding chapter, recruited a partner for capital and set up a hamburger stand. Berry Lind worked as a commodities broker and then bought a seat on the commodities exchange to start his own firm, as did Donaldson, Lufkin, and Jenrette in stock brokerage. Ross Perot sold computers and hit upon the idea of selling computer services with a company of his own, as did Sam Wyly. Thus thanks to prior employment it appears that thinking of a venture idea did not require any great imaginative leap, although in fairness to the entrepreneurs it should be noted that many others also working in their lines of business pre-sumably also could have done the same but did not.

Who else could have started the company that turned out to be Wang Laboratories? It began with the invention of magnetic core memories. IBM certainly had many research and engineering projects under way in mid-1948 when An Wang began working on the problem, but it could also have had one on this important topic. Similarly, Eckert and Mauchly at the University of Penn-sylvania were working on the first electronic digital computer, later to become the basis for Univac. It needed memory and could have used this device. The other main site of computer pioneering among U.S. universities was Harvard, and there the impetus to work on the key problem came from the head of the Computation Laboratory, Howard Aiken. As Wang recalls:

◆   "When I walked into the Harvard Computation Laboratory in the spring of 1948, I had no idea that my work there would contribute to the development of computers and start me on the path to founding Wang Laboratories. I had a much more practical concern: I needed a job.... A day or so after I started work, on May 18, 1948, Dr. Aiken gave me a problem to solve on the storage of information in a computer.... When I made my breakthrough, I had no idea of its eventual importance.... My invention [the magnetic core memory] emerged from the clut-ter of this era only years later.

"I tried to think of a way to read the field [of a magnet] by applying only a little current, or by using some other method to read it that wouldn't affect its state, but each solution I came up with proved unworkable for one reason or

[9] Harry Miller, *The Way of Enterprise* (London: Deutsch, 1963).

another. At that point, a few weeks into the project, I felt that I had exhausted all possible solutions to the problem.

"But then one day I was walking through Harvard Yard, an idea came to me in a flash. Like everybody else, I had been so preoccupied with preserving the magnetic flux as it was read that I had lost sight of the objective. I realized in that moment that it did not matter whether or not I destroyed the information while reading it. With the information I gained from reading the magnetic memory, I could simply rewrite the data immediately afterward."[10]

Subsequently, Dr. Wang applied for a patent on the magnetic core memory idea in 1949 and then presented a paper on the topic. This led to industrial inquiries and contacts. The opportunities for commercial work through these contacts, coupled with a Harvard decision to cut back on computer work because it was becoming too commerical, motivated Dr. Wang to quit the laboratory and start his own company in July 1951. His earnings for the last half of 1951 from the startup were 20 percent higher than his salary from Harvard for the first half of that year. From there his company grew at 50 percent per year for the next thirty years.

Why prior jobs are the most common source of venture ideas is not hard to imagine. Those are the activities in which the entrepreneurs have become professional and have developed sufficient competence to compete with other firms. This competition has put them close to the frontier of knowhow of the products and services involved, their shortcomings, and how they are changing. They know who the customers and suppliers are, and how the business is done. They should also have some feel for costs in their particular lines of work, the significance of location, quality control, sources of labor, regulations that may apply, and so forth. An example of one who acquired such expertise and then moved into competition with his former employer was a man who went to work for a company that manufactured pipe threading machines for plumbers:

◆   He was not planning to start his own company when he first signed on as a salesman. "I just wanted to do a good job and get ahead," he recalled. What he was supposed to do was call on distributors of plumbing equipment, demonstrate how the machine would cut and thread pipe, and try to persuade them to stock the machine and sell it to plumbing firms. This sounded simple enough, but when he actually tried to work the machine he found that it was not all that easy to run it properly.

"My first couple of tries made it obvious that I had some learning to do," he said. "I figured that to make anyone want to buy it I ought to become so skilled and smooth at whipping pipe through it that the whole process would look as easy as tying shoes." He took one of the machines home and mounted it beside his garage, bought a load of pipe, cut it into a large number of pieces and started threading. At first it was slow. Pipe would stick in the chuck. Threads would have trouble starting or run too far. The switch was awkward, and it was hard to set the adjustments properly on the machine. But gradually as he practiced hour after hour, his skill increased and he was able to turn out threads with smoothness, ease, and flourish. His efforts at selling the machines also went well.

But another thing he had not counted upon also happened. He began to get ideas for improvement of the machine's design. Intrigued with these new insights, he refined his design ideas as he learned more from his customers about

10 An Wang, *Lessons* (Reading, Mass.: Addison-Wesley, 1986), p. 46.

their preferences. Drawing on these ideas, he designed a new machine with substantially improved appearance and performance. This became the product of his
own company, which ultimately prospered and made him a wealthy man.

This man's particular line of work clearly gave him advantageous knowhow. First were technical details of the *product,* including the kinds of weaknesses it had which allowed entry with a better design. With these he also
became closely acquainted with strengths and weaknesses of *competitive units*
on the market, so he had intimate knowledge of the *state of the art* in such
equipment. Part of this knowledge was an understanding of who *customers*
were, what they wanted, and why they would make the decision to buy a particular unit. Finally, he developed personal *power to sell* such products. By the
time he was ready to launch his own company, he had already developed a
very strong capability to compete in this particular line of work. As part of the
argument for obtaining such specialized experience prior to startup, it can also
be noted he had not become especially equipped to enter any other line of
business.

The nature of the product is also significant. It was one that allowed
significant technical improvements, unlike heating oils or nails, which tend to
be stable commodities. It was one that customers could evaluate for themselves,
unlike paint or tires, which are harder to judge and may therefore be bought
more on establishment of a brand over many years. The product was within
the capacity of one man with modest resources to design, as opposed to an
executive jet or a power generating station, which would require many experts
and much capital.

The combination of characteristics that gave advantages to this job as a
venture idea source is only one of a vast number of combinations, many others
of which can also be effective. A different pattern, for instance, is illustrated by
an example from Murphy.[11]

◆   When George Moore of Washington, D.C., was separated from the air force,
he took a position with Ford Motor Company and was put in an intensive indoctrination course. Part of the cycle was spent with Ford dealers, and in the dealerships Moore saw his opportunity. "For years," he says, "I wanted a business of
my own. What really decided me was the indoctrination course. The dealer's
independence appealed to me."
Moore, then twenty-six and making $12,000 a year, asked friends to assign
him a Lincoln-Mercury dealership, then researched to find the best city among
those available, and finally borrowed money to open in Washington. Moore-Grear
Management Service grew to own three dealerships and manage six others. It
gave George Moore considerable independence. At the time Murphy described,
his net worth was over a half-million dollars.

Unlike the previous entrepreneur with the pipe threading machine, Moore
dealt with a service rather than a product, and he did not create anything new
beyond "another" dealership. But it was his prior job that gave him the idea
and the opportunity, as well as "friends," presumably with the motor company
for which he worked, who could "assign" him a dealership. Finally, his new

---

[11] Thomas P. Murphy, *A Business of Your Own* (New York: McGraw-Hill, 1956), p. 48.

company did not compete with his former employer, as did that of the previous entrepreneur, a difference that can sometimes be very important.

Legal Constraints

When a new venture competes directly with a prior employer, the startup, especially if performed by an engineer or scientist of the prior employer, which the pipe threading machine entrepreneur fortunately was not, can be stickier in a legal sense. Cooper learned this in his study of technical startups and observed:

◆   In my research, the one question that always touched a raw nerve was when I began to ask them how similar they were to the businesses they had just left. I found it very hard to get straight answers.[12]

Obligations and rights between employers and employees concerning ideas emerging from employment are a somewhat muddy area legally. In general, the law says a person has the right to employ skills and knowledge to earn a living, but at the same time an employer has the right to protect property fairly paid for, including information employees may be aware of. It has been held, for instance, that employees cannot keep from their employer information of value to their employer's business and then go start a company to use that information in competition with their employer. Real estate agents, for example, who had learned of a sales opportunity could not keep the information to themselves rather than sharing it with the firm they worked for, start their own firm, and make the deal.

It would not be legal while on an employer's payroll to organize his employees to leave and start another company in competition with that employer. It is all right to plan a new business, but not to "cheat" on an employer to facilitate it. What would constitute cheating is something courts might have to decide in specific cases, but in general it is recognized that responsibilities and loyalty should go both ways between employers and employees. Sharing information with each other is one aspect; use or misuse of a position of advantage is another. Three others that deserve attention concern (1) trade secrets, (2) solicitation of former employers' customers, and (3) inventions and noncompetition agreements.

A trade secret is commonly defined as any formula, pattern, device or compilation of information that is used in one's business and gives him or her an opportunity to obtain an advantage over competitors who do not know or use it. Many qualifications may enter into defining it further; it must be something not generally known, and not easy to figure out or obtain. The employer must indicate its secretness and make efforts to keep it secret, and the violation of it must do some damage to the employer competitively. One precaution an employer (and later perhaps the entrepreneur too) can take is to have employees sign an agreement such as the following:

---

2 Arnold C. Cooper and John L. Komives, *Technical Entrepreneurship, A Symposium* (Milwaukee: Center for Venture Management, 1972), p. 162.

◆ I will regard and preserve as confidential all trade secrets pertaining to the company's business that have been or may be obtained by me by reason of employment. I will not, without written authority from the company to do so, use for my own benefit or purposes, nor disclose to others, either during my employment or thereafter, except as required in the line of my employment with the company, any trade secret or confidential information connected with the business or developments of the company's specifications, drawings, blueprints, reproductions, or other documents or things.

There need not be such a written document for the company to be able to stop a former employee from developing a new business to utilize trade secrets. At the same time, there are many things an employee may learn on the job that can be used for starting a new business. Any general skills learned at the company, for example, can be used for earning a living, and also general knowledge. The salesman mentioned earlier, who came up with a better pipe threader, could not be prevented from doing so by his former employer. In another case, a chemist who worked for a wax company and developed some new products was sued by the wax company to prevent him from selling those products. The suit failed when the court found that

◆ There is nothing in the record to indicate that the formulas in issue were specific projects of great concern and concentration by Buckingham [the wax company]; instead it appears they were merely the result of Greenberg's [the chemist] routine work of changing and modifying formulas derived from competitors. Since there was no experimentation or research, the developments by change and modification were fruits of Greenberg's own skill as a chemist without any appreciable assistance by way of information or great expense or supervision by Buckingham, outside of the normal expenses of his job.[13]

Using customers of a former employer can also be a touchy area. If they are just personal friends, there is no problem. If they approach the former employee's new company and ask to buy from it, there is no problem. And it is legal for the former employee to make a general announcement of having quit the former employer and formed a new company in the same line of business. But if the former employee takes along a list of customers from the former employer, that may be regarded as stealing a trade secret. Or if the former employee goes out and solicits orders from customers of the old employer, using knowledge of those customers that is regarded as proprietary by the former employer, then there can be basis for a suit.

Inventions are another area that can prove troublesome for entrepreneurs and it is fairly common for employers to require an agreement such as the following:

◆ The employee agrees to disclose promptly to the employer in accordance with his or her employer's procedures all inventions conceived by employee, whether solely or with others, during employee's employment by employer, whether or not during regular working hours, which relate to any subject matter with which employee's work with employer is or may be concerned or which relate to business carried on by employer.

---

[13] Wexler et al., trading as Buckingham Wax Company, v. Greenberg et al., Pennsylvania Supreme Court, 1960, U.S. Patent Quarterly, Vol. 125, p. 471.

All sorts of variations of such a contract are possible, and it is therefore important to read with care the one being signed. For instance, some cover only inventions related to the business of the employer, whereas others may seek to cover any inventions at all. If there is no such written agreement, then both the employer and the employee have in effect royalty-free licenses to use whatever is invented. If there is such a written agreement, then the employer has the upper hand, though it is still not unusual, as will be illustrated shortly, for employers to grant rights of use to employees, particularly with regard to uses that the employer is not interested in exploiting, possibly because they lie outside the corporate strategic focus. If, in addition to having such an agreement, the employer is able to obtain a patent, trademark, or copyright on the product or service, then clearly the employer's hand is still stronger in determining what the employee might be able to do with it in developing a new business.

Another type of agreement that can be important in seeking to develop a new business around a job-inspired idea is the noncompetitive agreement. Under such an agreement the employee agrees in return for something, such as a job, not to leave and enter competition with his or her former company, possibly in certain carefully defined lines of work, within a certain geographic radius, and for a specified length of time. One way to learn a business, for instance, is to become a franchisee. The franchise firm as part of the deal will often train the franchisee in its way of doing business, which will presumably be a fairly well-proven formula for nonfailure, if not success. Another part of the deal, however, may be a noncompetitive agreement to prevent the franchisee from learning the system from the franchisor and then using that knowhow to go off and start a competitive business.

Thus a number of legal pitfalls can be associated with starting a new company around an employment-inspired idea. The fact that these pitfalls are real is attested to by the number of lawsuits against new companies which are brought by former employers of their founders. These suits may end up with the entrepreneurs being effectively prevented from continuing in business if the disputed product or service is key to their venture's survival and the court enjoins them from offering it to the market. If the former employer is able to prove injury, they may even be compelled to make restitution. More often, however, the decree will simply be that the new firm must pay some kind of royalty on business done. Combined with legal expenses of the contest, this may kill the new business.

Most employment-inspired new ventures do not encounter such legal difficulties. They proceed on a tack not in competition with the former employer. Or they may represent too small a competitive threat for the employer to spend legal service money squabbling about. Even if they do represent such a competitive threat, they are legally safe if (1) the product or service ideas taken from the former employer were not patented, and (2) how to make the product or service can be determined from examination of it in its finished form by anyone reasonably skilled in that sort of manufacture (i.e., it is not a trade secret), and (3) the employee did not sign a noncompetitive agreement. Finally, the entrepreneur may be able to ensure safety by obtaining permission to proceed with a new firm around the product or service from the former employer. A variety of such factors were explored by one new firm, which finally succeeded, as follows:

♦   An electronics engineer working in a small electromechanical controls company became interested in developing a special-purpose limit switch for which a customer of the company had expressed desire. As required by his invention agreement with the company, he disclosed the customer's desire and a proposed design he had developed, but the company declined to have him work on it further.

He quit to pursue the work on his own, and a month later as the result of a chance meeting at a dinner party went into partnership with a second electronics engineer, who had been laid off at another company. With customer orders in hand from the outset, the two men engaged a patent attorney to tie up rights on the device, and they and their two wives worked at assembly in the recreation rooms of their homes. A month after shaking hands on the partnership, the men hired another lawyer to begin the process of incorporation, and a CPA firm to set up books. Since financing was entirely from their modest personal savings, the expenses of these professional services were felt heavily, but in retrospect they agreed no money they ever spent had been better justified.

It soon developed that the former employer of the first entrepreneur had misgivings about their obtaining a patent on the product that had been originally conceived on his payroll, and a lawsuit was threatened. The patent attorney for the new company recommended that rather than attempt to obtain a patent with the search information he had gathered, they should instead build an argument that the device was not such that it could be patented. The former employer acquiesced to this argument. The entrepreneurs proceeded to design and encapsulate the device in such a way that for someone else to disassemble the switch it had to be practically demolished, hence virtually impossible to study and copy. With that protection the company proceeded and prospered.

It should be apparent from this brief discussion that legal aspects of employer-employee responsibilities regarding product and service ideas can be very intricate. The moral underscored by the last example is that a competent lawyer should be asked for advice on any of these matters that may apply to a particular entrepreneurial venture.

OBTAINING RIGHTS

Acquisition of rights to produce and sell a product or service developed by others is a feasible way of obtaining a new venture idea. At least four sources of such rights are the entrepreneur's prior employer, other companies or organizations, independent inventors, and the government. Instances in which prior employers have allowed entrepreneurs to "make off" with product rights occur typically when the employer develops something that it does not want to put on the market, possibly because the employer is big and the market is small, or because the employer wants to concentrate its resources in one market area and the development applies to a different market area. Obviously, another time when companies choose to make rights available is when they are not willing to bet that the development truly has a market at all.

If the employer is a nonprofit organization, it may allow acquisition of rights as part of a strategy of deliberately not going into commercial business. A success story of this variety was the following:

◆ William Moog, Jr., after studying engineering and working on technical projects during World War II, took a job in late 1946 at Cornell Aeronautical Laboratory, where he invented a servo valve that the lab patented. There was at the time no commercial interest in this product, and none arose until 1950, when Bendix ordered four units. Moog was given a leave of absence from the laboratory to fill the order. The components were made by a job machine shop, after which Moog assembled them in his basement and tested them at the laboratory. While he was doing so, an order came from a Philco subcontractor for seventy-five more units. Obtaining from the laboratory a royalty-free license, Moog incorporated in July 1951 with $3,000 of capital. To raise more capital he brought in other members of his management team who had capital to contribute. Breakeven occurred the first year, which showed a profit of over 5 percent on sales of $196,000 as the company's fortunes rose on the tide of a growing aerospace industry.

Although other success stories in which the idea for a new venture was taken under license from a former employer can be found, they are much more rare than those based on ideas found from other sources mentioned in this chapter. It is also possible to find a comparable if not greater number of startups that failed after obtaining their ideas in this manner. Why this is so is a subject that has never been studied, but it seems plausible that a combination of factors including the following may account for it:

1 The employee was involved with development of the idea and became enamored of it beyond justification.
2 The employee was a researcher or design engineer unfamiliar with selling and tended to make unrealistic assumptions about what the customer's point of view would be.
3 The employee was overly eager to leave the employer and enter independent business.
4 The employer chose to let the idea go because it was not worth commercialization.

At the same time, it is easy to find success stories such as those mentioned earlier in which the employee took an idea without any rights deal and developed it into a new venture. As will be further discussed later, there are many examples in which an idea was successfully transferred from one company or geographical area to another after it had demonstrated its commercial effectiveness. But effective startups using *licensed ideas* for the first time in commerce are rare.

Even more rare are startups in which the rights were obtained from sources other than the former employer. This is not to say that not much licensing goes on. Many companies—a leading example being General Electric—have whole departments devoted to selling licenses, and there is a national organization called the Licensing Executives Society, which publishes a substantial periodical, attesting to the high level of activity in this way of doing business.

It is not hard to find examples of products manufactured under license. A familiar example, for instance, is the Wankel engine in automobiles and other applications. But it seldom occurs that new companies are started around licenses, perhaps because there are simply too many disparate pieces of circumstance that have to fit together to bring it about. The entrepreneur must simultaneously know about a customer's need and find the product or service to fit in the possession of some company, individual, or government agency. At the same time, the possessor either must not be aware of that need or must not be interested in exploiting it. And the possessor must be convinced that the entrepreneur, who by definition of the startup process does not yet have a company, is in a good or better position to make the most of that product or service, to do a better job with it, and thereby to create more royalties for the licensor than any established company that might be interested in exploiting it under license.

Even established companies can find it difficult to prosper as licensees. Morrison estimates that losers outnumber winners in licensing deals by fifty to one, and observes:

◆　　There are literally thousands of products, processes and special equipment described by the developers as "99 percent ready" to go into profitable production and sale, but somehow that remaining 1 percent never gets done. I have viewed some of these; and when I observed them again a year later, no further progress had been made. Moreover, the estimate of "99 percent ready" had frequently been revised to 90 percent or even 50 percent.[14]

Thus in summary of licensing as a way of obtaining venture startup ideas, it appears that if the license is obtained from a former employer by the employee who worked on the product or process, the odds of the venture's succeeding may be fair. But the odds of the entrepreneur's finding a good startup license at some other company, from an independent inventor, or from a government agency are very slim at best. The way this latter is most likely to work out is if the entrepreneur first independently discovers the startup idea, and then happens to learn that some other person or organization has already laid claim on it and goes to them for a license.

Teaming with Inventors

Notwithstanding the unencouraging record of licensing as a source of startup ideas, a somewhat similar approach has yielded many successful companies. This is when the entrepreneur joins forces with an inventor and together the two share in the startup. In the two such examples that follow, two common characteristics at least are of note. One is that in each case the inventor had clearly demonstrated the existence of a need for the invention before the entrepreneur (or coentrepreneur) picked it up. They were not situations in which the inventor simply came up with something, hoped that there might be a need, and recruited the entrepreneur to work at fulfilling that hope. (Like one inventor who designed a new recreational game and offered a rights agreement to some business school students, who then went out trying to sell it and shortly failed.) Second, there was an effective complement of contribution between the inventor and his coentrepreneur.

◆　　A prominent surgeon in 1940 became injured in the hand by X-rays and had to have it amputated. He bought an artificial arm but found it very unsatisfactory

---

[14] Robert S. Morrison, *Handbook for Manufacturing Entrepreneurs* (Cleveland: Western Reserve Press, 1973), p. 38.

for holding implements such as eating utensils, pencils, and other hand-held items. He discussed the problem with his investment adviser, a man who, as it turned out, had been trained as an engineer and was currently doing some consulting work for a small machine company. The counselor outlined to the machine company a design that would use a chuck to hold different types of implements and asked them to build one. A feature of the design was that rather than using a carved wooden shell for fitting to the stump of the arm, it had a combination of metal and leather straps which made it cheaper, lighter, and easier to fit.

The surgeon was delighted and proceeded to display the new arm among colleagues and friends. He proposed that a company should be formed to develop the design further and make it available to others. Because of his age (eighty) and his handicap, he asked the counselor to organize the company. The counselor was reluctant and suggested instead that perhaps other companies would take it on. But the surgeon wanted the new company formed and agreed to advance the $20,000 that the counselor estimated would be needed to do so. A few machine tools were purchased, a machinist was hired, and development work began in the counselor's garage.

Meanwhile, through mutual friends of the surgeon, the Secretary of War had heard about the new arm, and ordered the Surgeon General to contact the counselor and inquire about obtaining limbs for wounded servicemen. Consumption of development funds was beginning to threaten continued work on the design when a $50,000 order arrived from the U.S. Army, and the A. J. Hosmer (after the surgeon) Corporation, which soon became the nation's leading limb maker, was in business.

An interesting aspect of this example is that neither the surgeon nor the counselor had previous experience in the artificial limb business. There were hundreds of limb shops throughout the world making their products as they traditionally had. There was no reason why those shops could not have introduced the same product improvements, but they did not, and the newcomers did without benefit of any special knowledge. The surgeon expressed the need, and the counselor took the initiative to fill it by reasoning freshly directly from the problem and then taking action to implement the solution he had thought out. After that, market forces came to bear and moved the venture ahead.

The next example followed a somewhat different interplay of initiative between the person who first became aware of the need, a salesman, and the person he sought out to help satisfy it, a technical specialist.

◆   A machine job shop in southern California employed a salesman in the late-1950s to solicit fabrication subcontracts from large aerospace firms. One of these firms asked if the shop could shape tungsten, a very expensive and difficult-to-work metal having desirable properties for use in rocket nozzles. Finding that nobody in the company or the local trade knew how to machine the metal, he contacted the eastern company that supplied the raw stock. He learned that a metallurgist working for that company had been experimenting with machining methods and had developed some effective techniques.

The salesman requested assistance from the metallurgist, who traveled to the West Coast to work on the nozzle-forming problem. Finding that the metal could be shaped into suitable nozzles and seeing that additional orders could be obtained for such work, the salesman then persuaded the metallurgist to join him in forming a company and also persuaded the owners of the machine shop to help with financing for the new venture.

Because the capabilities of this new company were at the outset unique, it was able to earn substantial profits on its work. There were some management disagreements with the machine shop investors, who felt that the salesman was not sufficiently conservative in taking on difficult jobs for the new firm. Before long, enough had been earned for the salesman and the metallurgist to buy out their interest. The two then obtained additional capital through a public (Regulation A) offering of stock.

Eventually, competitors entered the field and reduced the profit margins, and the company was sold out to a larger firm, but not before the two founders had made healthy profits for themselves.

A common factor to these episodes was that the entrepreneurs who became involved in them were out "circulating" when they encountered needs that formed the basis for startup. Clearly there were also other people who were aware of those needs, but these two men took the additional initiative to work out solutions for them. Three ingredients can be identified as important here: (1) actively circulating so that needs can be encountered, (2) alertness to recognize those needs when they present themselves, and (3) initiative to develop solutions. Possibly another factor is judgment in selection of needs to work on which have a venture potential, but it is hard to surmise the extent to which selection here took place. The extent to which other needs might have been ignored, rejected, or passed up for the sake of working on these because they appeared to have greater venture potential is not known.

SELF-EMPLOYMENT AS IDEA SOURCES

New product ideas may sometimes arise out of independent employment. Provided the entrepreneur was not doing his or her work for clients who can lay claim to the new product, there should be no danger of "piracy" charges, and the entrepreneur may be able to develop a new manufacturing venture alongside other free-lance activity without dropping his or her former means of support until it is no longer needed. That way, if the new venture happens not to work out, the entrepreneur can drop it without having lost so much. In the following example the venture succeeded:

◆   In 1948 Elmer Winter and Aaron Scheinfeld, independently employed attorneys, needed to have a brief typed in time for an appellate court deadline, but they could find no temporary typists. This experience gave them the idea of a company that would hire typists on its own payroll and farm them out as needed for a fee. In August 1948 they formed Manpower, Inc., to perform that function. Initially only a sideline, the business grew so profitable by 1955 they had dropped law practice entirely. In 1956 revenues of Manpower were $8.5 million with profits of 10 percent net before taxes, coming from ninety-one United States and ten foreign offices, two-thirds of them operating on franchises. (Franchise fee was $750–$1,500 plus 6 percent of sales.) Manpower was eventually absorbed by another subsidiary, and sales in 1987 were over $1.2 billion.

Like the two inventor-teaming examples earlier, this one began with encounter and recognition of a need followed by initiative in satisfying it and extending the solution to a broader market. It appears to have been another opportunity of which many people could have become aware and satisfied, one that did not require any high-powered expertise or heavy investment in assets. The entrepreneurs did not encounter the opportunity as part of any searching strategy. Presumably, they entered the law business expecting that would be permanent, and this venture represented simply a better opportunity that came their way and which they were astute enough to exploit very effectively.

This tendency of opportunities to be revealed through other activities was discussed earlier in terms of "side-street effects," which can produce sequential ventures. For instance, Edwin Land's first product was not intended to be the Polaroid camera or sunglasses but rather polarized auto windshields and headlights that would reduce the glare of oncoming cars, an idea whose time has still not come at this writing. But activity in this line of venturing led to the other products that made Land an enormously successful entrepreneur.

The following entrepreneur drew venture ideas first from his employment and then from two other ventures in turn even as they failed:

◆   For William Millard, high school was followed by jobs in ditch digging and copper mining and then three semesters of college. At age twenty-one he joined the Pacific Finance Company as a bill collector and advanced through several positions to become its youngest branch manager at age twenty-four. Two years later, in 1958, the company began to computerize, and he took the opportunity to become a trainee and eventually became a programmer and a systems manager in data processing. Then he was told he could advance no further in the company without a college degree.

He answered a want ad for director of data processing for Alameda County in northern California and got the job. "I was," he recalls, "a department head. I was able to meet with the chief of police, the sheriff, the heads of hospitals, the tax assessor, the whole thing. I got to play, 'How could computers help the hospitals? How can computers help the police, the tax assessors, the country controller?' I mean, hey, I was in my glory."

Next he worked at IBM for one year and then for the city of San Francisco for three years, again in data processing. In 1969 he quit to start a company "to sell system software right down the throat of IBM," he recalled. "Not smart. Really not smart. . . . we mortgaged our home, found some investment bankers, bet everything we had, and started this company. In May of 1972 we had to close it down.

"I learned there was a giant missing piece. I knew computers. I knew software. I knew the communications protocol and the stuff needed to make the terminals work. And I had directed many, many people—managed projects always—to completion and success. So I thought I had everything needed to go out and start a company and be its president and be a businessman. And the truth is I didn't. I was a manager, and I confused businessman with manager. I had giant gaps as a business person. I had never actually wrestled with a balance sheet. Never with a P&L statement."

Deeply in debt and jobless, he found that "no one is looking for a president that just closed its doors. You're an entrepreneur now." However, he did manage to bid on a contract with Los Angeles County for the design of an information retrieval system, form a new company, and win that contract and then others. It frustrated him to find that in consulting he was continually working his way out of business, and this prompted him to look for something proprietary and repeatable.

A job to develop a computerized accounting system for a General Motors dealer seemed to offer such promise. "Do you see what I'm saying?" he asked. "If we got it done, we had a product we could sell anywhere."

Seeking a solution, he and his engineer began looking at the new Intel 8080 microprocessor chip. This was the heart of the first microcomputer kit, the Altair, being sold by MITS, a company in Albuquerque. Millard bought two Altairs and reworked them for the General Motors job. Then he decided to start offering his version of the machine, which he called the IMSAI 8080.

To sell it, he placed a one-inch advertisement in *Popular Electronics,* the same magazine that had written up the Altair. He, his wife, and their three employees were amazed when he received a deluge of replies, 3,500 letters, some of which included orders for the machine and checks. "It was the first time we felt like we had a business," he recalled. "We had the opportunity to perform. The company sold 13,000 computers between 1975 and 1978, then failed." Product quality, customer support, and insufficient financial resources (Millard had refused to part with any equity to raise cash) were all blamed.

But in late 1976, well before the failure, Millard had started another offshoot. He had opened a retail microcomputer store, ComputerLand, under another president, and it was working. He began selling franchises in early 1977, and by 1984 his solely owned franchise company was earning about $30 million per year, giving William Millard an estimated net worth of around $1 billion.[15]

The ability to spot side-street opportunities and initiative to act on them can be enormously important, not only for discovering new ventures but also for keeping existing businesses in operation and successful as circumstances change. Thus one man in Pueblo, Colorado, watched his independent feed store fail as larger companies opened local branches that took away his customers. Meanwhile, in Edmonton, Alberta, another man shifted his retail hardware store that was faced with similar threats, first into wholesale hardware distribution and then into equipment financing and leasing. The result was continued growth as the hardware-retailing end of the business shrank and ultimately phased out.

Although the inspired discovery is probably more sought after by inventors and would-be entrepreneurs, the discovery of a need is probably a more reliable source. Studies of innovations have tended to find that innovations created in response to market needs usually fare better than those generated by "technology push" or simply advances in technical capability. There have been many exceptions in some high technologies such as electronics, however.

It is important to note that simply satisfying a need may not be enough. The need must also apply to a sufficiently large market. Innumerable clever devices are generated to solve "one of a kind" problems that do not lead to large markets or new business opportunities. The typical custom machine shop, for instance, continually solves problems for customers without ever generating proprietary products. Some of them do encounter proprietary opportunities, however, and being in business with resultant contact with customers and problems of the marketplace can be one way for a would-be entrepreneur to become exposed to many more startup opportunities than would a person shut up in the offices of a large corporation or government agency. Hence becoming self-employed in almost any form can be a reasonable way of seeking new venture ideas.

The self-employment from which the idea emerges can even be the startup

---

[15] Robert Levering, Michael Katz, and Milton Moskowitz, *The Computer Entrepreneurs* (New York: New American Library, 1984), p. 341.

itself, as perhaps illustrated best by AST research, which became a highly successful microcomputer company:

◆   The company's name came from the first-name initials of its founders, Albert C. H. Wong, Safi U. Qureshi, and Thomas K. C. Yuen, who recalled, "We wanted to manufacture a product, but we didn't know what, other than it would be microcomputer related."[16] Pooling $5,000 of their savings in 1980, the three engineers began by seeking consulting work and landed a job designing a local-area computer network for a firm that later scrapped it. When the IBM personal computer came out in mid-1981, they designed a memory expansion board for it. This turned out to be the first third-party product for the machine. The following year sales passed $1 million, and in the year after that $25 million.

VENTURE IDEAS FROM HOBBIES

To some extent there tends to be a built-in conflict between hobbies and successful venturing, in that hobbies are things that people are willing to do at their own expense,[17] which puts a strong downward pressure on profits. Margins are consequently often low in such things as model making, small-scale farming, small-plane charter flying, antique car restoration, and various types of racing. Nevertheless, profitable venture ideas sometimes emerge. One example seen in the preceding chapter was the retired construction man who invented a better bottle cutter from his hobby. Another was the medical equipment maker who built himself a pair of fiberglass skis so that he could use them himself, and then found that they fit a "hole" in the market. A third was the following young man:

◆   Bill Nicolai dropped out of college three weeks before graduating and hitch-hiked to Yosemite to mountain climb. For several years he worked sporadically, supplementing his income with food stamps while traveling to other ranges climbing other mountains. Then one night high in the mountains, an icy wind blew his tent apart, bringing death from exposure too close for comfort and setting Nicolai thinking about alternative tent designs to prevent such failure. He conceived a tube of fabric held open by circular metal hoops, borrowed a sewing machine, and created a new tent. It worked, and now he began to imagine an enterprise to fabricate and sell a product he would call the "Omnipotent."
          After sewing up more units he rented a booth at Seattle's annual Street Fair and put them on display. "I don't think we actually sold any at the Fair," he recalled, "but we did sell a few a short while later after people had had a chance to look over the flyer we distributed." Sales began to drift in and Nicolai moved from the friend's basement, where he began, to a store where he manufactured in the back. After two years he was employing four friends and sales were running at $60,000 per year. "It wasn't much of a living," he said, "but we were surviving and enjoying the work."

---

[16] Ann Lallande, "No Time to Write a Business Plan," _Venture,_ July 1983, p. 70.
[17] The idea of trying to profit from hobbies is not uncommon. See, for example, Scott Witt, _Second Income Money Makers_ (Englewood Cliffs, N.J.: Prentice-Hall, 1975); and Herbert and Lyn Taetzsch, _How to Start Your Own Craft Business_ (New York: Watson-Guptil, 1974).

At this point we might note where the business idea came from and where it led. Nicolai brought substantial experience to bear in conceiving his product and enterprise; not work experience, as did the entrepreneurs described earlier, but rather hobby experience. In a sense, his hobby had been like a job insofar as it had been a relatively full-time commitment over a period of years. It had given him knowledge of the available technology and of the market. The tent collapse and brush with death revealed a need. Pursuit of solutions to this need led to discovery of a product. Coupled with this product discovery the need to make a living triggered the idea of a business, which fairly straightforward actions then brought into being.

Although Nicolai's new enterprise was not very successful financially at this point, it had the most important virtues of being in operation and at least being marginally profitable. Simply achieving such a position in itself usually leads to more ideas and opportunities—as we shall see in the next chapter it did in Nicolai's case. Thus a hobby can lead to a startup concept, and execution of that startup concept can lead to other concepts for expansion of the business.

Other ventures will be seen later which, like these mentioned above, came from hobby-inspired ideas. Such ventures tend to be restricted to products whose prototypes can easily be financed and constructed by one person. (Though not always. One man's hobby venture was a railroad.) Many of them are products within some sort of recreational market, sporting goods or luxury items. Their development often involves a considerable amount of one-man tinkering, followed by sales starting with a very limited market such as through local stores or by mail order. Most of them are not initially conceived with the aim of starting a company but are rather for personal use of the inventor, who finds that others would like copies, and it turns out that a venture is a good way to provide them.

This last characteristic is a particularly important one, because it indicates how hobby-inspired ventures often manage to circumvent a pitfall of many new companies. It has often been observed that a cause of failures among many new companies is a kind of egocentrism. The entrepreneur conceives the company to provide something *he* or *she* would like to have, taking it for granted that many others would like the same thing and can therefore be expected to buy from the new company. Then it turns out that the desire was not widespread at all, and zero sales result. These hobbyist-entrepreneurs started out with a self-centered focus but then did not assume sales would follow, because they were not planning to have sales. It was only after the demand became evident that they developed ventures around the concepts.

That is not necessarily to say that would-be entrepreneurs should not try to parlay hobby ideas into ventures, or even try to choose hobbies likely to lead to commercializable ideas. But it is probably advisable to make a check on market demand before pushing ahead from the idea to the venture. Since hobby ideas typically are relatively easy to prototype, make two or three and take them around to stores. See how retailers and distributors react. Try a limited mail-order advertisement. Let some friends try the product or service on a small scale. Such limited market tests should be relatively easy to conduct and may be worth vastly more than they cost. The nice thing about hobby-inspired ventures is that if they do not work out as ventures, presumably, the hobbies are worth the endeavor for their own sake.

VENTURE IDEAS
FROM SOCIAL ENCOUNTERS

Connections, as discussed in the chapter on paths to startup, usually play a highly important part in the creation of a new company. Sometimes their function is to trigger the venture idea. Connections valuable in startup most often grow out of work relationships, but they can also come about socially. Murphy describes how one social conversation led to a new venture:[18]

♦   Bernard Berkeley is an easy-going New Yorker who prefers hard work—for half the year. "You can't pick me as an ambitious guy," he says. "I do what I have to do and still have six months to do what I want to do." It was during the "what I want to do" half of the year, when the Berkeley family was living in Miami, that Berkeley began conversing with his Florida neighbor. Since Berkeley had sold his successful radio repair business before moving down that winter, the conversation was about the neighbor's business. "I was left out of the conversation," says Berkeley a little defensively. "I wasn't in business so I had to listen."

It developed that the neighbor owned a series of rides on Coney Island. The more Berkeley listened, the more he though this might be the next business for him. He had bought a parcel of land, one of the few big ones left in Queens, before leaving the city, and it just might be ideal as an amusement park. When spring came, Berkeley returned to New York, and his first trip was to Coney Island. The friend he had met in Florida said, "Go over to 8th Street and talk to the ride manufacturers." Before going home Berkeley bought a kiddie merry-go-round, a fire-engine ride, a pony ride, a whip ride, and a sailboat ride. His Fairyland was the first kiddie amusement park in the City of New York and the prototype of many that followed.

In this example another key element may have been the fact that Berkeley already had enough money to walk into a manufacturer and buy a merry-go-round on the spot.

As a final illustration of the role that social contacts can play both in triggering venture ideas and in pursuing them, there is the story of Keith Barish, who dropped out of college to start a bank and shortly afterward became a millionaire.[19] In a 1969 radio interview he recalled that he had gone to Miami at age eighteen to work in politics for the right of eighteen-year-olds to vote. In a conversation with one of the state representatives he recalled being asked, "It's fine to go into politics, but what are you going to do for a living?" The sequence that follows, as he recalled it, was:

♦   And then I said, "What can I do?" And at that point there were a number of banks that had been chartered in Dade County and I thought, "That's a good business to start out in." So I decided I was going to start a bank and I went to some businessmen friends I'd known from politics, and organized a group, and applied for a charter in Hialeah. We got it, and I was in business.

Here there was a slight difference, in that the social contact did not directly suggest the particular venture idea, but rather simply the chain of thought that

---

[18] Murphy, *A Business of Your Own*, p. 49.
[19] Goodrich, *Horatio Alger Is Alive and Well*, p. 83.

led to it. Unanswered is the question of whether Barish would have thought of the same idea had he not been asked the question about what he was going to "do for a living" at that particular time. The idea might have still occurred from other sources, even "out of the blue."

PEDESTRIAN OBSERVATIONS

Occasionally, the inspiration for a successful new product or service will come simply from direct observation of a need in daily living, as the following examples indicate:

• The idea for "Q-Tips" hit Leo Gerstenzang when he noticed his wife's efforts to wrap cotton on toothpicks to clean their baby daughter's ears.
• The idea for cellophane soda straws hit Otto Diefenbach, owner of a small Baltimore machine shop, when he unwrapped a pack of cigarettes, idly twisted the wrapper around a steel rod, and noticed that it came away in the form of a tube.
• The idea for the safety razor hit King C. Gillette when he started to shave and found his razor dull. Ever since a conversation with the inventor of pop bottle caps, he had been looking for a product that people would throw away and reorder.
• The idea to build an outboard motor hit Ole Evinrude when ice cream melted in a boat he was rowing to a picnic on an island in Wisconsin one warm August day.
• The idea to form Diners Club hit Frank McNamara one night when he was entertaining friends at a New York restaurant and found he had lost his wallet.
• The idea for the automatic toaster hit Charles Strite when he got mad at the burnt toast in the plant lunchroom of the factory where he worked as a mechanic.

Often such needs could be contemplated and solved by many other people besides those who actually did it. But someone will always be first to act, and often a new business will be the result. The first step in this action is generally to recognize the need, and the second is to work out a solution. In the following case the need was presented in the form of a request.

♦   Lewis Salton's wife asked him to give her something to keep food hot at the table. As an engineer working for Radio Corporation of America the approach for solving this problem that occurred to him was an electrically heated tray that would hold serving dishes. He worked on the problem in his spare time and produced a device that satisfied his wife's need and also gave the basis for starting a manufacturing company. Sales of the company in 1978, thirty years after founding, were $10 million per year.

Expression of the need does not always come from someone else. The first one to see the need in the above case was Mrs. Salton, and had she had the inclination and knowhow, possibly she might have undertaken to develop the product herself instead of asking someone else for it. That pattern occurred in the following episode:

♦   L. L. Bean was orphaned at twelve, lived with neighbors, and later worked in his older brother's Freeport, Maine, store. Discomforted by wet, sore feet from a hunting trip in 1914, he decided that a useful piece of clothing would be a waterproof, chafe-resistant boot with a rubber bottom and leather top. The "experts," local shoemakers, said such a boot could not be made, so Bean cut tops from a pair of boots and sewed them to some rubbers. These worked well enough that his friends began asking for some, and this inspired Bean to print advertisements, which he mailed "to every man's name I could get hold of." This was the beginning of a successful mail-order business, which grew to sales in 1987 of $304 million.

Still another way of finding a need, as opposed to having a personal problem, as did L. L. Bean, or having someone else state the need, as did Lewis Salton, is simply to observe a need on the part of another person, possibly one he or she is not even aware of, or an opportunity in the form of a way to do something better. This sort of pattern appeared in the following case:

♦   In 1947 Louis J. Korter was a retail jeweler in Portland, Oregon, who got the idea of making aluminum shingles from watching a man covering a cedar-shingle roof with aluminum paint. Having earlier gained some knowledge of sheet metal forming as a young man, he created an aluminum shingle with interlocking edges in his basement and applied for a patent. The "experts" to whom he showed his new product did not show much interest in it, but his neighbor was sufficiently impressed to mortgage his house and borrow on his life insurance. The neighbor thus contributed $22,000 capital for one-third of the business while the remainder was held by Korter. Sales were virtually nil until in the second year of business use of the shingles on a model home began to draw orders. Annual sales in 1949 rose to $300,000, then $500,000 in 1950. By 1954 the company was grossing $3 million and netting 15 percent profit.

Again, as with the ideas that sprang from social encounters, it was necessary that the entrepreneurs first be alert to needs and then take initiative for doing something about them. They also had to be selective in choosing these particular needs for attention, rather than, for instance, going to work on hopeless causes. One way a would-be entrepreneur can operate is simply to keep waiting and watching for such needs. Another is to go actively looking for them.

DELIBERATE SEARCH

It would seem to be a straightforward conclusion that the appropriate course of action for a person who wanted to start a company would be simply to start looking for a venture idea and that the most logical way to do so would be to apply some sort of methodical approach in the search. In fact, most entrepreneurs do not find their ideas in this way, as can be seen from nearly all the examples considered in the preceding pages. Rather, most entrepreneurs encounter their ideas, sometimes without even recognizing them at the time, from more or less random events of work or everyday life.

There are no scientific studies demonstrating how deliberate searching can raise the odds of finding good venture ideas, but searchers do find them, as some examples to follow will illustrate. Coincidence and surprise still often enter in, but it can be seen that searching sometimes helps.

One author has defined the methodical search approach as being to "deliberately make contact with all the potential sources" of the kind of idea being sought, and illustrated application of this approach with the following example:

♦   "One experienced executive starting a new company asked all his business acquaintances to inform him of interesting new ideas. He also called up patent attorneys, inventors, industrial research departments, corporation lawyers, investment bankers, and venture capital firms. For three months, he devoted one day a week to a methodical search. The executive then selected a new-type automotive part which became the basis of a successful new firm. His reputation for being receptive to new ideas soon resulted in broadening the line with several additional meritorious new products."[20]

Presumably, this executive also conducted his affairs in such a way that those whom he contacted felt that there was good reason for them to make an effort to be helpful. The indication that people kept on passing ideas to him after his venture was going seems to suggest that he saw to it that there had been "something in it" for those who helped him.

Another person who applied this strategy was the engineer mentioned in the preceding chapter as an example of starting with corrections. He made it a practice to contact each day at least one person who might be able to help find a venture until he located a product developed at a university and obtained a license to manufacture it. Reflecting on how he came to adopt that searching strategy and what he learned in applying it, he commented:

♦   I tried looking at all sorts of possible sources, magazines, literature and the like, but it was no good. They could not answer questions and they were always obsolete. Talking to people was the answer, and in particular I learned that the best ones to talk to are often the marketing people, because they know what will sell and what will not. The best way to do it is first to pick an industry you want to work on, then start at the bottom. Talk to lower level marketing people and customers to learn the basics, then work your way up to the managers. The managers are the ones who are likely to have more opportunities than they can handle, but before you approach them it's important to be able to talk their language in the business so they will take you seriously. So you play work-up, learning as you go. This way you can reach a point where you can call the president and say, "I was just talking to your sales manager the other day, and I have some more questions. Will you join me for lunch?" Now you have somebody who really knows the business and can help you find the best opportunities.

A different view about whom best to contact was adopted by another entrepreneur who decided to make the rounds of purchasing agents, whom he asked about what things they found hard to obtain. This way he identified a particular product, the electronic delay line, and was able to form a company

---

[20] Cyril C. Hermann, "Ideas for New Business Firms," *Monthly Review* (Federal Reserve Bank of Boston, July 1953).

that produced it and made him wealthy. Still another type of contact of proven effectiveness is the plastic factory operator. E. Joseph Cossman said he made it a practice to write the plastic factories in his area at least twice a year to inquire whether they had any tooling they would like to sell. In this way he had found products that others had developed but had been unable to sell and which he could consequently acquire cheaply and sell with fresh approaches of his own. Trade shows are also cited by Cossman and others as particularly likely places at which to encounter people who know the market—both sellers and buyers—while at the same time receiving stimulation for ideas from seeing the new products of other companies on display.

Simply the act of searching persistently itself can help trigger ideas, because the mind is then more likely to take note of opportunities when it encounters them. Studies of creativity have consistently found that discoveries often occur at unexpected moments, *but only after* a person has applied sustained and often discouraging effort at trying consciously to work a problem out. In the following case a lawyer named Wendell Cherry had applied considerable effort to trying to find a profitable enterprise, including an unsuccessful startup, a coffee house. His search continued beyond this failure, however, until one day another idea cropped up as described in Armour:

♦   "One day Wendell (Cherry) and David Jones were playing golf, and talking about how to make money, when David mentioned that a friend of his, Bryan McCoy, had started a nursing home near Big Spring Country Club and was doing all right. This stuck in Wendell's mind because a few months earlier he had helped a client form a corporation to start a nursing-home business. The venture had never gotten off the ground, but during the effort Wendell had seen a promotion film stressing the need for better, more modern nursing homes. He and David decided to study the matter, and David went to look at McCoy's place."[21]

After further study the two men recruited other partners for architectural help, real estate, construction services, and so forth and entered the business. The beginning was modest, but the industry boomed and they went with it, Cherry accumulating over $5 million from it within a decade. As it turned out, the idea succeeded probably far beyond what he originally envisaged, so luck as well as effort were important. But without the deliberate search on Cherry's part, it might not have occurred at all.

The next entrepreneur was also searching, but not for what he found. His strategy was to find a going concern he could acquire, but he ended up starting a new company instead:

♦   He had been involved in modest ventures as a youth, taking opportunities as they came, then had managed through high performance on a test, and in spite of his somewhat lackluster performance in college, to land a job with a major computer company. Highly successful in setting sales records, he moved rapidly up the promotion ladder, finally reaching a point in the summer of 1973 where the next advancement would require leaving the West Coast location he loved and moving to the company headquarters back east. A better alternative, he thought, would be to pursue a company of his own.

[21] Lawrence A. Armour, *The Young Millionnaires* (New York: Playboy Press, 1973), p. 94.

But here he felt frustrated. The most likely type of company to start, he thought, would be one to distribute minicomputers. But there were two major drawbacks. It tended to take from four to six months to get such a product sold, which would require more sustaining capital than he thought he could raise, and he was also afraid there would not be enough repeat business, since each sale would satisfy the needs of the customer to whom it was made.

So he decided to seek an acquisition instead. He figured that he would be able to scout out plenty of prospects from his experience in sales. To get help in screening prospects he offered a two percent ownership in his future company to the financial vice-president of another company whose judgment he respected. The man offered to advise him without charge. Spending his evenings and weekends searching, the entrepreneur was able to locate a series of prospects. But there was always something wrong. Most involved very low profit for long, hard hours of work. The few that seemed to offer high profits also appeared to require that those profits would have to be plowed back to pay off the purchase price and sustain operations, so there would be a substantial sacrifice in lifestyle. In still others he feared that his lack of technical knowhow would be too serious a handicap. A year of searching passed and still he was frustrated.

Then in the middle of one night suddenly he awoke with an idea about how he could create the minicomputer distributorship he had originally thought of. He got up and wrote out a plan involving multiple scores of income to carry through the lean periods and gain repeat business; sources including sales, leasing, accessories, and leased equipment. Later he transformed his midnight notes into a fuller plan with organization and financial details. When he showed it to his financial adviser, he got another surprise. The man was independently wealthy and offered to advance the $100,000 needed to start the company personally. The venture was begun.

In hindsight it could perhaps be argued that this entrepreneur should have crystallized the idea for this venture sooner. But he did not, and neither did anyone else. Had he done so, he might still have rejected it as requiring more capital than he could raise. Performing the venture search with the aid of the financial adviser developed a contact with capital with enough confidence to invest in the idea, a resource he did not have initially. So it can be argued that the search was necessary, and as it turned out also sufficient.

One industry that has had to become highly professionalized at finding new products is the toy industry, in which some large companies are able to generate half their sales each year with new products. Others often immediately copy them, and many of the toys have brief market lives, so the companies have no choice but to keep moving on to new things very rapidly. How do they find their ideas? "By every means they can think of" was the reply of one toy inventor. They use brainstorming, licensing from inventors, internal pressures on their own organizations, asking customers, copying and modifying other toys of their own and other companies, adaptation of new technology, surveys, contests, marathons, anything that might yield results.

At the same time, they also find that some approaches work better than others. Many ideas come from independent inventors, for instance, but an extremely small fraction, something like one in a thousand, "pan out." Most of the ideas chosen come from professionals in the design areas of the company whose daily job is to develop new ideas. They were chosen for that work because they showed talent at it, and by practice they at least feel they get better at it, so that it is extremely difficult, almost impossible, for "amateurs" at this particular function to compete with them. Apparently practice builds competence in idea searching as it does in other lines of activity. It would seem to follow that a would-be entrepreneur should regularly and steadily practice venture idea searching if the odds of venture finding are to be maximized.

There appears to be some support for this view in a study by Bailey that found a positive correlation between "opportunistic questioning" wherein individuals tended to be constantly inquiring into possible new opportunities. At the same time there was a negative correlation with "social questioning" wherein individuals were inquiring about the status, well-being, and power relationships among others in social situations.[22]

Alternative Personal Tactics

Attempts to analyze the processes involved in discovering viable venture ideas as a basis for better prescribing how to go looking for them have been rare and so far not very successful. There have been studies of how successful scientists and other creative geniuses seem to find ideas, and these have generally led to acceptance of the preparation-incubation-insight notion as a consistent pattern in many discoveries. Elements of preparation, such as gathering information, working on problems, trying different approaches, and colliding repeatedly with frustration, can be identified by the discoverers. Then backing away from the problem and relaxing in a mode characterized as incubation can be recalled, and finally, the flash of insight, often a thrilling experience. But a gap always seems to remain in the story about just what was happening during the incubation stage. At this point the story seems to enter a phase where it cannot be observed, one where "intuition," the turning of unidentified and unseen wheels inside an impenetrable black box, has to be given the credit.

In one of the few attempts by scholars to study the entrepreneurial, as opposed to artistic or scientific, idea discovery process, Long and McMullan have proposed what they describe as a four-stage "model of the opportunity identification process": (1) provision, (2) point of vision, (3) opportunity elaboration, and (4) decision to proceed.[23] In this sequence the black box seems to occur between the first two stages, but what happens there remains a mystery. Certain life experiences are recalled as being related to having the business idea, and then the vision occurs. Thus for the three entrepreneurs studied:

- #1 attends chefs' school, works as chef, gets fired, sells food products, opens deli, applies friend's recipe with success . . . gets idea for medium-priced restaurant, at home cooks pancake breakfasts that people compliment, is visited by friend who operates franchised pancake restaurant . . . gets idea for family restaurant specializing in pancakes, studies friend's operation, expands to thirteen-unit chain.
- #2 studies microbiology through PhD, takes academic job and consults

---

[22] John E. Bailey, "Learning Style of Successful Enterpreneurs," in Robert Ronstadt, John A. Hornaday, Rein Peterson, and Karl H. Vesper, *Frontiers of Entrepreneurship Research, 1986* (Wellesley, Mass.: Babson College, 1986), p. 199.
[23] Long and McMullan, "Mapping the New Venture Opportunity Identification Process," p. 567.

on the side, clients offer full-time jobs . . . gets ideas to start genetic engineering company, recruits five colleagues . . . incorporate in 1980, acquire venture capital, reach revenues of $5 million by 1982.

- #3 has high school teacher who stimulates interest in economics, at age sixteen rides a train across the prairies and notices primitive conditions, water towers, and privies . . . gets idea of opportunity for better utilities, changes university major from law to engineering, works five years as engineer, starts utilities engineering consulting firm, observes inefficiencies in residential subdivision construction, starts commercial building and leaseback sideline, tries without success to influence construction industry members to use new methods . . . gets idea to start integrated land development company, is instantly successful, goes on to other successful ventures, including a chicken processor that was transformed from loss to profits through changes in government rules that the entrepreneur had anticipated.

These entrepreneurs variously described their discoveries of business opportunities as gradual or sudden, but in each case related to identifiable precedent actions and experiences. Some of the actions seemed based on a hunch that "there must be an opportunity here," while others were apparently taken without thought about further opportunity. Just what caused the ideas to strike is not clear. Therefore it is difficult to discern a "formula" for idea finding beyond simply taking initiatives and attempting to be alert to possible opportunity clues.

The forms that clues take is another subject rarely studied. Can an opportunity, for instance, be regarded as something that exists, like a body of ore, and awaits discovery, as opposed to being something that an entrepreneur creates? If so, what sorts of outcroppings might indicate presence of the ore? Does an opportunity send out "signals" of its presence, as might uranium ore from its radioactivity? If so, how far might those signals propagate, how fast, and what kinds of receivers might be most effective in detecting them? Are there definable signal detection zones and modes of detection? Or is the problem more one of decoding them, as opposed to detecting them? We don't know.

Gap Analysis

A technique called "gap analysis" has been suggested by White as a way of finding venture ideas:[24]

1 Make a list of the characteristics desired in the venture.

2 Select some general market in terms of types of customers and divide it into progressively narrower classifications (e.g., adults, leisure, workdays, around dinner time).

3 List the problems that might plague that market group in that particular circumstance.

---

[24] Richard White, Jr., *The Entrepreneur's Manual* (Radnor, Pa.: Chilton, 1977).

4 Narrow the problem list down by filtering it through the desired venture characteristics.

5 For each of the remaining problems, generate possible solutions through brainstorming.

6 Evaluate the solutions to select the most promising for the venture.

White reported that this approach yielded, if anything, far too many ideas. He also cited a few venture-finding examples. Unfortunately, the examples were anonymous, and no ventures created through this method have been described in other publications. Thus the proof of the method's utility in widespread application remains to be seen. What can be said of other idea-generating techniques may also be true of this one; namely, that generating numerous business ideas is not difficult, but discovering adequately profitable ones is.

In choosing a plan for deliberate venture search, there are many options open to the would-be entrepreneur beyond the alternative of simply waiting and hoping a venture idea would come. Some of these options include the following:

1 *Job selection* It was pointed out earlier in connection with success correlates that more entrepreneurs tend to emerge from some job and some companies in some geographical areas more than others, and also that successful entrepreneurs tended more often to have worked in several different functional areas—production, sales, finance—rather than only one. Implications for the would-be entrepreneur, therefore, might logically include seeking out such job circumstances and changing jobs as necessary to acquire breadth of experience in a geographical area and industry where startup is favored. Working for smaller companies, for instance, appears to be a better tactic for reaching toward self-employment than working for larger ones. Another straightforward tactic can be to seek employment in a firm owned by someone likely to entertain the possibility of selling out on some basis. The example of James Treybig mentioned in Chapter 1 appears to be a successful example of this approach.

Other tactics for utilizing employment as a means of strengthening entrepreneurial potential can be to accumulate methodically lists of connections—suppliers, potential employees and partners, sources of expertise, potential customers and middlemen, and sources of capital associated with the industry in which the entrepreneur works.

2 *Venture alertness* In each of the examples it can be seen that there could have been others who took advantage of the ideas besides the entrepreneurs who did. The entrepreneurs were the ones who were sufficiently alert to spot the opportunities, however, and to do something about them. Hence cultivation of sensitivity to venture possibilities by constantly looking for ways to find needs and desires of other people and to satisfy them is a logical tactic for would-be entrepreneurs. A possible way to cultivate "customer empathy" is to study what people choose and why, and to ask them what else they might like to have.

3 *Personal exposure* Generally, action is better than simply thinking, as noted in the chapter on success correlates. Such actions as discussing

venture possibilities and desires with others and taking advantage of opportunities to participate in ventures of others, to speculate about venture possibilities with other businesspeople, and to offer ideas and see what sorts of reception they get can help. In short, the would-be entrepreneur should try out new ideas, just for the learning experience if nothing else.

4 Seeking contacts Possibly the most effective deliberate search tactic of all is to make it a practice to seek out and meet people who may be able to help. These may include marketing people, customers, inventors, entrepreneurs, prospective partners, patent attorneys, purchasing agents, venture capitalists, engineers, suppliers, and many others. Association can be sought with others who have venture ideas and desires.

5 Hobby choices Hobbies less likely to spawn venture ideas can be replaced with other hobbies more likely to do so. Bowling or golfing with more entrepreneurially oriented people may be more productive than with "organization people" or routine operators. If a hobby includes making things, it may be better to reach toward things that potential customers can use, as opposed to the entrepreneur's repairing the home that only he or she uses, and it may be more productive to work ideas for new products rather than ones already made—new biofeedback devices, for instance, rather than furniture designs taken from magazines. The objective should be to be creatively productive for other people.

6 Study One way to cultivate greater sensitivity to venture opportunities can be to study entrepreneurial patterns that work, such as those illustrated in these pages. This should enable the reader to be aware of more possible strategic combinations that can work and consequently increase the circumstances offered by life.

Any successful entrepreneur can testify to the tremendously wide range of knowledge that must be brought to bear to accomplish a venture. Consequently, it makes sense for a would-be entrepreneur to expand his or her base of knowledge into many subjects. The entrepreneur mentioned earlier who made it a practice each day to contact, outside working time, at least one person with the aim of locating a venture opportunity (and succeeded) also took advantage of all opportunities he saw to attend courses, seminars, conferences, and symposiums pertaining to entrepreneurial subjects. A list illustrating the kinds of subjects in which useful learning may be available can be quickly generated from topics on publications lists of the Small Business Administration and from tables of contents in books on small business management available in any library.

7 Moonlighting A logical approach for minimizing new venture risk is to work up to the venture on a part-time basis while retaining a full-time regular job. Weaver advocates this approach, indicating that the shift from regular job to sideline venture should be made only after the entrepreneur has achieved some minor sideline commercial successes and has learned about starting companies through experience.[25] This approach, which was illustrated earlier under Sideline Ventures in Chapter 3, can be summarized by the following suggestions:

[25] Peter Weaver, You, Inc. (New York: Doubleday, 1973).

a Seek out and talk to others who have successfully developed sideline ventures into full-time occupations.

b Seek opportunities to develop business skills in different directions. Keep some books, do some selling, do some business purchasing, do some payroll work, deal with some government agencies. Do some volunteer work if possible in the line of activity you intend to pursue.

c Collect venture ideas on scraps of paper whenever they occur. Buy a used file cabinet and collect information on these.

d Involve your family in the project, but discipline them not to bother you when working on it at home.

e Set up a home office somewhere in a corner. Pick a logo and obtain letterhead stationery. Set up accounting books. Obtain Internal Revenue Service booklets on business taxes and deductions. From City Hall learn about state and local regulations and requirements.

f Seek out ways, such as through trade associations, of replacing company group insurance and other fringe benefits.

g Call around and locate an attorney, an accountant, and a banker. Briefly inform them about your venture ideas and learn what they can do to help for what prices. (They do not charge for telling about prices. But ask at the outset, particularly with lawyers.)

h Save money. Buy used rather than new things. Cut down on luxuries. Throw away the credit cards. Squeeze the household budget.

i At your regular job be a conscientious, model employee. Take every opportunity to learn about how different facets of a business work. But do not talk about your moonlighting or venture plans.

j Actually start some small-scale ventures, whether service, mail order, small fabrication, or whatever. Be prepared for some failures, but learn from them and move on to more ventures. Stick with full-time employment until you achieve some small-scale successes at least.

8 *Life-style* Implicit in the above suggestions is a kind of venture-oriented life-style. Saving money for a stake, looking for opportunities, trying things, seeking to learn can all be part of such a life-style. An additional facet can be developing connections and working relationships through patterns of socialization. The young insurance man who encountered the pennies opportunity (and subsequently many others) believed in joining clubs where he would meet people with wherewithal. Such people, he found, are often approached by many other people who are aware of or otherwise involved in venture opportunities, and in these situations there is sometimes room for participation by additional enterpreneurs. Such people, he found, are also sometimes well informed about others who can help with ventures, including professional advisers and potential investors. By moving in such circles socially and through his behavior indicating that he was seeking to become an entrepreneur, this man believed he substantially raised his odds of encountering venture opportunities.

In the chapter on starting points it was shown that some entrepreneurs go from one venture to another, regarding themselves as "starters" rather than "runners" of organizations. Such a pattern is another illustration of what might be regarded as an entrepreneurial life-style.

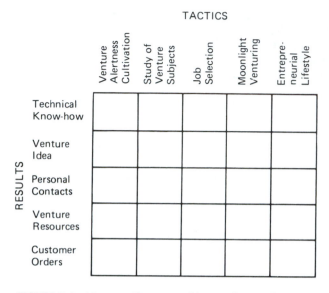

FIGURE 5-1 MATRIX OF TACTICS AND VENTURE STARTUP FACTORS

Strategies for Deck Stacking

It should be possible to work many different combinations of the above tactics into strategies for obtaining the five key venture entry factors mentioned earlier. A matrix for considering possible combinations appears in Figure 5–1. With this the reader may find it worthwhile to think about possible strategic combinations that might have been used either for "stacking the deck" to maximize odds of success in some of the venture examples discussed earlier or for some potential new ventures.

An illustration of effective personal strategy in developing a new business is the story of Vern Anderson and the formation of Vidar Corporation, a multimillion-dollar electronics company on the San Francisco peninsula:

◆   Trained as a mechanical engineer, Anderson decided that the time to take risks in entrepreneurship was while young, before family responsibilities precluded them. At age twenty-four he enrolled in Stanford Business School, and by the spring quarter of his second year, 1957, just before graduation, he began venture discussions with a friend who was working on a PhD in electrical engineering. Together with an engineering faculty member, and an electrical engineer from the Stanford Research Institute, and his friend's father, who happened to be an attorney, he began to have regular meetings once a month.

"Although my training was in mechanical engineering, I decided to go into electronics manufacturing," he recalled, "because I liked the local area and it was a good one for electronic companies, it allowed low capital entry, it involved a challenging and rapidly developing high technology, and it was a growth industry.

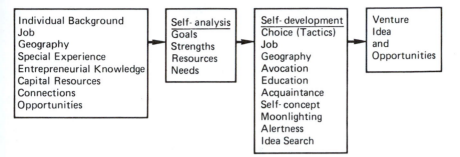

FIGURE 5-2 Deck Stacking

"Since I knew nothing about electronics, I gathered a group of guys who wanted to learn about it like I did, and set up a seminar which ran for one year at night. We went through Terman's text on *Radio Engineering,* all 750 pages of it, working out all the problems in the chapters. After that I felt I could adequately talk to electronics engineers, although I couldn't do their work."

He went to work for an electronics company after graduation "that had never been anywhere and was never going anywhere" because it gave him the chance to learn about the electronic equipment manufacturing business. "My boss was the general manager," he recalled, "and he said he wanted me right outside his office, so that whenever he wanted to chew I would be right there. I had gone from the school of enlightened management at Stanford to the school of very unenlightened desk pounding."

Nights and weekends, however, were a different matter, as the entrepreneurial team explored various venture possibilities. Plans and policies for the new company were hammered out over brown bag lunches on their station wagon tailgates in the parking lot. "We didn't have an idea at the beginning," he said. "We started with the desire, then went to the idea, and then went to the reality." Some ideas for electronic products, such as specialized power supplies, were generated and preliminarily designed, but the group had no capital whatever to enter manufacturing. "We landed a contract with Ampex and then told them if they wanted us to get started they would have to provide some money. They gave us $5,000 for an R&D program, and that was the beginning of Vidar. We built that to $63,000 in twenty months of nights and weekends, $55,000 of it in the form of cash. With that nest egg we were able to begin manufacturing our own products, quit our other jobs, and develop the new company."

A more generalized scheme for describing possible personal strategies for "stacking the deck" in favor of discovering more venture ideas is depicted in Figure 5–2. In effect, this scheme provides a missing link for the Swayne-Tucker startup model presented in the preceding chapter (Table 4–1), particularly for steps 5 through 8, which presumed prior identification of a product and market.

Generating ideas is, of course, only part of the venture discovery process. The ideas must be screened and a selection made of candidate ideas worth further investigation, eventually leading to one that is to be pursued as a startup. This chapter has concentrated on the idea-generating process. In the next chapter attention will shift to the process of screening and selection of which ideas to pursue.

SUMMARY

If sources of venture ideas were divided into two general groups, those encountered mainly by unforeseen coincidence and those found through deliberate searching, the majority by far would be of the former type. This chapter illustrated how sometimes ideas come through invitation from other people for the entrepreneur, who may not have been considering it at all, to undertake a particular type of venture. The greatest number of venture ideas arise out of employment, one of the career starting points noted in Chapter 3 and a consistent finding throughout examples of the book. But they also occur out of hobbies, social encounters, and chance observations of need, as when Mr. Evinrude's ice cream melted in the rowboat and stimulated the idea of an outboard motor. Many people may have been exposed to the same needs and venture opportunities; what sets the entrepreneurs apart is that they take action to do something about it, namely devise a solution for the need and follow through to make that solution available to others. Hence it is possible for entrepreneurs to influence discovery and follow-through and not remain entirely at the mercy of circumstance. Eight categories of action were suggested that can help the idea-discovery process. Emphasis, however, should be on the word "action," because it is by circulating about in the world, doing business, and encountering new situations and people that needs and venture ideas are more likely to be discovered rather than by simply sitting and thinking about it.

Evaluating
Venture Ideas

How to select among many potential venture ideas those that are most worthwhile is a question bound to arise for venture-seeking would-be entrepreneurs. It is easy to generate a great number of venture ideas. Most will be discarded quickly, particularly those that come from brain-storming or armchair speculation, because of obvious failings. Others, particularly those coming from encounters with other people and representing more definite needs, will merit various degrees of further investigation before rejection or possible acceptance and implementation. Much more time in the searching process will likely be spent on checkout than on hunting for ideas, and ultimately the success of the venture will depend heavily on how well the selection is performed. This chapter will discuss possible selection criteria, describe some ways of classifying ventures, and suggest some procedures useful in the evaluation process.

Evaluation should operate in two dimensions. One is a screening process to eliminate unsuitable projects. The other is a searching process to seek ways of adapting, modifying, and improving on ideas to find ways of making them work as well as possible. The checkout of ideas should include a search for how to make the most of them.

A place to begin can be to develop a scenario, projection, or visualization of the venture as described in Chapter 4 under the heading "Foreseeing the Venture." That process can be mentally adjusted, modified, and tuned to assess the best that can be done with the venture concept as a basis for evaluating it.

SELECTION FACTORS

Ultimately the criteria that a given entrepreneur uses for choosing a particular venture idea become personal. They may be very specific, such as that the future company should be located in a certain geographical area and should manufacture custom racing camshafts, or they may begin in a much more general form. One young business school graduate set out with a somewhat general approach by writing down the characteristics of the company he wanted as follows:

◆   I want a business where I can be boss, which rewards me for achievement rather than passage of time, where I can be a capitalist—without capital, for I have very little, whose product fills a basic requirement of the economy, a product for which there is a built-in-demand—I do not want to depend on luxury market, where I can make a little on a lot of business, not a lot on a little—if my margin is high, others will be attracted, and they may be willing to live on a little less than I. Where I can make money on what others do, and not only on what I can do— I want to multiply the return on my efforts. Where there is repeat business—I do not want to have to continually sell new customers. Where there is a substantial growth potential. Where I can grow without additional capital investment—I recognize that I have to grow to give my people opportunity, but I do not want to bring in new capital to do it. Where there is no credit risk. Where I have little or no competition. Where I will have a reliable net profit.

This entrepreneur, according to Professor Frank Shallenberger of Stanford, reached his goal. He built his company up to $60 million annual sales, then sold out in good shape to venture again. Which particular line of work and what opportunity within that line this man utilized may be of no particular relevance for another entrepreneur, because that opportunity has already been exploited. What is important is that the next entrepreneur be able to identify his or her own good opportunity. Both happenstance and rational scheming are likely to play important parts in the choice process.

It might seem most logical to choose a venture based entirely on systematic analysis of success factors such as those described in Chapter 2, or by following a methodical set of steps as set forth in the model described in Chapter 5. Real life is usually not that orderly, however, and, in fact, many other factors tend to play a part. These factors can be grouped in the following four categories:

1   *Head start factors*   The role of coincidence in causing a given entrepreneur to start a particular venture is usually very strong, even though deliberate and planned searching may have been involved. Most entrepreneurs in fact do not search and then carefully decide on their ventures, but rather tend to stumble into them. In hindsight it can be seen that the choice was in effect influenced by things that gave the entrepreneur a head start on that venture which other people did not have. These advantages may include any or all of the key ingredients described in Chapter 4, technical knowhow, personal contacts, physical resources, the venture concept, and even customer orders encountered by coincidence in the course of pursuits other than the venture itself.

2   *Apparent feasibility*   Three questions are key to exploring the apparent feasibility of a venture concept: (1) Are people going to want this product or service? (2) Would they buy it from the venture I could manage to start? (3) Could the venture make a profit on what they would pay? Each of these successive questions implicitly includes the other. Each successively also takes

more work to answer. Hence screening may be done more efficiently by starting with the first and applying the second and third in turn only to concepts that survive the earlier questions.

For instance, to find products and services people want is easy. Plenty of hungry people in the world want (question 1) food, for example. But they would not buy it from a venture (question 2), because they have no way to pay for it. Therefore it is not necessary to plan the activities and estimate the costs to see if the venture would be profitable (question 3).

As another example, there are many people who wanted (question 1) a pocket calculator (as hindsight reveals). And they were willing to buy it from the venture that introduced it, Bowmar (question 2). But that company was not in a position to profit from it (question 3) because it could not survive the entry of such powerful competitors as Texas Instruments, Hewlett-Packard, and Casio. Hence, it failed.

3 **Price of the venture** Two main categories of demands are imposed by new ventures. One consists of activities the entrepreneur must perform. These can include preparatory activities, such as acquiring knowhow and saving money, and work activities in setting up and operating the venture, probably at a very high cost in terms of hours. The other category concerns the *gamble* the would-be entrepreneur must make to undertake the venture. This may include both a career gamble in terms of leaving a prior line of work and a financial gamble in terms of both the amounts of money the entrepreneur must invest in the new venture and the risk the entrepreneur must take, possibly pledging other assets such as a house and other property to back the venture in the face of odds that it may fail.

Entrepreneurs may pass up some ventures in favor of others that offer more "fun" or take less time or require less in the way of taking chances. Someone who is relatively content with a job and has substantial savings, for instance, would have more to lose and might be more inclined to prefer a part-time, low-capital startup, whereas someone who was unemployed or had a distasteful job and not much in the way of savings might be more willing to go full time and gamble his or her total assets on something more risky. The notion of *downside risk* often plays an important role in venture choice, with the entrepreneur exploring the question, "*What can I lose?*"

4 **Payoffs** Greater independence, wealth, opportunity for self-expression, and the chance to follow through on pet ideas are among the common reasons of many entrepreneurs for seeking ventures. But among these and other desirable features are often tradeoffs that make one type of venture more attractive than another. Some prefer to buy a franchise as a way of entering business, because the risk is thereby lowered. Others avoid franchises because they impose restrictive operating rules. Many who discover venture ideas out of hobbies say that they chose to pursue those ventures for the same reasons they chose the hobbies—they simply liked sailboats, or high-fidelity sound systems, or airplanes, or camping. Tasks required of the entrepreneur all day long vary among ventures, as do travel requirements, tax deductions possible, discount purchasing advantages, and other perquisites that matter to some people more than others. A particularly important concept in assessing most ventures is the notion of *upside potential*. Here the question for the entrepreneur to explore is, "*How much can I win?*"

PRELIMINARY SCREENING QUESTIONS

Some screening tasks are easy and quick to perform in checking out venture ideas. Those are often worth doing first in order to determine whether harder checkout tasks, such as prototype construction or market surveys, are justified. This section will describe some of the easier tests; the next section will treat those that demand more time and/or money to perform. This is not to imply a "correct" order for the checkout questions, however. In a given venture situation all sorts of variations may be appropriate, particularly including jumping back and forth among checkout questions to explore each progressively deeper as the facts may justify.

Tracing back the mental process through which venture ideas are generated and screened is a type of research that remains to be done. Nobody knows how many ideas occurred to entrepreneurs such as those described in preceding chapters and how they went about rejecting the ideas they did not use. Probably there were many ideas that occurred to them but were rejected with little or no reflection for such reasons as "It wouldn't work," "It isn't legal," "I don't know how to pursue it, " "I don't have time to bother with that now," "Nobody would buy it anyway," "I couldn't muster the wherewithal to carry it off," or "If I got started with that one, the established competitors would quickly overwhelm the enterprise." Also, most of these out-of-hand rejections were probably appropriate, although again, nobody knows how many good ideas were thereby rejected, if any. If inventors or entrepreneurs are later asked, "How many times has it happened that you rejected an idea and later regretted doing so after someone else thought of the same idea and carried it through successfully?" they typically have difficulty recalling any examples.[1]

Once an idea passes through this first quick intuitive screen and begins to intrigue the would-be entrepreneur, some more conscious and rational analysis may take place. Hunch has now told him or her that this idea just might work, and might sell, and just might make money. It is worth setting other potential ideas aside and applying more investigative effort to this one?

The degree of personal appeal in the work required by the prospective enterprise is one early question to consider. One man who bought a pizza restaurant after having been a schoolteacher found that he had solved one of his personal problems. The restaurant greatly increased his earnings. But it caused another serious problem he had not anticipated. "It bores me to death," he said. "The work is terribly monotonous, and the deepest conversation I engage in all day long is whether somebody likes pepperoni better than mushrooms on a pizza."

Closely related is the issue of personal talents and resources versus requirements of the venture. The odds of succeeding with a venture are less, as pointed out earlier in the chapter on success factors, if the entrepreneur does not have prior working experience and consequent high competence in the line of business he or she is creating. An acquisition, as opposed to a startup, is a

---

[1] The author has tried this, but not in a formal way whose results are publishable. Incidentally, with regard to investments as opposed to new venture ideas, the responses are quite different. Many can think of ideas or propositions brought to them by others for investment which they rejected only to see the ideas turn out to be successful.

different matter in this regard, for prior experience appears to be much less critical in an acquisition, as will be further discussed in a later chapter. It is also important that the entrepreneur either have or be able to obtain sufficient resources, particularly money, to carry the enterprise through, and this therefore needs to be weighed early in the screening process.

If the concept of the new venture involves a new and untried product, process, or service, then the feasibility of creating the innovation and having it work as it is supposed to must be established. In early thinking it may be assumed that this can be done, with the entrepreneur reasoning that some way to do it can probably be figured out if it looks as if people would buy at a profitable price. Consequently, the question of operational feasibility may be shifted back and forth from "back burner to front burner" as other aspects of the analysis are worked out. Particularly if there are precedents in the form of similar products or services already in existence, it may be fairly safe to assume temporarily that feasibility is solvable provided that economic and market justifications are strong.

Who the probable customers of the new enterprise will be should be thought through next. A great pitfall awaiting the would-be entrepreneur is that of egocentrism, assuming that because the new product or service or concept of the venture appeals to him or her it follows that other people will buy. It is important to beware this tendency and also to beware "the deadly 2 percent syndrome." The latter refers to a line of reasoning that says, "The total market for this product or service is around a hundred million dollars per year. So if my company just picks off 2 percent, it will have sales of two million per year. Surely we can get something as small as 2 percent." There are two things wrong with this reasoning. The first is that it will probably be very difficult to get 2 percent of the market unless the company has a strong competitive advantage. The second is that 2 percent is likely to be an unprofitable share anyway, as will be discussed later in this chapter.

A much better approach to estimate the market in a preliminary way is to describe several different individuals, either actual or hypothetical ones, in fairly extensive detail and to describe how they will probably go about making the decision to exchange some of their money for the product or service to be offered by the new company. This estimate should be extended to include how often each of these people will buy from the company and how much they should be expected to buy each time. It should also describe how they will hear about the opportunity to buy, whether from a salesperson, an advertisement, or through a chain of middlemen, each of whom in turn will have to be persuaded to offer the product or service. Then estimates should be made of how many such people there are and what the consequent total sales volume might be. All this can be done in an "armchair" fashion with pencil and paper, plus possible study of library references or knowledge of similar enterprises. Without further cross-checking, as will be discussed shortly, the estimates will be very tenuous. But they are important, and the temptation to sidestep them in favor of simply hoping and assuming that a market will exist because the entrepreneur wants it to must be avoided.

Finally, the preliminary analysis must contain some sort of potential profitability estimate. The starting point here is usually with the question of margin, which was discussed in Chapter 4. If the margin cannot be seen to compare

TABLE 6–1 Expenses of Five Small Manufacturing Companies

	Commercial Electronic Instruments	Consumer Hi-fi Amplifiers	Wooden Furniture	Restaurant Equipment	Sawmill Machinery
Labor	10%	13%	41%	19%	28%
Materials	30	33	18	36	42
Manufacturing overhead	15	10	9	14	7
(Cost of sales)	(55)	(56)	(68)	(69)	(77)
Selling	10	20	15	8	3
Administrative	15	7	15	13	3
Engineering	4	5	0	0	2
Pretax profit	16	12	2	10	15
Sales as a multiple of labor and materials	2.5	2.17	1.69	1.82	1.43

favorably with what is typical for companies in similar lines of work, then the venture idea either must be modified to improve margins or must be dropped. For consumer products manufacturing, for instance, a rule of thumb is that the product must sell at retail for at least four to five times the cost of labor and materials, or it will lose money. Briefly, the reasoning here is that wholesalers typically receive around 50 to 60 percent off retail price as a discount, which cuts the manufacturer's share of that price to less than half. Costs of administration, overhead, and selling typically at least equal those of labor and materials. So what is left for labor and materials and profit is less than half the manufacturer's selling price or less than one-fourth the retail price; hence the required ratio of between four and five to one. For service firms the typical rule is three times labor cost.

Another way of looking at this is to note that a manufacturer has to receive about double the labor and material costs in order to cover administration, overhead, and selling and still make a profit. This is true of commercial as well as retail products. But it is only a very rough first approximation for manufacturers. In practice a considerably wider range can be found, as illustrated in Table 6–1, which shows actual operating figures for five small manufacturing companies in different lines of business whose gross margins range from 23 to 55 percent and whose multiple of labor and materials to selling price ranges from 1.4 to 2.5. Margin figures for still other lines of work, including nonmanufacturing, can be found in the library from published sources such as those of Robert Morris Associates.[2] Some of these are displayed in Table 6–2, in which it can be seen that cost of sales percentages (of factory selling price, not retail) range from 53.5 percent in surgical instrument manufacturing to 79.2 percent in millwork. In wholesaling cost of sales percentages tend to be higher, in the

[2] Financial Ratios (Philadelphia: Robert Morris Associates, 1978).

TABLE 6–2   A Sampling of Income Statements

Type of Company	Cost of Sales as a Percentage of Sales		Pretax Profits as a Percentage of Tangible Net Worth	
	Companies with Sales Up to $250,000	All Companies	Companies with Sales up to $250,000	All Companies
Manufacturing				
Cutlery and hand tools	74.5%	70.7%	17.8%	22.1%
Auto parts	72.7	76.9	20.7	28.4
Sporting goods	69.0	71.2	23.1	29.9
Jewelry	68.2	70.5	15.9	23.3
Men's and boys' pants	—	77.6	—	17.0
Millwork	79.2	81.6	15.5	17.9
Surgical, medical instruments	53.5	59.5	—	27.9
Drugs	63.5	58.2	5.4	28.0
Nonferrous foundries	71.5	80.5	29.8	27.2
Wholesaling				
Hardware and paints	69.2	75.3	21.6	20.4
Auto equipment	68.0	72.3	27.7	22.2
Sporting goods	76.8	76.3	12.3	17.5
Jewelry	76.9	77.1	23.5	22.2
Men's clothing	81.3	75.0	14.2	16.9
Lumber and millwork	87.8	85.7	23.1	21.2
Drugs	73.5	80.5	31.1	18.1
Retailing				
Hardware	65.7	69.1	19.7	19.2
Tires, batteries, accessories	64.8	68.9	29.6	25.9
Sporting goods	67.2	68.1	29.6	21.6
Jewelry	56.8	56.2	24.5	19.3
Men's and boys' clothing	60.0	62.9	14.4	13.8

70- to 80-percent range, while in retailing they tend to be lower, in the 50- to 70-percent range. Return, before tax, on tangible net worth also tends to be higher in wholesaling than in manufacturing and still higher in retailing. These are only averages, however, and can be greatly affected by how accounting is done. Whether the owner's draw is regarded as salary or profits, for instance, can greatly affect the profit percentages.

MORE-DETAILED CHECKOUT

An idea that survives the preliminary pencil-and-paper checkout may call next for action to validate the potential. Actions to check further on physical feasibility may include checking for patent infringement, for zoning regulations for a contemplated location, and for other legal constraints that may be involved, such as safety and pollution restrictions. It will also likely include construction of a prototype, if it is a product, to prove that it will work and refine it. If a service is involved, there may still be prototyping work connected with how it operates. This prototyping should allow operation and trial to see how well the product or service works and to learn about problems that may be associated with it. How difficult it will be to perform this prototyping can range widely from making a pasted-up layout, say for a new magazine idea, to extensive research and development, as might be required for a new computer design. Pencil-and-paper theoretical analysis is usually the best way to begin the prototype testing. Beyond that there are varying degrees of commitment that can be applied, depending mainly on what the product or service calls for and on the resources available to the entrepreneur. Each of the following three entrepreneurs applied a different level of commitment to the prototyping stage.

◆   Walter Meyer, a laid-off aerospace engineer, conceived an idea for a better fireplace heat exchanger. After tinkering with rough ideas in his home workshop, he made drawings of a design and took them to a custom sheet metal shop, where a prototype unit was fabricated. After testing in his home fireplace, he made a series of modifications and improvements and had other units custom-fabricated as he perfected his design.

_____

◆   An advertising agency executive conceived an idea for a computer-type terminal on which people could record their responses to television programming. His plan was to offer this as a service to advertisers to evaluate the effectiveness of their efforts, and his experience in the business plus conversations with colleagues persuaded him that it would work. But not being technically experienced in terminal and software design, he was in no position to create the unit. Consequently, he began by raising capital, then hired Stanford Research Institute to design and build a prototype unit.

_____

◆   Alejandro Zaffaroni, a Syntex Corporation executive, conceived of new approaches to administering drugs. As mentioned earlier in Chapter 4, his approach was to capitalize a company starting with $2 million of his own money, to hire a team of experts, to raise additional capital, and then to go to work on development. Later he commented, "There's always an opportunity to make a better switch or something. Now, to go from the idea to prototype in some cases is a major hurdle. But to go from the prototype to the product—that is the mountain."

Once a prototype of some sort exists, further testing of the market becomes possible. Prospective future customers can be shown the product or service and asked whether they would be willing to buy it, and how they would feel about various prices for it. Bob Howard, the MBA described in Chapter 3 in connection with curricular startups, who had to find a concept for a company in one of his classes, illustrated an effective pattern in this regard. It may be recalled that he met a fellow student who suggested the idea of selling a mix that people could use for making hot spiced wine without having to look up a recipe and gather all the ingredients. The two students agreed that they would have appreciated such a product to take along on ski trips. But given the idea, now what should they do? The student recalled:

♦ We went out into the kitchen and mixed up a batch, put some into a thermos bottle and drove to a supermarket. The store manager listened to our description of the product, then took a taste from the thermos. He told us that if we would package it to sell for under one dollar retail he would order a couple of cases and let us put it on the shelf. From there we went to some more stores and got similar reactions from the other managers. That convinced us we at least had a market for getting the product tried.

In this case the person approached to test the market was a store manager. Depending on the particular product or service, there are other types of people on whom the prototype could be tested. All department stores and chain stores employ professional buyers who keep regular office hours and who generally are glad to provide informed opinions about the viability of new products. The procedure is simply to call the store, specify the type of product, and ask what hours the buyer who specializes in that line will be available for interviews. For other products and services not suited to such retail outlets, other people can be identified who will also provide opinions and possibly sales orders. These include wholesalers and agents (listed in the Yellow Pages), governmental purchasing agents, purchasing agents of other manufacturers, and of course potential end users themselves. Inventors' shows, trade shows, and fairs are other places where it may be possible to exhibit the product or service for reactions, although generally this is not done until it is fully ready for sale. The entrepreneur may choose either to rent a booth at such shows or to rent permission to share someone else's booth for less cost.

Cost estimates must be refined and made more accurate as the detailed checkout proceeds. Construction of the prototype should help considerably, but only as a starting point. Improved versions should incorporate cost-cutting improvements, and production models should allow still greater savings as volume increases. If a product is involved, cost estimates for various volumes can be obtained by taking the prototype and/or drawings to some custom manufacturers, job shops, or the like and asking them for bids at various levels of output. Generally, it is advisable to obtain these from two or more shops as a cross-check for accuracy.

In the case of a service the only way to go beyond pencil-and-paper estimates is either to obtain bids for having someone else do the work or else to try performing some of the work, see how long it takes, and then estimate labor costs for hiring people of appropriate skill levels to carry out the work.

If any of the physical resources needed to perform the work pose a special problem, for example, lead time in obtaining machinery or materials, that too should be checked out at this stage. The procedure is simply to identify suppliers of what is needed and ask them for quotes of price and delivery time.

MARKET ANALYSIS

A particularly weak spot in the planning of many ventures appears to be the analysis of who will buy and how much. A survey of venture capitalists by Hills found that, in their estimation, entrepreneurs[3]

1 Don't place much importance on in-depth potential market analysis
2 Rely primarily on intuition in estimating market potential
3 Are less systematic in analyzing market potential than they should be
4 Are biased and ignore negative information when interpreting market information
5 Underestimate what is required to market their products
6 Underbudget marketing activities

As a result, over 90 percent of the entrepreneurs, according to venture capitalists, overestimated their market forecasts by 40 percent or more, and over 60 percent overestimated by 60 percent or more. A majority of entrepreneurs who failed, they said, could have avoided failure through better advance market analysis.

The answer may be to engage professional help in market analysis, although according to the venture capitalists interviewed, most entrepreneurs do not consider it worth the cost. An alternative can simply be to apply more time and follow common sense to estimate and to some extent verify just who will buy what the venture offers, why, and at what price. Some elements of the task, such as facing up to negative information realistically, simply call for self-discipline.

A more general industry analysis can be another crucial factor to look at in assessing the market. It is not just the demand but also the supply offered by competitors that is important. Moreover, it is not the present that is most important, but rather the future competitive situation that the new venture will face. Who else will likely be operating in that market, not only from existing companies but also from other new ventures that may enter? Who might be in a good position to do so, and how would their strengths compare with those of the startup in the future?

FINANCIAL ANALYSIS

All this collection and refinement of market and cost information should put the entrepreneur in a better position to improve on the first margin estimates and to make fuller and more accurate financial forecasts that can be used not only as a more complete check on advisability of proceeding with the venture but also for raising capital if it is needed. The procedure begins simply with

---

[3] Gerald E. Hills, "Market Analysis and Marketing in New Ventures: Venture Capitalists' Perceptions," in John A. Hornaday, Fred Tarpley, Jr., Jeffry A. Timmons, and Karl H. Vesper, *Frontiers of Entrepreneurship Research, 1984* (Wellesley, Mass.: Babson Center for Entrepreneurial Studies, 1984), p. 43.

making up some blank forms for income statements and balance sheets and then filling in the numbers. Normally, these begin with estimates of sales by month. Costs for labor and materials are then filled in, based on estimates gathered and scaled to the sales volumes. Other expense items are estimated from a listing of what the company will need to operate: supervisory personnel, rent, utilities, advertising, and so forth. From a listing of the materials, equipment, and other physical resources needed to operate, a pro forma balance sheet can be worked up, beginning with the assets—receivables and inventory representing so many months' sales, and so forth. The liabilities side then follows from estimates of the amount of trade credit, depending on sales, other borrowings, and capital to be put in by the investors.

As these financial forecasts begin to come into focus, there are three key questions to be explored. The first is what sales volume will be required for the venture to break even. The second is how much will be lost if the venture fails. The third is how much can be made if it succeeds.

Breakeven should be considered in two forms, profit breakeven and cash flow breakeven, both of which can be illustrated with a simple hypothetical example. Suppose a poverty-stricken jewelry maker rents part of a storefront for $40 per month, including all utilities, to make and sell copper bracelets. He borrows $120 to buy tools and copper, which is to be paid back at $10 per month. The bracelet materials cost him twenty-five cents each, and he sells the bracelets for $2.25. Also assume that he has decided to take no salary but will instead pocket any net income as profit.

Profit breakeven is the level of sales at which the company manages to cover all its expenses. Profits and losses are zero. In this example the jeweler receives $2.25 per bracelet but must give out copper worth twenty-five cents (his variable cost) to receive it. So he can keep $2.00 on each bracelet (this $2.00 is called the contribution) to pay the rent (in this case equal to the fixed cost). Since the rent is $40 he will need to sell twenty bracelets per month to cover it at a contribution of $2 per bracelet. This represents sales of twenty bracelets times $2.25 each, or $45 per month to break even. The formula is therefore

$$\frac{\text{fixed costs}}{\text{contribution}} = breakeven\ volume.$$

Cash breakeven takes into account the fact that there are other expenditures besides variable costs (copper) and fixed costs (rent) that the jeweler must pay, in this case $10 per month, which he must repay on the loan he used for buying copper and tools. To cover this additional payment he will have to sell another five bracelets per month, which each give him a contribution of $2. The formula is therefore

$$\frac{\text{fixed costs} + \text{other payments}}{\text{contribution}} = cash\ breakeven.$$

In this case it is

$$\frac{\$40 + \$10}{\$2} = 25 \text{ bracelets per month,}$$

which is a higher required volume than the profit breakeven. Usually the cash breakeven is higher than the profit breakeven, as in this example, but not always. In apartments with high depreciation charges, for instance, owners often break even on cash flow without showing a profit, which is why high-income people such as doctors like such investments.

Real-life breakeven is more complicated, but the principles are identical. The pro forma statements can also be used to ascertain breakeven more accurately than the above fixed and variable cost formulas. The procedure is simply to develop the pro forma statements for several levels of sales and then to plot profit versus sales volume on a graph to see where the line crosses zero, which is the breakeven point. The important thing is to determine both profit and cash flow breakeven points by some means or other, because if it cannot be seen that the breakeven sales volumes are attainable, then the venture is bound to fail and should be rejected.

Downside risk refers to both how much the venture can lose if it fails and how likely it is to fail. The losses in some kinds of ventures, such as investment counseling, magazine publishing, or manufacturing where no plant or equipment is owned by the venture, can wipe out virtually everything that was invested. In other types of work, such as capital intensive manufacturing or real estate, there can be substantial liquidation value in event of failure. The way to explore the question, "How much can I lose?" is to consider alternative scenarios of failure and estimate the liquidation value. In the above example, for instance, if the closed shop after a week because of inadequate sales, he might sell off the tools and inventory to pay off his loan. To the extent that they fell short, he would lose the amount of money plus time and effort he had spent.

Upside potential refers to both how much the venture can make if it succeeds and how likely it will be to succeed. Usually there are two ways to explore this question. One looks at operating revenues to be received by the entrepreneur, and the other contemplates selling the venture off to take a capital gain. In the jeweler example if sales were one bracelet per hour on the average eight hours per day, five days per week, fifty-two weeks per year *beyond* the number needed for profit breakeven, the profit would equal $2 per bracelet times the number sold above breakeven, or $4,160 per year, from multiplying (one bracelet/hr) × (eight hr/day) × (five days/wk) × (fifty-two wks/yr) × ($2/bracelet), before taxes. This would be the rate of income that he could consider against the time, effort, and risk required.

On the other hand, if he supposed a venture like this could be sold to someone else for two times its earnings before tax, then his potential capital gain would be a one time only income of two times the $4,160, minus the amount he invested, which was zero since he borrowed the stake, or $8,320. Again, he could consider whether that profit was worth the time, effort, and risk involved.

The way to explore the question, "How much can I make?" is to consider alternative scenarios of success and to compute the possible operating profit and capital gains profit. The jewelry entrepreneur might explore other assumptions about sales or other key numbers. What if sales were two bracelets per hour instead of one, but $1,000 had to be spent on advertising to bring that about? What if the store operated seven days per week instead of only five? What might the upside potential be if other product lines were added, such as buckles and earrings? Determination of upside potential calls for dreaming happy fantasies and pressing the most from creative imagination to see what can be gained.

These are not the only questions to consider in assessing startup feasibility and attractiveness. Other major ones include how much money the venture will need, where it will come from, and what rate of return will be realized on it, as well as questions about what the other alternatives are for applying the effort and money. A more complete list of checkout questions, beginning with those raised so far in this chapter and others, appears in Table 6–3. Ultimately, however, the questions must be determined by the nature of the particular entrepreneur, situation, and venture, and no general list can fit all cases without being overly voluminous and boring. Rather than picking into ever finer detail about startup feasibility, it may be better to return to the most generally important success factor, the nature of the business, and to the question of whether it fits the entrepreneur's objectives.

LONGER-TERM PROSPECTS OF THE VENTURE

Whether the entrepreneur plans to keep and operate the business or to sell it off to someone else, the long-term viability should be considered. The reason is that if the entrepreneur keeps the business, he or she is bound to have an interest in how it prospers. If the entrepreneur wants to sell the business, then a buyer will be concerned about the long-term prospects in considering price. So either way the long-term prospects—the kind of business the enterprise is destined to become—are important in evaluating prospective venture alternatives.

Most new companies begin small, but among small firms there is an enormous amount of variety, some types being more attractive than others. Although most are bound to remain small, a few will grow larger. Generally, those with higher growth potential offer greater economic payoffs. But those are not the only kinds of payoffs that are important, and some stably small ventures provide very pleasant and lucrative employment. For convenience here, three types of ventures will be considered:

1 *Low-Pay, Stably Small Ventures* These include most "one-man shows" and Mom n' Pop ventures, taverns, gas stations, restaurants, dry cleaning shops, and independent small retail stores. Typically, their owners make modest investments in fixed assets and inventory, put in long hours, and earn considerably less income and fringe benefits than the average un-

TABLE 6–3 Some Other Venture Idea Checkout Questions

Basic Feasibility
1. Can the product or service actually work?
2. Will it be legal?

Competitive Advantages
1. What will be the specific competitive advantages of the product or service?
2. What are those of the companies already in business?
3. What will competitors' likely countermoves be?
4. How will the initial competitive advantage be maintained?

Buyer Decisions
1. Who will decide to buy from the company and why?
2. How much will each such person buy, and how many such people are there?
3. Where are these people located and how will they be sold?

Marketing
1. How much will be spent on advertising, packaging, selling?
2. What share of market will the company get by when?
3. Who will personally perform the selling functions?
4. How will prices be set, and how will they compare with competitors?
5. How important is location, and how will it be determined?
6. What channels will be used—wholesale, retail, agents, mail, direct?
7. What specific sales targets should be met?
8. Can any orders to obtained before starting the business? How soon?

Production
1. Will the company make or buy what it sells?
2. Are sources of supply at suitable prices available?
3. How long will needed delivery take?
4. Have adequate lease arrangements for premises been lined up?
5. Can needed equipment be available on time?
6. Are there special problems with plant setup, clearances, insurance?
7. Who will have the appropriate operating skills?
8. How will quality be controlled?
9. How will returns and servicing be handled?
10. How will pilferage, waste, spoilage, and scrap be controlled?

People
1. How will competence in each area of the business be ensured?
2. Who will have to be hired when? How will they be found, and recruited?
3. How will a banker, lawyer, accountant, and other advisers be chosen?
4. How will replacements be obtained if key people leave?
5. Will special benefit plans have to be arranged?

Control
1. What records will be needed at what stages?
2. Will any special controls be needed? Who will take care of it?

Finance
1. How much will be needed for develoment of product or service?
2. How much will be needed for setting up operations?
3. How much will be needed for working capital?
4. Where will money come from? What if more is needed?
5. To which assumptions are profits most sensitive?
6. Which assumptions in financial forecasts are most uncertain?
7. What will be the return on equity, on sales, and compared with the industry?
8. When and how will investors get their money back out?
9. What will be needed from the bank, and how does the bank feel about that?

TABLE 6–4 HIGH VERSUS LOW PAYOFF FIRMS

Higher Payoff Types	Lower Payoff Types
Harder to find or enter	Easy to think of and enter
Small minority of small firms	Most small firms
Higher capital investment	Lower capital investment
Higher skill and specialization	Lower skill, more generally available
Tight patents, trademarks, or secrets	Nothing very proprietary, easily copied
Established and respected reputation	Not particularly well known
Strong customer ties or contracts	Easily formed customer relationships
Leadership position	Not a leader
More innovative but not radical	Ordinary or highly eccentric
Examples:	Examples:
High-technology firms, successful franchise chains, very high skill manufacturers	Most single outlet retail and food establishments, single operator services, small contractors

skilled auto worker or union craftsman. Upside potential in resale also tends to be low.[4]

2 *High-Pay, Stably Small Ventures* Many small manufacturing firms, larger restaurants and retail firms, small chains of gas stations, and other multiestablishment enterprises are in this category. Usually they involve substantial capital investments—from roughly $100,000 on up. Some owners put in long hours, while others do not. Most enjoy a variety of fringe benefits, such as tax deductions and company-paid cars and travel. Upside potential in resale can be high to a buyer who sees both an attractive job and a profitable investment.

3 *High-Growth Ventures* More rarely than either of the above two, although also typically more publicized, these are small firms that have the capability to become large ones. They include many high-technology companies that are formed around new products with substantial potential markets, and also some of the above high-pay small firms which, due to such factors as having amassed substantial capital or having hit upon a successful formula for operating, can be expanded many-fold. Often ventures of this type are bought up and absorbed by larger companies. Very high upside potential on resale often results.

These three types and characteristics that tend to be associated with them are illustrated graphically in Table 6–4. As might be expected, low-pay small firms tend to be associated with assets easier to come by and are easier to start than either of the other two. High-growth firms are the typically hardest to hit

---

[*] Sometimes a low price works to the advantage of an entrepreneur. Through buying low and selling less low, a good profit can be realized on a low-priced venture.

upon and correspondingly offer the greatest financial rewards. Each of these types is worth illustration and closer examination to appreciate why it is the way it is.

STABLY SMALL FIRMS

Although most of the country's industrial output is produced by big companies, the largest number of companies in the country are small. Just 3 percent of the companies in manufacturing, for instance, employ over 70 percent of the manufacturing workers. The number of firms has also tended to decline over time, from 327,000 U.S. companies in 1956 to 313,000 in 1963, while between 1947 and 1962 the 200 largest companies increased their share of value added in the economy from 30 percent to 40 percent. A study of small manufacturing companies in Washington State found that the average small company expanded its sales at an average annual rate of less than 1 percent between 1950 and 1959, substantially slower than the growth of the gross national product.[5] Even most high-technology companies stay small. This was pointed out in a study of 500 companies formed between 1950 and 1970, which turned up the fact that only 60 had grown to one hundred employees, while the great majority had stayed under forty employees.[6] Thus not only has the number of small manufacturing companies declined, but among the survivors growth has been the exception rather than the rule. Among services, retailing, and wholesaling, moreover, growth is even more rare. A hamburger stand that does well generally does not grow. It may expand to other outlets, but it does not expand the successful unit itself nor do gas stations, shoe repair shops, retail stores, and so forth.

Looking at firms one at a time, we see that each has its own reasons for surviving, perhaps, but not for growing large either as a single unit or in chain form. Proprietors of the firms often have not even considered trying to expand substantially, and if asked why, they will first look perplexed, then go on to suggest reasons like the following:

- "I'm too busy doing the work I have to do to keep this operation running as is. A bigger one would be more than I could handle."
- "There aren't enough customers in this area to support an expanded operation, and customers won't travel from other areas for the sort of thing we provide, because they can get it easier from other similar operations in their own areas."
- "Expansion would require more capital for facilities, inventory, advertising, recruiting, and operations, and I just don't make enough from this business to build up the capital I'd need to expand."

[5] Joseph W. McGuire, *Factors Affecting the Growth of Manufacturing Firms* (Seattle: Office of Business Research, School of Business, University of Washington, March 1963).
[6] Albert Shapero, "Do Small and Medium-Sized Businesses Have a Future in a Large Market?" (Austin: Working paper 72-9, School of Business, University of Texas, July 1971).

- "With more employees it would be harder to keep track of how everything was being done, and the work would get sloppy, as it does whenever I can't stay right on top of it."

- "Our expansion is just limited by the number of orders we get. If that number were to grow, the company would grow with them."

- "If we grew larger, we would start running into more governmental regulation and red tape, and then if we grew still more the unions would be after us. We were bigger for a while, but we encountered some of these things and found our profits were lower than before."

- "My business is comfortable just the way it is. It makes me a good living and leaves me plenty of freedom. If it were larger, it would be more demanding and tie me down more, and I wouldn't like that."

Such responses should not be interpreted as invalid excuses for not growing in an age in which the popular view has tended to hold that more of anything good is better. Many small firms continually try to grow but are stopped by events beyond their control. Some fail by pursuing expansion in the face of good reasons not to.

◆   Ted's, a restaurant serving simple but high-quality steak dinners in Santa Monica Canyon, became well known during the 1950s and flourished. At dinner time there was regularly a waiting line to enter, and customers kept suggesting to the owner that he expand. "Why not?" he thought. A second branch was opened a couple of miles farther up the coast and also began drawing good traffic. More branches were opened in the local area and also showed initial promise. But then problems of maintaining quality began to arise as the owner became burdened with keeping tabs on more things. Traffic at some locations leveled off before they reached profitability, and at other outlets it declined. Difficulties in meeting expenses and debt service prompted the owner to take some economy measures, which reduced food quality and in turn led to further declines in business. Events spiraled, and shortly afterward the firm failed. Even the originally successful first outlet was boarded up and remained closed.

Possibly this particular business could have been expanded successfully had different tactics been used by its owner, but most food establishments cannot expand successfully. Services like TV repair and home remodeling fit into the same category. Such companies are easy to start, and those who want to work in them often tend to start their own shops rather than work for others. This tendency breeds many competitors who drive margins down, so that none of the firms grows large. Floral shops, hobby stores, and bookstores face similar obstacles. However, some lines—e.g., radio parts, home furnishings, and convenience grocery stores—do lend themselves to expansion through franchising or establishing chains.

Some kinds of manufacturing regularly defy extension, for example, job machine shops, plating plants, foundries, and ornamental iron works. In these shops each job tends to be special, requiring careful individual pricing and negotiation with the customer of technical details in the work to be done. The margins, moreover, are typically slim, so that employees whose motivation is slightly less than that of the owner can quickly run work into the red and cause the firm to fail. Still, there are some custom manufacturers that do grow large. Typically these are suppliers to very large purchasers—e.g., the government or auto manufacturers—and each order involves a very large contract which requires the effort of many to fulfill.

For a would-be entrepreneur the significance of these patterns is threefold. First, some lines of work hold less potential for growth of small companies than others. Second, many factors may influence the ability of a given firm to grow. Third, most new firms are destined to remain small regardless of their lines of work or how their managements operate. However, within the category of firms that are destined to remain small, there are some that nonetheless offer high pay and other rewards and there are some that do not. It is important for the would-be entrepreneur to be aware of both these types.

Low-pay Small Firms

Most of the small firms visible around town are not only stably small but also likely to produce very limited incomes for their owners and operators.[7] They have been characterised as "marginal businesses; the small cafe, the cab owner, the corner grocer . . . about 2 million businesses with very limited resources and annual net receipts below $5,000 that come and go rapidly.[8] One man recalled his family's enterprise of this type as follows:

◆ My dad had a business for years that was a failure without his realizing it. He ran a small grocery store that paid him much less money for working much longer hours under worse conditions than he could have had working for another organization. He thought he was making a profit because his books said so, but in effect the store was losing money and he was subsidizing it out of his income by taking a low enough salary to keep the till even. After his many years of hard work in his own business he died a poor man.

The average small business operator, even though he or she is a manager, is risking savings to capitalize the enterprise, is working longer hours with less job security and fringe benefits, and is more poorly compensated than the average unskilled auto factory worker, although some small business operators do considerably better. Typically, the level of compensation to the entrepreneur is dependent on the capitalization of the business and the degree of skill needed to operate it. As can be seen from the ranges of investment and owner incomes for various types of stably small ventures listed in Table 6–5, the range of incomes, particularly after subtracting a rate of return for the invested capital, is quite low. Moreover, to earn this income, owner operators typically work at least six days per week, often seven, for

---

[7] Of course, there are also companies with high growth rates that are losing money and therefore are low in income. Generally these are transient circumstances, however, and if the companies continue at high growth rates they either shift into high-income products or else fail. Consequently their existence represents a trivial exception to the above generalization.

[8] *Business Week,* July 31, 1965, p. 36.

TABLE 6–5 Investments and Payoffs of Typical Stably Small Firms*

Type	Investment Required	Annual Sales ($000 omitted)	Owner Income
1. Construction contracting	2	24	6
	90	600	35
2. Beauty shop	2	15	9
	20	85	17
3. Janitorial service	2	18	10
	5	65	25
4. Machine shop	3	40	13
	25	250	22
5. Mobile catering truck(s)	5	100	10
	15	325	15
6. Photo portrait studio	6	25	6
	12	50	12
7. Contract dressmaking plant	10	125	12
	25	375	22
8. Industrial laundry	20	50	10
	80	200	27
9. Dry cleaning	25	50	9
	40	100	16
10. Children's clothing store	35	100	12
	85	300	22
11. Convenience store	50	150	6
	120	250	16
12. Supermarket	75	1,000	9
	150	2,300	46
13. Furniture store	75	250	10
	150	600	24
14. Bowling alley	150	46	16
	500	250	45

*Based on Small Business Administration data c. 1975.

between nine and twelve hours per day, not counting time at home spent on keeping the books and other paperwork.

These income figures could appropriately be discounted still further to recognize the probability of failure. This depends on the line of business, but in most of those that, like those of Table 6–5, require only modest skills and low investment, it is very high, with something like 80 percent of the companies failing within two years. Consequently, most stably small businesses are high in risk as well as high in work demand and low in return, and unless a would-be entrepreneur either simply does not care about these things, or is willing to put up with them for the sake of obtaining an educational experience, or has no other choice, such businesses should be rejected in favor of staying with higher-income employment until a venture with higher payoff potential can be identified.

STRATEGIES OF SIZE

Not all stably small firms are low payoff, however, and those that offer greater rewards are the ones that manage to exploit some sort of competitive advantage. A concept often associated with the small firm that identifies and obtains for itself a particular competitive advantage is the notion of "industrial niche." This refers to a specialized activity in service or manufacturing in which the company concentrates and becomes very good relative to its competitors. It has been found that types of specialities wherein smaller companies tend to have advantages over larger ones include the following:

1 Where demand is limited either by a small national market, as in some types of medical instruments; or where the market tends to be regionally dominated, as in heat treating and plating, or where local convenience is a major factor.

Big companies usually avoid small markets because coping with them demands too many bureaucratic inefficiencies. Unusual products, such as crew racing shells or top-quality musical instruments, tend to be in this category, as are local services such as real estate. Where national demand is less than $5 million total, for example, the likelihood of smaller firms dominating, rather than divisions or departments of big companies that must support greater overhead, is high. Whereas a large company may need sales of $300,000 or more per year to break even, a smaller one may be able to do it on sales of $60,000 or less. When big companies embark on diversification programs, they invariably rule out pursuing any activities whose markets are small relative to the total firm. No big company would dream of going into buggy whip manufacturing, but a small company that entered that business in 1961, Wonder Whip of Fostoria, Iowa, prospers on sales of around one-half million dollars per year. Most large companies have phased out of aircraft propeller manufacturing, for them a declining industry, thereby creating a field of greater prosperity for some smaller firms.

2 Where flexibility and innovation are at a premium. Big firms have a penchant for tidiness, order, and hence regimentation that works against change, especially rapid change. As a larger firm turns out increasing volume of any given thing, it finds incentive to spend great money and effort at maximizing efficiency. A small savings per unit multiplies quickly into thousands and millions. This commitment to finely tuned efficiency then becomes a block to any innovation that would disrupt the system and wash out the accumulated investment.

Small companies, on the other hand, especially new ones, have much less to lose and may have everything to gain by introducing innovations, and consequently they excel in areas of fast change. Familiar examples of small-company innovations have included automatic transmissions and electric starters for cars, xerography, ball-point pens, color film, low-priced wristwatches, electronic watches, jet engines, plastic skis, and pocket calculators. It was later, either through growth or acquisition, that these products became fields of big business.

Flexibility is also an important advantage for small firms in some areas where there is not much innovation. Highly seasonal businesses, such as some kinds of construction, resort operations, and itinerant combine wheat harvesting are often done by smaller firms. Subcontract manufacturers and job shops that must continually adapt to shifting needs are typically small. Short runs, special lots, custom models, and small-scale mass production are abhorrent activities to big companies.

3   Where close supervision and very careful work without excessive costs are vital. Chain restaurants are fine for producing dependable mediocrity, but for exceptionally outstanding cuisine a gourmet must turn to independent enterprises. High-quality artistic outputs similarly calls for small producing units. Large companies proved they could produce extraordinary precision in spacecraft fabrication, but only at enormous expense applied to red tape for checking and cross-checking. When exceptional precision must be produced more economically, it generally must be done in smaller firms.

4   Where custom or personalized service is important. Architects, portrait photographers, private schools, and custom tailors are examples. Sometimes customers prefer to deal with the presidents of their most important suppliers, and if their suppliers are large companies, that is simply not possible. The president of General Motors cannot delve into complaints of individual customers, but the president of a firm manufacturing race cars for the Indianapolis 500 must.

5   Where government policies are designed to aid small firms. Because there are so many small businesses in total, they together represent appreciable political "clout." Responding to this, the federal government, and in turn some state governments and even big firms, have adopted policies within certain areas deliberately intended to foster and assist small firms. Certain federal contracts are set aside for small companies in particular. Certain types of financing are available to small firms that are not available to larger ones; certain tax benefits and types of assistance are available to small firms. These vary with the tides of political fortune, but a good place to learn about those in force at any particular time is the Small Business Administration.

HIGH-PAY STABLY SMALL FIRMS

Although the types of firms shown in Table 6–5 generally yield only low returns for their owners, there are almost always exceptions, firms of the same types that have high returns. Sometimes the key will in large measure be associated with greater investment making possible expanded operations. Thus, while the owner of a single beauty shop may be able to earn only $9,000 per year, the same entrepreneur might, by expanding to two or three shops and hiring subordinate managers, be able to raise that income to $20,000 or more. Similarly, the construction contractor who does only electrical subcontracting with a partner may earn only $6,000, while a housebuilder who manages to put up and sell twenty homes in a year may take home $35,000 or more. Or a job machine shop that obtains special machines, perhaps a numerically controlled mill allowing high-volume precision machining, may be able to substantially increase its profitability. The owner of a job machine shop in one major city, for instance, had acquired machines that allowed him to handle larger parts for machining than any of the other shops in town and was earning net profits, including his draw, of over $130,000 per year on a half-million dollars in sales with a quarter-million dollars invested in equipment. Here a part of the advantage was investment, and part was specialized skill possessed by the owner and his employees.

High incomes are not always dependent on having made larger investments, however. Even among low-investment and low-skill businesses, there are always some that manage to pay off highly. Often these exploit one or more of the above small business competitive advantages plus other special competitive advantages or tricks of doing business which others in the same line of business lack, such as unusually good location, more effective advertising, lack of competitors in the immediate area, and temporary surges in demand. Among dry-cleaning firms, for example, Table 6–5 indicates typical owner incomes ranging from less than $10,000 per year on sales under $50,000 to around $16,000 per year on sales of $100,000. Around 85 percent of all dry-cleaning firms gross less than $150,000, but some go as high as $200,000 per year and generate profits in the range of $60,000. Thus profits are highly dependent on sales volume, which in turn is highly dependent on one crucial factor, location. Firms located with good access to parking on streets with very high traffic to and from work appear to do best in dry cleaning.

One entrepreneur made a business out of locating service firms that seem to prosper particularly well, studying how they do it and then selling the information through a service called *Insider Reports*.[9] He told, for instance, of finding a two-store dry-cleaning business with combined annual sales of $456,000 and annual net profit before taxes of over $200,000. Prior to obtaining the two present locations, the owner had owned three shops elsewhere. None grossed over $60,000, and he sold them. Then he found a new location, which grossed $196,000 its first year. Examples of other service enterprises and the kinds of competitive advantages that allow some entrepreneurs to earn high returns with little specialized knowhow and small investments according to *Insider Reports* are listed in Table 6–6. It is important to bear in mind, however, that these are the exceptions, the "fortunate sweepstake winners," in fields where few earn more than meager incomes at best and most entrants go broke.

Also, usually such high-profit exceptions do not continue to thrive for long, either because the basis for their prosperity is temporary, as in fads, or because the opportunities for high profits that they are exploiting draw competition. This is especially true of enterprises selling directly to consumers, because they are exposed to so many people who can see how they work and become aware of the opportunity to "muscle in."

Longer-lived high-profit records tend to occur more frequently in lines of work that are more invisible to consumers and require either specialized knowhow, an established performance reputation, significant fixed asset investment, or some combination thereof. Even there, however, there is constant threat of competition from customers and suppliers alike, who may become aware of additional profits they can glean by integrating forward or backward. Thus the manufacturer considers buying direct or selling direct to eliminate wholesaler

[9] *Insider Reports,* Chase Revel, Inc., 1445 Fifth St., Santa Monica, Calif. 90401 (The successor to these reports is *Entrepreneur* magazine from the same publisher.)

TABLE 6–6 CHARACTERISTICS OF HIGH RATE OF RETURN INDEPENDENT SERVICE ENTERPRISES*

Type of Business	Investment Required ($000 omitted)	Annual Owner Income	Competitive Advantage Angles
Helium balloon concessions	0.4	0.7/wk	Obtaining good location
Janitorial service	0.5–1.3	60	Policing quality, selling contracts
Flower concessions in cafes, etc.	0.45	80	Obtaining good location
Ice-cream-bar-making concessions	0.5–7.3	3/wk	Obtaining good location
Parking lot concessions	0.5–1.7	54	Obtaining contracts at good locations
Parking lot stripping, maintenance	0.6–0.8	25	Personal scouting, selling, bidding
Weekend parking lot art shows	0.9–2.7	30	High-traffic location, artist clientele
Consignment auto sales	0.9–4.0	30	Location, good consignments, reputation
Custom T-shirt shop	1–3.9	30	Location, novelty
Local dwelling rentals listing	1.5–6.1	40	Suitable area, advertisement writing
Xeroxing shop	3.6–9.5	36	Obtaining good location, advertising
Quick printing shop	6.7–17.0	35	Location, advertising, personal selling
Specialty foods and cheese shop	7.5–42.3	60	Location, decor, inventory, service
Muffler shop with tailpipe bender	9.8–20.0	100	Modern bender, discount pricing
Dry-cleaning shop	18.4–36.5	100	Parking location on high-traffic street

*Derived from *Insider Reports*.

charges, while the wholesaler thinks of the possibility of opening a manufacturing plant to cut purchasing costs.

The line of work where the largest percentage of participants manage to derive high profits from stably small ventures is commercial manufacturing. These little companies are often invisible to the average consumer, but a close look will reveal owners who derive very attractive incomes, often without putting in long hours, if they choose not to and instead rely on management by hired shop supervisors. A few examples follow:

◆   Small manufacturer of lapidary equipment for laboratories, not selling to the general public. Parts manufacturing is mostly subcontracted. Two men perform assembly in a small shop. The owner, arriving in his late-model Cadillac, spends about twenty hours per week at the business, mostly handling correspondence and processing rock samples sent in by oil companies. The books he keeps at home.

◆   The young owner of a heat treating shop, who acquired it from its aging founder with a down payment borrowed from the bank against plant equipment, spends about two hours per day at the company and the remainder on various civic activities. He is in the final stages of acquiring a ten-man metal stamping shop in the same way, where he expects to spend another two hours per day.

◆   A supplier of aircraft control cable pulleys commutes in his late-model Cadillac between his home in plush Bel Air, his hole-in-the-wall three-man West Los Angeles shop, and the nearby aircraft plants. His pulleys, although not difficult to make or patented, have been extensively tested, and his company has been formally approved as one of very few suppliers from whom they can be bought.

◆   The owner of a company making proprietary eyedrops visits her post office box to pick up the company mail. The orders received from drugstores and physicians are forwarded to a contract laboratory, which formulates, packages, and ships according to her instructions. She sends out the instructions and billings from her home and deposits the receipts in bank-by-mail envelopes. Although the company does no advertising or selling whatever, it provides her a high income and the orders continue to grow.

◆   A recycler of second-hand shipping cartons buys both used cartons and others which for some reason, perhaps incorrect labeling or improper size, were not used. In a small warehouse with the aid of three other men, one of whom mainly drives the truck, he strips tape from the used cartons, stacks and catalogs his inventory, occasionally manufactures short runs of special sizes, and takes orders by phone from customers who can use the cartons. Selling at over three times his cost of materials, he and his wife, who keeps the books, draw an income of over $65,000 per year on sales of less than $200,000.

It is perhaps not a surprising coincidence that a Case Western study of

120 successful small metalworking plants turned up the fact that most of their managers were not particularly striving to grow but rather were happy with their companies at their existing sizes.

It can be amazing how many small, virtually unnoticeable plants around town, often run by proprietors whose dress and demeanor are undistinguishable from those of the others working in the grime of the shop, manage to make millionaires of their founders. Always there is a reason that they are able to do it: a contract the entrepreneur was able to land at favorable terms, a market that is unknown to others or too small to attract competitors which therefore allows a high margin, special skills or knowledge on the part of the proprietor, so that in effect he or she is like a medical doctor who is able to charge enormously high rates for his or her time because the commodity owned is in short supply. The advantage may be a particular location, perhaps purchased for a low price many years earlier before its advantages could be foreseen, or a patented or secret process that others are not able to copy, or plant capacity of a type that happens to be in short supply at the time. It can even be simply a brand that is protected by trademark and which has become known over the years or through successful advertising. Sometimes a successful small company will be "made" by a fad that dies out before competitors gain a foothold and yet has enough residual market to continue providing well for one small company. Even a declining market can be advantageous for a small company that is able to capture residual customers from larger companies that formerly dominated the market and have been squeezed out or withdrawn to apply their resources elsewhere.

HIGH-GROWTH VENTURES

The highest economic payoffs of all tend to be associated with high-growth ventures. Virtually every large company was once small, and along its history of expansion made many people wealthy. In his study of twenty-one exceptionally successful British entrepreneurs, Miller observed at least five patterns that yielded high growth:[10]

1 Founding new industries (by innovating and by transferring proven ideas from other countries)

2 Participating in expanding industries (in high-technology areas such as biological science, metallurgy, and electronics)

3 Innovation in backward industries (such as scaffolds, greeting cards, farming, and clothing)

4 Breaking into established industries (home heating and toys by innovation, appliances by copying other countries)

5 Improving standards of service (in advertising, engineering, printing, and moneylending)

---

[10] Harry Miller, *The Way of Enterprise* (London: Deutsch, 1963).

Many writers, like Miller, tend to emphasize the role played by effective management in accounting for substantial growth, but the importance of choice of industry can also be seen. Those Miller describes in manufacturing of proprietary products, for instance, clearly show greater employment growth than those in services. Moreover, it is clear that often growth of the industry as a whole plays a large role in determining growth patterns of new startups in that industry.

Which industries are seedbeds for high-growth companies is in part a function of the times. Following World War II there were, as a result of pent-up demand from the war, many opportunities in consumer products and home construction. The 1950s saw many banks and savings and loan institutions begin, along with some spectacular success stories in discount store merchandising. Also, the Korean War led to a substantial amount of government contracting in high technology and resulted in many high-growth companies initiated by engineers, particularly in weapons, but also in industrial electronics. The high-technology success patterns continued through the 1960s, accompanied by "high-flying" business successes in computer services, conglomerate pyramids, equipment leasing, and franchising, especially in fast foods. The bloom came off these last three categories as the 1970s began, though high-technology successes continued to be initiated, particularly in medical electronics, but at the same time there were substantial declines in other fields such as space and weapons. Thus, which areas are most fertile for high-growth startups tends to shift with time.

Generally, however, there has to be some sort of property of the business that can readily be multiplied by that company but cannot easily be duplicated by others for there to be a high-growth potential. In manufacturing, the extensible thing is ability to turn out more of the company's product and to sell it to a broader market efficiently. In franchising, it is a format for doing business that has proven itself exceptionally effective and can be taught to others, coupled with effective support in trademarks, purchasing, site selection, and sometimes financing. In high technology, it is specialized knowhow in creating something at a hard-to-reach frontier of engineering for which there is a demand, possibly something patented, but often not. If a technology is common knowledge and not too capital-intensive, then companies providing it do not grow. For example, heat-treating companies and electroplating companies are invariably small. What they offer is needed by large markets, but many people know how to provide it, and this makes the number of competitors large while keeping the size of each small.

High-growth companies are not always companies that started out growing fast. In fact, a review of case histories of some of the most successful growth companies found that close to half began as inauspicious one-man shops and only later shifted to trajectories of high growth, either due to shifts in demand imposed from outside or to changes in strategy, often without clear prior vision as to where it would lead.[11] Franchise and chain expansions often represent shifts in growth trajectories. During the 1950s and 1960s some companies started on limited government contracts and managed to shift into commercial products with higher growth potential. Among machine shops are some, a small

[11] K. H. Vesper, "Venture Idea Sources," *Proceedings of the American Institute for Decision Sciences Annual Meeting*, 1978.

minority, that manage to shift away from custom work into proprietary manufacturing with higher growth potential.[12] Most do not succeed in such aims, but some do, as the following:

◆ Lesney Products, which makes the familiar "Matchbox" toy vehicles, began as a two-man diecasting firm in 1947. They did fairly well as a commercial job shop, but to diversify began making a toy steamroller and a few other vehicles. These too did fairly well until the Korean War provoked a government ban on use of zinc in toys. Later they were again able to start making toys but decided this time to make them much smaller, and in 1953 the "Matchbox" line began. Suddenly sales exploded, and the company, which had not even employed a typist before 1954, grew to employment of 1,500 people in 1962.

Two-stage growth can also arise in a proprietary manufacturing company whose initial product is not outstandingly successful. This happened in the case of Bill Nicolai, the entrepreneur, introduced in the preceeding chapter, whose invention of a different type of tent grew from his mountain-climbing hobby. After two years in business his tentmaking company was grossing only $60,000 per year to support him plus four friends he employed, and after paying for materials his net income still left him living on food stamps. Then suddenly things changed:

◆ A salesman called and tried to interest Nicolai in using a new tent fabric. Gore Tex, as it was called, boasted the unique property of being able to vent vapor without leaking water; breath moisture could escape the tent but rain would not enter. "They went to all the big companies first, because we were nobody," Nicolai recalled, "but each big company assumed the material was no good because none of the other big companies used it." Seeing little to lose, Nicolai introduced a tent of the new material and threw all the resources he could muster into advertising it. Within a month sales leaped from $5,000 per month to $6,000 per day. Over the next three years sales rose to $2 million annually, all handled direct at high margin through the company store and through mail order.

In both of the above cases the founding entrepreneurs were also the managers who later shifted their companies to accelerated growth trajectories. Probably more often, however, the trajectory shift is brought about by a new management moving in with a fresh approach of some sort. Sometimes this results in "takeoff" of a stably small venture, and at others it produces the more spectacular result of "turnaround," wherein a company that was clearly on the road to closure has its trajectory transformed into one of both profitability and growth. The approach of moving into a losing company and turning it around can be immensely alluring for an entrepreneur who happens to have high self-confidence, but it is also enormously risky and usually does not work out satisfactorily. ("I thought the company was failing because management was making crucial mistakes. But it turned out that the crucial mistakes had been made long ago, and by the time I got the company management really didn't much matter. It was too late, a hopeless situation.") When it does work, however, it can be greatly rewarding.

In addition to the two-stage types of trajectories, there occur multistage

[12] K. H. Vesper and D. R. Haglund, "Strategies and Barriers to Growth in Job Machine Shops," *Proceedings of the Academy of Management Annual Meeting, 1978.*

trajectories in which companies may go through a series of ups and downs or various degrees of ups. Eddie Bauer, a Seattle hardware store, shifted from stably small to a growth trajectory by entering manufacturing, then later embarked on a stage of still more rapid growth by introducing mail-order selling, thus going through three distinct growth stages.

COMPETITIVE SHIELD

The survivability and profitability of a company can be regarded as a function of the strength of whatever shield protects it from competitors. Initially this shield may consist of the fact that it presents its product or service to customers ahead of the competition. The startup hence initially enjoys a competitive shield characterized by Peter Drucker as being "Fustest with the Mostest" with what it offers to particular customers.[13]

If the market truly has profit potential it is possible that competitors will fail to notice it, but they unlikely to do so for long. When Bob Carver founded Phase Linear utilizing a new circuit design that permitted him to offer 750-watt amplifiers to rock groups for less than 250-watt amplifiers were selling for on the market, he expected to be copied immediately. In fact, competitors amazed him by failing to copy his ideas for nearly three years. But that was exceptional. Usually competitors will move in faster, especially if either the market looks highly attractive or the new venture looks vulnerable or both.

The proprietary shield must then be built with other advantages besides simply being first. By being aware of the need for these, the entrepreneur can think ahead at the outset to increase the odds of survival by seeking to build up one or more of the following competitive advantages:

1 Working harder for less and with fewer constraining formalities such as red tape can give the venture an edge. It can be a demanding way to win to the extent that it relies on a combination of longer hours, lower pay, and/or lower return on investment, but many small companies that lack other elements of a protective shield find it is what they must do. Unfortunately, it may not be enough, since it leaves little or no reserve capacity to match additional price cuts or extra efforts that competitors may resort to.

2 Legal protection for ideas through patents, trademarks, and/or copyrights may give the company a monopoly on a product, process, and/or design that wins customers. To get these, the startup must exercise exceptional creativity and innovativeness as well as following through on legal procedures.

3 Ownership of such things as advantageous location, licenses, ready inventory, or contracts with key employees, suppliers, agents, distributors, or customers. The owner's personality, ability to perform some tasks, charisma, and personal relationships are vital to certain firms. Some of these may be obtainable through a shrewd maneuver or purchase. Most of them, however, must be earned through performance over time. Hence the startup must find other ways to last until it is able to earn them.

---

[13] Peter F. Drucker, *Innovation and Entrepreneurship* (New York: Harper & Row, 1985), p. 209.

4 Financial capacity in terms of both cash available and ability to obtain credit to take advantage of buying opportunities, provide credit to customers, perform development work, advertise and support expansion can be a major competitive advantage, particularly for companies whose top managers must spend their time raising money to make moves rather than concentrating on performing the moves. Unless the startup enjoys an extraordinarily high profit margin, which few high-technology startups do, financial capacity may have to be purchased by sharing ownership.

5 Information in files, such as customer lists, supplier lists, product or service specifications, standard procedures, and brochures. Trade secrets may also allow it to perform with a competitive advantage. Some of this "special-advantage information" may be what the company already has. Over time it should acquire more.

6 Knowhow in the minds of the entrepreneur, partners, and/or employees, can also give the company superior performance capability in such areas as

a The company's technology—how to innovate on its performance frontier

b The company's customers—what they care about, how they buy, and what they can be expected to value from the company

c The company's operations—how to perform them, possibly including secret or little-known processes, and how to do them as well as or better than anyone else

7 Habits of buying by customers and of work by employees, and holding suppliers to standards as high as or higher than those of competitors can give the company an edge over them. Starting with employees who bring reputations and skills from their prior work should help initially, but there will probably be need to retune them in the startup and then add to them if the venture is to succeed.

Discerning, designing, and developing a competitive proprietary shield is the most crucial task of the entrepreneur for the survival and prosperity of the venture. It is, however, not simply a one-shot task. Rather, it requires continued vigilance and adaptation, as the following illustrates.

♦   Jugi Tandon had two degrees in engineering, plus an MBA and several years' experience at Memorex as a project engineer, mostly on magnetic heads for computer floppy disk drives. He had also started a floppy disk manufacturing operation for Pertec Corporation before he left to start on his own with $7,000 in capital. He figured the risk was low because "if you are a good engineer you can always get a job," he recalled. "That gave me the courage."[14]

In 1975 he started to manufacture magnetic heads for floppy drives, with his wife helping to cut and solder the cables. Making them for $12 and selling them for $18 against competitors at $50, he broke even the first month. Managing his company for the first three years with no other technically experienced people, he began to build sales, customer base, and product lines. By 1983 sales were

[14] Robert Levering, Michael Katz, and Milton Moskowitz, *The Computer Entrepreneurs* (New York: New American Library, 1984), p. 316.

over $300 million, the line included drives of all types, and there were 480 customers. The drives, moreover, included design innovations such as double-sided recording, which made them superior to those of competitors. He locked up all the business of such major drive users as Radio Shack and, later, IBM. And through his relatives and Indian background, he was able to manufacture them abroad cheaply. Tandon himself was able to live lavishly. The day his company went public in 1981, he bought a $130,000 Rolls Royce. Thereafter he built up his collection of Ferraris and other luxury cars to over thirty vehicles.

Competition was coming, however. IBM began developing second sources of supply. Japanese companies began introducing designs similar to Tandon's but at lower prices. Then new generations of drives more advanced than Tandon's began to appear. In late 1984 Tandon had to write off $137 million of obsolete inventory. And Indian suppliers run by Tandon relatives were found to be draining great amounts of cash from the company. By 1987 the company had become the target of a class action lawsuit for mismanagement, a Singapore subsidiary was being sold to raise cash, Tandon stock was "in the cellar," and management was said to be working on a turnaround.[15]

Tandon's company initially had the advantage of his ability to produce a sophisticated product that not many people could make and to sell it to a growing industry where demand was high and shakeout had not yet occurred, hence where profit margins were wide, allowing either high profits or easy price cutting. Later the competition greatly intensified, but by then his company had moved down the cost curve through experience and economies of scale, allowing it still to compete and prosper. Over time, however, competition made inroads on each of its competitive advantages while the company itself allowed them to weaken, resulting in a downward turn of its fortunes.

For other companies the proprietary elements may be entirely different. In rentals, for instance, it appears that tying up attractive sites through leases has been a most powerful element. Long after Hertz had been in operation, Warren Avis entered car rentals by opening offices at airports, which Hertz had failed to do. Franchise companies of various types seek to tie up certain sites in shopping centers, while others look for certain kinds of neighborhood locations. In some cases, such as fast foods, they find it advantageous to have other similar companies nearby, whereas in others, such as tool rentals, they seek to dominate the area. No company has been more successful than U-Haul at the latter:

◆   While in the navy in 1944, Leonard Shoen was hospitalized for five months with scarlet fever. With much time to think he began to envisage the possibilities of a trailer rental business. He had seen rental lots with one or two dozen trailers for rent at two dollars per day in Los Angeles, but the trailers, which were typically made of old car parts, were unreliable and had to be returned to the same lot after use.

Upon discharge from the navy he went to work on a better scheme. With $5,000 in personal savings he began buying trailers and building his business. He would sell the trailers to anyone he could, thereby recovering his capital, and then have his company lease them back. Thus the investors got an investment

---

[15] Jonathan Littman, "The Karma of Jugi Tandon," *California Business,* June 1988, p. 29.

tax break and he got trailers he could rent. For rental sites he lined up gas stations, thereby gaining wide geographical distribution that enabled him to offer one-way rentals. G.I.'s returning after the war provided a booming market, while the trailers themselves served as moving billboards to advertise the company name.[16]

Shoen's idea, initial capital and willingness to put it at risk, gave him the jump on possible competitors. After that, he managed to spread geographically faster than anyone could economically catch up.

Each company must identify its own combination of competitive advantages among those listed in the seven categories above. For Shoen it concentrated on the third of these, while for Tandon it was the first and sixth. For Polaroid it has been more in the second category, protection through patents. Ray Kroc began developing McDonald's by purchasing the rights to the name and recipe, but in the longer term it has been customers' perception of the product and service they know they, and more importantly their children, will get that keeps them coming in to buy.

ECONOMICALLY IDEAL VENTURE TYPES

Two concepts that appear to have a major bearing on long-term prosperity of a business are the notion of *distinctive competence* and *market share*. The two are related in the following way: A company with larger market share in its particular line of business gets more practice in performing that business than a company with a smaller market share and consequently should be able to develop through that practice a higher level of competence. At the same time, by having a larger market share a company enjoys economies of scale—quantity discounts on purchases, thinner spreading of advertising costs, and justification for greater investment in tooling and automation and for more research and development. Consequently, it has an advantage in lowering unit costs, which in turn can allow it to lower prices and thereby outsell the competition to gain still more market share, and so forth. Research data indicate both that more sharply defined competence, often as a result of narrower specialization, leads to greater growth, and that larger market share lends to higher profits.[17]

In evaluating prospective venture ideas it therefore makes sense to ask, "What will the company's distinctive competence be?" In other words, what will it be able to do better than other companies can and why? It also makes sense to ask what share of market the company will have as compared with competitors. If it seems likely to have only a very small share of market, such as the "deadly 2 percent" mentioned earlier in this chapter, and competitors enjoy larger shares, then it will need either some major performance improvement such as significant special innovation or else a lot of financing to increase its share and be able to survive.

One ideal approach is to begin early in a new industry. When the industry is small, it should be possible for the new company to obtain a significant share

[16] L. S. Shoen, *You and Me* (Las Vegas: AMERCO, 1980).

[17] Vesper and Haglund, "Strategies and Barriers"; and Boston Consulting Group, *Perspectives on Experience* (Boston: Boston Consulting Group, 1970).

without having to be large to do so. As the industry grows, the company can then grow with it, still maintaining its market share, with consequent high profits. This type of enterprise is ideal not only from the entrepreneur's point of view, because the company prospers, but also from a venture capitalist's point of view, because rapid growth of the company will create a profitable application for capital to expand the company's capacity to handle increasing business. Thus to capture a major market share at the opening stage of a new industry is an ideal pattern for a growth-oriented venture.

A second ideal type of venture is one that captures a major share of an existing but more mature industry. The major share will generate high profits, but if the industry, because of its maturity, is not growing, then the company will not have to grow in order to maintain its market share. This will mean that it will not need external venture capital. From a venture capitalist's point of view it is not particularly attractive. But from the entrepreneur's position it is, because the profits will not have to be plowed back but can rather be taken as salary, dividends, and other benefits. The trick, of course, is to capture a major share in an existing industry, and this can be done by choosing a very small industry to start in, by entering through purchase of a going concern that already has a respectable share, or by entering with a strong innovation or other competitive advantage. The nature of such competitive advantages will be the focus of the next two chapters.

TRIAL AND ERROR

Going through checkout questions can be the cheapest way to test a venture idea, but the surest way is simply to try the idea out by implementing it. By doing so not only will more certain feedback result, but through encountering problems and being forced to live with and solve them solutions will be found that could not be anticipated in an "armchair think through." Also side-street opportunities, as discussed in the preceding chapter, will probably be discovered. The creation of Analog Devices, a Massachusetts company specializing in digital processing equipment, is illustrative:

◆   Six years after graduation from M.I.T., Raymond Stata was selling instruments in Massachusetts for Hewlett-Packard when he bumped into former classmate Matthew Lorber, who was working at the M.I.T. instrumentation laboratory. The two found they had in common the desire not only to save money by sharing an apartment but also to start a business. They began building electronic power supplies on weekends and evenings, and in 1962 Stata quit his job to pursue the enterprise, Solid State Instruments, full time. He recalled its lack of success: "We didn't have any capital, we didn't have any experience and the business was badly strategized—it was really a bad deal. But the thing that really sustained it was the urge to try something on our own."

The two men viewed the power supplies as "just something to take off on. Having done that we pooled our relative skills and experiences and looked around for more meaningful products. . . . we shared a knowledge about gyro instrumentation and we developed this product which turned out to be pretty good," Stata observed.

Because of their product another company, Kollmorgen, took an interest in hiring the two men and bought their company to get them. They each received fifty thousand dollars worth of Kollmorgen stock in return for their year-old company plus their agreement to stay on for at least two years and help continue to build the business.

As their two-year obligation drew to a close, Stata and Lorber began discussing the possibility of starting a new company. As Stata recalled it, "We would find something else and get the hell out of there." The opportunity they found was to make operational amplifiers. These were items they had been designing and making as part of their gyro instrumentation product. They stopped making them when they found that they could obtain them more cheaply from other companies. But then they further discovered that those companies provided very poor service and support.

"Getting information, help or support was like pulling teeth," Stata said. "The salesmen never showed up, and the companies just weren't sales oriented. Well, countless other companies had made the same decision to buy rather than make and we presumed a whole bunch of people are going to start doing that. We could see some ways of developing, selling and marketing the products better than what was being done. So we came on the idea: well, that's it, we will strike out and set up a business to make operational amplifiers in competition with our vendors."[18]

The resulting company, Analog Devices, was established in 1965. Twenty years later it was publicly held with its shares valued at $500 million.

How did the selection analysis take place in this sequence? It appears to have been largely intuitive with Stata and Lorber. They had knowledge of what they could do and of what things a market was likely to want. When there was a match between the two they went ahead and tried a company around the idea. The first one, power supplies, apparently did not pass the profit test very well, and possibly this could have been foreseen with more extensive analysis. But it did pass another test, which was to serve as an entry wedge on which the two could get started, develop some experience, and stand to look around and leap after a better prospect.

SUMMARY

After noting four sets of factors that determine the choice among venture possibilities—head start factors, apparent feasibility, cost factors, and payoff potential of the business—this chapter described procedures for evaluating the attractiveness of alternative venture ideas. Key questions include how much can be made, how much can be lost, and how likely breakeven can be attained. A key element in this assessment is analysis of the venture's market. Longer term prospects of ventures were considered both in terms of the kinds of businesses ventures can ultimately become, whether low-paying, high-paying small, or high-growth companies, the latter two types generally being much more attractive than the former. Both recognition of strategies of size and attention to creation of the company's competitive shield can be important to its longer term viability.

---

[18] A. David Silver, *Entrepreneurial Megabucks* (New York: Wiley, 1985), p. 408.

chapter 7

Main Competitive Entry Wedges

The world of commerce generally does not welcome a new competitor for the customers and resources needed to create profits. Established companies do their best to maintain proprietary shields, as discussed in the preceding chapter, to ward off prospective as well as existing competitors. Consequently, the entrepreneur who would create a new competitor to attack them needs some sort of "entry wedge," a strategic competitive advantage for breaking into the established pattern of commercial activity. There are many ways of characterizing the kinds of "gimmicks" or special edges that can help. One is the familiar slogan to "find a need and fill it," which Miller elaborates in slightly more detail as follows:

♦ It must be either something that the community does not know it needs but will want when it hears about it; or it must fulfill a known and still unsatisfied need; or it must improve upon existing goods and services in a market that believes itself to be well served.[1]

This brief statement of Miller's makes several important points. One is that the heart of the entrepreneur's task is discovery of something customers will want. Another is that ways of satisfying those wants can take different forms, as a few brief examples can illustrate.

- *Present Unknown Need* When Alex Manoogian developed and tried to sell single-handed faucets in the 1950s, plumbing suppliers declined to carry them. He mounted his own selling campaign and succeeded, ultimately building the nation's largest plumbing supplies manufacturing company.

[1] Harry Miller, *The Way of Enterprise* (London: Deutsch, 1963), p. 125.

- *Future Unknown Need* When Gary Kildall, an instructor at the Naval Postgraduate School, developed the CP/M (control program/monitor) operating system in 1973, he had no idea that it would form the basis for a company. He offered it to Intel, but they took no interest in it. Two years later, after he had worked on other projects such as an astrology machine, Kildall found that demand for CP/M was rising due to the introduction of microcomputers, and he had the basis for his new company, Digital Research.[2]

- *Known Need* The need was apparent when Tom Fatjo's subdivision could not get adequate garbage collection. When he proposed that the community members themselves take up the task of collecting it, one of them suggested that he buy a truck and do it himself. He did, and from that built Browning-Ferris, a major corporation in waste collection.[3]

- *Existing Goods Improvement* Digital computers were already widely available by the mid-fifties when Ken Olsen, a thirty-one-year-old circuit designer at MIT Lincoln Laboratories, got the idea for creating a smaller one, the minicomputer, for certain segments of the market. Because established computer companies were blind to that opportunity, he was able to start the Digital Equipment Corporation, which became IBM's largest domestic competitor.

- *Existing Service Improvement* Airmail service had long been available when Fred Smith, a Yale student writing a term paper, got the idea that it could be improved through offering overnight delivery of "time sensitive goods" via a "hub and spokes" routing system. For Federal Express the hub became Nashville, and the company became an industry leader as other similar companies followed.

To explore this important concept further, the ensuing chapters will identify a series of different types of strategic entry wedges, beginning in this chapter with three general types most frequently used. The categorization will simply be an artifice for revealing a wide variety of possibilities. The different types are not always mutually exclusive, nor are lines between them always necessarily sharp. The more variety a would-be entrepreneur can discern, however, the more complete should be his or her kit of strategic tools for working with whatever opportunities for new ventures he or she may encounter.

The three main competitive entry wedges to be treated in this chapter are

1 *The New Product or Service* Among the three main wedges this is the least often used but can also be the most powerful.

2 *Parallel Competition* Here the product or service already exists, and the company's advantage derives rather from minor variations in what is offered and/or in how it is provided. This is the most often used entry approach.

[2] Paul Freiberger and Michael Swaine, *Fire in The Valley* (Berkeley, Calif.: Osborne/McGraw-Hill, 1984), p. 138.
[3] Thomas J. Fatjo, Jr., *With No Fear of Failure* (Waco, Tex.: Word Books, 1982).

3 **Franchise Entry**   This employs a proven product or service without variations but in new geographical areas under license.

Other variations of wedges will be described in the next chapter.[4]

ENTRY BARRIERS

Barriers to entry, created mainly proprietary shields of established companies, which the wedges must penetrate, can be grouped into three categories, each of which in turn can be further subdivided. The three are (1) customer characteristics, (2) competitor employee capabilities, and (3) required assets. Two facts about these barriers should be noted. First, they are usually not absolute, but rather matters of degree. For instance, employee capabilities may be similar in established competitors and in a would-be startup, but the established companies may have them to a higher degree. By coming close enough on some and by exceeding those of competitors on others, the startup may be able to accomplish entry.

Second, the relative importance of barriers is also a matter that differs with line of business. In some lines of work the major barrier may be customer beliefs and loyalties; in others it may be company assets such as special production machinery. A closer look at each of the three categories of barriers will clarify these distinctions, as a basis for examining how the barriers may be overcome.

Customer Characteristics: Why Should People Buy from a New Company?

Generally, people find it easier and safer to buy things they have bought before rather than new things, and to buy them from established suppliers rather than a startup. Customer characteristics can be divided into *customer habits, customer beliefs,* and *customer constraints.* In the first of these, *customer habits,* competitors usually have a clear advantage. As creatures of habit, people may continue to buy from an established supplier even though a startup offers something better. For example, some people consider digital watches and microwave ovens clearly superior to what they used before but nevertheless were slow to make the change. It was easier not to change, even though the change was worth making.

Also at issue are the *customer beliefs* as to whether it would be desirable to switch from competitors and buy from the startup company. These beliefs may be based on analysis of fact, such as whether the startup offers something other companies do not, is cheaper to buy from, can give faster delivery, has a better-performing product, and/or can give better service. They can also be based on suppositions or emotions.

This is where deal making can enter. What will it take to persuade the customer to buy from the startup? Exploring that question with a potential

---

[4] Not included are entry by way of inheritance, marriage, and illegal means, such as robbery.

customer may both help the sale and help the startup tune its product or service to other similar customers at the same time. Ability to do this is what allows startups in general to be characterized as more flexible than established companies and is often what enables them to prevail against much larger and generally more powerful competitors.

There may also be *constraints* on customers, which are the basis for entirely rational beliefs about whether it is wise to shift to buying from the startup. Porter has characterized these as "switching costs."[5] They apply mostly to companies buying from other companies, as opposed to consumer buying, and fall into four general categories:

- *Relearning* If the new product or service is not identical to what was used before, then there may be a need for the buyer to retrain workers to use it.
- *Dependability* In the short term there may be costs of checking out the new item, and developing or modifying specifications for selecting and testing it. In the long term, and often more important, there is the potential cost of having the new supplier fail and consequently running out of supplies, having to switch again, having to explain to customers, and possibly having to cope with delays for changeover.
- *Physical Accommodation* Modification of machinery, logistical systems, and possibly even the buyer's product may be needed to accept the startup's new offering.
- *Recontracting* Not the least of the switching costs may be the time and effort required to check out the new supplier and develop a working relationship. The change may also produce problems with old suppliers who may still be needed but irritated because of the loss of expected sales.

The first step in developing a remedy for each of these problems is to recognize its potential existence. The would-be entrepreneur may then be able to devise a solution, identify some other advantages that outweigh the problem, or work to develop satisfactory answers with the prospective customer.

Competitor Employee Capabilities: What Can the Startup Do Better Than They Can?

Two forms that employee capabilities can take are technical knowledge and polished working skills. The reason these are barriers for a firm that needs them to get started is that people cannot acquire them quickly. *Technical knowledge* may in part be formal, such as education in engineering or science, but the more important part will be that obtained by working experience dealing with the technology needed to produce what the new venture will offer the marketplace. The entrepreneur may possess this knowledge personally, and if not the specific knowledge, then he or she may have leads to it through knowledge

[5] Michael E. Porter, *Competitive Strategy* (New York: Macmillan, 1980), p. 10.

about key contacts. But the venture will probably also have to recruit it by persuading others to join the company, a task that can be challenging for a new and unproven enterprise.

To do so the company may have to overcome such unattractive features as lack of job security with other positive ones such as opportunity to work in a small group atmosphere, to grow with the business, to make a noticeable difference in what happens, and possibly to share rewards through participation in ownership.

If the company does succeed in hiring people with the needed capabilities, they will still have to develop *polished working skills* in the new company environment. An employee who has worked for a larger company may be accustomed to greater specialization and may have to develop the ability to handle different kinds of tasks. He or she will also have to learn how to work with new associates, suppliers, and customers and will have to operate with fewer resources, a lack of company specialists in such areas as employee relations or law, and probably a greater urgency to get things done. In short, the employee may need to develop both new work habits and new attitudes toward the job, some of which may come as a refreshing change and others as an annoyance.

Required Assets: How Can the Startup Acquire What Would Be Needed?

Assets for getting things done in a startup can differ considerably from those in an established company. Some can take the form of intangibles, such as *reputation, name recognition,* and *market breadth.* Others may involve formal documents, such as proprietary *patents, copyrights,* and *trademarks,* or *contracts* with suppliers, landlords, or distribution channels, as noted in the preceding chapter. The contracts may also be less formal but nevertheless represent monopoly arrangements possessed by the company. A new company, seeking to break into competition, may find itself up against advantages of *location* or *economies of scale* possessed by established competitors which are difficult or impossible to match. Those competitors may, for instance, have an established distribution system, complete with nationwide advertising and a service network supported by an ongoing sales volume that is large compared with zero for the startup.

Often the hope is that enough startup capital, combined with ingenuity and contracts to tie in with existing channels and service networks belonging to others, will be able to overcome them. But a great amount of cash, initially not justified by any sales volume, will be needed for *working capital* and possibly also for *technical development, capital equipment* and *custom tooling* to produce what the startup will offer. To justify such investment the startup must have some sort of "entry wedge" that will enable it to penetrate these entry barriers and prevail against established competitors. The greater the barriers, the greater the need for a more powerful entry wedge. In situations where barriers are high, it may be newness in the product or service of the startup that is needed for overcoming them.

NEW PRODUCT

Relatively rare is the invention of a new product in an area where nothing like it has been available. Such a development may be made possible by the advance of technology, as when discovery of transistors led to pocket radios, or by the emergence of a new customer desire, such as the market for backyard bomb shelters in the 1950s. Or it can occur simply as the discovery of a way to meet a need that had not been recognized or that nobody had found a way to satisfy before. Such a discovery led to the formation of this successful biomedical equipment company:

◆　　　Early in his training as a surgeon overseas with the Marine Corps in 1952, a young doctor observed that deaths often occurred due to heart stoppages during operations which were not noticed quickly enough by attending doctors. He knew of no instrument available for monitoring heartbeat and signaling when it stopped, but drawing upon prior electric experience as a radio "ham," he was able to create one and obtain a patent on it. After leaving the service he met through friends a senior partner in a prominent Boston law firm, who helped form a corporation in return for $300 plus a small share of stock. Selling more stock to friends, he opened a small shop and made three or four units before running out of money. He sold a license on his product to a large company and began work on a second new product which would deliver an electric shock to stop heart "twitching" during open-heart surgery, and then which would operate externally for heart attack victims, obtaining additional research funding from the National Institute of Health.

This case clearly illustrates that just having a good idea may not be enough to get a company started. The idea had to be developed into a working model, and that took special knowhow in electronics. It also had to be developed into a product and presented to a market where it was unfamiliar, and that took more financing than a young medical doctor could muster from his own income. Finally, he had to share his idea through a royalty arrangement in order to keep his company going. Later, still further compromises were needed in ownership before the company became fully established in the market, even though the inventor managed to come up with additional successful products that were new and unique and for which the market also was new. Although procedures in medicine are constantly being researched and experimented with, they are in many ways slow to change and new products can have a hard time "breaking in."

A contrast is the toy industry, where a stream of new products pours forth every year, particularly at Christmas time. Some large toy companies generate as much as half their sales year after year with new products. Most such products come from professionals who develop new toys all year around and are highly experienced both in the kinds of things the market will accept and in the combinations of materials and ideas from which new toys can be composed. Toy companies often keep themselves open to independent inventors too, however, because occasionally one of them will submit a new product idea worth large-scale development. Also occasionally an independent inventor will carry the new product all the way to market by forming a new company to exploit it. This would be a case of taking a new product, the novel toy design, to an established market, which includes the existing channels of toy distribution, the toy purchasers, who are most often parents, and toy users, children and sometimes their parents. An example is the following:

♦   Model rockets existed when in the late 1960s an engineer who was employed by an aerospace firm began in his spare time to work on a new design. The trouble was that all existing rockets used a pyrotechnic propellant which was highly combustible and could injure users, and when stored in warehouses posed enormous danger. He devised a scheme to propel instead with compressed freon gas loaded into the rocket from an aerosol can and then released through the nozzle during launch by using a small battery to melt electrically a thin wire which held back a sealing plug in the rocket. A partnership was formed with $3,000 from the engineer plus another $2,000 from one of his colleagues at work. Work began in the engineer's basement in 1965, with development of prototypes. By 1968 the partnership had been changed to a corporation, patents had been applied for in the United States, Japan, Germany, etc., and the design was ready for production.

Now more capital was needed, and the founders began selling stock to friends at one dollar per share, which soon raised an additional $15,000. They located a small shop to rent and began seeking suppliers to subcontract parts manufacturing. By soliciting bids they found it more economical to have some machining performed 150 miles away in another city. Enough parts were ordered for an initial production run of 1,000 units.

The marketing plan was to sell initially through mail order, and as the company grew in strength, to drive competitors off the market by lawsuits concerning product safety. At the same time it was expected that legal permission would be needed for selling the new product across the country. Letters were written to state authorities explaining safety features of the new product compared with those already on the market. To the entrepreneurs' surprise the responses were often unfavorable, threatening litigation if the product were sold in the responding states. An exception was New York, whose bomb squad pronounced the product safe. The entrepreneurs concluded that no safety lawsuit could win against them and decided to ignore the threats.

Advertisements were placed in magazines like *Boy's Life* and *Popular Mechanics* soliciting twenty-five cents for information which would include an order blank for a rocket at $10.95 postpaid. The company figured each unit would involve direct costs of $5, which would leave roughly a 50 percent gross margin. This price represented the high end of competitors' prices. Sales began to trickle in, but not fast enough. By the end of 1968, the owners had left their former jobs and capital was short.

The engineer approached an investment banker friend, who agreed to help raise another $50,000. This capital was used for rudimentary production equipment and presentation at the Chicago toy show. The show stimulated orders from toy distributors and chain stores, which were then shown to the investment banker to raise another $200,000. Aided by an article in the March 1969 *Popular Mechanics,* sales began to grow, then expanded further as distributorships across the country took hold. Sales went from $50,000 in 1969 to $150,000 in 1970 and $300,000 in 1971. Breakeven was achieved in 1970, but sales were cyclical, peaking at Christmas time and dragging the rest of the year. Capital was insufficient to sustain the growth, and the founders' equity was now down to 30 percent. Rather than approach the stock market—which was now having problems of its own—for more capital, the owners decided to sell at a substantial profit.

The founders of this toy company based their strategy on a product that was new and clearly better in one important respect, safety. In addition, it included other novel features, such as an automatically deploying return parachute, plus instructions with great sophistication about how to arrange payload and launching angle to achieve selected performance goals. But they also faced substantial obstacles. How much readers of the advertisements really were concerned about safety and whether they believed the claims that this product was truly safe (as many state agencies apparently did not) were open questions. The high price of the product and relatively thin margin (toys often retail for more than five times direct costs) made competition difficult in spite of the novelty. So although the company was able to gain entry, it never made substantial profits, and although the owners realized a gain on their investment in selling out, they did not become rich. Thus the entry wedge of novelty in this case was only marginally sufficient at best.

Finally, as an illustration of a "right product at the right time," we can note the case of Osborne Computer. Although it ultimately failed (as will be further discussed in the next chapter), it combined features that initially provided an entry wedge of tremendous power:

◆   Adam Osborne's venture began as independent technical writing. Trained as a chemical engineer, he had joined Shell Chemical, only to find himself unwanted. "So I went into business for myself," he recalled, "more out of necessity than desire—and by the mid-seventies I was running a small Berkeley-based publishing company that sold books about microcomputers."[6] He became a computer authority who lectured on assembly language programming and wrote a column for *Interface Age* magazine. He also wrote technical documentation for microprocessor manufacturers in the early seventies before introduction of the first microcomputer kit, the Altair. To distinguish himself from other microprocessor experts, he wrote and published in 1975 what turned out to be the first book on microcomputers.

IMSA1, one of the first microcomputer manufacturers, began ordering copies of this book in ever greater quantities in 1976, prompting Osborne to tell his secretary that "either these guys are raving lunatics, or they are on to something big." He began spending more time on writing and publishing, observing that it had clearly become a better business than consulting. Until 1977 his were the only microcomputer books on the market.

As the microcomputer industry developed, Osborne began to include more stories about startup companies in his column, and he began to think about venturing beyond publishing himself. By 1978 Apple, Radio Shack, and Commodore were becoming industry leaders, and Osborne's own company had become the leading microcomputer book publisher with some twenty-five titles and a half-million dollars in sales, all from an equity base of $3,000. Osborne himself wanted to try manufacturing, and when McGraw-Hill offered to buy him out, he sold his company, staying on for a time to manage while under contract, but thinking about his own computer design.

The idea of a very low priced machine occurred to him, but Sinclair, a British company, beat him to it in 1979 by introducing a $99 computer. But the low-price aspiration remained with Osborne as he developed his design. Other guidelines he later recalled adopting included "To be number one, you don't have to be the best, you don't even have to be good. All that is necessary is that your product be adequate, properly supported and readily available. IBM proved this point . . . Apple Computer is another example. . . . With these lessons in mind, I

---

* Adam Osborne and John Dvorak, *Hypergrowth, The Rise and Fall of Osborne Computer Corporation* (New York: Avon Books, 1984).

designed my computer to include everything that was necessary for low-cost computing and excluded all extras."

He added two other ideas to his own. One was to combine drives and screen into the same box with the computer, instead of separately with wires running between. The other was to make it small enough to fit under an airplane seat. Two other choices later to haunt him were the use of single-sided disk drives and a small five-inch screen capable of displaying only fifty-two characters, twelve more than the Apple II of the day but fewer than the eighty becoming available elsewhere. For help on the hardware he hired a well-known pioneer of the microcomputer industry, Lee Felsenstein, in July 1980 for subsistence wages plus 25 percent of the company's stock. By the end of 1980 Osborne himself had invested $100,000 and a venture capitalist, Jack Melchor, had invested $40,000.

"My greatest coup," he recalled, "was the software bundled with Osborne 1." Some of the software he bought at bargain prices and some was bought with shares of Osborne stock, bringing the total cost for inclusion of an operating system, a word processing package (Wordstar), and a spreadsheet program (Supercalc) to less than $10 per computer.

As 1981 began Osborne raised another $900,000, roughly one-third from venture capitalists and the rest from friends and personal sources, based on Visicalc financial projections. At a March trade show the first prototypes were exhibited, and Osborne recalled that "our booth drew huge crowds, largely because of the announced retail price: $1,795 was roughly half of what any other microcomputer cost, including the same software."

After the trade show, development of production began to fulfill July delivery promises made for ninety computers ordered at the show. A plastic case was acquired; suppliers were lined up for other components. Publicity helped sales: one *Wall Street Journal* article saturated the company's switchboard for days. The first computer was shipped on June 30, and by fall 1981 the company was "buried under an avalanche of orders." By year-end sales totaled 7,053 computers versus an original forecast of 9,530. In the fiscal year that followed and ended February 1983, the company posted sales of $100 million.

Unsuccessful New Products

For many new product ideas the market interest is simply not sufficient. Examples can be seen in advertisements of older magazines for products that are not, and possibly never were, on the market. Such failures come as much from big companies (Ford's Edsel, Kenner's Steve Scout, Warner-Lambert's Listerol, and the quadrasonic radio receivers of several major makers) as from small ones. Mark Twain observed, "The man with a new idea is a crank, until the idea works out," and then proceeded to buck the naysayers by backing a series of inventions (including, for example, self-adjusting suspenders) all of which, in spite of his genius as humorous speaker and author, were failures. Many other examples of products that will never work out can be seen at inventors' expositions held by a number of state chambers of commerce. An important fact that can be observed at these fairs is that despite the fact that few of the displayed inventions will prove commercially successful, virtually all of their inventors display absolute confidence in the promise of their creations. It has often been observed that unwarranted confidence has been necessary for the achievement of many successes. But it has regrettably been responsible for many expensive failures as well. Sometimes it may be the result of an inventor's infatuation with his or her own creation, but it often catches people in apparently "objective" positions of judgment as well, many of them experienced professionals in the evaluation of new ideas. Below is one example of each:

♦   A burly truck driver became annoyed with the task of pulling staples out of the many invoices, bills of lading, and numerous other forms required in the business. After trying the existing devices, which were either too easy to lose, too bulky in the pocket, or too awkward to use, he struggled along with a penknife until one day he got an idea for a small pincerlike device which could slip over the end of a pen or pencil for easy carrying and recovery from a shirt pocket. In his home workshop he fashioned a prototype out of tin, reworking and adjusting it until it fit snugly on a pen and still worked properly to grip and remove staples. He then used it in his work and as he became more adept at operating it, he started showing it to others in truck stops along his route. When they asked for duplicates he began asking the stop proprietors if they would put them up for sale if he supplied them, and received what he regarded as encouraging replies. Now he was ready for his major move. He invested $35,000 to have a progressive die made for stamping out and forming the parts in high volume. Taking a few samples, he then started looking for sales, pointing out that he was now ready to deliver in any volume desired. He visited store operators, who either declined or referred him to their buyers. These buyers, in turn, referred him to the wholesalers from whom they purchased. And the wholesalers referred him back to the store operators and store buyers. Nobody told him they thought the product would not sell. They just didn't order any.

♦   In the early 1960s an experienced, sophisticated, and highly respected San Francisco venture capital firm "dropped a bundle" on a new product with the catchy name (they thought at the time) of "Steam-Stir." This device was designed to pass steam up through food to cook it in the home kitchen and was demonstrated to perform an excellent job of cooking rice and heating a variety of other vegetables and foods. It made little mess, could not burn or dry out the food, and was easy to use. The venture capitalists made a careful assessment, and it was easy to see from the number of households in the world that the total potential market was virtually limitless. The trouble was that after investments had been made in development, tooling, and initial marketing efforts, it became apparent that people simply did not want to buy the item. The product was terminated and the investment written off.

How can such mistakes be avoided? If there were a perfect answer, there would be many fewer made. Often it is necessary to make an investment as a test and write it off if the test fails. The young men who developed the titanium frame bicycle described in Chapter 4 lost over $25,000 on the venture. Their conclusion in hindsight, however, was that it was necessary to make that gable in order to test feasibility. There was no way, they felt, to learn whether the idea would work without investing in a prototype and in travel to potential suppliers and investors to see whether the venture would work.

Importance of Degree of Advantage

New product advantages can come in all degrees of strength, and generally it is desirable to avoid ventures where the likely margin of success is close. From one day to the next in such a venture it can appear that the company's fortunes shift from success to failure and back, and it can even take years for the situation to settle out clearly, years during which investors and management alike live through considerable grief. Many who have followed such a course have in hindsight proclaimed, "I'd never do it that way again," even though the enterprise eventually succeeded and made them wealthy.

◆   In 1966 a man who had obtained eighteen years of experience in engineering, sales, and general management with several computer manufacturing companies, both large and small, decided to start a company of his own. With savings of $500,000 he decided to start the company around two computer peripheral products that he considered promising. To reach two million in sales, he reasoned, they would only have to capture around 2 or 3 percent of their respective markets, and in case one of the two failed, the other should serve as a fallback. To recruit additional investors, he prepared formal plans for product development, marketing, and financing, including extensive details, time schedules, and dollar forecasts. Five alternative financing plans were worked out involving some nineteen different financing schemes with various tax advantages and other investor appeals. Market surveys and profit analyses were performed and yielded encouraging information, which was further supported by enthusiastic responses of different user groups to whom the plans were presented. Money-raising efforts were successful in obtaining $900,000. By 1969, this had been consumed by losses and an additional $300,000 was raised through public offering. Losses continued, however, and still further funds were obtained through an SBA-guaranteed loan for $388,000, then a rights offering for $500,000, further infusions of $200,000 from the founder's savings and a $600,000 private placement. By 1973 one of the two original products had been sold to a foreign company after having earlier been dropped, and the other had been dropped as well, other products meanwhile having been developed. Losses continued until early 1974, when the company announced a twelve-weeks' profit and said they were "highly optimistic."

This case is particularly of interest for the light it sheds on detailed planning and market research. Although these two "good management practices" may often be helpful and apparently did help this company—particularly in raising capital and perhaps in other respects as well—they still did not ensure success. In hindsight the plans simply proved to be in error and the market research misleading. Management's conclusions from the experience were the following:

1   Talk is cheap in market research, and it is easier to get optimistic answers than it is to get orders from prospective customers.
2   It would have been more worthwhile to spend early sales efforts on obtaining orders directly rather than on advertising and trade show presentations that did not yield direct orders.
3   It is better to make smaller capital commitments and make them contingent on shorter-run results as a company progresses rather than make larger commitments and await longer-run results on faith.

More solid progress toward success was exhibited in the creation of the following publication venture:

◆   As free-lance publicity agents, Robert Peterson and Robert Lindsay had worked together publicizing the first Hot Rod Show sponsored by the Southern California Timing Association in 1947. From this experience, and inspired by the fact that other work was hard to come by at the time, the two came upon the idea of publishing *Hot Rod Magazine*. The first 10,000 copies were published with a borrowed $400 and quickly sold out, convincing them that they had a viable product. *Motor Trend* and other hobby magazines followed. Lindsay sold out for $250,000 in 1952, and the company continued as Peterson Publications.

In this case, had the magazine not proven to be an early success the founders could quickly have cut it off without a substantial loss, although they then would, of course, never have known whether it ultimately would, like the computer company above, have become profitable. *Careers Today*, a magazine introduced by the management of the highly successful publication *Psychology Today*, was an example of this pattern. After trying only a few issues the founders concluded that the sales trend was insufficiently promising, and simply cut it off. This left them with a loss, but at least did not aggravate it.

A rule advocated by one very successful entrepreneur is that any new product should have at least three different substantial advantages over competitors to justify support. These could be in performance, quality, appearance, lower cost, higher markups for distributors and dealers, novel service provisions, faster delivery, more custom treatment, easier customer credit, and so forth. In his own company that particular entrepreneur built sales from zero to over $1 million on very little capital within a year through a combination of (1) direct selling to distributors through personal sales calls by himself and the other company officers (while the large competitors whose market he was attacking used only salesmen, not executives), (2) a technological innovation in the product substituting an electronic readout in contrast to competitors' mechanical displays, (3) a larger price spread for distributors made possible through lower manufacturing cost than competitors, and (4) a service policy that meant more rapid turnaround for customers who had any troubles with the product. Thus in effect his company had four special selling advantages for its new product. In general, it is probably less important how many there are than how great the competitive advantages are. But nevertheless two very useful questions for the would-be entrepreneur to consider are, How many competitive advantages does the new product or service offer? Can any others be added to make the number greater?

NEW SERVICES

As pointed out in an earlier chapter, services have a vastly higher failure rate than manufacturing enterprises in general. Typically, there is less required in terms of either effort or capital to start a service, and as a result more are started, leading to a proliferation of the variety already available, intensified competition, and lower margin of profit. Whenever one is successful, others quickly enter, thus reducing the market potential per firm and depressing prices. This, in turn, multiplies the failure rate.

Most service company startups largely represent duplications of businesses already in existence except for minor, though important differences (about which more will be said shortly)—another beauty shop, another restaurant, gift store, or television enterprise. But occasionally new ideas emerge (and/or reemerge), such as the following:

◆   A group of young men fresh out of graduate school with their MBA degrees were determined to have their own business. After exploring a number of possible ventures, particularly in connection with setting up some sort of firm to retail mutual funds, they hit upon a different idea. Why not offer to relieve homeowners of the fuss and bother of locating a suitable repairman every time something went wrong with their house? The new company would provide comprehensive home repair services, guaranteed to please, on a contractual basis. Thus the company would in effect become the expert on whom to call, do the calling, arrange the work, keep track of the results, and take a cut on the fees for itself.

A plan was developed, venture capital was sought and successfully raised, contractual arrangements worked out, space rented, and soon a new sign appeared along the San Francisco Bayshore freeway over the new building of the Homesmith Corporation. The service was advertised, customers were obtained, services begun, and the company was in business. But in spite of energetic efforts by the young entrepreneurs, the concept simply didn't work. Not enough customers could be obtained at prices sufficiently high to cover the costs of hiring the work and covering problems with the work to customers' satisfaction. So within a couple of years the business was closed and the young founders moved to other things.

◆   A former Nevada casino dealer with a college degree in engineering encountered an opportunity to buy a small bar for $6,000. He took it, improved its performance, and sold it eighteen months later for $88,000. He then moved to the West Coast, bought a small yacht and a diesel-powered Mercedes with part of the money, and took a job in the used-car business. In the summer of 1973 the diesel engine in his boat needed replacement, and in looking for it he learned that marine diesels had incorporated modern design improvements which the diesel in his Mercedes, unchanged in design for thirty years, lacked. This observation gave him the idea of converting U.S. cars and small trucks to operation on modern marine diesels. Chrysler-Nissan, he found, made a diesel that was relatively light, operated in the right RPM range for existing automotive gearing, offered good economy, met EPA emission standards, and had parts suppliers nationally. Buying one of these and a new Dodge van, he removed the gasoline engine and put the diesel in for a total cost of $6,800. Then, satisfied with the improved mileage and the performance, he decided to make such conversions a business, quit his used-car job, and began organizing the venture.

Figuring that it would take about $25,000 to get going, he went to see a banker for a loan. The banker not only liked the idea but volunteered to invest. The two men then each invested $17,000 to provide the $25,000 plus an extra $9,000 for contingencies. An attorney was engaged to set up the corporation for only $100 (it worked out fine), a consulting firm was paid $900 to develop a written plan ("It was a complete waste"), and a "big eight" accounting firm was given $500 to set up books ("They did a poor job and we regretted it"). Through a real estate firm several possible sites were located and one signed up on a year-to-year lease. Shop equipment, such as jacks, grinders, and welding equipment, was bought for $6,000, three mechanics were hired at union scale, and machine job shops were contacted for fabrication of conversion parts. Obtaining sales through dealers and referrals production began in October 1973 with plans to perform around four conversions per month working up to twenty per month by mid-1974. Moderate problems were encountered with some adapters that did not work quite right, engines that needed more tuning, and others that proved too weak for the vehicles and consequently needed supercharging, but these were not too difficult to cope with. By December 1973 the firm was doing ten cars per month.

Then the big problem hit. The Arab oil boycott and energy crisis struck and news media started mentioning the company's conversions to diesel operation as an antidote to the gas shortage. A local newspaper article, spread further by the AP wire service, and TV coverage suddenly brought inquiries and orders from all over the nation. The company doubled its work force and added a secretary, but plant space limited further expansion, and growing numbers of customers had to be turned away. Then the banker announced that he had to withdraw from the business because of possible conflict of interest seen by his employer. The two partners began looking for someone to buy the banker out. By April 1974 other partners had been obtained and most of the production problems cured, except for the insufficient volume, which was now restricted by lack of expansion capital. The new partners came up with $13,000 more, but not nearly enough. The president was spending nearly all his time looking for money.

As the fuel crisis eased, production was stabilized at around twenty-five cars a month, selected from among potential customers on the basis of ease of conversion. One of the companies contacted for money, a large auto firm, indicated that it too planned to set up in the business but on a nationwide basis and offered to either buy 51 percent of their stock on its terms or enter competition. The entrepreneur and his partners decided to sell, taking with them a healthy profit, but regretted they had not been able to raise enough capital to go national themselves and thereby stay ahead of the competition.

Several contrasts, some in line with "conventional wisdom" and others not, can be noted from these two examples. Whereas the MBAs whose venture did not work out were inexperienced in the line they entered, the engine converter began with knowledge of engineering in general, some knowledge of diesels in particular, prior work in the automobile business (although used cars, not conversion), and a previous successful entrepreneurial venture. On the other hand, the often-claimed cause of failure, weak financing, certainly did not apply to the MBAs because they had strong venture capitalists behind them, and had their venture appeared to merit further support, it would undoubtedly have been given. The engine converter began with a considerably larger stake than have many entrepreneurs, but even that proved too little when a large market demand made itself felt. Most striking, though, may be the effect of the unforeseen Arab oil boycott on the engine converter. He was doing fairly well before it came, and its occurrence was both his blessing and to some extent his undoing. It gave his sales and profits a great boost, but it also outran his capital and attracted competition that combined in forcing him to relinquish control. Thus while the MBAs appear to have chosen an idea whose time never came, the converter his upon one that was almost too timely, though it made him a healthy profit.

PRODUCT-SERVICE SEQUENCES

A recurring theme that may be noted in entrepreneurial experiences is that action leads to opportunities, usually unforeseen, particularly when the action is aimed at solving a problem or creating something to satisfy a need others share. This pattern not only tends to play a crucial role in revealing opportunities for startup but also goes on after a company has started to reveal additional opportunities for expansion. New products lead to other new products or services, and vice versa as the company comes into contact with customers and as people learn about the company's capabilities and seek out its assistance on problems they have. The following two examples will illustrate first how a product can lead to a service, and second how a service can lead to a new product.

♦   A salesman of metal products had given serious thought to starting his own company with a new product idea he had conceived, but he dropped it when terms proposed by his prospective financial backer proved unacceptable. Then one night his wife invited to dinner another woman, whom she knew from work, and the woman's husband. The salesman found conversation tedious because the other man declined to discuss common topics like sports and politics and instead kept coming back to a design project he was engaged in at work. His employer, a very large manufacturing company, needed to form in moderate volume an important part out of very difficult-to-work metal for one of its products, and he found no machine on the market capable of doing the forming. Hence the man had been asked to design one. He added that the large company had no interest in the forming machine except for producing that part, and did not expect to patent it. What finally caught the salesman's attention, however, was his impression that the forming capability might be useful on occasion to other companies. The visitor was intrigued by the idea of starting a "moonlight" venture to produce another such machine and offer its services on a job shop basis. A third partner was located who provided financial backing, and the company was begun in the salesman's garage. The machine was made, sales followed, other machines were added, and within ten years the company was doing an annual volume of over $1 million with a healthy profit.

———————

♦   Two engineers in a large aerospace company, had become expert in strain gage instrumentation. One day they were surprised when a subcontractor to the company submitted a bid that included a charge for strain gages on a product at a rate roughly ten times what the two men estimated such work should sell for. Thus alerted to a potential market, the two began asking manufacturers' representatives in the strain gage business about potential customers for a new strain gage application service. Small contracts resulted, which the two began to serve on evenings and weekends. However, they noticed that such work tended to be sporadic and undependable, and that to make it a permanent, full-time business some sort of proprietary product line would be needed. One possible idea they thought of was to make strain-gage-based weighing scales, and to test this idea they visited a large lumber company to see if it would have any interest in some sort of platform scale they might develop to weigh trucks. The lumber plant supervisor, however, suggested instead that they design an on-board load-measuring system for trucks. The partners tentatively declined, feeling that they were not familiar enough with the sort of application that would be needed. They did discuss it further with loggers, however, and concluded that the appeal of such a system, which would make it possible for truckers to load their trucks to the legal limit accurately without exceeding it, would be an attractive market if it could be tapped. Bringing in additional partners to complement their existing expertise and resources, they went ahead with the design. It was successful, other weighing products followed, and six years later, only eight years after the original part-time service business began, the company was well in the black with sales over $1.3 million.

The second of these two patterns, where a business begins as a service and later moves into products, is more common than the first wherein the order is reversed. It is a pattern that many consulting services and job machine shops seek to follow, to get away from the easy-entry competition, which keeps margins thin in most services, and reach the shelter of proprietary designs and capital equipment. But it is not a particularly easy route, as illustrated by the fact that most such services never manage to achieve the shift.

The sequence of one opportunity's leading to another is not confined to occurrence within the same company, of course. A major new product such as television may create opportunities for many new independent companies, television repair shops, not connected with the innovating company itself, and those in turn may lead to opportunities for still others, such as the companies that manufacture instruments for TV repair shops and others that offer technician training. The advantage tends to lie, however, with those that are active in the industry and in better positions to see the opportunities coming.

PARALLEL COMPETITION

It is not necessary to have a new product or service to start a business and succeed. In fact, most do not. Competitive duplications, "me too" products and services, are being introduced all the time both by new companies and by existing ones. Professor Arnold Hosmer even suggested that procedures for such "me too" entry might be formalized in a strategy he referred to as "parallel competition."[7] Although he intended this method as one for small companies to use in competing with larger ones, the words also fit well to describe the entry wedge by which most new companies get started, namely by introducing a product or service that is already available on the market, but with variations sufficient to gain entry. The distinction between a product or service that can be called "new" and one that instead is "parallel" is a matter of degree, including a "gray area" where assignment to one category or the other requires arbitrary judgment and is not likely to be very useful. But in clearer cases the distinction can help to highlight the degree of newness, which is an important strategic dimension.

The opening or "market hole" that allows parallel entry may exist because existing firms have not expanded sufficiently to fill demand, or because the new firm offers advantages to customers through small innovations or by simply working harder. Sometimes competitors have been left alone long enough to grow slack. One successful entrepreneur commented, "Any company is bound to have some unhappy customers, and if it doesn't have many competitors it will tend to have a higher percentage of customers who would like to buy from someone else."

---

[7] Arnold W. Hosmer, "Parallel Competition" (Teaching Note #SME 59, Harvard Business School, 1961).

A study of 120 small metalworking plants noted in Chapter 2 concluded, "In most industries there are enough marginal operators with inferior quality, high prices and poor service to permit success to a competent and determined beginner."[8] Hosmer went on to point out that many companies with wide product lines tend to have one or more items that earn exceptionally high margins and may therefore be especially vulnerable to parallel competition. Other clues to opportunity may be the presence of big companies in markets that have turned out to be too small to inspire their careful attention, product difficulties, labor troubles, expired patents, slow deliveries, and technological obsolescence.

Included in the parallel competition category are many of the traditional success stories of solo self-employed individuals who become team builders such as the man who buys a truck and offers freight services, then adds a second truck and driver as his traffic grows, and so on until one day he has a large trucking company; or the fry cook who manages to save a little money, one day buys a small counter, finds his food popular, expands to larger quarters, thereby increasing profits, eventually opening several similar restaurants which become well known and highly successful. The service or products offered are not substantially different from what was available to customers before; competitors were already offering them, though perhaps with not quite the same personality or location or service flair.

The most extreme form of parallel competition appears in certain professions such as real estate and insurance sales, where anyone can enter with little or no capital and many do. Here competitors have virtually identical offerings and seek the same customers. Much of the public feels overly harassed to begin with by salespeople in these fields, and those few who become highly successful typically do so only after persisting through many failures. An example was Michael Braunstein, a life insurance man whose annual production reached an average of $20 million in sales. After dropping out of college, he went into selling life insurance, "like a lot of people. Something goes wrong with their original career and they go into insurance because they think it's an easy way out." In fact, for Braunstein it didn't turn out to be very easy, at least not at first:

◆   I had a lot of discouraging experiences starting out. It was very difficult, mainly because I had no one to see except the fathers of my friends. It was a case of twenty-one talking up to fifty or fifty-five. And fifty-five doesn't listen well to twenty-one, particularly when twenty-one doesn't know what he is talking about, which I didn't.[9]

With time, Braunstein developed expertise in how to use life insurance to reduce taxes, particularly through pension and profit-sharing trusts for small corporations, and as his expertise increased so did his prosperity. Had he somehow had the expertise to begin with, presumably the starting would have been easier, but the selling job would still have been a difficult challenge against direct competition, and development of clientele would still have taken time.

In some cases selection of parallel competition as a means of entry may

---

[8] Kenneth Lawyer et al., *Small Business Success: Operating and Executive Characteristics* (Cleveland: Bureau of Business Research, Case Western Reserve University, 1963).
[9] David L. Goodrich, *Horatio Alger Is Alive and Well and Living in America* (New York: Cowles, 1971), p. 145.

be a matter of choice, while in others, as illustrated by the following example, it can be for the entrepreneur a matter of perceived necessity:

◆   Following the death of his father a young man had taken hold of a fish brokerage business (mentioned in Chapter 2). But then he found that the other brokers from whom he was buying fish were cheating by providing him with inferior products. The company was consequently losing money and he knew he would have to straighten out his sources of supply or else shut down shortly, because his capital would give out.

He elected to enter directly into competition with the brokers who were cheating him. Buying a boat of his own, he began making the rounds among fishermen as soon as they had landed their fish, and buying from them directly. This provided him with good fish, and his customers responded with increased sales. Soon the company was in the black with rapidly rising profits. Eventually his former suppliers came around to providing him with dependable products, enabling him to sell his boat and operate as a successful broker as he had originally intended.

Parallel Services

Most parallel competition startups are, like the preceding examples, in services. Every doctor or lawyer who opens a new office in a metropolitan area, for instance, faces a market with numerous established competitors. The same is true of drugstores, barber shops, and furniture shops in cities. Direct competitive entry occurs most often where requirements in terms of capital and special knowhow are least. House painting, janitorial service, gardening, and simple appliance repair fit these conditions. Most such businesses never grow large, but a few become highly prosperous, as did the following manufacturers' agency:

◆   Morton Levy was a toy salesman when he met Jerry Fryer, office manager of a toy manufacturer. In late 1948, both earning less than $8,000 per year, they became partners, borrowed $10,000, and opened an office as manufacturers' representatives on commissions between 6 and 7 percent of sales. Traveling and selling any accounts they could get hold of, they managed to earn over $30,000 between them the first year on sales of $500,000. By 1954 they had incorporated and built a sales force of seven men selling nationwide for seven toy manufacturers.

Retailing is a field where parallel competition is virtually the only possible mode of entry. It is easy to rent an outlet in which to "set up shop," easy to obtain goods to sell, provided that there is some capital with which to do it, and easy to sit back waiting and hoping for the customers. The problem of entering the retail business, clothing sales for instance, can be very straightforward. The path to failure is also very short for a majority of retail firms, and among those that survive the net income per manager is very low. Exceptions exist, among those who early recognized the potential bonanza in discounting during the 1950s for example, and those who franchised some chains such as 7–11 grocery stores, but these are a most tiny fraction of the retailer population.

◆   Farrell's Ice Cream Parlour Restaurants grew out of a 1962 Portland, Oregon, church supper where Kenneth E. McCarthy and Robert E. Farrell met. McCarthy worked with Carnation Dairies, and Farrell was sales manager for a large food packer. Both had worked with restaurants for years, Farrell as an expert in promotion, while McCarthy was skilled in training programs. Both had dreamed of operating a distinctive eating place.

"For the next eighteen months," McCarthy recalled, "we practically lived at each others' houses while we planned our restaurant. Sometimes we worked until two or three in the morning."

Both were apprehensive when in 1963 they opened their first 108-seat basement in Portland with an 1890s decor, candy barrels, quaint lights, ceiling fans, an elaborate soda fountain, and marble-topped tables. But the customers came. "They kind of pinned us against the soda fountain, and we stayed there for six months." Before long the restaurant was grossing over $300,000 per year and netting 15 percent before taxes, far above the average.

What was the key to successful parallel competition with other ice cream outlets by Farrell's? The decor? The service? Different ice cream in quality or flavor? Location? Probably it was a combination, and clearly they felt it was one that could work repetitively, because the company expanded to other company-owned outlets and also via franchising to span the coat from Seattle to San Diego.

In most cases it is easy to identify some fairly distinct competitive advantages that account for success of the new company in breaking into the market, even though the service is not really new. The following examples will illustrate a variety of such advantages. In the first it appears that a combination of pent-up demand left over from war, plus initiative in seeking out customers while competitors sat back and waited for them, accounted for successful entry.

◆ T. C. Morss had been a metalworker before World War II, in which he served with the RAF. After discharge following the war he started independently doing body and fender repair, traveling from one garage to another on a motorcycle to serve several shops in South London. Then he rented a shed just large enough to hold one car and established his own location. As his trade grew, he moved to large quarters and added more men. He also started taking other fabrication jobs besides auto repair. By 1950 the company was building its own 80 × 120-foot factory to take on custom design and construction of prototype equipment, sheet metal and structural fabrication, machining and short production runs of hard-to-make metal products, such as those involving skin-milling and sculpture milling. Sales reached $750,000 by 1955 and over $2 million by 1961, in a country experiencing general economic decline.

In several lines of business it is common for employees to develop a clientele with their employer and then leave to start their own companies, taking some of the clientele with them. Real estate, stock brokerage, and insurance are all fields where this is fairly common. Another is advertising:

◆ John Hobson had been director of a leading agency and was well known in the advertising trade when at age forty-five he resigned and started his own agency. In an industry tending increasingly toward individual specialization in subfields such as copywriting, market research, art work, and media, he was qualified by virtue of varied experience. He opened up in first-class rented quarters using savings of $12,000 and borrowings of another $36,000, with two major clients plus a smaller one aggregating accounts of over $1 million. Although no additional accounts were landed within the first eighteen months, the company was able to pay off its debts within eight months. The number of employees, which began at seventeen, grew to three hundred within six years, making Hobson's agency one of the largest in England.

Another common pattern in parallel competition is the formation of a new company that competes directly in any bidding contest. Government contracts at all levels are continually placed out for bid, for example, and although the vast majority of these are snapped up by existing companies, they are also occasionally sought by new bidders. The construction industry is another wherein jobs are frequently put out for bid, and within the home-remodeling sector of that industry private buyers frequently make their purchase decisions based on price from the lowest bidder, who may be either an established company or a new one. Every town of any appreciable size will have at least one job machine shop that stands ready to give price estimates on metal-machining work of all types, and in every metropolitan area there are many such shops, all offering about the same service and competing mainly on delivery time and price. These shops clearly compete in parallel, although many develop distinguishing specialties. The following example is typical:

◆ The son of a poor North Dakota farm family could not afford the $6 needed for books to finish high school. He found jobs, first as a laborer and then as an auto mechanic, saving his money to attend trade school as a machinist. After serving as an air force flight engineer in World War II, he obtained a series of machine shop jobs, first as machinist, then tool and die maker, and finally as mold maker for plastic injection molds. Every year or so he would change jobs, "After I learned what I could from them," he said. In 1967 he was working in a medium-sized injection molding company, designing and constructing molds, installing them to start production, and performing general troubleshooting. Because of his extensive experience he was given the most difficult problems to solve, but his pay was identical to that of the other mold makers with lesser skills. Fed up, he quit.

He had no formal plans for starting his own company, only the observation that he knew how to produce and the conviction that if others could survive in the business so could he. Lacking capital, he recruited two relatives as partners to contribute $10,000 each and borrowed $10,000 himself, taking 51 percent control in return for that amount plus his knowhow. The three men located a building to rent and used their capital to buy equipment and set up shop. Unanticipatedly large expenses for hookup of the machines and small items needed in startup consumed their capital, and somewhat dejectedly the founder approached a bank for more. To his surprise the bank loaned him $8,000 on the three men's signatures.

At first the company worked very long hours, offering low bids on all the work they could find. They found that the difficult part was to convince customers that they could perform the work properly, and as a result most of the jobs were small and low-margin. With time, however, their capabilities became known and they were able to attract more appealing work, gradually phasing out the low-margin work and taking larger, more profitable jobs. The controlling founder kept the three men's pay to a subsistence minimum, although they paid their other employees above union scale, to increase the company's financial strength. Dispute among the partners ensued, and the other two were bought out by the founder so that they could obtain employment elsewhere. The company, however, prospered, and by 1974, sales were exceeding $600,000 and the owner's profits were well in excess of $100,000 per year.

This pattern, wherein an entrepreneur becomes highly skilled in manufacturing, opens his own shop, competes for minor jobs on price, builds up a reputation, and gradually increases his margin, is common among job shops.

A number of similar examples, including the phasing out of partners, can be found among the studies of Collins and Moore.[10] The competitive edge begins largely as one of price, being willing to work longer hours at the same cost to the customer to get the work, and shifts over time to being one of reputation for dependable work combined sometimes with the cultivation of personal relationships with customers. Because this pattern is so straightforward and there are so many with the capabilities to try it, however, the competition is extremely intense, the work is very hard, especially at the start, and many fail.

In consumer, rather than industrial, service industries similar entry patterns are often attempted, and again the failure rate is high. Chances can be greatly improved, however, if the owner is able to create some special twist to distinguish the company from its parallel competitors. Farrell's, above, did it largely with special decor, while Morss used initiative to provide more convenient service. The next example, a window repair company, used several techniques:

◆   A young man who had studied animal husbandry and held the ambition to become rancher found himself unemployed after discharge from the navy in 1956. Going to the unemployment office, he picked the first skilled trade he could find, glazier, and applied. Lacking union connections, he had some difficulty but managed to wangle a job anyway and learn the business. Although still planning eventually to become a rancher, he began at the same time to prepare for starting a glass business. He changed jobs several times, and at each employer kept a book in which he made notes of deficiencies, listed distributors', suppliers', and customers' names, and wrote down procedures, costs, and ideas for ways to do the job better. One idea that particularly impressed him was the way another business, Roto Rooter, managed to operate from trucks with each service man working largely as a decentralized branch of the business.

In 1962, six years after beginning as a glazier, he bought an old truck, quit his job, and with $600 savings plus $2,500 in credit from a supplier began his own window replacement service, operating out of his home. Unlike his competitors, he gladly took jobs any distance away. En route he looked for new construction sites and broken windows, often stopping to make a sales pitch or leave a note. Also unlike his competitors, he gladly worked fifteen-hour days and 100-hour weeks. Short on working capital, he approached his banker but was turned down, and so took in a partner. Within ten years the two had expanded to a fleet of radio-dispatched trucks, opened a branch in a second metropolitan area, and were earning profits of over $100,000 on sales of over $1 million.

Competitive advantages thus differ among parallel ventures. Some take the form of highly personal qualities such as special knowhow or personal contacts, while others may hinge upon resources of the entrepreneur or original ideas for ways to operate. The most common of all, however, is a very simple difference, namely location of the enterprise. A type of venture that is successful in one area can often be opened with equal success in another. Ways of utilizing this fact will be discussed in the section on franchising later in this chapter and under the heading "Geographical Transfer" in the next chapter. At this point it can be noted, however, that there are many ventures with thin potential for parallel startup in different locations. Some possibilities with their respective competitive angles were listed in the preceding chapter.

[10] Orvis Collins and David G. Moore, *The Organization Makers* (New York: Appleton-Century-Crofts, 1970).

Parallel Products

Somewhere along the borderline between products that are new and those that because of relatively minor differences actually represent parallel competitors are products in which only styling or themes vary. Ford, Chevrolet, and Plymouth, for instance, differ mainly in styling to compete in parallel. Examples of products that differ mainly in themes include greeting cards, as illustrated by the following three startups.

◆ David Kaye, a young Englishman, began in 1947 at the suggestion of a friend, to sell birthday cards to stationers' shops. Though totally lacking in experience, he bought a secondhand car and on his first day sold out his supply. A year later, still selling, he met two former RAF acquaintances who combined stationery sales with printing in a basement shop. Because he had encountered requests for cards with "mother" on them, he asked his friends to print some. They entered partnership with around $1,500 between them, started producing their own cards, first buying prints which they attached, then later hiring an artist to help with designs. Sales grew and within ten years had passed $1,000,000.

◆ Jim Jones, a freelance artist, with a successful advertising agency, began designing Christmas cards as a favor to his clients. Encouraged by the praise of his customers for the custom cards, he sent designs to two card companies. At one company the sales manager, Joe Wallace, was favorably impressed. It also happened that he was interested in a job change. The two formed Citation Cards, Inc., in late 1953 with $3,000 pooled capital, and printed two thousand each of twenty-four designs. Out of 750 stores to which samples were sent 300 placed orders, and Citation was under way. Within a few months stocks were selling out coast to coast and volume was $30,000 per month.

◆ William Box and William Kennedy worked nights together as parking attendants. Although they had no capital, they often spent free time discussing ways of making money. In November 1953 Box, who attended art school on the GI Bill during the day, designed four Christmas cards featuring zany "bebop" men with big glasses and watch chains. Showing them to Los Angeles dealers brought sales of eight thousand cards in five weeks. Box designed more cards, and Kennedy—who happened to have a car—joined Box in selling the cards by day; both continued to park cars at night. Sales totaled less than $4,000 in 1954, but then grew rapidly, reaching $250,000 in 1956 with profits of over $60,000.

These three examples illustrate that, in spite of some similarities substantial variations can occur among the ways ostensibly similar companies get started. The last two in particular, however, clearly share the feature of product distinctiveness as part of the starting wedge. Competition was still head-on in the sense that numerous other companies already offered cards for exactly the same occasions, but the newcomers managed to be different in their designs within limits acceptable to the same customers.

Every major metropolitan area in the country typically has at least one and often more companies competing in parallel to produce sliding glass doors. Sometimes newcomers manage to enter by devising changes in design which add features or enhance appearance, but often the inroad has simply been lower price, sometimes made possible through redesign but often simply through working harder for less to break in. A successful example of the lower-price tactic was the startup of Arcadia Metal Products in Southern California:

◆   Henry E. North had studied mechanical engineering at Yale and business administration at Stanford, had worked his way from trainee engineer to head of the materials laboratory at Douglas Aircraft, and had built a small company manufacturing oil heaters. When oil was phased out by natural gas in southern California, the oil heater inventory was sold off, ending that business. An architect suggested to North that he enter the manufacture of sliding glass doors, and in 1948, North and his partner incorporated Arcadia to do so. The doors then available were all custom built and cost up to $1,000 each. By standardizing North was able to cut costs to as low as $75 per unit. Riding an architectural trend that favored more glass, sales grew rapidly, reaching $2 million with profits of $98,000 within seven years.

The "twists" that may be used to enter parallel competition with products either identical or just slightly varied are virtually limitless. E. Joseph Cossman made a success of selling "Ant Farms" (two transparent panels held parallel in a frame to make something like a small aquarium in which ants can be watched digging tunnels and living their lives). Several such products were on the market when he introduced a farm that, unlike the others, could be disassembled and cleaned, and mounted an effective mail-order advertising program to sell it. The authors of *Insider Reports* have proposed that readers examine mail-order advertisements to find products that could be copied directly and advertised in parallel competition but with advertising being beamed at markets different from those being served by existing advertisement.

But not all parallel product startups are so humble, as the following two examples illustrate. In the first of these the entrepreneurs capitalized on obtaining certain fixed assets, manufacturing machines, and a plant made possible largely by government financing, to give them an edge in startup to produce a product others were already offering. In the second the entrepreneur used sheer technical expertise and his reputation for possessing it to enter competition with the giants of his industry.

◆   "Chip" Clark, forty-eight, a vice-president for Celanese Fibers Group in New York, had become impatient with his employer of twenty-one years after a series of policy disputes. He decided to leave, but rather than seeking an executive job, preferred to strike out on his own. He discussed the idea with "Rusty" Lovin, forty-four, a former subordinate who had subsequently left and become a marketing vice-president for Genesco, and as a result the latter suggested, during a joint ski trip to Vermont with their families, the idea of entering manufacture of warp knits of menswear. A few large companies were already producing the product, which was a cheaper and lighter competitor for the already established double knits, but the market appeared headed for substantial growth.
The largest maker of machines for warp knitting was the Karl Mayer Company in Germany. Clark contacted an old friend who worked for Mayer and arranged for an option to buy forty machines. Then he approached Bob Adelman, forty-one, a lawyer who had become assistant treasurer at Celanese, for help on legal and financial aspects of the venture. Adelman, it turned out, had also been thinking about leaving Celanese, and as Adelman recalls, "We put some numbers

together. I didn't believe them, because they were outrageously profitable." He also estimated, however, that startup would require around $4 million, beginning with the forty machines at $20,000 each. The two men's combined net worth was only around one-half million dollars, so they began looking for capital and a site.

Bankers and insurance companies turned them down. Venture capitalists all wanted control, which the entrepreneurs were unwilling to yield. The search for a plant, however, turned up possibilities of government financial assistance in South Carolina. The Economic Development Administration of the federal government would loan money at low rates if 5 percent of the loan amount could be raised from a local community desirous of having the plant to increase employment. After some frustrating months of struggle with rejections from various sources, government red tape and delays, the entrepreneurs managed, mostly through borrowing, to obtain the needed starting capital as follows:

$ 200,000   Land and site improvements donated by county
  1,750,000   EDA loan, less the $2,200,000 requested
  1,140,000   First mortgage, more than the $800,000 planned on
    400,000   Equity investments from personal savings and friends
    450,000   Equity from another yarn and cloth manufacturing company
$3,940,000   Total, just $60,000 less than estimated need

◆   In addition, a factoring company agreed to loan $700,000 for working capital, and suppliers agreed to extend trade credit. Within a little over a year from the time the venture idea had been conceived by its three entrepreneurs, Calina Industries, Inc., was in operation with a work force of over one hundred employees.

◆   Gene Amdahl left IBM in late 1970 with the idea of competing with his former employer in the design and manufacture of full-scale computers. For most companies that particular year was a difficult time in which to raise venture capital. Another company with similar aims, Computer Operations, Inc., had not been able to do so because, according to a consultant in the business, "they had no name player." Amdahl's name, on the other hand, had been established by his leadership of the technical team that designed the most widely used computer in the world, the IBM 360, and his subsequent assignment as director of IBM's advanced computer systems laboratory. Further, he had been named an IBM fellow, which gave him a charter by the company to pursue his own interests at their expense.

Instead, he resigned, saying he was "really disenamored with working for IBM," and in 1970 became a competitor of IBM in "the design, development, manufacture, marketing and maintenance of large-scale, high performance, general-purpose computer systems." After raising $2.5 million in venture capital from Heizer Corporation of Chicago, he obtained another $25 million, also partly from Heizer, from Nixdorf and Fujitsu. By March 1973, several months before his first expected product announcement, Amdahl had obtained a $35 million backlog of orders. No sales were actually made, however, until 1975, by which time the company had piled up total accumulated losses of over $44 million. Sales in the first six months of 1976, however, brought in a profit just over $3 million, and in the fall of 1976, the company went public at $27.50 per share. Multiplied times the total number of shares then outstanding, this gave the company a total market value based on its stock price of around $165 million. Amdahl himself, as owner of 135,196 shares, thus realized a book value of over $3 million, and in the public offering would realize cash of more than $841,000, on top of his annual salary of $92,384.

The examples of parallel services and products to this point have only partially completed the picture of parallel competition as a general form of entry wedge. It will be seen that several of the entry wedges yet to be discussed can be regarded as simply other specialized forms of parallel competition. Because of their number and variety, however, they merit separate discussion in the next chapter.

Product Service Combinations

Neither cosmetics nor cookies are new products, and retailing is certainly not a new service. But the following two entrepreneurs managed to combine these old products and retailing in ways that created very successful new businesses.

◆   Mary Kay Ash did not invent pyramid selling ("direct sales") schemes. In fact, she had worked for two other companies that used them, Stanley Home Products and World Gift, prior to founding her own cosmetics firm. She opened a storefront in Dallas in 1963 and began selling a cosmetic she herself had been using by recruiting and training other women to be "beauty consultants" who would give home demonstrations and recruit still others to do the same. On sales they would earn commissions, and on recruiting they would receive further commissions from what the recruits sold. Her competitive ability was that of being able to recruit and motivate other salespeople through commissions, organizational recognition of them, and charismatic preaching to them. Sales grew from zero in 1963 to $31 million ten years later and $384 million ten years after that.[11]

◆   Debbie Fields, as nineteen-old community college dropout, also began with a storefront, but selling cookies, not cosmetics, and selling them directly rather than through representatives. When not enough passersby came into the store, she went outside and dispensed samples. The store turned profitable within a week and she went on to open a second one eight months later. First-year sales were $200,000. Ten years later she had two hundred stores with total sales of $50 million. Quality and service were highly emphasized, with centralized computer monitoring of sales and direct communication with outlets by phone on a continuous basis to control freshness and inventory.[12]

It should be noted that both these enterprises were in tune with the general trends of their time. Other direct sales organizations such as Avon, Amway, and Shaklee were also growing along with the Mary Kay Ash company. And other cookie store chains were growing at the same time as the Debbie Fields chain, the first apparently having been Famous Amos, who started seven years earlier than she did.[13]

---

[11] Curtis Hartman, "The Spirit of Independence," *Inc.,* July 1985, p. 64.
[12] Lewis Beale, "Young Entrepreneurs," *Venture,* October 1983, p. 46; and Tom Richman, "A Tale of Two Companies," *Inc.,* July 1984, p. 38.
[13] L. D. Bershad, "Smart Cookies, Handsome Profits," *Venture,* October 1979, p. 29.

Another common factor of these entrepreneurs was that both seemed to motivate their employees to high performance largely through independence, since the employees in many ways ended up operating *their* own businesses, even though technically they did not. They would rarely see a "boss," they operated their own individual business locations, and they prospered directly according to the business results they produced. These factors of freedom and self-determination are also present in startups accomplished with the aid of franchising, the next main entry wedge to be examined.

FRANCHISING

Help in getting a parallel competitive firm going is often purchased by would-be entrepreneurs through franchise deals. Under the franchise contract an established company with a formula for success that has already proven workable for them provides help to the new firm in breaking into the market. In return the entrepreneur typically pays a fee to obtain the contract, invests money to set up and provide working capital for the business, gives a royalty percentage of sales in return for the help, and promises to operate in accordance with rules specified by the franchisor or firm providing the help. Forms this help may take include such things as the following:

1 Rights to sell the franchisor's product or service
2 Use of the franchisor's established brand or logo
3 Use of operating procedures and systems that have worked for the franchisor, probably a manual
4 Training in how to operate the enterprise
5 Assistance in location finding
6 Plans for the physical plant, decor, and possibly supplying of special equipment
7 Financial help, leases, or loans for physical assets
8 Advertising support
9 Purchasing assistance, large-volume discounts, and possibly direct supplying of proprietary ingredients
10 Centralized research and development support
11 Monitoring, review, audits, advice, consultation, and guidance on management
12 Opening-day and possibly longer direct hands-on startup help from a professional team

In short, the franchisee buys and/or rents from the franchisor the use of a proven (it is hoped) proprietary entry wedge and competitive shield.

The total U.S. industry operating on franchises in 1988 ranged upward of 509,000 outlets with total sales of $640 billion, according to the U.S. Department of Commerce.[14] The largest category, accounting for 70 percent of these sales, consisted of automotive dealers, filling stations, and soft-drink bottlers, which offered mainly the first item on the above list. The number of filling stations had declined drastically.

"Business format franchising," which included more items on the above list than those three types, had been increasing, as had the number of different franchises being offered. Franchisors with more than one thousand units, such as McDonald's, dominated this field, fifteen of them accounting for half of all outlets and sales. Familiar names among these were Radio Shack stores, A&W Root Beer, Shakey's Pizza, Burger King, Kentucky Fried Chicken, Holiday Inns, Roto Rooter, and convenience stores such as 7–11. Some idea of the variety of format franchises that became available when that type of business was expanding rapidly in the early 1970s can been seen in the following sampling of 1973 *Wall Street Journal* advertisements:

- Golfomat—Electronic indoor golf . . . using real clubs and balls . . . $10,000 required to qualify. . . . no franchise fee
- Management Recruiters—Personnel placement . . . over 150 offices. . . . investment of approximately $25,000
- Lollypops Pantyhose—Hosiery business . . . your own home . . . service merchandising displays in stores, beauty parlors, and gift shops. Absolutely no selling involved . . . Financing available . . .
- Aamco Transmissions—Over 500 shops . . . No mechanical skill necessary. Home office management training course included. Minimum cash required $16,000–$26,000. Total price $23,301–$38,740.
- Binex Financial Services— . . computerized services for small businesses including profit and loss statements, accounts receivable, accounts payable, income tax, business taxes, custom management reports, and more.
- Kiddie Shops— . . children's ready-to-wear stores . . . proven operating techniques and group buying advantages . . .
- Sir Speedy— . . printing centers . . . guarantees your success in six months or your initial cash investment of $20,000 is returned . . . we train for four full weeks . . .
- Yogi Bear's Jellystone Camp-Resorts— . . Investment of $40,000 and up . . .

By 1988 some of these names, such as Golfomat, Lollypops, and Kiddie Shops, had faded, but others had entered, particularly franchises in fast oil change, video rentals, and computer stores, which were unknown in the early seventies. Fastest growing, according to the March 1988 *Venture* magazine survey, was an industrial cleaning franchise firm, followed by a yogurt shop, a video store, a hotel chain, and a cinnamon roll store. Largest in terms of numbers of franchises, according to *Entrepreneur* magazine's annual (January) franchise issue in 1988, were the following:

---

[14] U.S. Dept. of Commerce, *Franchising in The Economy*, 1988, U.S. Govt. Printing Office.

Rank Franchisor	Franchise Outlets	Company Outlets
1 McDonald's	7,274	2,280
2 Century 21	6,833	0
3 Kentucky Fried Chicken	5,480	1,920
4 Dairy Queen	4,956	6
5 H&R Block	4,900	3,966
6 Servicemaster	3,568	0
7 Jazzercise	3,370	0
8 Budget Rent-A-Car	3,200	154
9 7–11 Stores	3,058	4,854
10 Pizza Hut	2,603	2,660

Another listing and brief description of franchises available is the *Franchise Opportunities Handbook* published by the U.S. Department of Commerce.

The great advantage of utilizing a franchise as an entry wedge is that by choosing a proven franchise formula, the chances of success in the new venture are enormously increased. Some franchisors, such as McDonald's, claim never to have had a franchisee fail. And they can point to enormous numbers of franchisees of theirs who have done well for themselves.

The main advantages are two. First, because the franchisee must obey rules set down by the franchisor ("for the good of the business"), the new business never really becomes an independent operation. "It's just the same as working in a branch of a big company, except that they make you invest money to become their employee," grumbled one franchisee who chafed at not being able to try out his own ideas in what he offered customers, how his establishment was decorated, or what prices he charged.

The second main disadvantage is that most franchises are not very lucrative for those who run them. Most franchisees put in very long hours for pay that is low, particularly when the return on investment has been factored out. The president of one large and successful franchise company at that time, Chicken Delight, described the picture to prospective franchisees this way:

♦   Are you working for $20,000 a year but want to make an easy $50,000 a year? We don't have that for you. Are you making maybe $60, $80, $100 a week and you'd like to make about $10,000, $15,000, or $20,000 a year, and are you prepared to work hard for it, at least in the initial year? We have lots of opportunities for you.[15]

A 1971 study by the Conference Board noted that franchise companies claimed average profits of $22,000 per year for outlets, but that when it polled operators the figure was closer to $20,000, with auto dealers pulling the average up substantially. For fast-food franchises the figure was less than $12,000 per year (including both salary and return on investment for the owner) for working "hours that would make a farmer buckle." Half of gas station operators make

---

[15] Large and successful at the time of this statement, Chicken Delight later was dissolved because the federal government decreed that tie-in sales through which a company makes money by requiring franchisees to buy supplies from it were illegal.

less than $6,000 per year, though they work an average of seventy hours per week. One-third fail each year. Figures in the September 1985 *Venture* magazine indicate that the average franchisee's salary among the fastest-growing one hundred franchises was $22,629, although the average return on investment among them was 44.6 percent overall.

There have been many sad stories associated with franchising. At the relatively benign end of the spectrum have been those who simply did not like the work involved. Other people have lost their entire investments, sometimes by investing in franchises for enterprises that would not work in new locations, and even in franchises that were total frauds. Some sent in their money for a franchise, then sent more money for inventory of one kind or another, and never heard from the franchisor again. Resultant governmental investigations of the industry began to shed more light on "horror stories"—Howard Johnson accused of raising prices on goods that had to be purchased from the parent firm so that franchisees would more willingly sell back (once 80 percent of Hojo outlets were franchisee-owned; today only 20 percent), Chrysler terminating dealers in areas where it wanted to replace them with factory outlets, Pepsi-Cola terminating all eighty-five dealers in the New York area on the same day, March 31, 1971.

In the early 1970s many states began passing restrictive legislation to control franchising. It remains for the individual entrepreneur, however, to decide whether franchising is a desirable opportunity and if so, which one to bet on.

High-profit Franchisee Strategies

To make large amounts of money as a franchisee, the following three strategies have been shown to work:

1 *Take on a larger rather than a small franchise.* A Holiday Inn or metropolitan Chevrolet dealership typically pays much higher profits than a fried chicken franchise. However, it also requires a great deal of capital. That cliché that "it takes money to make money" clearly applies to this strategy, and a major task of the entrepreneur who would like to apply this approach will be that of raising the starting capital.

2 *Add units to build a chain.* An Indiana attorney who took on an Econ-O-Wash coin-operated laundromat franchise as a part-time occupation became so intrigued with the avocation that he added another unit and then still others. He found that they typically paid back the startup investment in three years. Shortly thereafter he dropped his law practice and expanded his chain to seventeen outlets, which earned him over $100,000 per year.

With time this approach seems to be getting increasingly difficult for newcomers to use. As the industry matures, established franchisors are tending not to accept new one-at-a-time franchisees but rather favor company-owned outlets, granting additional franchises individually only to established and proven franchisees, or selling territorial franchises only to large established companies such as existing restaurant chains. The man who owns the territorial rights to the Seattle area for Kentucky Fried Chicken now has some forty outlets with seven hundred people doing $14 million worth of business per year. But he obtained that territory some thirty years ago, and it would be difficult for others to acquire comparable privileges today without enormous capital.

3 *Acquire, then sell units off for capital gain.* A proven franchise is typically worth more than a new one. A profitable franchise is worth more than one that is losing money. Consequently, capital gains can often be realized by obtaining either relatively new franchises or ones that are not operating well and by application of effective management proving them out. When Midas mufflers began in 1955, its franchises sold for $5,000 each. Five years later franchisees found they could sell them for five times that amount. Tastee Freez franchises were given away free in the company's early days. In the late 1950s its franchise for Puerto Rico sold for $1,000. Eighteen months later the company repurchased it for $20,000, and by 1962, its value was estimated at $1 million.

The trick with this approach, of course, is to be able to spot a new franchise that is going to be successful. After it has proven so, the capital requirements will be high, creating profits for the others who gambled on it, but not necessarily for the next set of buyers.

A fourth strategy that has been suggested at times is to buy a franchise simply to obtain the training and experience and then leave it to apply that knowhow independently. This would appear to have the advantages of using a proven formula and yet being able to operate freely, to try variations on the approach and at the same time to escape the franchise royalty fee to increase profits. One difficulty with this approach, however, is that the franchisor may have foreseen this possibility and included a provision against it in the franchise contract. A second is that tampering with the proven formula may not be all that successful. When Denny's started buying back franchises so that it could impose even greater control than the contracts allowed, they found it possible to increase earnings by 60 percent. Thus there is evidence that hewing to the line closely produces better results and departing, the opposite. Finally, the importance of the advertising and franchisor name, which would be lost by leaving, may be very great. The executive in charge of a chain of Burger King franchises commented: "I could walk down there today, take down the Burger King sign and put one up that read Fred's Burgers, and volume would drop 60 percent before the end of the day." Thus starting from a franchise base and branching off independently, even if it is possible, can be a very chancy strategy at best.

Becoming a Franchisor

The largest fortunes in the franchise industry have been made not by those who bought franchises, the franchisees, but by those who sold them, the franchisors.

♦ In 1937, after working at jobs ranging from real estate salesman to piano player to paper cup salesman, Roy Kroc made a deal to become the executive sales agent, worldwide, for a new soda fountain machine capable of mixing six shakes simultaneously, the Multi-Mixer. The business prospered, but Kroc continually looked for something better as he traveled among his customers, all types of eating establishments. By 1954 he was fifty-four years old and successful, but not sufficiently so to suit himself. Then an unusual sales order suddenly caught his attention. Somebody wanted to buy eight Multi-Mixers. What sort of enterprise, he wondered, needed to be able to mix forty-eight milkshakes at once? He went to San Bernardino, California, to see for himself

What he found were crowds of customers waiting in lines to buy hamburgers at a stand under two bright arches owned by the McDonald brothers. The two men had already sold six other franchises but had passed up chances to go further because they liked their lives the way they were and they did not wish to travel. Kroc offered to do the expansion for them, and after some sales effort managed to obtain rights to the name and system for opening in new areas in return for 1.4 percent of gross sales while the brothers retained their original business. Within a few months Kroc opened his first outlet in Des Plaines, Illinois, and then went on to sell franchises, beginning in California. The Des Plaines store grossed $158,000 its first year. By 1959 some one hundred outlets were operating from coast to coast and the gross per site was $204,000. In 1960 Kroc began negotiations to purchase everything from the McDonalds—contract, trademarks, copyrights, formula, systems, and all. The deal eventually cost $14 million, but it went on to become the nation's leading fast-food operation, with sales in 1987 of over $3.5 billion.

The approach used by Kroc, finding an enterprise successful in one spot and forming a business to sell its formula for operation in many other locations, has produced spectacular results for many other entrepreneurs, such as John Y. Brown, who did the same thing with the formula of Colonel Sanders and his Kentucky Fried Chicken. Three things required to carry out this strategy are identification of a successful pattern to replicate, knowhow to set up the franchising system, and resources to carry out the franchising campaign. Most difficult is the first of these, finding a successful formula. The owner of a successful business will often be alert to the possibility of franchising, and if the formula seems to have that potential may try to franchise it personally, as both the McDonald brothers and Colonel Sanders did. Consequently, the would-be freelance franchisor must have an additional edge beyond ability to spot ventures with unexploited franchising potential.

Some aspects of knowhow that must be brought to the franchising task include the following:

1 A "pat" formulation of the system to be franchised, which includes
   a Standard procedures for running the unit.
   b Bookkeeping and other paperwork systems, forms, and procedures.
   c Any special equipment, tools, signs, or parts.
   d Supplier contracts for any special deals or buying, or custom ingredients such as labels, boxes, printed napkins, and displays.
   e Sample pro forma operating figures backed up by the "track record" of a flagship unit.
   f A written loose-leaf manual covering all phases of the operation for franchisees to use. Included would be such things as operating instructions, policies for monitoring performance, ordering supplies, hiring and firing, "canned pitches" for dealing with prospects and customers, and pricing rules.

2 Legal coverage, which should include

a Protection of the system, any patentable designs, trademarks, and copyrights to protect written and graphical materials, logo, and so forth.

b The franchise contract, spelling out obligations of both franchisor and franchisee fees (typically 25 percent of the setup cost will be the franchise fee), royalties (typically one-half to 5 percent of gross sales for tangible goods, 6 to 8 percent on services), and provision of terms for termination of the agreement.[16]

c Protective advice for the franchise firm concerning state and other laws that govern and restrict franchise operation. These tend to change continually; hence an attorney who specializes in them and is thereby kept constantly up to date on them is needed as adviser.

d A selling method, "pitch" for salespeople, and compensation plan.

e Competent salespeople. Someone in the firm must be a good "closer" who can get franchisees' signatures on the contract.

f Forms and methods for recording and screening data on applicants.

3 A training program. Depending on the type of business, this may include classroom lectures, working in the field with a trainer, practicing the operation of the business in the flagship or other existing unit, and franchisees taking turns serving each other. During this period franchisees should all become familiar with the operating manual mentioned above and how to use it.

4 A followup program, which may include

a Direct help with initial advertising and in opening for business the first day.

b Encouraging, supportive, educational, and stimulative literature from the home office to help franchisees operate their units better. The looseleaf manual should be updated with new pages as better ideas come into view.

c Checkup on franchisees to make sure that they are operating according to the franchise agreement, not departing from the proven formula, maintaining standards of quality, following effective accounting and cost control practices, hiring and managing employees well, and generally "running a tight ship."

d Weeding out of ineffective franchisees, either by legal action to enforce the contracts or by buyback of franchises that are not working out, possibly followed by resale of the franchises to others.

Expert help in the setting up and operation of franchises is available. There are accountants, consultants, attorneys, and other professionals who specialize in this sort of work and whose experience can be immensely helpful.[17]

Clearly, it may require substantial resources to carry out a franchising

---

[16] Sample franchise contracts are easy to obtain, either from other enterprises or from published references, such as Harry Kursh, *The Franchise Boom* (Englewood Cliffs, N.J.: Prentice-Hall, 1962), which contains several.

[17] Leads to such sources of expert help can be obtained by contacting other successful franchisors to ask who helped them and also through franchise associations.

campaign including such ingredients as the above. Money will be needed for pulling together the package, for legal and accounting fees, for mounting the advertising program, and also simply to live on as the franchisor goes about pulling the package together. The large expansion of franchising over the past decade has brought many companies into the business and has included shake-outs in which the weaker zones went out of business, leaving the stronger ones in dominant positions. Many of these are owned by large holding companies with enormous resources. Hence the competition has now become extremely intense in many fields, such as fast foods and automotive repair, and it is often difficult for new companies to enter.

At the same time, however, this maturation of the industry has made available proven techniques for setting up franchisor firms and has also created markets for sale of such new firms as entrepreneurs may create. Moreover, there are now many experienced people in the business who can help would-be franchisor entrepreneurs either as advisers or employees. As a result opportunities remain, although different in form from those that were encountered by earlier pioneers such as Ray Kroc, and it is to be expected that there will still be entrepreneurs emerging from time to time, showing that successful company building as franchisors can still be done.

SUMMARY

This chapter described general types of advantages most new companies use to break into the stream of established commerce. Most desirable is to have a significant innovation, a new product or service with substantial advantages over the competition. But most new companies do not have such an advantage. Rather, they capitalize on less dramatic features—longer hours at a lower rate of pay by the owner, better location, more service, different advertising or merchandising, and so forth. In franchising, the advantages come from things provided by the franchisor: a proven formula, advertising support, managerial help, possibly financial help. But these come at a price—less freedom to manage by the franchisee, lowered profits as a result of royalties paid to the franchisor, and an initial cost for the franchise. As a result, when the investment, hours, and return after royalties are considered, becoming a franchisee tends not to be a particularly lucrative occupation, although the risk of failure can be correspondingly lowered. A limited number of ways in which a franchisee can make substantial gains were suggested in the chapter, and a brief discussion about becoming a franchisor was presented.

Other
Entry Wedges

The preceding chapter described three main types of startup wedges—the new product or service, parallel competition, and franchise entry—and also indicated some of the main subclassifications within those three categories. This chapter will introduce eleven more entry wedges which can be regarded to some extent as variants of the three main wedges. They are more specialized and tend to occur less frequently than types of the preceding chapter, but they are no less powerful in the right situations, and consequently they can be just as important to learn.

These other eleven wedges can be grouped for convenience into four categories: exploiting partial momentum, customer sponsorship, parent company sponsorship, and governmental sponsorship. They will be discussed below in this order, as listed in Table 8–1. The table also shows how they might be cross-classified against the three main wedges plus that of acquisition entry. Neither overlaps nor distinctions between wedge types are always sharp. Nor is that the point. Sometimes the strategy used for a given venture may fit under more than one wedge classification. The objective of identifying types, however fuzzily at times, is to expand the reader's awareness of options. In the concluding section of this chapter it will be noted that wedges can be used in combinations, often to increase their power. But first, the alternative types must be identified.

TAKING ADVANTAGE
OF PARTIAL MOMENTUM

The notion of building a new business upon a proven and very similar precedent is one that applies to many of the entry strategies to varying degrees. Franchising, which was discussed in the preceding chapter, clearly exemplifies such

CHAPTER 8

TABLE 8–1   CROSS-REFERENCING OF ENTRY WEDGES

| | Main Entry Wedges | | | |
Other Entry Wedges	New Product or Service	Parallel Competition	Franchising	Acquisition of Going Concern
Exploiting partial momentum				
1. Geographical transfer			X	
2. Supply shortage		X		
3. Tapping unutilized resources		X		
Customer sponsorship				
4. Customer contract		X		
5. Becoming a second source		X		
Parent company sponsorship				
6. Joint ventures	X			
7. Licensing			X	
8. Market relinquishment		X		
9. Selloff of division				X
Governmental sponsorship				
10. Favored purchasing		X		
11. Rule changes		X		
Combinations				

an approach, and many of the examples in parallel competition also incorporate this element. Generally, the more successful and more closely similar the precedent, the more likely the new venture is to succeed. In a sense one can build upon momentum of established enterprises, applying the venture concepts they use but extending them to customers not yet served. Three types will be described in this section (although it will be seen that the concept applies to others as well)—geographical transfer, shortage of supply, and exploitation of unutilized resources.

Geographical Transfer

It is not necessary to buy a franchise in order to transfer a venture idea from one geographical area to another. All a would-be entrepreneur need do is spot a type of venture that works in one place and then devise a way to emulate the example in another location with similar characteristics. *Insider's Report,* for example, pointed out the relative ease with which someone with a cash investment of between $3,000 and $25,000 could open a fried chicken fast-food store that would serve food similar to that of chains like Kentucky Fried Chicken but without paying a franchise fee or royalties.[1] Cooking recipes are simple and

[1] *Insider's Report #600* (Santa Monica, Calif.: Chase Revel, Publisher, 1976).

easy to obtain, prices can be read from competitors' menus, equipment can readily be purchased and installed, and although there are subtle profit-raising tricks, these too can be picked up from sources such as *Insider's Report,* competitors, or simply experience. Probably the main drawback will be lack of advertising support and pull which the more familiar logo would provide. Location choice might also require help.

One entrepreneur who accomplished geographical transfer of a fast-food enterprise and ultimately built a successful pizza chain began by doing his own location study as a student report:

♦   After eating and enjoying pizza when he was a pilot in the navy, Pete Utter had developed a thriving pizza business during college by renting one side of an Oxford, Ohio, tavern and selling both to tavern patrons and through delivery to dormitory students. Not knowing how to make pizza dough, he bought it from an Italian bakery in nearby Cincinnati. The bakery had been near failure, but Utter's business helped it, and soon the baker decided to try selling pizzas also in Cincinnati. While Utter continued his studies, the baker developed a successful pizza chain.

When it came time for Pete, whose major was statistics, to write a master's thesis, his adviser directed him to select a topic dealing with multiple correlation. Pete decided to analyze the baker's pizza chain and, on the basis of demographics, predict where else such a chain could be developed west of the Mississippi. He isolated what seemed to be the critical factors in Cincinnati and identified three western cities with similar demographics and no pizza chains, Denver, Phoenix, and Seattle.

Upon graduating he went off to work in the headquarters of a major advertising firm. Eight days of working in New York City convinced him that he had chosen the wrong town and the wrong line of work. In need of another job, he decided to follow the advice of his thesis and start a pizza restaurant. He had sold his Oxford location, leaving him with a $2,500 stake to start anew, and recalled, "It was either Phoenix, Denver, or Seattle next. Since I had already lived where there was a lot of land and not much water, I decided to try Seattle."

Moving with his wife to Seattle, he looked for a site. Because he had become familiar with the college trade, he chose a spot next to the University of Washington. "Pizza was new to the college crowd in Seattle," he said. "There were only four places in town with pizza, all of them Italian restaurants of the traditional type. Nobody was doing what had been done in the East, namely modernizing and merchandizing in pizzas." His store, opened in October 1957, was soon thriving. He opened a second near Seattle University, then others. Within nine years he was able to make good on a promise he had given his wife when they moved to Seattle. Keeping only a summer residence in Seattle and delegating management of the chain to others, he established a home in Coral Gables, Florida, where Utter returned to college work, this time as a teacher.

In this example three instances of venture idea transfer can be identified. First, Pete Utter took the idea of pizza making that he had encountered in the navy and set it up in the Oxford tavern. Second, the Italian baker from whom he bought dough noted his success in the tavern and expanded on that formula in Cincinnati. Third, Utter took his own Oxford experience, improved on it with ideas developed in the baker's Cincinnati chain, and transferred it to Seattle.

Who else could have exploited this venture opportunity in Seattle? Probably many people. The Italian restaurants could have opened at college locations had they spotted the idea of no-frills, low-cost fast service. Other college students who had seen that idea could have done it, and in fact one did. Ron Bean transferred the same scheme of a pizza store from Provo, Utah, where he worked as a college student, to Seattle at almost identically the same time as Peter Utter, and he too built a successful chain starting near the University of Washington. He did not do it on the basis of a demographic survey like Utter's but simply as a source of income during law school. The starting capital needed—Utter had $2,500, Bean had $3,000—was in the range possessed by many people. The technology was simple and could be learned by anyone through simply taking a job in a pizza store for a couple of weeks. Even the location may not have been terribly crucial, for the Cincinnati baker, Utter, and Bean all soon opened successful stores in other areas. The main essential ingredients may simply have been perception of the transfer possibility plus initiative to try it.

How could a would-be entrepreneur deliberately go about preparation to perform a geographical transfer? Whenever a new type of enterprise opens in town and is successful, the potential to do it elsewhere is likely present. A demographic search like that of Pete Utter may give clues as to where. If the would-be entrepreneur happens to be moving, possibly because of a job change with his or her employer, he or she could take note of differences in available services between the former and new locations. Even on vacation trips it may be possible to notice transfer opportunities. The entrepreneur may be able to recruit a knowledgeable employee from a transferable enterprise in another town, perhaps as a partner to exploit a hometown opportunity. Periodicals like *Venture, Inc., Entrepreneur,* and *In Business* may reveal opportunities. Clearly, the key to bringing the transfer about, however, will be not just to discover the possibility but to act upon it. If the would-be entrepreneur does not provide that action, someone else likely soon will, as the constant transferring of venture concepts, particularly in service industries, continually demonstrates.

Geographical transfer is not limited to services, however. It also happens in manufacturing, though typically less rapidly. Initially, a product may begin with one company and be shipped to other regions. As its market matures, economic tuning and price shaving may cause freight charges on raw materials, finished products, or both to become more important, thereby making branch plants desirable. If the manufacturer for some reason fails to set up such plants, or does so poorly, there is opportunity for entrepreneurs in effect to open the branch plants themselves as independent enterprises.

◆   A machinist who had long felt the urge to have his own company, and who had tried several new enterprises without success, joined several other partners to set up a company in Los Angeles that would manufacture "loadbinders." These are small ratchet-type winches that mount along the sides of flat truck beds. Ropes or cables to hold down cargo on the truck are tied to the loadbinders, which can then be ratcheted to pull them tight and thereby secure the load. There were already companies in this business in Los Angeles, but the partners believed that by lowering the price and doing more advertising they could realize sufficient volume to break in on a mass-volume basis. The company succeeded, but the machinist soon realized that the relatively large number of partners involved caused serious dilution of the profits so that his share would always be limited to less than he had hoped.

Searching in his mind for ways to find a business where he could own a larger share, he took note of the fact that patents on the loadbinder had long since expired, and it occurred to him that he could make them on his own. He did not see a way to gain any appreciable advantage over his present firm by manufacturing locally. Another approach would be to produce loadbinders for the original equipment market by obtaining a contract from a truck maker, but that would require tooling up for mass production at the lowest possible cost, which would be expensive. Besides, other loadbinder companies already had that market.

But how about setting up a shop similar to his old one serving the retrofit market, only in a distant market where there was no local producer? There he could reduce shipping charges to local customers and in addition could offer within that region shorter lead times on special orders, lower inventory levels for wholesalers, and more convenience in dealing directly on quotes, questions, and service. He identified a city several hundred miles away where customers were currently paying a fifty-cent freight charge per $7 wholesale unit. He estimated the labor and material should cost around $2.50 per unit, and commissions and overhead another $3, leaving him a profit of $1.50 per unit, which would retail at $11.

Selling his interest in the partnership, he moved to the new city and calculated his capital needs. His computations showed he did not have enough to start the new firm, even combining his savings with proceeds from sale of his share of the Los Angeles firm. He began discussing his idea with friends, and one, another machinist, volunteered to contribute capital and join him in the venture. Through a CPA selected to set up the company books, a third partner was located to provide still more capital, shares of ownership being divided both according to the amounts of money provided and according to the effort being contributed to the startup by the partners.

The valuable capital was economized in several ways. The entrepreneur worked up his own sales catalog and advertising brochures. Manufacturers' representatives were engaged for sales channels rather than hiring salesmen, so that no money would have to be paid out for sales until shipments were billed. The partners also agreed that no salaries would be paid to owners until the company was above cash breakeven. By locating used equipment, which at $30,000 was available far below the cost of new, and by installing it themselves, the partners further saved in creating a plant that could produce 10,000 units per month, enough for sales of $840,000 per year and profits projected at $180,000 per year when full volume was reached.

Who else could have spotted and exploited this opportunity? Someone connected with the business, the Los Angeles or other established company, a customer or supplier who noticed the freight charges, or perhaps someone else who simply happened to hear about them could have investigated and acted. Knowhow in the manufacture would probably not have been too hard to come by. General machine shop talent is widely available and could have served. For this capability and the needed capital, an entrepreneur who spotted the idea could have moved on it by appropriately recruiting partners.

Supply Shortage

Occasionally situations arise where entry is facilitated by inability of existing companies to satisfy demand. Such circumstances may exist when supply has been curtailed by some major event, such as war or natural disaster, or when some new product or service has "caught on" and its demand is expanding faster than existing suppliers can catch up.[2] An entrepreneur who is quick to spot this imbalance and to create, corral, or geographically transfer a source of supply may then be able not only to break into the market but to realize exceptionally high margins in doing so, at least until other suppliers manage to catch up with demand. It should be noted, however, that while such conditions may facilitate entry, the startup process may still not be easy. Existing firms in parallel or even unrelated lines of business may also enter the competition to expand supply. An entrepreneur who is fast enough may even be able, shortly after setting up his or her supply, to sell out on favorable terms to larger companies wanting to enter the business who might be big enough to wipe the entrepreneur out anyway if he or she did not sell.

The following illustrates an exceptionally spectacular success in this approach. It can be seen also that the entrepreneur benefited by the unusual circumstance of wartime plus a substantial stake of financial savings.

◆   Kemmons Wilson was stationed in the army during World War II in Memphis, where he noticed the shortage of housing. Having earlier built a jukebox and pinball machine business (starting with a single secondhand popcorn machine), which he had sold out for $200,000 before enlisting, he was equipped with capital. As a sideline he began building houses, completing forty before being transferred to duty in India. After the war he returned to house building, and then in 1952 built his first motel in Memphis, which he called the Holiday Inn. Expansion into a chain of motels followed via franchising into a worldwide chain. By 1987, the total assets of Holiday Inns was $2 billion.

It does not require a war to generate housing demand in which startups, most of them small, become very profitable. Many did so in the real estate booms of the early 1970s in southern and central California. Nor does shortage born of wartime, although it served Wilson well, guarantee success for suppliers. The auto shortage following World War II, for example, lured entrepreneurs like Tucker and Kaiser-Fraser into starting auto companies that failed because they were too small in competing with established makers. The following, on the other hand, was a peacetime success prompted by supply shortage.

◆   An executive with a medium-sized space technology company learned in 1968 that his employer was encountering very long lead times in obtaining parts made by screw machine. These were parts for which it was most convenient to utilize local suppliers, but upon checking into who the local screw machine shops were, he found that only one existed locally and the next closest two were 150 miles distant. Although important, the relatively small volume of screw-machined parts needed by his employer was nowhere near sufficient to justify purchase of a screw machine for in-house production. Although he knew next to nothing about such machines, the idea occurred to the executive that he might be able to set up a screw machine shop of his own to service not only his employer but also other local customers.

He began by asking an engineer at work about screw machines, how they operated, what they could make, skills needed, and what would be required to set

---

[2] Another occasion of supply shortage occurs when it has been curtailed by government action either rationing it or making it illegal. The resultant black market is then created by entrepreneurial activity. Because such activity is illegal, however, it lies outside the scope of this discussion.

up a screw machine shop. Then he visited two existing screw machine shops to see what they looked like and how they worked. Concluding from this self-education that he might be able to start such a business, he approached the chairman of the board of his employer, who said he saw no conflict of interest in the executive's retaining his job and pursuing the startup on the side. Now he felt ready to move seriously on the venture.

On the engineer's advice, he visited a local machinery dealer, who told him that a new screw machine cost $30,000, but a used one was available in another city two hundred miles distant for around half that.

The dealer also told him of a substantial screw machine job soon to be let and agreed to help arrange purchase of the used machine. The prospect of this job, though he never got it, added major impetus to the project in the entrepreneur's mind. He proceeded to seek financing from a local bank, which agreed to loan $10,000 against the machine, provided that the entrepreneur came up with cash for the rest of the price, the other machinery needed for the shop, and working capital.

Next he looked for location, and after scouting a wide radius decided it would be worth premium rent to have his shop as close to home as possible to minimize personal travel time, particularly considering that the venture would be an after-hours and weekend time consumer on top of his regular job. While waiting for the building to be readied for occupancy, he arranged purchase of ancillary equipment for the shop and paid $500 to have a lawyer prepare a corporation that included 100 percent ownership for the entrepreneur plus a stock option plan for future use with employees. When the building was ready, he accepted shipment of the screw machine and other equipment needed to start operation, spending long hours on evenings and weekends building cabinets and setting up equipment.

Now the entrepreneur felt he was ready for orders. The job the machinery dealer had first told him about had long since passed, but the dealer told him of other possibilities and he began preparing bids, estimating the material and labor costs, adding an overhead rate plus 10 percent for profit, then checking the price against competitive bids expected. After a month with no results the first order finally arrived, for one hundred small parts, and the business was under way.

There followed a series of problems. A part-time man whom he hired worked sporadic hours, and the executive had to fill in with extra moonlight hours of his own to keep production up. A salesman had to be found who would sell half time and work half time in the shop. Receivables proved hard to collect, and the company's cash stretched progressively thinner, causing the executive to draw the lesson that "The amount of cash needed to start a business will be three times as much as you estimated." As sales grew toward breakeven, a second screw machine had to be bought to handle the increased volume. The part-time man quit and had to be replaced. The executive's wife became distressed that the family was seeing so little of him as the new venture consumed all his free time.

Then, just as the company passed breakeven, a little more than a year and a half after inception, matters came to a head when the executive was offered a promotion by his employer and a seat on the board of directors. The board said, however, that they would regard his continuation of the venture as too great a time demand and a conflict with his new duties. But they went on to say that because their company was interested in diversifying they would be willing to buy him out. A price was arranged that rewarded him well for his investment in the startup, and the venture was merged to become part of his realm of responsibility as vice-president.

This entrepreneur "happened" to encounter a supply shortage because of his job, but many others could have seen it or found it too: other employees of his company, other people who bought from screw machine shops and encountered slow delivery times, and employees of the screw machine shops themselves. In fact, one approach for finding venture opportunities can be to go looking for supply shortages, as did the following entrepreneur who was mentioned briefly in connection with deliberate search methods in Chapter 5.

♦   He began making the rounds of purchasing offices in local companies, asking what sorts of things they were having trouble obtaining or on which they were being quoted long delivery times or prices that appeared excessive. In this way he identified need for a particular electronic product, a "delay line." He then set about recruiting the talent and money to produce it and built a million-dollar electronic company on which he cashed in by going public.

This is an opportunity-seeking approach that any would-be entrepreneur could employ. What it requires is application of time to go out and make the calls plus persistent initiative to tolerate rejections until a suitable opportunity is found.

Tapping Unutilized Resources

Throughout the world are resources waiting to be discovered for demands that exist. They may consist of oil, ore, unused equipment, sunken treasure, unemployed labor, or even products that have not been presented effectively or refined. The traditional independent mining prospector is a type of entrepreneur who makes a career of seeking and exploiting such resources. Others discover unused resources with profit potential almost by accident.

♦   Two high school brothers in the late 1950s bought themselves old cars, the only kind they could afford. After refurbishing them they found they could sell them at a modest profit, so they repeated the process to earn pocket money, coincidentally accumulating old parts for repairs and storing the ones they did not use in garages of their parents and relatives. Occasionally someone needing an old car part would learn of the brothers' hoard and approach them to obtain it. The sale of $150 worth of parts on one Saturday triggered the idea of going into the antique car parts business seriously. With $300 cash, plus $400 borrowed from their father, an old pickup truck, and their collection of parts, they located a vacant store and leased it for $85 per month. As business grew they moved to larger quarters, eventually constructing their own 10,000-square-foot store and an entire wrecking yard full of antique autos. Fifteen years later sales were around $400,000 per year with a high margin and inventory accumulated over the years valued at $800,000.

Discovery of unutilized resources need not be so accidental. E. Joseph Cossman, for example, has taken products originally developed by others and added some refinement or effective merchandising to achieve success. Each of the following examples from his experience illustrates a different discovery and exploitation strategy.[3]

---

[3] The cases involving the plastic soldiers, the "fly cakes," and the "spud gun" are from *How I Made $1,000,000 in Mail Order* by E. Joseph Cossman (Englewood Cliffs, N.J.: Prentice-Hall, Inc.) © 1963 by Prentice-Hall, Inc. Used with permission. The case of the small plastic diver is from *How to succeed in Your Own Business*, a cassette tape published by Cossman International, Inc. (Palm Springs, Calif.). Used with permission.

◆   Cossman read in the newspaper about a toy company going bankrupt. It had tried selling small plastic soldiers at fifty for a dollar and failed. He bought the abandoned tooling for $2,000, mounted a new advertising campaign offering 100 for a dollar, and soon sold two million sets.

◆   Cossman read in the Business Opportunities section of the *Los Angeles Times* classified advertisements about a new type of fly killer available. The government had spent thousands of dollars developing a cake form, which was being manufactured and sold by two men with very little success. Cossman offered to promote the product in return for exclusive sales rights, and they accepted. He gave the product a new package, mounted an advertising campaign, and sold over two million "fly cakes" the first year.

◆   Cossman read in *Playthings Magazine* an article about U.S. Divers Corporation, makers of the Aqua Lung, which had tried introducing a toy product, a small plastic diver that rose and sank in the water when a bulb attached to the diver by a small hose was squeezed and released. Customers found that the bulb and hose did not work properly, and consequently great numbers of the product had been returned, causing the manufacturer to take it off the market. Cossman called U.S. Divers and offered to buy the tooling. New, the tooling had cost $25,000, but now it was regarded as virtually worthless, and he was able to obtain it for $500. Cossman engaged an engineer to modify the tiny diver to eliminate the bulb and hose and make it work with baking powder pellets instead, a modification which cost approximately another $500. At this point he happened to mention what he had done in a talk to a Rotary Club, with the result that two men in the audience offered to buy a half interest in the product. For this Cossman accepted $35,000. The product was put on the market, and 100,000 units were sold at $2.98 each, yielding net profit of $50,000, of which $25,000 went to Cossman. The two men bought his half interest for another $35,000, leaving him with a total gain of $90,000 on the item.

◆   Cossman received a call from a plastics factory inquiring whether he wanted to buy tooling for a toy gun that would shoot tiny pellets dug from a potato. The caller said, "To tell you the truth, I made 100,000 guns ten years ago, and I have 90,000 guns left." Cossman obtained samples, which he mailed to 500 toy wholesalers across the country, all of whom rejected it. He contacted the U.S. Department of Agriculture to learn what he could about potatoes, and learned that there was currently a glut on the market due to a bumper crop. At this point he bought the tooling for the "spud gun" from the plastic factory for $600, then wrote to 100 U.S. potato grower associations telling them of plans to introduce the product at the forthcoming New York toy show and asking the associations to contribute potatoes to create a "roomful of potatoes" which would yield valuable human interest publicity both for the spud gun and for the potato. Subsequent sales of the gun, he predicted, would further help potato sales. His request yielded 50,000 pounds of potatoes, filling two New Yorker Hotel rooms. He then issued press releases and offered to give the potatoes to an orphanage. He requested that twenty-five orphans help demonstrate the guns with a "shoot out" on a truck loaded with potatoes in front of the hotel. Sales orders boomed at the toy show, and Cossman soon needed more tooling to expand production. (One of the original duplicate sets he tracked down had been used as a boat anchor and was unserviceable.) Over a million and a half guns were sold.

So effective did Cossman consider this strategy of exploiting unused plastics tooling that he made it a policy to write plastics firms twice per year asking whether any "old tooling, prototypes, or even inventory of 'dead' merchandise" was available for sale. Responses, he said, were always "tremendous."

CUSTOMER-SPONSORED STRATEGIES

In all examples of the preceding section and in most of the sections before that, the startup sequence involved first getting the business together and then either going after customers or hoping that customers would come to the business. Sometimes, however, that order is reversed, and the company's wedge for breaking into business is to enlist customer support first. If an entrepreneur can start by first obtaining a contract or other backing from a customer, then this commitment can be used to round up other needed ingredients, such as people, money, and equipment. Two variations on this approach will be described in this section. In the first, the entrepreneur's strategy is to obtain one or more major contracts to begin the company. In the second, the entrepreneur takes advantage of a special situation, one wherein the customer is anxious that a second source of supply for some needed product or service be made available. The entrepreneur then obtains support in the form of a contract or other types of aid to get a company going, which will be that second source of supply.

Customer Contract

The trick in this approach is first to identify a prospective customer who needs and can pay for something and then to convince that customer to make a commitment to buy it from the entrepreneur. What this requires is the kind of selling that goes on in business all the time, seeking out customers and persuading them to buy, but with an added difficulty, which is that they are asked to buy from an unproven firm, possibly one that is not yet established at all. Usually the entrepreneur either must possess very good credentials personally in the line of business or must have them all lined up in the form of people who agree to go to work for the business and who hold the credentials themselves. Many computer software companies began in this fashion. An entrepreneur familiar with the software business would locate prospective customers for programming, then persuade some competent programmers who were working for other companies that they could enjoy better financial rewards and/or working conditions in a new company. He could then take their résumés, with their names blanked out, to the customer as representative of the team that offered the programming service, and thereby establish the credibility to land a contract. Given the contract, he could then hire the programmers and be in business.

A source of many of the contracts around which new companies have been formed, particularly in high-technology industries, has been the federal government. Announcements of opportunities to bid on government contracts are published in the *Commerce Daily,* a newspaper regularly followed by sales departments of companies that sell to the government. In the following case, two engineers who worked for such a government contractor and who had written a book together entitled *Selling to the Government* (which they had been unable to sell to publishers) decided to follow their own advice by seeking a contract on their own.

◆   In 1965 Richard Smith and William Dell decided to leave relatively secure positions with United Technology, an established aerospace company in Sunnyvale, California, to start their own company. Smith described the rationale for leaving a secure position: "You were doing a job; really very much dedicated. But then things slow down and you eventually get where the vice-president who is your boss is forty-two and in great health. . . . I realized at the end of one year, I had spent the year doing pretty much the same type of thing I had done the year before, and that was very unappetizing. Running a big technical program was fun, but I had done that. And the idea of starting a business, you know, was sort of starting to grow.

"But I'm not a specialist. I haven't just invented a good transistor or some specialty item that we could start a business around—when you're somewhat of a generalist, how do you do it?"

The answer, Smith and Dell decided, was to quit UTC. "It was clear," Smith continued, "that as long as you were there in that job, devoting a major portion of your time to it, there was just too much inertia to do these things. It became very clear that if you wanted to kill the bull that you had to get in the ring. Everybody else was trying to do it from the bleachers.

"We had been working on the idea of how to get started, what to do, and what to work on. Being in the forefront of marketing, it was clear to several of us that the field of rocketry was going to go downhill. But we could see in the broad sense there would be a technical revolution of all things, all advanced things coming out of their niches in rocketry and space and out into the commercial world. So we started with the brilliant idea of transferring the technology out of the aerospace world and into commercial products. . . . and learned a lot and made mistakes."

The first contract landed by the new company, a $25,000 pump and compressor technology study for NASA, was in Smith's view not very satisfactory. "We were pinned down . . . reading volumes of reports . . . highly technical data . . . complex equations. Instead of learning about business, I was back redoing complex engineering I'd forgotten about. It took a couple of months longer than we had planned and we ran out of most of the money. . . . We discovered that you don't just go to a CPA and get an accounting system . . . they don't even know what the hell cost-plus accounting means. You get something that's just adequate for the corner grocery store. And we didn't know any better, so that got messed up.

"We tried to raise money, just based on broad ideas, and found out we couldn't raise a dime. Nobody can separate you from every other nut . . . It was really a good thing . . . because if we had been able to get a lot of money I'm almost sure we'd have gone right through it.

"Well, anyway, while doing the pump and compressor contract we had lots of ideas. Ideas are not the problem; we've got file drawers full of them. . . . One of the things we heard about just idly was the great problem of disposal of solid waste. We started thinking about it and we said, 'Well, hell, why don't we burn it in a gas turbine?' . . . we wrote a proposal and solved the solid waste problem by burning refuse in a gas turbine and we called it the 'refuse rocket.' . . .

"We found that you have to know not only the technology that's in the field currently, but also the people who are involved in it, the market, how they look at it, whether they think it's good or bad. That took quite a while to learn, because we knew nothing about garbage. Now we know quite a bit about garbage."

Smith emphasized that in his view an important asset to the new company was capability in dealing with government people. After two months in preparation a proposal for a solid waste disposal study was submitted which brought a $25,000 cost-plus contract, which was subsequently increased to $140,000. As of April 1969, the company had added a full-time secretary and two engineers besides the founders. Proposals were being prepared for further research and development contracts eventually leading to products.

Most contract work is not proprietary to the contractor. As a result, such companies find themselves continually working their way out of jobs and accrue a desire to develop products of their own, as did the above pair of entrepreneurs. Lamont found this shift of orientation common among contract startups, and he observed that entrepreneurs who had started a contract-type company and then later went on to start another company tended to prefer products the second time around.[4] A study by Baillie found that shifts from research contracting to proprietary products can be very hard to accomplish and tend to be a losing game for many small companies, although strategic rules can be suggested that make success more likely.[5] Contract startup is generally easier to accomplish with less financing than product startup, however, and sometimes the later shift to products can lead to very high success. The NYSE-listed company of Edgerton, Germeshausen, and Grier, for example, began when an M.I.T. Professor suggested to one of his thesis students that they become industrial consultants. The professor and the student undertook contracts for paper and printing industries, using M.I.T. laboratory facilities, where they developed and patented instruments that later became their product line. Another manufacturer that began as a service contract start was Solartron, a highly successful British electronics company:

◆   Two electronics engineers, E. R. Ponsford and L. B. Copestick, pulled together a few hundred pounds and set up Solartron Ltd. in 1947 to develop and manufacture electronic instruments. However, they found their capital too limited to produce the instruments, and consequently they undertook government contracts for repair and nonproprietary production work to survive. Not until 1949 were they able to put their own electronic instruments on the market. But then sales began, rising slowly at first. By 1951 the work force numbered only twenty, but in 1954 it reached 240. Five years later it had reached 1,330, and the company was producing a wide line of products in instrumentation, data processing, automation, industrial controls, and atomic energy. The manager largely credited with this growth since joining the company in 1951 was John Boulton, an accountant with Harvard Business School training, who operated largely "by the book." Thus in one decade the company grew from inception to a large and rapidly growing enterprise with trained professional management.

Thus, in summary, obtaining a contract as the starting point of a company

[4] Lawrence M. Lamont, "What Entrepreneurs Learn From Experience," *Journal of Small Business Management,* July 1972, p. 36.
[5] Allan Baillie, *Strategic Management of Small R&D Subcontractors,* (PhD Dissertation, University of Washington, 1978).

can be an attractive way to begin. It provides guaranteed sales, at least for a while. If the customer is large and strong, the contract can often be used for obtaining capital from investors who will have confidence that a responsible company has determined the entrepreneur's venture to be a satisfactory source of supply. The promise to pay from such a customer provides a reliable source of income, one against which even banks may be persuaded to advance money to the new company. By obtaining the beginnings of a "track record" through the contract, the entrepreneur should have an easier time obtaining more customers. And it is possible, as the EG&G and Solartron examples illustrate, to move from contracts to proprietary work with greater permanence.

The problem is that the shift can be difficult. Unless the company finds a way to make that shift, its future may be much less secure. Again, there are exceptions. Some companies, such as Arthur D. Little, Planning Research Corporation, and professional consulting firms, stay permanently in the contract business and prosper, but that can be a hard and relatively low profit way of life for a smaller firm that is unable to average out its contracts by carrying many contracts at the time.

Second Sourcing

Greater permanence can sometimes be built into a contract start if the new company can become a continuing supplier to its customers. The most attractive position to be in from the entrepreneur's point of view is that of sole supplier, so that the customer becomes dependent on the new company. But such a position can be hard to sustain, because the customer generally does not like it, and this in turn can create other entrepreneurial opportunities to start up as alternate sources of supply for the customer.

◆   Jerry Sanders wanted to become wealthy, he said, because he grew up impoverished. After "overachieving" in high school and graduating from the University of Illinois School of Engineering, he moved to California. "In Chicago," he recalled, "I would have always been identified with the University of Illinois and the south side of Chicago. I didn't go to Northwestern; my family wasn't from Winnetka. I was tired of it." To him California was "the transparent society where you will move as far and as fast as your abilities will take you without that excess baggage that you didn't go to the right school."

He worked for Douglas Aircraft designing air-conditioning controls and then for Motorola, first in applications engineering and then in semiconductor sales. "People in sales," he observed, "didn't know anything and made more money than I did, had an expense account and a company car. I was not in engineering because I had a great desire to create, or design or invent." When his driver's license was lifted for too many speeding tickets it cut into his mobility as a salesman, and friction broke out between Motorola and Sanders, who thereupon moved to Fairchild Semiconductor. There he rose rapidly in sales until he was fired because, he says, he was a "hot-shot and smart mouth."

With a year's severance pay to go on he decided to start a venture, observing that everyone told him a star should run his own company. Because he lacked a proprietary product idea, he decided to start his company as a "second source" by duplicating the semiconductors of other single-source suppliers.

He also lacked the technical expertise to create those products and the capital to produce them. To solve the first of these problems, he recruited seven engineers using ownership in his new company, Advanced Micro Devices, as an inducement. To raise money he approached venture capitalists and, with what he recalls as great difficulty, managed to obtain $1.5 million. His share of the company was 6 percent; that of the engineers he recruited was 4.5 percent each, proportions that he later regarded as unfair to himself. Sales in the company's first year, 1969, were zero. In 1970 sales began at $1 million, went to $4 million in 1971, $11 million in 1972, $26 million in 1973, $25 million in 1974, and $34 million in 1975.

The second sourcing strategy began to shift in 1975. David Drennan of Corporate Planning recalls that "for the first three or four years after our startup in 1969 we just sold 'me-too' products created by Fairchild or Texas Instruments or some other firm. The first important device that we designed ourselves (in late 1975) was the 2901 microprocessor using bi-polar technology." By 1979 the company had sold its millionth 2901 chip and sales had reached $220 million. By 1984 the company was larger than Fairchild Semiconductor and had sales of $330 million. Jerry Sanders' salary and benefits that year approached $1 million and his net worth was estimated at $28 million.[6]

Purchasers generally prefer to have more than one source of supply. Sometimes they consider it essential. If there is only one source and that source fails, the supply becomes unavailable until a replacement source can be developed, and such a delay can be intolerable. If there is a second source available to begin with, such a delay is avoidable. If the first source breaks down, or has a strike, a fire, a flood, or other interruption of output, the purchaser can then turn to the second source to keep supplies coming. Moreover, the second source may help keep the first source "honest" by providing competition in R&D refinements, delivery promptness, service, and price. The U.S. Defense Department always makes sure that weapons, spare parts, and other supplies can be obtained from at least two or more sources, and so do industrial companies when they have the choice. If providing purchase orders to a new and untried supplier is what it takes to open a second source, even though startup costs of the second source may impose slightly higher prices, the company may be willing to provide them, as in the following example.

♦   The vice-president of a clothing manufacturer, a man who had long considered forming his own company, was impelled to act on that inclination by two simultaneous events. One was knowledge of a forthcoming auction of production machinery by another clothing manufacturer, and the other was disagreement with his colleagues about how his present company should be run. "One of them suggested," he recalled, "that maybe I should go start my own company." Knowing that large chain stores dislike being tied to a single source for goods and that one company was supplying all the parkas bought by a particular chain, he contacted a buyer whom he knew at the chain and promptly obtained a purchase order, which he was able to use at the bank to obtain working capital with which to start. The 50 percent off retail price paid by the chain left him with a tight margin, but with no need for a sales force or advertising (his goods all bore the name of the chain rather than that of his own company), he was able to build a business that eventually expanded into other lines.

One distinguishing feature of second-source startups that can be noted

---

[6] Robert Levering, Michael Katz, and Milton Moskowitz, *The Computer Entrepreneurs* (New York New American Library 1984), p. 298.

in this example is that they generally involve manufacturing products, as opposed to simply providing services. Being already into manufacturing, moreover, can make it easier to move the company into proprietary lines, because the plant, equipment, and skills needed for production will already be in place, whereas they often will not be with a service activity. An even more important advantage in second sourcing, however, is that the customer not only may be willing to provide a contract for purchase from the new company but may also give direct help in marshaling the physical resources and knowhow needed by the entrepreneur to get started, as happened in the next example.

◆   Robert J. Schreiner, a former Fairchild Camera and instrument corporation engineer who briefly served as president of a money-losing company called Computer Microtechnology, attempted to start a new semiconductor manufacturing company but found it impossible to raise venture capital in the financial community. Changing his strategy, he decided to develop his new company as an alternate supplier to a limited number of companies that had become dependent on others for key components in their products and were uncomfortable about it. He was able to line up four larger companies to sponsor him at $250,000 each, American Telecommunications, Victor Comptometer, General Automation, and Bulova Watch. In exchange for 60 percent of the stock in his company, he thereby arranged for both the capital needed to start and sales to get started, while his four backers in return received a dependable source of vital supply.

In some ways second sourcing can become a highly secure type of startup, with sales and resources guaranteed, possibly even including followon orders and future expansion, at least until other suppliers enter the competition. However, there is always the possibility that they may. Moreover, the second-source supplier may find itself captive to a single customer who can control its margins and profits in discomforting ways. There is, for the second source, the option of attempting to diversify into supplying other customers, but if this generates competition for the initial customer, it may cause friction. The lack of need for the second source to invest in a marketing arm, because it has a guaranteed customer, may leave the company in a poor position to go after other business. Hence, in choosing a second-sourcing strategy it is important for a would-be entrepreneur to consider in advance the question of where the company will attempt to go beyond startup.

Being an only source can be ideal for the entrepreneur, and being a second source can be a good way to enter. But as the number of sources grows, the attractiveness of entry declines. As noted in Chapter 2, there were typical cycles of industry growth and decline as more competitors entered in automobiles and electronics. More recently, Sahlman and Stevenson observed such a shakeout in the computer disk drive industry where, it appears, the capital markets implicitly overestimated how big the total industry could become and consequently backed too many startups, many of which consequently failed.[7]

---

[7] William A. Sahlman and Howard H. Stevenson, "Capital Market Myopia," in John A. Hornaday, Edward B. Shils, Jeffry A. Timmons, and Karl H. Vesper, *Frontiers of Entrepreneurship Research, 1985* (Wellesley, Mass.: Babson Center for Entrepreneurial Studies, 1985), p. 80.

PARENT COMPANY SPONSORSHIP

Customers are not the only established companies that help new ones get started. Suppliers, financiers, advisers, and sometimes even competitors help. Franchisors, to take an example already considered in the preceding chapter, help sponsor companies to enter the lines of work that they themselves are already in through providing such things as knowhow, advertising, capital, and purchasing help. This section will consider five other major mechanisms through which startup is powerfully assisted by established companies: joint ventures, in which established companies support largely through financial, physical facility, and technological assistance; licensing, which is similar in many respects to franchising; and spinoffs of three types in which the new company picks up business either willfully or involuntarily relinquished by an established firm.

Joint Ventures

When an established company joins forces with one or more entrepreneurs to create a new company, it can be regarded as a joint venture.[8] Each contributes to the venture and shares in the rewards. This can be a way for an established company to participate in a new development without having to recognize or even to take responsibility for the venture beyond the initial contribution, and at the same time it can be a way for entrepreneurs to spot opportunities and obtain resources and other backing from a strong, well-equipped source. In the following example the venture grew out of a moonlight research project for what turned out to be a future customer.

◆   In 1960 a young man who liked to water-ski began making his own jumping skis while attending a Midwest university in chemical engineering. After graduation he joined a large chemical company where he rose to the position of regional manager on the West Coast, still water-skiing competitively and experimenting with new ski materials in his basement. During a skiing contest in 1968, he met the owner of a water-ski manufacturing company, who became interested in his ideas for fiberglass composite skis and offered to provide space in his factory and help in fabrication work and in development of production machinery in return for sales rights on the product. Working evenings and weekends in the plant, the skier gradually refined his new type of ski, which by 1968 was in his opinion beginning to look ready for the market. Now he felt that he needed capital, but the manufacturer who had helped by providing plant resources was short of it, so he had to look further. He mentioned the idea of forming a new ski company and his capital need to one of the customers of the chemical company which still provided his main employment. This man was familiar with materials fabrication, particularly bonding such as was used in the plastic skis. He knew nothing of water skis or their market, but he had capital. A partnership was formed between the

---

[8] There are other types of joint ventures. For instance, two companies sometimes merge to form a single new company, or several companies may contribute resources to form a new company or to carry out a project. The term here is used to refer to situations wherein one or more companies join in with one or more independent entrepreneurs, not employees simply appointed to start a new department, and create a new company. The emphasis is on use of this strategy by the entrepreneur rather than on its use by the established company.

two men, one providing the idea and water-ski expertise and the other providing the capital, while the established water-ski manufacturing company agreed to put its well-known brand name on the product and provide marketing channels. With the added capital work continued on development of the new skis, and sales began. In mid-1969 both partners left their regular jobs to work full time with the new venture as sales grew. By 1970 capital was running short, and a third partner was taken in to provide more money. Then in early 1971 the manufacturer in whose plant they were working was suddenly arrested and sent to jail. To cope with his own capital shortage he had attempted to smuggle cocaine from Mexico in hollowed-out skis and had been caught. Suddenly the joint venture was thrust on its own. Unable to collect $50,000 due from the arrested manufacturer, the partners withdrew manufacturing equipment and inventory from the plant and established their own plant, lining up another well-established sporting products company to market their skis.

In this example the entrepreneur fulfilled the classical role of pulling together the crucial ingredients for startup from wherever they might come, and it happened that one place they came from was an established company. What was provided by this company could also have been bought if capital had been plentiful, but it would have been less convenient to establish a new facility, probably less efficient, certainly more risky, while the product was in its early developmental stages. Having an established company provide the marketing channels was deemed by the entrepreneur so much to be preferred than setting up new channels of his own that he even continued doing so after losing the initial manufacturing company for that purpose.

Sometimes the initiative for a joint venture comes from management of an existing company as a way of developing new directions of growth. Analog Devices of Norwood, Massachusetts, for instance, adopted a policy of seeking to identify and support people from within the company who had new product ideas that might be developed through formation of independent companies. Under this policy Analog helped provide venture capital, assisted with marketing, and, as the new venture grew, bought more stock. Eventually, the new company might be bought out and merged, provided that its product line was compatible, with the parent company.

Generally, to make a joint venture strategy work, the entrepreneur must couple with a sponsor whose line of activity is close enough to that of the new company that the parent can appreciate the degree of promise and potential reward. At the same time, the startup should be different enough from activities of the parent so as not to duplicate or compete with them.

Manufacture Licensing

Sometimes, however, what the entrepreneur wants to do is emulate exactly one or more aspects of what the parent company does. This can be done through a license from the parent. Such an approach has cropped up in two preceding chapters, first in Chapter 5 as a way of obtaining a venture idea, then again in Chapter 7 in connection with franchising. The distinction with franchising is that franchising usually involves a service rather than independent manufacturing of a product, and also the franchise agreement usually includes use of the parent company's logo or trademark, which carries with it advertising support and sometimes other support as well. A straight license, on the other hand, may simply grant permission to duplicate a product or use a patent.

A license was the starting point for what became the largest manufacturing company in America, General Motors:

♦   In 1886 William C. "Billy" Durant became impressed with the ride of a road cart which, thanks to a new type of spring, made riding over road bumps less annoying. He bought the patent rights for $2,000 and formed a partnership with J. Dallas Dort to start the Durant-Dort Carriage Company. Within five years it had become the largest buggy manufacturing company in the United States.

Three years later, in 1904, Durant looked at the failing company of a plumbing supplier, David Buick, who had developed an automobile. Durant bought the company, capitalized it by selling $500,000 worth of Buick stock, and started promoting the experimental car it had developed. By 1908 it had become the leading automobile company in the country.

With stock from that company he bought others, such as Oldsmobile and Cadillac, which he combined to form General Motors. He almost bought Ford as well, but Henry Ford backed out.

Durant's fortunes rose further with General Motors but then fell in a 1910 recession when the company was taken over by creditors and he was ousted. Taking associates with him, he formed still other car companies, including Chevrolet, which prospered and put him in a position to recapture General Motors in 1915. In 1920 the economy again collapsed, taking with it Durant's fortune, and again he was out.

Again he raised capital and started another car company, Durant Motors, which designed and built its first product in just forty-seven days. Orders for thirty thousand cars poured in before production had even begun. Again Durant began buying other companies, this time to combine them into his Consolidated Motors, which would challenge General Motors. However, many of these companies did not fare well, and the enterprise collapsed even before the crash of 1929. By 1936, at age seventy-five, Durant was broke and filing for bankruptcy but was still forming companies, including an 18-lane bowling alley in Flint, Michigan, which he hoped would be the first in a chain of recreational centers.[9]

This example illustrates not only how a license can be used to start a business but also how that business can lead to others. Those aspects can also be seen in the next example, as can the critical role played by personal contacts both in locating and obtaining a license and in obtaining other needed ingredients for startup.

♦   By the toss of a coin Sig McGuire decided to seek employment connected to skiing rather than golf after being mustered out of the navy as a metalsmith following World War II. So he joined a friend and helped install rope tows for a ski lodge. When the lodge was unable to pay the full price of the work, McGuire wound up running the tows for a percentage of the revenues. Shortly thereafter, the lodge changed hands, and McGuire acquired ownership of the tows. Then the lodge began to fail. McGuire recruited the friend with whom he had put up the tows, plus another acquaintance in the restaurant business, and the three of them took over the lodge while McGuire negotiated payouts with the lodge's creditors. The lodge survived but did not prosper, and the three eventually sold out. During

[9] Joseph R. Mancuso, "William C. Durant, the Forgotten Entrepreneur," in *The Entrepreneurial Manager's Newsletter*, Vol. 9, No. 1 (October 1987), 1. New York, Center for Entrepreneurial Management.

the ski venture he had become acquainted with people in the logging industry, and one of them gave him a job running a logging operation on the lonely undeveloped northern end of Vancouver Island. "It was a living," he recalled, "but I had a family and wanted to move us back to a city." One day while in town to pick up income tax assistance from an accountant, he decided to look up a former skiing friend, whose office was near the accountant, to have lunch together. During lunch the friend told him about a new business he was in, distributing under license a drapery track invented in Switzerland. When the friend exulted in how successfully it was selling and mentioned that a license for the U.S. might be available, McGuire became interested. Stepping across the street to a recently built bank where one of the drapery tracks was in operation, McGuire became even more impressed. Maybe this would be his opportunity to move with his family back to a U.S. city. Obtaining the address of the Swiss who had the U.S. rights, McGuire immediately sent off a night letter expressing interest.

The Swiss man, who held rights throughout the British Commonwealth plus the U.S. and had his factory in England, phoned McGuire the next day and suggested they meet halfway, in Montreal, to discuss it. "It was a fairly expensive ticket," McGuire recalled, "but the product really looked promising, and you don't get anything for nothing. You always have to extend yourself in either time or money or both. I'd had a successful season logging and could afford it, so I went."

The two men got along well, and McGuire arranged to obtain samples of the product. These he carried around to architects, designers, and decorators, soliciting reactions. "They were all impressed and seemed eager to buy," McGuire said, "so I went ahead with getting a license. Essentially, the Swiss man turned over his U.S. distribution rights to me by having the people in Switzerland from whom he had obtained them make the change. He seemed to feel a responsibility to them to help develop sales of the product, and I didn't have to pay him anything. Later I reimbursed him for his trip to Montreal, and eventually I wound up buying parts from his company in England, but there was no formal obligation to him. We just had a good rapport and figured we would collaborate more in the future one way or another. My agreement was with the Swiss parent company, giving them a royalty percentage of gross sales for exclusive rights in the U.S. It was a fairly standard form and no legal work was involved. I just signed what they gave and for their part they took me on the word of the man who recommended me."

After signing the agreement, McGuire first formed a corporation, and then traveled to Europe, where he visited several other companies that had licenses for the product, studying their methods of operation and spending a week and a half with the parent company and inventor of the product in Switzerland. In England he visited the man who had relinquished the U.S. rights to him, studied his manufacturing operation, and arranged to obtain some inventory for demonstrating the product in the U.S. During this visit the man told McGuire about another product, wire markers, for coding the ends of wires to facilitate installation, which he had himself invented and was selling very successfully in England. "I was not particulary interested," McGuire recalled, "but he said the U.S. rights were available and after I got the drapery track business underway, he'd like me to take on the wire markers too."

Returning home, McGuire set about raising money, roughly $30,000 for inventory, brochures, and other sales materials. "I managed to recruit some money from my accountant and some from another man whom I had been associated with in the ski business," McGuire said, "The accountant formulated the terms, giving me 51 percent for contributing the idea plus time and money I had already spent, while the other two took 49 percent in return for their investments. I guess it must have been a reasonably fair arrangement, because they're both still talking to me." Finding the potential national market much larger than a small company could handle, the partners soon sold out for cash plus sales royalties, only to have the purchasing company decide that the product competed with others in their line that were more profitable. "I had visions of grandeur from the royalties," McGuire reflected, "Rolls Royces, yachts, and all that. But they never materialized."

Now McGuire decided to move on the other product that had been offered to him on license, the wire markers. Calling England, he learned that the Swiss man who had offered it to him had died, but the English director of the company said he had been told of the verbal offer and was willing to go ahead on it. McGuire flew to England and spent two months working in different parts of the factory, learning the business. He signed an agreement stating that he would buy supplies from the English company and give them a royalty in return for exclusive U.S. manufacturing and sales rights. "The agreement was almost a handshake deal," McGuire commented. "It was only a half page long and ran for five years. But now we have been operating long past that time. I paid royalties for ten years, and although I no longer do so, we continue to exchange technological improvements and patent rights. For instance, I developed a packaging system for the markers, which I patented. They use it without any royalties. It's been a very cooperative relationship."

By the mid-1970s McGuire's business, although small with around thirty employees, was thriving. His main problem turned out to be that of obtaining supplies from England in quantities sufficient to meet sales demand. While looking for alternate sources of supply, he was keeping sales effort to an absolute minimum and also exploring ways to diversify in order to maintain growth. His main diversification was in the direction of assembling wire harnesses for pleasure boats, automotive vehicles, and other uses, an idea that had been suggested to him by the purchasing agent of one of his customers and was now proving highly profitable.

In hindsight Sig McGuire characterized many of the developments in this successful sequence as "lucky"—hearing of the drapery track opportunity from his Vancouver friend, hitting it off easily with the Swiss, and hearing of the wire marker opportunity. But in fact each of these events resulted from prior initiatives on his part. And the fact that he wound up with partners in each of his deals and continued pleasant relationships with each of them suggests both that he was willing to share ownership and rewards and that he conducted himself in such a way as to be seen as a compatible person to deal with by others. Also, it could be noted that he encountered some "bad luck" as well. The logging venture that resulted in his wanting to get out somehow, inability to develop the drapery venture independently to a scale called for by the market, failure of the royalties from the sellout to materialize, and chronic shortages of materials in the marker business might all be regarded as less than optimal outcomes. Most remarkable, perhaps, was the consistently satisfactory way that relatively informal and nonlegalistic agreements seemed to work out between Mr. McGuire and the licensors with whom he dealt. This was a result that he himself regarded as atypical, commenting, "It seemed to me that I was really fortunate on that score. Of course, that was some years back. I'm not sure I'd treat it that casually today."

Market Relinquishment

Quite a different form of assistance may be realized by a new venture when an established company decides to phase out of a market. There can be several reasons for such phaseouts. The parent company may find itself short of capital which it either needs for survival or feels it could put to better use elsewhere. Or an established company may conclude that the market has become unprofitable due to union initiative, more aggressive competitors, technological obsolescence, shortage of supplies, or shrinkage of demand below economic operating levels. A conclusion by top management, particularly in very large companies, that the market is incompatible with overall corporate strategy can be another reason for simply dropping it.

This can leave customers looking for somewhere to turn, and a new company with a different approach, better location, or smaller operating scale may be able to break into business at a profit by serving them. Its entry wedge thereby becomes the presence of a ready-made market, as the example below illustrates.

◆   In a large container company in 1961 a policy decision was made that because the company was making insufficient profit on small orders of corrugated boxes, no orders of less than 2,500 boxes would henceforth be accepted. Two salesmen who had been with the company for six years knew that although there were shops making smaller production runs in some major cities, none was closer than eight hundred miles to their own city. They decided to attempt startup of a firm that would specialize in producing runs smaller than 2,500 cartons and act as wholesaler for larger orders. Their first move was to visit three distant firms similar to the one they planned. Then they formed a partnership and rented a warehouse. All the money they were able to raise was $1,500, not enough to make down payments on manufacturing equipment or inventory. Instead, they managed to persuade their former employer to provide an inventory of precut boxes on consignment. The last of their $1,500 was used to print and mail advertising brochures announcing their service.

To their surprise, nothing happened. Several weeks passed without any apparent effect from the advertising campaign. A few small orders came in from former customers of their prior employer, but not enough to break even. As cash dwindled, the pair decided to attempt the only action they could think of. They walked out of the warehouse and started down the street, knocking on doors and asking for business. Orders came immediately, and soon business was brisk and profitable, providing money to buy inventory, manufacturing equipment, and eventually a plant to house a work force that grew to thirty employees. At that point the partners allowed the business to stabilize and continue at what they regarded as a comfortable pace. Despite the fact that they soon had many steady customers, knocking on doors remained an important part of their marketing program.

Insiders clearly tend to have strong advantages for spotting and exploiting opportunities of this type. They are generally the first to learn of the new policy phasing the big company out, and at the same time they have experience in the business without having to learn it fresh in the new company. The parent may also help by providing information about customers and, as actually happened in this case, by providing inventory on consignment to minimize needed startup capital. Understandably, such opportunities tend to be rare, nor are they without competition. At the same time that these men were setting up to exploit the relinquished market, several others from similar backgrounds were doing likewise, and several new companies resulted. Hence the relinquished market was not a complete gift. The companies formed to pursue it competed with each other and selling was consequently still an important part of the game.

Selloff of a Division

A more common way than market relinquishment for a parent company to withdraw from a line of business is to sell off the part of the company that is responsible for the business, particularly if it is already in the form of a somewhat autonomous division. Often the buyer will be another company, but sometimes it is an entrepreneur or entrepreneurial team, typically employees of the division. Through buying it, they obtain not only the market and rights but inventory, equipment, employees, and going concern as well.

How this can come about will be illustrated here with three examples. Each follows a somewhat different pattern, but in all cases the entrepreneur who ended up in charge of the newly independent company began from inside the parent as an employee of the former division. Also, each had to go outside to raise capital before succeeding with the venture.

◆   In May 1970 an advertising agency marketing director left his job for a new one. His agency had been asked by one of its clients, a large construction equipment company, to analyze a small company it had recently acquired as part of a diversification program. The small company operated in two lines of business, acting as distributor for audio-visual equipment used in schools, and performing "contract programming," or the preparation of special educational materials on contract. When his analysis concluded that the small acquisition was undercapitalized and poorly managed, the advertising agency man was hired to straighten it out with a promise that he would be supported with "unlimited capital."

Within a few weeks it became apparent that the promise would not materialize. The construction equipment company fell on hard times, and rather than adding capital to the acquisition decided to liquidate it. Faced with unemployment, the new manager offered to take over the enterprise for no money down and pay out its book value over time. The parent company accepted. A month later he purchased for 40 percent of his stock the assets of a second company, which principally consisted of a reading program for the mentally retarded. Now he controlled the assets of a company with three lines of activity plus advisory services of the research team that had developed the reading program.

But serious disappointments followed. The capital needed to develop the product line and mount a selling campaign proved elusive. Banks turned the entrepreneur away because, they said, he had no "track record" of line experience in the business. The SBA rejected his loan application six times. Friends expressed reluctance to invest in a company so thinly capitalized. The entrepreneur hung on financially only thanks to income from his wife's employment for eleven months until the SBA loan finally came through, for $105,000. Then friends invested another $55,000, and the pace of activity in the firm picked up.

Still profits did not come. As a distribution company the enterprise found itself unable to match prices of competitors whose larger volumes let them buy at higher discounts. Contract programming brought a trickle of income, but school districts were beset with tightening budgets and just not buying. The reading program for the retarded still needed development to transform it from filing cabinets of research work into commercially salable materials, and that consumed funds. Two years of long hours and hard work trying to develop sales passed, and the company, now approaching the end of its financial resources, had yet to break even.

This man had no intention initially of becoming an entrepreneur. Rather, he was thrust by circumstance into a position where he either had to become one or was out of a job. The division was doomed if it stayed with the parent company, so the parent was willing to let it go for no money down and a note in the amount of the book value, which was more than liquidation would bring. But was it a bargain? Although he was not putting in much money to keep operating, the entrepreneur was in effect working for free and thereby contributing the salary he could have earned elsewhere. The bank and potential investors did not think much of the company's chances. Even the SBA, which is continually in the business of making risky investments, shied away. The company appeared to be clearly headed for failure and, in fact, nearly did fail but for the intercession of a government policy change that gave it new business, as will be described further in the next section.

In the next example it was not so clear at the outset whether the division to be spun off was in dire straits or not.

◆   A young man who, as a college student, had worked in the document-handling department of a bank took a job with the bank after graduation. He continued there in data processing, attending short courses run by IBM and NCR and then an eighteen-month executive development program run by the bank. By 1968, after spending two years as sales manager for a department of the bank that offered computerized accounting systems for small businesses, he felt himself caught up in what he regarded as too impersonal an organization with insufficient prospect for further advancement. Resigning, he moved to a CPA firm to direct startup of a computer service department similar to that of the bank. Within a few months, however, he concluded that the management of the CPA firm was not strongly committed to supporting growth of the new service. He was left largely alone to run it, but it was not set up as a profit center, and this made it hard for him to use its performance to argue for pay raises. He asked management if he could arrange to set it up as an independent profit center and personally acquire a share of ownership as compensation.

Management said no. Now he saw only three options for moving ahead: look for a new job, quit and take two key employees who were willing to go with him and start a new service company to compete with his employer, or buy out the service department. Job hunting so soon after he had just done it did not appeal, and some calculations quickly revealed that startup would require considerable cash for computer rental deposits and working capital, plus much work in redevelopment of software. He decided to try buyout first, and approached the CPA partners with the argument that the service department had not turned out to be of great interest to them anyway. He also let them know that he saw startup and competing with them as an option. Somewhat to his surprise, the partners readily accepted the buyout idea. The young entrepreneur now prepared some pro forma financial projections for the business and approached possible investors with his buyout idea. By proposing to set up the new corporation in such a way that high-income investors could write off startup losses against their taxes, he was able to recruit capital from ten of the twelve people he approached. He also persuaded them to guarantee a bank loan for working capital. Soon the deal was closed. In a year and a half the new business was in the black and growing.

In this case the ambition, will, and action of the entrepreneur played a substantial role in creating an opportunity. The division was not marked for phaseout, as was the education service division in the prior case, and the entrepreneur was not faced with unemployment if he did not move toward takeover. Rather, he acted because he was dissatisfied with his present position.

Had his offer of buyout been rejected, he likely would have moved on to the option of either taking another job or starting a new company.

In the next example the entrepreneur probably could not have started a company comparable to the division he took over. The effort required to start something so complex would probably have been simply too great relative to the effort he could apply and relative to the expected level of profitability.

◆   In 1966 a young MBA two years out of school left the large company he had joined "to take the edges off" and joined a smaller company that had been growing by diversified acquisitions. A year later he was made controller of the company's nuclear products division, which seemed at the time destined for substantial growth. After another three years, however, it appeared that the opposite might be the case. The parent company had undergone a severe sales decline, and although the nuclear products division had remained stable and profitable, cash was extremely short, making reinvestment for growth impossible. When the parent began selling off some of its other divisions, executives of the nuclear division began discussing their futures. The young MBA decided that he could either wait out the apparent stagnation, quit, or throw his energies into an attempt to buy out the division. He and the other division executives felt that the division was missing great opportunities because of the parent company's management' preoccupation with its own troubles.

He began making the rounds of financial circles in the city, commercial bankers, investment bankers, financial advisers, wealthy inventors, and others, soliciting advice about a price and terms as well as potential sources of capital for buying the division and putting it on a new track. Meanwhile, strains grew within the division and dissension broke out sporadically among the division's managers as they struggled with terms for an offer to the parent company and worried about what would happen to the division and their jobs if it were re-fused.

Finally, they settled on a cash offer of $650,000 that they had been able to line up from a group of prospective investors. To their great disappointment it was turned down by the parent management. Even more disturbing was the news that the president of the parent company was being replaced with a new man, who was expected to come in "with his ax swinging."

The young MBA reflected briefly on what to do, then decided to wait and see what happened, going about his job as usual, while others either did the same or went looking for new jobs. A month later the new president's ax took a favorable swing. Overruling the rest of the parent company management he accepted the cash offer. The MBA became president of the spinoff as it went its own way, operating in the black and expanding its product line.

In addition to being more capital-intensive than the other examples, several other differences in this spinoff can be noted. It was more a team effort on the part of the entrepreneur(s) than were the others, in part, perhaps, because the division was bigger to begin with, but also because the technology involved was both greater in breadth and more industrially specialized, hence harder to re-place in event of breakoff. A more significant difference, though, was the fact that unlike the two preceding examples, the division in this case was clearly profitable prior to spinoff. The result was that it was profitable during and after spinoff, whereas the prior two examples lost money for many months before breaking even. This was a desirable feature of the spinoff, but to obtain it the entrepreneur had to come up with a better offer, a cash buyout of several hundred thousand dollars. Fortunately for the entrepreneur, the parent company was sufficiently desperate for cash to let the division go. Otherwise, the spinoff likely would not have been possible.

There was considerably more than luck involved, however, because the parent company could also have found another corporation to buy the division. The entrepreneur simply could have awaited this eventuality, as have most employees in such circumstances. But by taking initiative to set up an offer, he was able to move faster, preempt such a sellout, and obtain the prize for himself and his team.

GOVERNMENTAL SPONSORSHIP

Governments, both state and federal, tend to be sympathetic to startup of new enterprises and they do make efforts to provide assistance, but for the most part this assistance is aimed at small businesses that are already under way, rather than startups. That assistance which is given to startups, moreover, generally does not provide an entry wedge, but rather complements whatever main wedge the entrepreneur has mustered independently. For instance, governments publish enormous amounts of information, trade statistics, SBA booklets on how to operate businesses, NASA lists of new product ideas, and books on a huge number of subjects. They provide counseling services for entrepreneurs and business managers and courses in how to prepare business taxes, how to operate businesses, and how to start them. Information about foreign sales channels, laws and regulations of all types, and protection from unfair competition is available without charge from various agencies. The federal government also assists many firms in obtaining capital, both through the direct means of guaranteeing bank loans and also in some cases making grants, as well as indirectly through support of small business investment companies. But none of these activities itself constitutes an entry wedge for breaking into business. At best they are complementary to the means of entering into production and sales activities.

Favored Purchasing

There are some circumstances where governments do more directly provide entry wedges. One already mentioned is that of granting contracts, where the government is the first customer. With such a contract an entrepreneur can often go to the bank and borrow money, go to suppliers and obtain credit, lease the necessary equipment, and start producing. Consequently, a would-be entrepreneur may find it of interest to learn about how governments do their buying and how such contracts can be obtained. Two main types of references can help in this regard. One is a daily newspaper, the *Commerce Business Daily,* which is available from the U.S. Department of Commerce and advertises contracts of the national government open for bid. The other type consists of publications telling how to deal with various levels of government and different agencies. One entitled *Doing Business with the Federal Government* tells in plain language how to sell to federal agencies. Many of the agencies themselves also publish "How To" books describing their purchasing practices, as do many state and local governments. The purchasing department of the city of Seattle, for instance, has a booklet entitled *Selling to Seattle,* while the Department of Defense puts out one entitled *Selling to the Military,* and so forth. A contact point for learning about sources of federal contracts in general is the Small Business Administration, which is specifically charged with helping small firms obtain such contracts wherever possible.

By contacting purchasing offices of governmental agencies an entrepreneur can obtain information about contract opportunities and how to take advantage of them. Many governmental agencies practice discriminatory purchasing designed to give advantages to small versus large companies, also to certain geographical regions such as those of disaster or high unemployment and to certain racial groups. Under "small business set asides," for instance, it is specified that certain types of products and services must be obtained from small firms, while under the Minority Vendors Program and 8(a) Business Development Program, minority races are given preferential treatment in purchasing supervised by the Small Business Administration.

Rule Changes

Profit opportunities sometimes arise from governmental rule changes. When the government condemns land to put in a new building or freeway, for instance, the landowner may be able to exact an attractive price. Consequently, those who are able to anticipate the condemnation may acquire the land and make substantial profits, as many with political connections have done. It is also possible sometimes to bring about rule changes that enhance the value of property. One entrepreneur, for instance, bought an old mansion in a residential district for a low price, arranged to have the area rezoned, transformed the mansion into a sanitarium, and made a $750,000 profit almost overnight. Another governmental rule change was the break that allowed the educational service and publishing venture mentioned in the preceding section to change from losses during startup to profits, as follows:

◆   After two years of struggle the company had failed to break even and was now having difficulty even keeping up payments on the SBA loan interest. Contract programming was at a low level, and there appeared to be no way to expand audio-visual equipment sales to a profitable volume. Many similar small firms in that line of business were failing already. But a break occurred in the company's third area of business, publication of a reading program for the retarded. In May 1972 Pennsylvania passed legislation entitling retarded children to public school education. Suddenly there was a large potential market for the reading program and virtually no established competition.
        Now the problem was how to finance $100,000 worth of production in a company with a record of losses, a negative net worth, and substantial due debt. The answer turned out to be formation of a new partnership for selling the reading program. The original corporation received 50 percent ownership in the new partnership as general partner in return for the program. The investors, all personal friends of the entrepreneur, received the other 50 percent as limited partners in return for the $100,000. Thereby the new enterprise was shielded from overhanging debts of the original company, the creditors of the original company were

in a position to be paid off from profits of the new company, and the new investors were free of liability for all former debts. Within a few months the first order had been shipped, a sales campaign was generating followon orders, and the company was operating well in the black.

This entrepreneur was, in effect, sponsored by a governmental rule change that happened by good fortune rather than planning. The previous entrepreneur who started the sanitarium was able to plan on the change because he brought it about.

A type of rule change available to would-be entrepreneurs exists in some foreign countries, although not in the U.S., and is designed by governments to stimulate industry through *import substitution*. Those governments in effect give a monopoly through cutting off imports on any product whose manufacture is initiated locally. In the Central American Common Market countries, for instance, if a local entrepreneur decides to start manufacturing certain vehicle replacement parts currently being imported, the government will clamp import restrictions on those parts, thereby giving the entrepreneur a captive market.

COMBINATIONS OF WEDGES

The main reason for classifying different types of entry wedges has not been to delimit rigid and inviolate categories, but rather to display a spectrum of strategic options open to would-be entrepreneurs as an aid in triggering awareness of more venture possibilities. But it should be noted that lines between categories are often blurry. Strategies used by a given venture often may straddle categories and be hard to place in one versus another. What is a new product or service versus one that is parallel competition is usually a matter of arbitrary definition. In fact, virtually any venture can be classed as parallel competition if the category is regarded broadly. Second sourcing can be viewed as a form of parallel competition, or customer contracting. Franchising and geographical transfer are in many respects similar, and so forth.

Moreover, startups often combine several of the categories at the same time. A given company may have a *new product* that *exploits unused resources* during a *supply shortage* via sponsorship through a *customer contract* and thereby combine four different entry wedges at once. It may even be an effective strategy to attempt deliberately to combine as many as possible and thereby enhance the venture's chances for success.

APPLICATION

The choice of basic strategy may be largely or even entirely dictated by circumstances. Thus an entrepreneur does not create a supply shortage or the availability of unused resources. Instead he or she simply spots them and through awareness of them as strategic options takes advantage of them before others do. The same could be said of virtually all the entry wedges.

However, once the strategic option is recognized and chosen for exploitation, any number of choices can still be made about *how* the wedge is employed, including such aspects as the following:

1 *Differentiation* In what ways, how sharply, and at what stages in development of the market and the venture?

2 *Market segments* How will these segments be defined? And how narrowly will they be targeted by the product features or the selection of products offered?

3 *Scope* What territory will be covered? Which products or services will be offered?

4 *Marketing mix* What will be the balance of elements? Will sales push start slowly and build or go "all out" early to head off competitors?

5 *Degrees of integration* Is selling direct or through others? Which things are bought and which ones are produced by the venture?

6 *Degree of leverage* To what extent is capital borrowed to retain more ownership versus raised through ownership sharing to reduce borrowing risk? How readily will ownership be shared to recruit key people and retain others?

7 *Speed of product introduction* At what stage will development of second and later generation designs begin? To what extent will speed of introduction be traded off against testing and refinement?

8 *Formalization* To what extent will informality be retained versus the regimentation to provide a basis for growth? When will audited accounting begin?

Very little research has been done on the question of what combinations of application tactics and strategies work best in what circumstances. From a study of seventeen startups Sandberg and Hofer found some indication that the most promising industries for entry were those that were young and turbulent and had heterogeneous products.[10] In more mature industries focused strategies worked best, and in high-growth industries broad scope plus differentiation worked best. Generalization was difficult because of the small sample, and even strong findings would not necessarily apply to any particular venture. But it does seem clear that there is no single answer, that these factors do matter, and that they work in combinations.

DEVELOPMENT DOWNSTREAM

Beyond startup lie other problems as a venture grows and matures, as a number of authors have noted. As the number of people in the business expands, problems of leadership and delegation arise, needs for more formal procedures

---

[10] William R. Sandberg and Charles W. Hofer, "The Effects of Strategy and Industry Structure on New Venture Performance," in Robert Ronstadt, John A. Hornaday, Rein Peterson, and Karl H. Vesper, *Frontiers of Entrepreneurial Research, 1986* (Wellesley, Mass.: Babson Center for Entrepreneurial Studies, 1986), p. 244.

and controls emerge, and so forth. Kazanjian summarized downstream growth patterns as falling into various models of three, four, and five stages plus some other types.[11] Based on case studies he found statistical support for claims that certain problems tend to crop up at certain stages, although it also appeared that the stages were often overlapping and more complex than earlier articles about them had suggested.

The extent to which it is possible to anticipate during startup other stages of company development that will occur, and to capitalize on that knowledge by taking action at the outset that makes those stages more likely to develop successfully, is also a relatively unstudied area. The story of Osborne Computer illustrates how a promising startup can fail even though it began with a winning idea and operated in a booming market:

◆ As noted in the preceding chapter, Osborne had achieved sales of over $100 million in the fiscal year ending February 1983, just 20 months after shipping its first product. Seven months later, in September 1983, the company filed for bankruptcy. From Osborne's account it appears that many events combined produced the failure.[12]

Early choices of small screen size and single-sided disks forced expensive later redesign, but that difficulty did not show up immediately. A problem that did show up was the production of circuits that did not work. Engineers blamed faulty components; suppliers blamed incomplete engineering specifications and documentation. A production manager claimed the problems were solved when in fact they were not. Osborne himself was off in Europe setting up a subsidiary, thousands of faulty circuit boards were piling up, and the company's bank was becoming nervous about the level of accounts payable.

Technical problems also arose. The CP/M operating system turned out to have "bugs" that imposed the need to modify circuits. The keyboard needed revisions. Internal designs of the machine needed changes, whose introductions caused still other problems. In late 1981, after about four months of shipping products, the company had to recall all of them for modification.

"But the product recall was just the tip of a huge iceberg," Osborne said. "There were endless design changes that resulted from a lack of real engineering or manufacturing experience in Osborne's management. And we urgently needed such management experience, since no company before us had ever attempted to compress so much electronics into such a small space. The interaction between the many components of a microcomputer—the disk drives, display units, power supply, and logic boards—was complex, especially regarding radio frequency emissions and their effect on disk electronics.

"Davidson's method of solving problems was to collect Lee Felsenstein, Pat McGuire, and any other active participants and scream at them until they promised to have the problem fixed by the next morning. Fixes were dutifully reported, whether they worked or not. It was beginning to be clear that Davidson was over his head."

Engineering changes to enlarge the display and change to double-sided drives were relegated to outside consultants, but instead of being ready for ship-

---

[11] Robert K. Kazanjian, "Operationalizing Stage of Growth," in John A. Hornaday, Fred Tarpley, Jr., Jeffry A. Timmons, and Karl H. Vesper, *Frontiers of Entrepreneurship Research, 1984* (Wellesley, Mass.: Babson Center for Entrepreneurial Studies, 1984), p.144.

[12] Adam Osborne and John Dvorak, *Hypergrowth, The Rise and Fall of Osborne Computer Corporation* (New York: Avon Books, 1984).

ment by December 1981, they were ten months late. This, said Osborne, began to erode the company's credibility with the press. Upgraded cases for the machine were also two months late in arriving. Other problems arose in purchasing as design changes obsoleted agreements with offshore suppliers before delivery could be made. One company employee, according to Osborne, "mimed an atomic bomb explosion before his startled [Japanese] hosts to make the point that he was in Japan fighting for really low prices."

In the accounting department at one point accounts receivable billing fell two weeks behind while company employees tried to correct a problem in the company's own computer billing system. At another point the company failed to pay a bill because it was the same size as a bill that had been paid to another supplier. "It was April of 1982," Osborne said, "before a reasonable semblance of a financial reporting system was installed. . . . each department was developing its own numbers by hand. Departments would be told they were over budget or out of money for no apparent reason, and it was mid-summer before adequate controls were in place."

Shipments fell behind forecasts in the first half of 1982 and then rebounded in the second half as these problems were solved. Work began on future designs for second- and later-generation products, and Osborne, noting his lack of training and experience in business functions where he was now making most of his decisions, began looking for a successor to run the company. Robert Jaunich took on that role in early 1983.

As February 1983 arrived it appeared that the company had concluded a $100 million year with a small profit. Actions were taken to make a public stock offering. Orders were running high and new products were coming.

Then revised figures indicated there had been a loss of $1 million for the year, then $4 million, then $10 million. The public offering was first changed to a private offering, but that too was canceled as losses on microcomputers at other companies such as Atari and Texas Instruments hit the news. Osborne's financial position became progressively more precarious as an inventory of obsolete computers began to pile up, news of problems at the company undermined confidence, and creditors closed in, precipitating bankruptcy in September 1983.

Several points should be noted in observing this chain of catastrophes. First, some things are always going wrong in any company or any startup, especially those that are operating in a rapidly changing environment such as Osborne faced. Second, many other complicated tasks were being performed effectively while these problems were arising. Osborne, for instance, was coping with the complexities involved in entering the markets of other countries, which had different rules and standards. Many of the computers were operating properly, and others were being adequately serviced. The company's sales were growing, and many customers were becoming happy and loyal Osborne users, for all of which, in addition to its innovations, the company deserves credit.

Problem stages or typical crises the entrepreneur should anticipate in development of a company over time have been suggested by several authors and include the following:

1 *Too much to do at once*   During startup the entrepreneur must tend to all areas of the business. The length of the list of tasks is enormous, and when divided into the number of hours per day or week produces a virtually

impossible figure. No single person can be expert in all areas, but the entrepreneur must somehow get them all covered.

2 *Cash runs out*   In forecasting it is impossible to think of everything. Hence forecasts of cash needs tend to fall short, and the entrepreneur must work on raising money when there are many other things to be done.

3 *The entrepreneur loses track*   Having started doing too many things personally out of necessity, the entrepreneur falls still further behind as the company begins to take hold. Others should pick up some of the tasks but have not yet learned how.

4 *Borrowing capacity runs out*   The capitalization of the company is too small to accommodate expansion and equity must be sold to keep growing. This brings new owners and with them a new set of problems.

5 *Employees become disorganized*   The number has grown beyond what the entrepreneur can personally supervise. Intermediate management layers are needed but not available, and new procedures for cooperating are needed. The company may lose focus, spread itself too thin, or alternatively stick to a diminishing opportunity.

6 *Rigidity sets in, creativity slows, and morale drops*   The organization starts to become too formalized. People begin to feel impersonally treated, middle managers begin to work on politics instead of the job and to focus their attention on the boss instead of the customer. Top managers may become complacent.

7 *Subempires develop*   Each works autonomously for its own advancement but at the expense of cooperation with other units.

8 *Shakeups ensue*   The company recentralizes, reorganizes, introduces new managers. Red tape proliferates. Top managers worry that the entrepreneurial spirit has been lost. Some of the most creative employees leave to start their own companies, in which the cycle begins again.

A common remedy for these problems is to obtain help from people whose talents and abilities differ from those of the entrepreneur. The founders of Apple Computer recognized the need for such help from the beginning when they hired an experienced executive to become CEO. Later, as the company expanded, the executive of a still larger company, Pepsico, was brought in to take charge. And still later Steven Jobs, one of the original founders, was deliberately cut off from active management, at which point he left to start another company, Next.

At Apple and many other startups this replacement approach worked. At others, however, the founders managed to develop their own managerial capabilities as the company grew and to stay on top of it. Hewlett-Packard, Polaroid, Ford Motor, Douglas Aircraft, and McDonnell Aircraft all had founders who stayed in charge from inception through growth and did so successfully. Ordinarily the company never becomes large and the entrepreneur is able to stay in charge until the company ultimately changes hands as another entrepreneur enters the business via acquisition. How this happens will be the subject of the next two chapter.

SUMMARY

Expanding on the three main entry wedges—parallel competition, new offerings, and franchises—examined in the preceding chapter, this chapter has suggested other variations. Although the other wedges described in this chapter can be to some extent cross-classified against the main wedges, it will probably be more useful to concentrate instead on their distinguishing characteristics. Three wedges that build on proven formulas or established partial momentum are those having to do with transfer of an effective strategy from one geographical area to another without using a franchise, and two other wedges that capitalize on imbalance in supply and demand, either by spotting a supply shortage and finding a way to satisfy it before others do or by spotting a resource that others have not found and bringing it to market. Sponsorship by either customers, established companies, or governmental action is sometimes used by entrepreneurs to start new companies with any of a variety of strategies described by this chapter or, preferably, with a combination of strategic advantages. It was pointed out that although these other entry wedges tend to occur less frequently than the main three described in the preceding chapter, they are no less powerful in the right situations. Hence a would-be entrepreneur should be aware of them and how they can work.

No clear rules have been discovered for which strategies will work best in which circumstances. By being aware of the options and the fact that selecting them cannot be done by rule but rather must be based on individual judgment, the entrepreneur may have a clearer picture of the job to be done and the decisions to be made. Over time the role to be played by the entrepreneur typically changes, and early awareness of this fact may also help him or her make decisions that bode well for the company's longer-term success.

chapter 9

Acquisition Finding

To enter independent business in a line of work where the entrepreneur lacks prior work experience, generally the best approach is to buy a going concern rather than to start a new company. It is relatively seldom that people start successful companies in lines of work new to them. When they do so, it is generally in very low technology enterprises such as retailing or food service, and even then the odds of their succeeding are considerably lower than those of people with prior work experience in such businesses. But it is not at all uncommon to find entrepreneurs who acquired going concerns in lines of work completely new to them, even quite substantial firms and firms in high technologies, and succeeded handily. Consequently, business entry through going-concern acquisition is a most important strategy for would-be entrepreneurs to know, since it so greatly expands the variety of business types in which any given entrepreneur is likely to succeed.

A second main reason for taking over a going concern in preference to starting a new one is that future performance can be better estimated. If the company has had a record of stability and profits over several years, the odds of its continuing to profit are quite high, even with new and inexperienced management. It can be surprisingly hard to kill a profitable venture, as the following example indicates.

◆ A small manufacturing company in southern California was taken over by a former middle manager of a charitable organization. Before his association with the charitable organization, he had been a preacher and then a missionary in the South Pacific. Upon buying the small manufacturing company, which had experienced roughly level sales and operated in the black for the preceding decade despite substantial neglect by its owner, his first move was to change the company's name, which had built up a good reputation with customers, to his own. Next, he hired an attractive secretary and utilized working capital that had been obtained through a bank loan to pay travel expenses of the secretary and himself on a trip to Europe. Upon his return he purchased a small sailing yacht upon which he lived and began to take sailing trips. When cash became short, he negotiated a loan from the Small Business Administration, which also helped him install new management systems. Part of the money he used to pay off the remaining note held by the former owner for payment on the business. This he was able to do at a substantial discount, pointing out to the note holder that unless his reduced principal proposal was accepted, the business would probably go broke. Another part of the SBA loan was used to hire a competent shop manager. The business continued.

This enterprise survived despite the imprudent moves made by the acquiring entrepreneur in running it and his lack of experience in the business. Customers kept buying, as they had during several years of neglect by the former owner, largely out of habit plus the fact that the company's products were basically all right. Prices of all companies in this line of work were close to the same, and it would simply have been more trouble for customers to change suppliers, so they stayed on. For a while quality suffered in the product as shop work declined during and following the transition, but it was corrected by hiring a competent man who knew how to operate the plant before too many customers "caught on." Suppliers kept delivering, employees kept doing the work as they had been, and deliveries continued under the new owner largely from inertia. It has been said that "a company is mainly a collection of habits," and these are the main things that carry a successful company on, regardless of who acquires it and, to some extent, regardless of what the acquirer does with it. Mistakes can kill it, but they have to be substantial and may have to be applied for some time to do so.

If, on the other hand, the acquiring entrepreneur applies sound management practices to the company the results obtained, still despite lack of capital or experience in the business, can be impressive, as the following illustrates.

♦   Dave Ederer spent nine years with Price Waterhouse following graduation from the University of Washington Business School, eventually becoming a manager in mergers and acquisitions. In mid-1974 one of his clients, the owner of a local heat-treating company, asked Dave if he knew anyone who might be interested in buying the business. "I said, yes, I sure do," Dave recalled, "and three weeks later I was the proud owner of a new business."

This he was able to accomplish starting without any appreciable personal capital, without personally putting a penny into the business, and without any knowledge of heat treating, a technical art whose correct performance was absolutely crucial to the company. Nonetheless, during the following year he managed to increase sales by roughly 30 percent, and company earnings, after paying Dave a suitable salary, were enough to pay off more than one-fourth of the $475,000 purchase price.

"It's not so important for me to know the technical aspects," Dave commented. "My job is to make sure we have somebody in here who does. Just after I took over the company, I lost two of my key men. One moved away and the other got himself jailed. It was my job to replace them. I ran an advertisement in the classified and then interviewed the forty-six people who showed up. After selecting those who seemed to be the best ten, I had the men in the shop interview them and decide whom to hire. It was my responsibility to see that this process was carried through and completed, which I did, and it worked out fine.

"Other odds and ends I do include such things as going down to the airport to pick up parts, delivering other parts to one customer or another, dealing with the bank, buying stamps. Last week I was up on the roof sweeping so that we could re-tar it. I also go out and try to sell our services, something that astonishes many purchasing agents, because most heat-treating companies never make sales calls."

Within the first year Dave found he was able to reduce the total time spent managing the business to around two to three hours per day and was concluding a second acquisition, which he also planned to oversee part time. "I think it's important not to get too close to the business," he said, "or you may become overcompetitive. One of our competitors is that way. His sales are a lot higher than ours, but he gets them by pouncing on every job that comes along. As a result, he has a backlog of work and most of it is low-profit. This prevents him from quoting fast delivery when a big order comes up with high margin in it. He has to run hard all the time and isn't all that well paid for it." Dave, in his spare time, was active in a number of civic affairs, juvenile court, community theater, Boy Scouts, election campaigns, Rotary, a local college, and several church committees.

Even more spectacular as an acquisition success story was the takeover of the Remington Razor company by Victor Kiam in 1979. In this case the acquisition involved takeover of a failing division of a major corporation by a lone individual.

◆ Although most of the career that Victor Kiam describes in his book *Go for It* was in selling and sales management, particularly for Lever Brothers and Playtex, he had become involved in startups on the side. He had also explored acquisitions with others and was working in one of them, Wells Benrus, when Remington was brought to his attention as a possible acquisition in 1976. The account manager at Young and Rubicam who serviced Kiam's employer, Wells Benrus, learned that Remington, which also employed Young and Rubicam, was for sale and told Kiam about it. Too busy at the time, Kiam let it pass.

Two years later Kiam with two partners was negotiating to acquire a Hawaiian company that harvested coral for making jewelry. Coincidentally, he had noticed that Remington was still for sale. When his partners fell into disagreement and pulled out of the coral-harvester deal, he shifted his attention to Remington and called its chairman to track the possibility down.

First, he studied the company's books, noticing that there were operations other than shavers that might be shut down. Second, he bought a variety of shavers and comparison-tested the company's product. Third, he talked to shaver dealers, whom he found dissatisfied with Remington's policy of continually changing models but nevertheless desirous of being able to carry a stronger competitor to the dominant brand, Norelco. His conclusion was that Remington management, dominated by engineers, had the best product on the market but did not understand how to exploit it. Even though the company had lost $13 million in the preceding four years, he decided to try to buy it. After about two months of negotiations, which will be further described in the next chapter, he did.[1]

Many attractive features of buying, rather than starting, a business can be

[1] Victor Kiam, *Going for It* (New York: William Morrow, 1986), p. 182.

seen in these examples. The purchaser does not have to develop the product or service. It is there. With the business comes knowhow in the minds of its employees about how to perform the operations, who the suppliers are and what supplies should cost, how the plant should run, and how to maintain it. There are always startup "bugs"—unanticipated problems that in an established company have already been met and solved. In the records of the business are already prepared price lists, customer lists, accounting systems, various licenses and permits, a plant lease or ownership title, advertising literature, letterhead, and the many other small details that each take time during startup. The company Dave Ederer took over included another very attractive feature as well. Its prior owner had already tuned the enterprise for absentee operation. The employees knew how to run it from day to day, needing only partial management attention to see that the routine was maintained and to make sure that problems were properly solved when they arose. Thus, when Ederer took over, he was soon able to operate the company with only part of his time.

Notwithstanding these attractive features associated with the use of acquisition as an entry mode, there are sometimes good reasons for rejecting it in favor of startup. Often they center on the problem of finding the "right" company to buy. In some cases the entrepreneur simply cannot find one that is attractive, although it is easy to find losers, as can quickly be seen by checking out a few companies advertised in the "business opportunities" section of the classified advertisements of any metropolitan newspaper. Other times, although an attractive company may be found, it may simply be impossible to work out satisfactory terms with a seller. In the following case the entrepreneur found an attractive company and thought he had good terms, but the deal fell through and he chose the option of starting a new company instead.

◆ In early 1963 the district manager for a large international airline decided to look for another job. In the last twenty-five years he had worked his way up from clerk to district manager, but for the next promotion he would have to compete with twenty-five other managers, and if he prevailed he would then have to move to New York, in his view a step down. He quit and for three years worked in sales with a tour company that had been started by one of his former colleagues at the airline. But that job too was disappointing, and when he learned of a California tour company whose owner had said he wanted to sell out and retire, the former district manager decided to attempt acquisition.

His problem was how, with relatively little money of his own, to make an offer for the firm, which was employing five people and turning a net profit of $80,000 per year, that would be attractive to the owner. The solution he developed was to become vice-president of the company and work for it for one year without pay in exchange for 25 percent of the stock plus an option to buy the rest for $300,000. Thinking he had an agreement with the owner to that effect, he put in a year of work, only to have the owner back out on the deal.

But as a result of the year, the former district manager had learned how to operate a successful tour company. He had also spotted some areas, such as the Canadian Rockies, where no tour companies were presently operating. So he decided to start his own. To make ends meet, because his savings had been depleted by the no-salary year, he took another airline job while he spent a year obtaining his broker's license and developing contacts with hotels and other enterprises that would be important to setting up his tour company. Finally, he took out a mortgage on his house for working capital, quit his job, and opened up.

The new firm was in the black almost from the very start, showing a net profit of $23,000 the first year and growing rapidly from there on.

Whether the balance swings in favor of startup or acquisition for a given entrepreneur generally depends most heavily on prior experience and opportunity. In the above case both of these factors clearly supported the tour business, but the entry mode could have gone either way. The objective of the entrepreneur regarding such issues as full- versus part-time venturing, managing or being a more silent partner, investing heavily or only a little bit all may influence the choice. One former research laboratory director told of a millionaire who wanted to purchase the company and move it from Washington, D.C., to his home town of Alice, Texas, "just so I can walk through it once in a while."

For many, however, the main objective in acquisition is "to buy a better job" for themselves. Most who do so find themselves, unlike Dave Ederer whose policy was to spend only a couple of hours per day at each company, required to devote enormous amounts of time, particularly during the first year or two during takeover. Dr. E. Norman Hernandez, who acquired a failing instrument company and made it into a success, commented, "On a scale of one to ten buying a business should be rated a solid nine in terms of disruptions to your life-style. Marriage and nuclear holocaust come in at 8.9 and 9.9, respectively."

In favor of acquisition as an entry strategy, a final important argument is that acquisition lends itself particularly well to a deliberate search and to fairly straightforward procedures for shaping and closing the deal. Finding and screening potential acquisitions, the first two steps, will be the focus of the remainder of this chapter. The next chapter will focus on pricing, deal formulation, and negotiation.

The objective of these two chapters is not to provide a complete handbook on acquisition or make the reader expert in how to accomplish it but rather to highlight some important considerations, illustrate a variety of ways acquisition can work, and enable the reader to undertake acquisition with the assistance of such specialists as attorneys, accountants, tax experts, and valuation appraisers. Part of the acquiring entrepreneur's plan should ultimately be to engage one or more appropriate professionals to review and help with the fine tuning of any purchase agreement before signing.

ACQUISITION OPPORTUNITY SITUATIONS

In looking for companies to acquire, there are several types of situations for an entrepreneur to be aware of. In all cases the paramount question to be kept in mind is, What will the future earning power of the company under the new owner be? Examination of prior history, present conditions, and seller motivations is important only insofar as it helps answer that question.

The most attractive type of acquisition is frequently one wherein the present company owner wishes to withdraw from it for personal reasons having nothing to do with a business that is doing fine. The way this most often happens is when either the owner dies and leaves the company to heirs not interested in keeping it or the owner wants to retire and change life-style. Sometimes the owner will plan for such events and groom a successor in advance or take time to find the most attractive proposition, in which event the buyer is less likely to pick up a bargain. Often, though, especially in smaller companies, the owner will not have planned for succession and the desire or necessity to depart will come up suddenly, in which case takeover may be attractive. Aging owners who look for buyers sometimes offer very attractive situations, as Dave Ederer found in an earlier example and as the following man found.

◆   James N. Abbott, Jr., was working in his father's Gloucester, Massachusetts, boat yard in 1947 when he was asked by an aging Walter Henderson, owner of the Henderson and Johnson Paint Company, if he would like to buy the firm. Abbott was a Penn graduate of 1934 who had worked as a statistician for the government, taught accounting and statistics at the Wharton School of Finance, and spent World War II in the navy. "The company looked like a good buy to me," he said. "It was making money, though I wasn't sure how much; it had a sizable inventory and $14,000 in the bank. There were no accounts payable, because Mr. Henderson paid bills as they came in."
        The company, which manufactured boat paints, had annual sales of around $100,000, and for it Abbott agreed to pay $15,000 down plus $15,000 per year for three years. "Walter Henderson left the day I moved into the company, and since I didn't know anything about making paint, I told everybody to continue what he was doing until I learned what we should be doing. Then I started learning about paint." Sales and profits continued to grow steadily as the firm stuck to its specialized marine market, and Abbott acquired another small paint company with sales of $60,000, also from an aging owner. By 1960 combined sales were over $700,000.

In the case of Abbott, the role of coincidence was very important. He was not looking for a company to buy; the owner approached him. But the opportunity likely could have been found by someone who was looking, as many have. The role played by personal confidence was also important, and that is generally the case. Abbott did not know the paint business, but the owner believed in him and presumed that by selling to Abbott on contract he could be sure to get the money due him. He may also have cared, as sellers of successful small firms many times do, that Abbott could be expected to take good care of the business and carry it on in a respectable way, as in fact he did.

Easier to find but typically less attractive is the company open to acquisition because it is in trouble. Bank loan officers are especially good sources of information about companies of this sort, because by the time a company is in trouble it is usually in debt to the bank, and the bank would like to see someone else come in to pull the company out before the loan goes bad. The company may, in fact, be in such deep trouble that it cannot be saved, except perhaps by injection of an unjustifiably large amount of money along with new management. It has been estimated that over 15 percent of acquired companies fail even when they are merged with larger companies, which would surely be expected to have the talent and financial strength to save them.[2] For an individual entrepreneur the task, and consequent probability of success, may be even more discouraging in a troubled company. Still, many examples of successful turnarounds can be found, such as the following:

---

[2] "Merger Lemons," *Mergers and Acquisition,* Vol. 1, No. 1 (Fall 1965), 36.

◆   Eric Wade took over a small British company in 1947 with the intention of
liquidating the assets of an operating but hopeless venture. The company had
been formed to make a new product, a home-heating radiator consisting of an
oil-filled metal shell heated by an electric coil. The product was plagued with
technical problems, and in trying to cure them the company had run out of money.
        Although not experienced in that line of business, Wade became intrigued
with the product and decided that it offered enough promise for a further effort.
He managed to arrange for further bank credit, initiated continued work on the
product design, obtained from the government the required manufacturing permit,
and began to advertise. Two small newspaper advertisements suddenly brought
1,500 replies, and sales began. The product became a familiar sight in British
homes as rapid growth of the company followed. By 1960, thirteen years later,
the company, Dimplex Ltd., had gone public, and its outstanding shares carried
a market value of over $7 million.

Trying to emulate such success stories as Wade's quickly reveals the
difference between hindsight and foresight, as will be seen from some sadder
acquisition stories shortly. Before the product was advertised, it was not obvious
at all that it would sell, and before the advertising test could be performed, the
product had to be fully developed and into production. Thus a substantial
gamble was inevitable, and had it not happened to work out, failure would have
been all the greater for having made the one additional effort.
        Still less attractive to buy than a company in trouble can be one that has
failed completely, and yet sometimes that can be a better time to move in. A
still-going company has the advantage of rolling inertia: the employees are
already signed up, the machinery is still working, and the customers are informed about the company's existence and know what they can get from it.
But it also carries a burden of obligations, principally to creditors to whom it
owes money, but also to those employees whose morale and performance are
low but whose firing would disrupt things, to customers to whom it owes deliveries and warranty work, and sometimes to suppliers with whom it may have
purchase contracts that it no longer wants but cannot terminate. On balance
it can sometimes turn out to be better to let such a company fail and then to
pick up the worthwhile pieces out of bankruptcy. In that way the slate of prior
obligations can be wiped clean, and the successor company can start fresh.
The trick is to retain as much as possible of the former momentum along with
the clean slate, as was shrewdly done in the following case.

◆   Production at the water-ski manufacturing company was zero. The plant
had lain quiet and dark for over two months since August 1974, when the young
executives who owned the company had been arrested, convicted, and jailed for
attempting to smuggle cocaine concealed in a hollow water-ski across the border.
Before the company had been bustling and growing. Annual sales had reached
close to $2 million in the eight years since the company began and were expected
to increase another 40 percent in 1974. People driving by the growing plant had
jokingly referred to it as a Mercedes dealership as they saw the row of expensive
cars owned by the company's managers. But underneath the company had become stretched very thin financially. Nearly $500,000 was owed to the bank on
an SBA-guaranteed loan, and the expanding sales created need for still more
capital. Dope smuggling was the wrong solution.
        The bank, whose loan was secured by tangible assets of the business, began
looking for someone to take over. One of the people who looked at the deal was

a young man affiliated with the bank who himself had developed several successful businesses, including a successful gas station, ski shops, a stereo store, and nearly a dozen other enterprises as a limited partner. The bank offered him the water-ski company if he would personally guarantee the loan. The thirty-year-old entre-preneur looked at the financial statements, the silent plant, and his lack of any manufacturing experience whatever, and the fact that others had been approached by the bank on the same basis without success. He declined the deal at first, but then kept discussing it with business associates, officers of the bank, and key former employees of the ski company and began to change his mind. The com-pany's products had a good reputation; there were nearly $500,000 in outstanding orders, and the market appeared to be growing.

Bringing a merger and acquisitions consultant, a lawyer, and an accountant into the discussions, he began working on legal arrangements for takeover. The SBA guarantee would have to be extended, as would leases on the plant and some equipment. New financing had to be set up, raw materials ordered for delivery, sales orders reconfirmed, and employees signed up. After six weeks of negotiating through fourteen-hour days the takeover was finally arranged at the end of November 1974. Bankruptcy was shortly declared, which in effect erased former creditors' claims from the books (including one hundred individuals who had paid for skis but never received them) and turned the assets over to a new corporation owned by the entrepreneur and his team. A month later production resumed without major difficulties; orders came pouring in from existing dealers and a January trade show, and the company was under way. By March 1975 the company's income statement showed a profit to date in the new corporation of $126,000.

Buying a company can be more difficult when the present owner is rel-atively comfortable and not contemplating sale. But virtually every company can be bought at some price, and if the plan for utilizing the company is good enough a high price may be justified. One such strategy is that followed by conglomerators. Amassing first a pool of capital in a corporation and formulating a statement of objectives for building it into a larger company, they would then approach a company that seems to fit the strategy and offer to buy it with a combination of cash from the parent corporation with an ongoing business. If this first company bought had continuing profits, then the overall corporation would now be both financially strong from the combined assets and profitable. With these advantages it could approach a second acquisition target with an-other similar deal. But this time the stock used for buying the acquisition would be more highly valued due to the greater strength of the acquiring company. Moreover, growth of the acquiring company would cause its price/earnings ratio to increase. With that higher P/E ratio the next acquisition would be still more favorable to the acquirer, and the effect would be compounded through buying a company having a lower P/E ratio absorbing it. If it then took on the P/E ratio of the acquiring company, the total company's valuation would be correspond-ingly higher, investors would be pleased at the growth and bid the P/E ratio still higher, and so forth.

Following the lead of the best-known practitioner of this game, James Ling, many large "conglomerate" (built out of acquisitions in unrelated lines of business) corporations were built in the late 1960s. His Ling-Temco-Vought (LTV) was overblown and collapsed, as did others, but some conglomerates such as Textron and Teledyne, prospered.

On the average, the acquisition of companies by other companies has not paid off for the shareholders of the acquiring companies, although it has paid off for the sellers. Presumably, it has also paid off for executives of the acquiring companies. Unfortunately, no statistics have been gathered on the performance of companies acquired by entrepreneurs. Their performance as acquirers is probably better than that of corporations if the impressions gained in gathering information for this book is indicative. However, they typically tend to acquire firms different from those that corporations seek, smaller for instance, which might make comparisons difficult.

Entrepreneurial acquisitions frequently are made from owners who have become, for one reason or another, discontented with that ownership and would like to find a way out. Three such reasons can be: the aging owner (or other family member) desirous of retiring, a wife who inherits a business from her husband and does not want to run it, and the situation wherein problems exceed the present owner's capabilities or resources. There can be any number of variations on these patterns and others as well. Three others that might briefly be noted are as follows:

◆   *Domestic breakup.* When the founder of a small aircraft manufacturer died, his wife inherited controlling interest, and his partner took charge. Later the partner married the widow, and the firm prospered. But after a while the marriage failed, the partner quit, and both looked for ways to sell out. Neither would give terms to the other that the other could accept, so both hung on. The firm declined and ultimately had to be sold to avert bankruptcy.

◆   *Absentee owner loses interest.* A young man desiring his own business found a large sheet-metal shop whose owner, a wealthy man with several businesses, lived over a thousand miles away. The young man realized that the business could be much more profitable if closer attention were paid to it. This led him to offer a price that, in view of the company's present performance, was quite high. The absentee owner took it, and subsequently the young man was able to buy out other minority stockholders who worked for the firm.

◆   *Owner sees a better opportunity.* Some prefer to start firms rather than run them, and such persons may sell out so that they can take their winnings and begin again. Others may simply want to cash in and enjoy it or to take advantage of other investment opportunities offering higher returns. Such businesses are more likely to be of the stably small variety rather than the high-payoff or high-growth potential types.

ACQUISITION STRATEGIES

As noted earlier, there are different types of acquisition approaches. They can be characterized along a few dimensions, and such combinations as the following are possible.

1 *Who is Doing it* Whom to bring in as collaborators can be a major

part of the acquisition strategy. The buyer may be an individual, a partnership, or a corporation. The individual may be an employee, a relative, or a stranger, may have substantial financial backing or none, and may be familiar with the line of business or entirely new to it. Assistance in the process may be coming from other stakeholders such as a union or an economic development agency interested in preserving jobs, the prior owner seeking to preserve the buyer's ability to keep payments coming, and advisers such as attorneys and accountants who may take a share of interest in the deal as compensation for their services. Lenders, such as banks and finance companies, may be crucial to the deal. Finally, there may be other shareholders either private or in the open market who have a stake and a say in how the acquisition goes.

2 *What is Bought* Stock in the open market, assets only, selected assets are all possibilities. The entrepreneur or acquiring team can seek to obtain only control and then possibly over time increase ownership through buyout of other shareholders. Or the objective may be to obtain full ownership immediately. Factors influencing this decision will likely be the size of the company, whether it is publicly or privately held, and how much in the way of resources the buyer can muster. Total ownership can afford the buyer greater freedom of operation and less drain of time and energy in dealing with shareholders. However, there can also be advantages to having other shareholders, since they may be able to provide further financing for the company, as well as a market for the company's stock, so that the buyer can sell shares to gain more personal liquidity.

3 *Relatedness* If it is a first acquisition, is it related to what the entrepreneur did before or is it a new field for him or her? If it is a second or later acquisition, is it related in some way to what the other companies of the acquirer do, and how? One thing common to the strategies of both Ling and Ederer was that both acquired unrelated companies.

That is not to say they were indiscriminate in what they bought. Ederer, for instance, wanted companies that were successful, capital-intensive, and privately held by aging owners and that dealt in commercial, not consumer products and services. But other than that they were unrelated and included for instance, a heat-treating shop, a metal-stamping company, an industrial supplies distributor, a job machine shop, and a cardboard box producer.

The following entrepreneur started in a different manner, first acquiring two related companies and then going on to others that were unrelated.

♦   In 1978 William Zimmerman resigned a $200,000-per-year job at Monogram Industries in Los Angeles to enter independent business. In the ensuing year and a half he bought four companies by borrowing against assets to raise a cash down payment, with the seller to receive the remainder over time. The first was Standard Wire and Cable, a thirty-five-year-old southern California manufacturer and distributor of aircraft electrical wire. The second was Alpine Wire and Cable, a Chicago-based wire distributor, which became a division of the first acquisition. The third was a manufacturer of nonwoven fabrics, and the fourth was a small trucking delivery service. "I wanted," he said, "variety."[3]
His criteria, except for Alpine, were that the companies be based in southern

---

[3] Marcella Rosene, "Building a Mini-Conglomerate," *Venture,* January 1980, p. 24.

California, that they be in easily understandable low technologies, and that they be purchasable through borrowing. His mode of operation was to retain the companies' managements, put them on incentive compensation, and allow them to continue having high autonomy. He himself would serve mainly as a "banker" for their financial needs.

As a contrast, the next example, Pedus International, was a company built through the acquisition of related enterprises. The creation of Pedus also illustrates that it is not always clear just who the entrepreneur is—there may be more than one sharing the role.

◆   Peter Dussmann, who had started a janitorial firm in Germany and built it into a major European company, decided he wanted an American investment. Rather than buying stocks or bonds he decided he would create his own company. In 1979 he engaged a management recruiting firm to help find an American who would undertake the project.

Dick Dotts, whom the recruiter found, had quit other jobs, twice at AT&T and once at Bekins Moving, when he found his upward career path stymied. With Dussmann, Dotts agreed to build not just another janitorial company, but one with a broader range of semiskilled labor services. The first acquisition was a security firm for $85,000, with Dussmann providing the money and Dotts acting as chief executive officer on a seven-year employment contract with lifetime renewable options. Subsequent acquisitions were also security firms as well as janitorial firms. By 1984 Pedus International led *Inc.* magazine's list of fastest-growing companies, with sales of over $60 million and 6,300 employees in janitorial service plus 2,500 in security service.[4]

Whether related or unrelated businesses are preferable in an acquisition program is a debatable issue. The argument most offered for related firms is that top management can concentrate on knowing its business completely and doing a limited number of things well while benefiting from economies of scale. In favor of unrelated acquisitions is the argument that they may provide greater stability, since a turndown in the market of one division need not mean that corresponding declines will occur in other divisions. With unrelated firms what seems to work best, however, is to give them high autonomy.

4 *What is Paid* If the entrepreneur making an acquisition already has a company, there may be two choices of exchange media: stock from the company already owned, and cash on some kind of terms. Ling used stock, successively parlaying ownership of one company into others by paying with stock. Ederer bought each company separately with cash, mostly borrowed and with payments spread over time. This approach, known as a leveraged buyout (LBO) and illustrated by the cases of both Ederer and Zimmerman above, will be further discussed in the next chapter. Still another option may be to float a public stock offering for the purchase.[5]

5 *Condition when Acquired* Some problems may be apparent from the company's financial statements, and for each of those it may be possible to think of potential solutions fairly quickly. However, making the solutions work will undoubtedly be more difficult than inventing them. Moreover, there may be other problems that are not so obvious, as illustrated by the following two cases.

Curtis Hartman, "The Cleanup Crew," *Inc.*, December 1984, p. 61.
Udayan Gupts, "Buyouts Go Public," *Venture,* May 1981, p. 18.

◆   Ken Carpenter was a financial expert in the California headquarters of Wyle Laboratories. Well paid but feeling bored, he became interested when the company decided to sell off a losing Midwest division, Curtis-Toledo. Financial data with which he was familiar as a company insider indicated to him that it wouldn't take much effort to make the division pay.

After working up an offer of $4.5 million, he found it hard to present it to company management. "It took me two weeks to work up the courage," he recalled. "It traumatized me—the thought of giving up the Cadillac, the stock options, and California. And I wasn't sure what I was doing."[6] Rejection of his offer ensued, and he worked up another of $5.6 million. His employer spent two months trying to find someone who would pay more, and when that failed, accepted Carpenter's offer.

Carpenter then moved to St. Louis, took over his new purchase, and learned about problems he had not been able to discern from financial analysis. The plant was located in a run-down area where employees were afraid to travel and where thieves slashed the fence to steal castings. Worker discipline was so poor that repeated orders from Carpenter to repair a roof leak that was dripping water on electrical panels were ignored for three months. Workers were in the habit of littering the plant and leaving it disorderly and dirty. Machines that broke down were ignored. Workers arrived late, took long breaks, and left early. Foremen and managers did nothing about it, and when Carpenter attempted to crack down he found all his time being consumed in meetings with the union and arbitrators over a flurry of employee complaints.

In a recent plant move the company had lost employees who knew manufacturing details that were not recorded anywhere. Consequently, the company was shipping products it did not know how to make correctly. This had lost some customers and angered others. Other products were shipped with missing parts and poor workmanship. To stem losses, one action taken had been to defer maintenance, leaving the plant in bad repair. Another action had been to raise prices on products for which the company was a sole supplier. As a result, customers were developing second sources of supply and had stopped making purchases from Carpenter's company.

Carpenter's problems by no means exhaust the list of what can be found wrong after purchase. An experienced appliance store operator from Texas, Elias Zinn, ran into a different combination when he took over a New York chain, Crazy Eddie's, as described in an *Inc.* article:

◆   New management soon discovered that the company's banks had withdrawn $100 million in credit and its vendors were refusing to ship any goods until they received $35 million in overdue balances. An inventory count Zinn ordered after taking control came up a startling $65 million short. About half the stock was missing. For the first nine months of fiscal 1988, ended last Nov. 29, just after Zinn took the helm, Crazy Eddie lost a whopping $83.3 million, compared with earnings of $9.8 million reported for the same period the preceding year.[7]

6   *Management Intervention* Management options for the acquirer range from heavy hands on action to leaving the company essentially alone. Because they bought healthy companies, Ederer and Zimmerman, who were mentioned

[6] Harrison Moore, "You Can't Run a Company by the Numbers Alone," *Inc.*, September 1981, p. 74.
[7] Laurel Brubaker Calkins, "The E.Z. Way," *Inc.*, May 1988, p. 52.

earlier, were largely able to avoid management interference. The examples of Carpenter and Zinn just noted, however, demanded it. Both of them had to spend full time working at their acquisitions. Carpenter became more forceful in his personal actions, brought in a new plant manager, and traveled to meet with customers personally. Slowly, the company turned around.

Zinn turned Crazy Eddie's around by concentrating initially on controlling costs. "Every penny counts," he said. *Inc.* further observed: "Zinn keeps costs low by constantly minding the details. For example, he insists on using both the front and back of computer paper to print reports. An electronic voice mailbox answers his phones at headquarters instead of a clock-watching receptionist. Every conceivable warehouse and paper-shuffling function has been automated. Members of his bare-bones headquarters staff punch in 60- to 70-hour workweeks on a regular basis. And Zinn keeps strict tabs on salespeople by pulling computer report cards of their sales activity daily and comparing them with their monthly goals."

7 Disposition Possibilities for longer-term disposition of the acquired company once it is healthy include keeping it as an investment, keeping it also as a job, building upon it through other acquisitions, trading it for something else, or selling it, either to another company or to the public through a stock offering. If the objective is to sell it, then the acquisition process can be a learning experience from the buyer's point of view, which the buyer can use to become a more effective seller.

LOCATING LEADS

Finding companies for sale is easy. There are dozens listed every day in the "business opportunities" classified section of every major metropolitan newspaper and most small ones as well, not to mention weekly listings in the *Wall Street Journal.* However, to seek out an attractive acquisition matching the desires of a particular entrepreneur can be very time consuming and difficult. What will be found in the classified sections are mostly motels, restaurants, bars, and numerous sales agent and franchise propositions, almost all of which will be found to be some combination of low profit, high risk, and time demanding which makes them unattractive to most people. Many are failing or clearly headed for failure and some are outright frauds, although there are some entrepreneurs who located opportunities in this way and became very successful.

There were over 18 million businesses, either full or part time, in the U.S. in 1987.[8] Although roughly half a million failed while a comparable number started, many continue indefinitely, and they all have to change hands sometime. Consequently, there are many companies being bought and sold every day, and it should be possible for a would-be entrepreneur to find one that appeals. The would-be entrepreneur who goes searching will certainly hear about some, but most companies will regrettably already have been acquired by someone

[8] Small Business Administration, *The State of Small Business* (Washington, D.C.: Government Printing Office, 1988), p. xv.

else. The reason is that every business has its sphere of contacts, some people close to it, others more distant, who have firsthand awareness of the owner and what is happening at the company. When symptoms of willingness to sell appear, the first to detect them will be people within this sphere of direct contact, and from there the awareness will emanate outward to others whose contact is progressively less direct. This emanating takes time, and generally the first to encounter it are those closest to the company and the last are those farther out. If a given entrepreneur has not been directly dealing with the company at the time when the emanation is triggered, then his or her odds of learning about it early are correspondingly reduced. While the emanation and the entrepreneur are working toward each other, somebody closer to the company will likely hear of the opportunity and take advantage of it.

Hence it turns out that most acquisitions are made by people who happened to have active business relationships with the companies when the acquisition possibility popped up. The following are some examples:

◆   An investor who had loaned part of the money to start a water-ski company called his loan and bought out the owner when the company got into trouble and could not make its payments.

◆   An engineering professor who wanted a company of his own was performing some technical consulting for an instrument company. When the company ran into management troubles, he proposed buying the owners out, and they accepted.

◆   Two brothers with a diesel-powered boat were having repairs made to their fuel injectors. The owner of the injector shop had just died. His widow asked the brothers if they might be interested in buying the firm. They bought it.

To wait and hope that such opportunities will come along may not be sufficient for the entrepreneur determined to acquire a business, and for that person the other alternative is to go looking. In doing so, there are two contrasting strategies, the "shotgun" approach versus the "rifle." The first begins with the question, "What companies are for sale?" and screens to find those most attractive. One argument favoring this approach is the fact that not all that many firms tend to be for sale at a given time, especially firms attractive to buy, and it may be important not to miss any good possibilities. A second argument is that when a firm is for sale, the seller tends to be committed to the goal of selling, and this gives the buyer an advantage. Against this approach is the fact that the majority of firms for sale tend to be unattractive, and screening them consumes time that might better be spent focusing on better opportunities. Most of those for sale tend to be losing or marginal ventures with little if any profit potential—filling stations, taverns, and the like—and the searching entrepreneur who looks at them may simply be wasting time.

The opposite strategy is to formulate specific criteria for the acquisition, and then find the firm that fits and proposition the owner to sell, whether the owner is trying to sell or not. In this approach the entrepreneur can take time to learn about the particular type of work the company is in, maybe even take a related job for a while, and then contact every company in the line of work to learn which can be obtained on the best terms. One advantage associated with this strategy is that the entrepreneur can know better what he or she is getting into with the acquisition so that the odds of disappointment may be lower, both in terms of what the new company demands of the entrepreneur and in terms of the entrepreneur's ability to make the acquisition succeed. Another advantage is that the entrepreneur becomes better informed to be able to judge the potential acquisitions and choose the best one. Perhaps most important, however, can be that the entrepreneur's knowhow about that line of work can make the entrepreneur a more credible purchaser from the company owner's point of view. Sellers tend to take more seriously someone who has invested time and effort to obtain "savvy" in the line of work and who is committed to pursuing it. Hence through this approach the entrepreneur may become aware of purchase opportunities that a shotgun approach would never reveal at all. The risk is, however, that by concentrating on a particular line the entrepreneur may happen to choose one where nobody wants to sell out and at the same time may be shutting out opportunities that are attractive in other lines.

In the following case, the entrepreneur had only a hazy concept of the type of industry he was looking for, and then found his first acquisition in the Yellow Pages of the telephone directory. Kirby Cramer, it may be recalled from the section on Sideline or Moonlight Startups in Chapter 3, was one of three young entrepreneurs who pooled a total of $900, gave their company the name "Seadyne," and then began looking for acquisitions.

◆   While searching for companies to buy, Cramer, who was employed full time as a mutual fund investment analyst, began trading the $900 seed capital in the stock market. In researching stocks he noticed that Charles River Laboratories, an eastern supplier of laboratory animals, had been growing at a rate of 30 percent a year.

One of several approaches Cramer used in searching for companies Seadyne might buy was scanning the Yellow Pages. At about the same time that he noticed Charles River, he spotted the small listing of a research and development company in the Yellow Pages. He picked up the phone, called the company, and learned it produced an automated rat cage for medical researchers. Was there a promising industry here, one in which this small company participated along with the prospering Charles River Laboratories? Cramer contacted one of his former finance teachers at the University of Washington, who suggested having a team of MBA students investigate the industry as a class project. The students pieced together the concept of a "life sciences" industry connected with laboratory animals. They estimated this industry had national sales of about $35 million annually and that it was growing at a rate of 14 percent a year.

The small company from the Yellow Pages was operated as a sideline venture by an electronic systems engineer who had developed rat cages that fed animals and flushed itself automatically at periodic intervals. Advertisements in psychology trade journals between 1965 and 1968 had brought orders for twenty-five cages at $2,200 each. But by mid-1968 orders had slackened and the operation largely lay dormant in the engineer's garage. Still, the engineer thought the product had promise if more advertising could be mounted.

So did Cramer. He began to see a goal for the company he and his two partners had formed—to become a conglomerate in the life sciences industry. The $900 stake had been growing rapidly, thanks to some extremely successful investments, and Cramer began to negotiate with the systems engineer to buy the small cage company. By February 1969 the Seadyne stake had grown to a book value of $44,000. With this money a new company, Environmental Science Corporation, was formed and a deal was negotiated to acquire the product line and $6,000 worth of assets, mostly machine tools, from the systems engineer. The engineer received about 10 percent of the ESC stock plus an option to buy another 10 percent for $6,500; he was also given an eighteen-month contract as general manager. Cramer now sold another 25 percent of ESC for $200,000 via a public stock offering. He also began looking for other "growth industry" acquisitions.

The striking thing about Cramer's search for acquisition was its great flexibility. He and his partners did not even know what their company, Seadyne, would do when they named it. Their first acquisition—the rat cage outfit—was selected on the combined basis of the record of the Charles River company, the student report on the "life science" industry, and the discovery that the rat cage company could be brought. Seadyne took on a "life science" direction which it continued, as will be described later. But in spite of this direction, Cramer and his associates were still looking for all types of "growth industry" acquisitions in the early stages, whether or not they fitted with the cage company.

Sometimes entrepreneurs formulate specific search criteria. One may search exclusively for companies whose owners are old and, hence, ready to retire. Another may seek companies with absentee ownership (i.e., companies whose owners are rarely there—as determined by the entrepreneur's phone calls). Still another entrepreneur may look for companies with troubles that appear to be curable. Since any one of these criteria may succeed, the way to maximize the odds for finding an attractive opportunity is to maintain a high degree of flexibility. One banker recalled how his brother had entered a different field than he planned:

◆   My brother started out with the intention of entering the boat business. He had always like fishing, and it seemed to him that would be a pleasant kind of place to work. So he studied up on marinas, boat repair, and the recreational boating industry. Then he started contacting people to find some sort of boat business to buy. But before he found a boat business that appealed to him, he ran across a motorcycle dealership for sale and decided to pick that up instead. It's worked out very well for him.

An inevitable part of the search process is the task mentioned by this banker of contacting people to learn about opportunities. Regardless of what combination of strategic approaches is tried, there are many potential sources of leads. One expert on acquisitions, for instance, advised entrepreneurs that "the most probable source is an insurance agent. I've obtained more credible leads from this source than from any other. By the very nature of their business the more successful agents are well connected—often to top people they've dealt with for year and years."[9] In Table 9–1 is a list of twenty different lead sources, which have been grouped into five more general types. These types are listed roughly in order of promise for finding attractive companies, starting with the most common source, which is contact through other business activities, as discussed above.

[9] Gary B. Anderson, "Defining the Game Board," in Stephen C. Diamond, Leveraged Buyouts (Homewood, Ill.: Dow Jones-Irwin, 1985), p. 16.

TABLE 9–1   Twenty Sources of Acquisition Leads

Contact through other business activity
1. Employer, suppliers, customers

Direct independent contact by entrepreneur
2. Walk-in cold calls on potential acquisitions
3. Chamber of Commerce directories
4. Trade associations
5. Placing acquisition wanted advertisements
6. Reading business opportunity advertisements
7. General business news

Professional middlemen
8. Business brokers
9. Commerical real estate brokers
10. Consultants

Confidential advisers
11. Bank trust officers
12. Bank commercial loan officers
13. Securities brokers
14. Public accounting firms
15. Law firms

Other sources
16. Small Business Administration
17. Factoring companies
18. Venture capital firms
19. Personal friends and social acquaintances
20. Insurance brokers and agents

Next on the list are methods of direct independent contact with prospective acquisitions by the entrepreneur. If the entrepreneur walks in and talks to the owner directly, he or she may be able directly to learn of a potential acquisition as soon as or even before the news of availability of the company can spread out to others who might preempt the entrepreneur, as mentioned earlier. One entrepreneur who had successfully performed several acquisitions described his approach as follows:

♦   I personally have most success with direct contact, simply knocking on doors. In driving around town either looking for a company or on other business, I don't hesitate to walk into a company and introduce myself "cold turkey." I tell them my story and try to learn whether there might be any interest at all on their part in selling out. Other times I may use the phone. If I happen to notice a company or type of activity that might be of interest, I'll try to call a few people to learn about it and see where they might direct me. I may also obtain Dun and Bradstreet data on the company, which will tell who the principals in the company are, when it was founded, what the sales are, products, distribution, and so forth. Once a company has been on the market, I consider it too late. In my view it's better to start working on the deal before the present owner has decided to put the company up for sale.

In effect, this cold-call approach takes advantage of the truism "Any company is for sale if the price is high enough." But the entrepreneur will find some owners who are willing to discuss the matter just to find out how high a price someone will pay. These can waste a considerable amount of search time if the entrepreneur is not careful.

Kirby Cramer of Environmental Science Corporation used a cold-call approach in locating the rat cage company through the Yellow Pages. He also simply drove through the industrial districts of Seattle looking for companies that might be interesting to Seadyne, and he became aware of possible acquisitions as a result of the contacts his mutual fund stock analyst position afforded him. But the companies Cramer later actually closed deals with came through the business itself.

Because he was in the laboratory equipment business, Cramer attended a trade show where he met the owners of a midwestern animal equipment company. He got the feeling they might be willing to sell out. They denied it, but he pursued the matter and a year later they sold.

◆   Through conversations with the systems engineer who had sold him the rat cage company and through advertisements in the trade, Cramer learned of another nearby company, Kirschner Manufacturing (whose startup by an unemployed mining engineer was described in Chapter 3), that produced splints for animals. After six months of negotiations, ESC acquired Kirschner Manufacturing.

Cramer learned from an employee that a Virginia-based company that bred laboratory animals might be for sale. Cross-checking with other companies in the business to verify this information, he also learned that a European laboratory subsidiary of TRW was for sale. Both companies were acquired by Cramer through an exchange of ESC stock. ESC stock thereby took on greater value as the company grew.

The focus of ESC became more firmly established in the life science field when ESC acquired still more companies in that field. Eventually, ESC changed its name to Hazleton Laboratories Corporation because Hazleton was better known in the industry. According to *Moody's* net revenues in 1987 were $81,754,000.

Another way to single out companies for direct contact, companies that more definitely are for sale, is through advertisements. The entrepreneur can run these either in local newspapers or in national ones, such as the *Wall Street Journal*. Some of the larger banks also circulate newsletters carrying advertisements both by people who want to buy businesses and those who want to sell them. The advertisement need not be complicated. One entrepreneur said simply, "Capital and management available, send proposals" in a local city newspaper, and through this located three different ventures into which he bought, but as a partner rather than sole owner. Another who advertised in the "Capital to Invest" section of the *Wall Street Journal* received six replies on a small advertisement, five of whom were business brokers soliciting contracts to do the searching. With a bigger advertisement in the same section, however, he received five hundred replies in three weeks. Most, again, were from middlemen seeking to represent him, some offering vague company descriptions. Eventually, the list was boiled down to four companies worth serious consideration.

The same papers also carry sections, commonly entitled "Business Opportunities," in which companies for sale are advertised. In local papers these are most often very small and failing or marginal firms, as mentioned earlier.

But every now and again there crop up companies with greater potential. Bank newsletters are particularly likely to contain these. Such newsletters are not widely circulated but are confined usually to customers of the bank or others with whom the bank does business. Moreover, the newsletters usually do not name the companies, but only list them under a code. An interested entrepreneur then must gradually work through the process of being referred to the company by some personal contact at the bank.

Next on the list come several types of professional middlemen. These are people who typically work at bringing buyers and sellers together for either a flat fee or a commission. (Commissions typically range according to the size of the deal—a large percentage on small deals and smaller percentage on larger ones. An average is around 5 percent.) The number of people nationwide who are able to specialize solely in business brokerage because they can put enough deals together is fairly small. More frequently, a broker will deal in both real estate and businesses for sale, since both require being familiar with large numbers of firms and both often go together in deals. There may be a natural inclination to avoid such middlemen because of the cost of paying them. The advantage is that they can be a quick avenue to many leads, because they already know the territory. By restricting payment to a commission, the entrepreneur can avoid having to pay unless he or she finds the company and deal (including commission) that seems satisfactory. Either way, it can be important to sort out these agents and brokers according to whether they know mostly about firms of the type the entrepreneur is interested in or simply about properties and small firms of no interest.

Consultants span an even wider range of specialties. Most in the Yellow Pages under "Management Consultants" are personnel recruitment agencies and public relations firms likely to know little about acquisitions. Others are people who specialize more in problem finding and solving. One entrepreneur said that they were much freer with advice than leads, commenting, "A consultant is someone who knows a hundred ways to woo a girl but doesn't know any girls." Another observed, "Often a consultant is just somebody who was fired from a management position and hasn't found another job yet. If he sees a good acquisition opportunity, you can be sure he isn't going to pass it along to anyone else." Nevertheless there are cases where entrepreneurs have located highly rewarding acquisitions through consultants who specialize in acquisition work.

The contacts who most often come to mind first as possible sources of acquisition leads are several types of confidential advisers. Trust officers in banks come into contact through their work with individuals planning their personal estates. These sometimes include older people who may be eligible to retire from family ownership or who may want to sell their companies in conjunction with plans to minimize estate taxes. Through trust work banks also frequently become involved with carrying on companies that have been left to heirs as part of estates. Since banks are not in business to manage other firms, they generally look for ways to move these estate companies along to other owners.

Often these buyers turn out to be other companies that are financially strong and reliable buyers, as opposed to individuals whose financial resources are smaller. Moreover, their relationship with clients is confidential, and before you can discuss the names of potential clients with a would-be buyer, they must obtain the permission of those clients. At the same time, clients who may be interested in selling companies may not want that interest revealed to employees, suppliers, or customers, lest it have an adverse effect on business. Hence the confidential adviser such as banker, broker, public accountant, or lawyer is usually slow and cautious about revealing such interest. Moreover, when they do reveal it, they most often do so first to other clients of their bank or professional firm with whom they have developed confidence over a period of time.

Hence, although such professional advisers may often know about good leads, it can be very difficult for a searching entrepreneur who has not developed a working relationship with them to gain access to that information. In attempting to do so, the best way to begin is often to start with the closest personal acquaintances available in those professions and work through them to others by personal referrals. Each of these contacts may have its own strengths and weaknesses. Commercial bank lending officers, for instance, may tend to pass along as leads those clients of the bank about whom the bank is concerned regarding loan repayment. Securities brokers sometimes have clients who want to sell businesses and whom they would like to move into stocks. Other times they simply know about companies that want to sell stock to raise money. The best deals seen by public accountants and law firms may be picked up by them personally or otherwise tend to be passed along directly to other clients of their firms.

Companies in financial difficulty often turn to the Small Business Administration and to factoring companies and so can sometimes be located through these sources, although their client relationships are confidential and clearance from the clients must be obtained before they can be revealed to prospective buyers. Venture capital firms also encounter clients looking for money, but unlike those approaching factors and the SBA, the venture capital clients tend to be more expansion (as opposed to survival) oriented. Many of them also tend to be startups, as opposed to going concerns, and few of them have the objective of selling out. The venture capital firms try to invest in those with greatest promise, but these are a very small fraction, typically less than one-half percent, of those who approach them, and consequently there are many who are turned away to seek their funds elsewhere. Although these did not set out to become totally acquired, some may be open to it, particularly after rejection by the venture capitalists.

All companies, including acquisition prospects, are approached by many salespeople constantly seeking to serve them in one way or another. Consequently, some types of salespeople may be reasonably likely to run across companies of interest to a would-be buyer. Some insurance brokers and agents, for example, specialize in types of insurance such as key-man insurance, pensions, and profit-sharing plans. This puts them in touch with top executives of small companies, some of whom may be owners interested in selling. When an owner does want to sell out, he or she may tell many people, including salespeople and others who may, through chains of acquaintance, be known to individuals with whom an entrepreneur may come into contact. Consequently, once an entrepreneur has some idea of what he or she is looking for, it can pay to let out the word to many possible sources. Any of these may talk to someone who knows someone else who may have heard about an opportunity. The odds of its making its way back to the prospective buyer without being plucked off by another may be slim, but it takes only one to win. The network will soon go quiet if it is not continually reactivated, however. The entrepreneur will need to keep reminding people of his or her acquisition interest, so that when an opportunity flashes into view the message has a chance to be sent the "right" way.

Which lead sources to tap will be a function of many factors for a given entrepreneur, including time available, whom he or she knows, which ones seem to work best, and what kind of company is being sought. Experimentation can be used to "tune" the approach, with, it is to be hoped, better effect than the following three entrepreneurs encountered.

◆   All three were successful, well-paid executives in larger companies, and between them they could personally contribute $300,000 to be extended further by borrowings. They agreed that two would keep jobs to support the third for up to three years of search for the acquisition that all three would later manage. They printed five hundred copies of a list of specifications indicating that the company should be a manufacturer of some established basic product with a relatively high volume, broadly based market and capable of "continuous technical improvement."

Nine months later the searching partner had screened over three hundred possibilities and had made more careful personal investigation of fifty without finding one to buy. He reported that few leads had come from firsthand personal introductions, but that rather they had come through sources, such as those listed in Table 9–1, to whom he had been introduced by personal acquaintances, such as family friends, classmates, professors, and business associates. Most helpful, he found, were commercial and investment bankers, and least helpful were business brokers and risk capital firms, which, he gathered, were giving him "culls" that they had rejected.

So many leads came from his inquiries that he tightened his search criteria to restrict the flow to manageable size. Companies with annual sales of less than one million dollars he ruled out as too small to support and adequately challenge the management team; those in declining industries, such as New England textiles, were scratched as holding too little promise, and those in glamour industries, such as electronics, he excluded as typically overpriced. He also eliminated family companies employing several relatives and "one-man shows" in which the current owner's expertise seemed crucial to success.

Of the remaining fifty followed up in depth, most owners indicated price ranges—around five times earnings—beyond what the partners considered attractive. It appeared that owners tended to envisage a price range roughly double what buyers would pay. By following the experiences of one hundred of the companies encountered, the searching partner found that during his nine months' search only five were sold. Three were dissolved and sold their equipment at auctions, and the other two were merged into larger companies. None sold to entrepreneurs.

In the next example things turned out more satisfactorily, although it started out the same way as the preceding, with formulation of broad specifications for the company to be found, followed by full-time methodical searching.

◆   This entrepreneur spent the first nine years following his graduation from business school working for others, two years as a Lever Brothers salesman "to get some practical apprenticeship," five years as an IBM salesman "to interact with more company presidents," and two years with a smaller computer leasing company "to get some experience in higher management." Meanwhile, he was thinking about how to get his own company.

Buying an existing company rather than starting a new one seemed preferable for reducing risk. He started looking full time for a firm that would generate enough cash flow for payments, allow him a $24,000 annual salary, and produce an additional 10 percent return after taxes on investment. The most helpful sources of leads he found to be commercial realtors and chambers of commerce. Less helpful in his view were commercial bankers (later he decided he had talked to the wrong ones at the wrong banks), other companies, the SBA, newspaper advertisements, and business brokers.

Some possibilities he investigated included a tire company, sporting goods distributor, sporting goods retailer, small airline, several machine shops, marina, furniture wholesaler, paint manufacturer, radio station, door manufacturer, investment counsel, and securities sales (got his license). He unsuccessfully tried to raise financing to enter office equipment leasing. He also tried to buy a screw machine company, but lost to a faster buyer. The company went bankrupt six months later.

After four months of search, private business colleges caught his interest when a man (who, he later learned, was regarded in the industry as a crook) told him they averaged 12 percent net profit on sales. He approached the owner of such a college to learn of any for sale and discovered that that college was available for purchase. It had been one of the top schools in the area a few years earlier but had recently declined. He checked pro forma statements. With a $14,000 down payment plus annual payment, he figured the business could pay for itself in five years.

In fact, it took only three. He contracted to have the owner stay and teach him the business for six months but released him after two weeks. He took no salary himself for the first year, put in eighty-hour weeks for the first two years, and fifty-hour weeks for the ensuing three. This left him working longer hours for the same salary that he earned working for others, but he felt the greater independence and chance to grow were worth it. The return on investment had now reached his planned 10 percent and he had now acquired another firm training motel, hotel, and mobile park managers which he expected would lead to further growth and profits.

What made the difference between the two cases? It can be noted that the second search became successful when the entrepreneur had decided specifically on a type of business he was interested in and went looking for it. Another difference was that he ended up making an offer on a firm that was ostensibly not for sale. Effectively he was not competing with other bidders, and this may have strengthened his hand. Other entrepreneurs could have found this opportunity, but didn't. Maybe the difference was luck. There are many maybes, and many other methods have worked for other entrepreneurs.

PRELIMINARY SCREENING

Victor Kiam's first action after calling the CEO of Sperry to confirm that Remington was for sale and being referred to the person in charge of divesting that division was to look at the books. He recalls:

♦   "Commandeering a cab, I raced over to Sperry headquarters and lugged the books and records back to my apartment. There were twenty-six volumes of material and countless pieces of paper packed with facts and figures. These numbers told the story of Remington's entire domestic and overseas operations. It took me an hour and a half to arrange and spread out the material on the dining room table.

"When I started to pore over the books, I saw that Remington was more than just shavers. They had operating companies that were producing or distributing a wide range of products for different countries: watches in Mexico, steam irons in Italy, clocks in Germany, hair-care products in France. I didn't see any cohesiveness in the operation. The only product that was common to each nation was the shaver. Knowing that it was ridiculous to try to manage so many different products in so many different locales, I decided to rule out the secondary branches of the operation, and confined my study to the shaver business."[10]

Although bargain acquisitions are few and may require much searching to find, the most time-demanding activity is usually that of screening rather than finding the leads. One entrepreneur who teamed up with another to seek a company that they could jointly acquire spent some time searching, then sent the following comment to his partner:

♦   You will find no problem in picking up more suggestions than you could explore in a lifetime. I am finding that more and more of these prospects can be culled simply by keeping our own requirements and abilities clearly in mind. Too many times I have spent a full day exploring a situation only to find that some basic fact, which I would have determined by three minutes more discussion at the source of the suggestion, made the situation one we should not consider.

How narrow the criteria for selection should be is a matter of judgment. If they are too broad, the search becomes an endless checkout task; if too narrow, all the leads are eliminated. One decision that can affect the criteria strongly is the extent to which the entrepreneur wishes to operate alone. With partners a larger investment can be mustered and a larger work force can be applied to take over the business; hence it is possible to acquire a larger firm. How much time the entrepreneur wants to apply to the task of taking over can also be important. If the entrepreneur wants to pick up a part-time business so that he or she can retain a regular job, many types of acquisitions will automatically be excluded. Typically, those who acquire find them extremely time-demanding for at least a year or two, after which it may be possible to develop hired management to carry on. How much commuting the entrepreneur is willing to do is an important decision that automatically imposes a geographical radius within which to search.

At the same time, it is very important to be ready to suppress the criteria if a promising opportunity arises. A venture that is too big to fit the investment, time demand, or labor-force needs criteria can be tackled through recruiting appropriate partners. One that is too small can serve as a valuable training experience or steppingstone to get into the system and find something larger. If a business is of a nature that simply does not appeal, there is always the possibility of keeping it for a short time and reselling it at a profit. Alertness to the possibility of picking up a bargain, which generally tends to be something the other prospective buyers already looked at and decided was not attractive for some reason, should always be maintained along with willingness to subordinate preconceived criteria as necessary to take advantage of it.

[10] Kiam, *Going for It,* p. 183.

A common dilemma in searching is whether to spend more time on searching or to spend less on that task and more on screening. More searching will turn up more and possibly better leads, but fuller investigation of a given lead may reveal hidden advantages or ways to develop more from the company than others might perceive. The following case illustrates what can be found in a company even though many others have looked it over and rejected it.

◆   The company had been on the market for three years since the old man who had owned it died. Bankers, real estate, and business brokers had all looked at it and spread the word of its availability. Prospective buyers had visited the well-built plant, walked through the shop with its expensive but mostly idle machinery, looked over the list of medical instruments in the company's product line, which were many in number but not great in sales, walked past the shelves of inventory, somewhat dusty from sitting, scrutinized the financial statements, which bore a dismal record, and walked away uninterested in buying.

A young former life insurance salesman, who had recently lost his job as sales manager when the small aircraft company he worked for went into receivership, took more interest in the situation, however. "That machinery out in the shop looked awfully good," he recalled, "and it made me wonder how the company could have been doing so badly and still bought it. The financial statements showed that the company had been losing money for nineteen years straight, except for one year. It turned out that that year they had replaced their local CPA with a "big eight" firm. The funny thing was that after the big eight firm showed them a profit the old man fired it!

"Another thing that mystified me was to hang around the front office and listen to what was said on the phone to customers. They had no salespeople, and when customers would call in a secretary would take their orders. But what amazed me was how often the secretaries would try to talk them out of buying, saying they didn't know how the products worked and maybe they had better not experiment with them, and so forth.

Well, it turned out that the old man had been using the company as a tax dodge. He made a lot of money as a surgeon and ran the company as a hobby to make products he invented in his work. The expensive machinery he bought to get the depreciation write-offs, and he really didn't care about sales, because losses would help cut his taxes. He put his kids on the payroll, even sent them to college on the business. The company turned out to be a gold mine, and it was just lucky for me that somehow all those people who had looked it over never figured that out."

This insight enabled the young entrepreneur to strike a very attractive bargain on the company. Following takeover, he immediately threw himself into learning as much as he could about operation of the company and its products and then took to the road, selling. He also began to deluge overseas markets with sales literature, reasoning, "Although American medical people knew who the big equipment suppliers were and that we were only a small one, the foreigners did not. For all they knew, we were as big as Standard Oil but just beginning to go after foreign sales." The result was that within two months the company passed the breakeven point and a rapid growth of sales and profits followed.

The fact that many others had previously looked at this company and passed it by suggests two things: first, that there are many people looking for companies, hence much competition for any new would-be buyer; second, that it is easy to overlook good opportunities. Adding to the difficulty is the fact that an energetic search will turn up a considerable number of leads. So the entrepreneur needs a way to screen leads quickly while minimizing the chances of throwing out good ones.

Most experience acquisition entrepreneurs know what they are looking for, but they do not all look for the same things. One looks for companies whose principals are old and ready to retire. Another looks only at capital-intensive companies with clean balance sheets, so there is substantial borrowing capacity. Others stress the importance of solid earnings records over a period of years, or of successful operation under absentee ownership, while still others prefer to find "distress situations"—companies in trouble where there is a combination of turnaround potential plus pressure on the principals to sell out. Each entrepreneur needs to formulate his or her own criteria for screening leads quickly. A format in which such criteria can conveniently be cast and used appears in Figure 9–1. The personal preference of the searcher who developed this was to find companies where the check marks all fell toward the right-hand side.

One or more quick rules of thumb for checking price are also useful for screening leads. Serious final pricing can be a time- and effort-consuming matter, a subject that will be more fully developed in the next chapter, but for first screening something more simple will do, such as briefly exploring the following questions:

1 How much capital must be risked by the entrepreneur (personal cash plus personal debt), and how much cash will be generated by the company after allowing suitable payment for time the entrepreneur and any hired managers must spend? What is the cash rate of return?

2 What is the cash value of the assets that will be obtained in the acquisition, and how does this compare with the purchase price? If there is a gap between them attributed to goodwill, does it seem justified?

3 How much would it cost to start fresh, and how does this compare with the purchase price, noting the advantages and disadvantages of starting fresh?

4 How does the price compare with that of other similar deals?

5 How flexible is the owner willing to be about terms? Liberal terms (as will be discussed in the next chapter) can make up for a substantial portion of the price.

A host of other questions must race through the entrepreneur's mind in the screening process: Is the deal feasible or how can it be made so, maybe by bringing in partners? Is running this company something the entrepreneur can do successfully? (It is important not to underestimate the job being done by the present management, even though it may not appear to be exemplary.) Is it something the entrepreneur would have time to do and enjoy doing?

1. Company Name _____ Date _____

2. Owner _____ Phone _____

3. Product(s) _____

4. Size: Number of Employees _____ Valuation Guess $ _____

5. Ratings:

	Undesirable	Desirable	
a. Custom Products			Standard Products
b. High Priced			Bargain Price
c. Busy Workforce			Slack Workforce
d. Owner Long Hours			Absentee Owner
e. Many Competitors			Clear Niche in Market
f. Complex Product			Simple Product
g. Local Customers			Widespread Customers
h. Few Customers			Many Customers
i. Entry Costs Low			High Startup Costs
j. Low Growth Potential			High Growth Potential
k. Narrowing Markets			Expanding Markets
l. Short Profit History			Long Stable Profits
m. Owner Indifferent to Selling			Owner Anxious to Sell
n. High Capital Intensity			Low Capital Intensity
o. Obsolete Equipment			Equipment Current

6. Other Thoughts:

FIGURE 9–1 SEARCH CHECKLIST

TRAP SITUATIONS

Just as it can be surprisingly difficult to make a successful company fail through acquisition, as mentioned earlier, it can be practically impossible to turn a loser into a success, and a major objective of preliminary screening should be to discard basic losers. If the entrepreneur finds that the company has had a chronic history of operating in the red under several owners and there is no clear justification, such as a tax write-off objective, then probably there is a basic reason for failure that likely is uncorrectable, such as an unworkable location for a retailer or a manufactured product that simply does not fit the market. In the following case it was clear that something was wrong, but what was it? The searcher recalled:

◆   The owner said that he wanted to sell out because the company had been draining off his personal savings and his banker had told him to drop it. I asked if he could show me some financial statements. He said, "Sure," and fished an August income statement out of a desk drawer. Where were the others? Well, he fished other months out of other drawers here and there. They were in a computer format, and back a year the format shifted to a different one. The owner explained that he had not been able to understand them, so he changed accountants. But they still didn't make sense. Part of the puzzle, he said, was that two years earlier his bookkeeper had embezzled money from the company. He wasn't sure how much but said they had been able to prove $35,000 at least. But he didn't know why the company was still eating money, and I couldn't figure it out either. Apparently cost of goods sold was too high, but the shop superintendent had carefully measured time and materials, and based on this the shipments should have cost less. It was clear that the company would need substantial cash for resurrection, and besides their product had become somewhat out of date, so engineering would be needed as well as government approval inspections on any new designs. Here was a going concern with a pretty good reputation in the market, receiving orders, even though the owner had stopped sales efforts to conserve cash, and shipping out products, but I could not see how to keep it going, even if the owner gave it to me for nothing, without pouring in cash that might simply disappear.

The searcher walked away from this venture. So did several others, and shortly afterward the company closed up and auctioned off the equipment. In a way the searcher considered himself lucky that the fact the company was a loser had been so clearly apparent. Otherwise he might have gambled and lost ability to move on to more attractive deals. More dangerous and worrisome are companies wherein the weaknesses are not apparent, except perhaps to the present owner. The following trap situation caught the purchaser completely by surprise.

◆   After six years in the controller's department of a very large corporation, a young man quit his job in 1973 to look for a small company to buy. His wife also took leave from her job as a schoolteacher to look with him. As a stake they had managed to accumulate a net worth of $170,000. For six months they searched out and screened possible acquisitions, finally becoming rather discouraged, until they came upon a company with a net worth just under $300,000 which had never lost money, had earned profits after taxes of $71,000 in the preceding year, and was being offered for $240,000. The company appeared neat and well run. The financial statements were certified by a respectable CPA and the owner, although only in his fifties, said he wanted to move to Florida and leave the pressures of managing a company behind. Visits with the CPA and the company's banker confirmed that the company's record had been good and it was well run. Inquiry with twenty of the company's customers revealed satisfaction with its work and intentions of continued sales.

The couple bought the company and took over. For two weeks all went well, with orders coming in and production rolling out. Then the catch appeared. Upon contacting suppliers to obtain materials needed in production, the new owner learned that a critical ingredient had become scarce and the suppliers had notified all customers, including the prior owner, that allocations were being cut back 30 percent. This put the company below breakeven.

More frequently trap situations involve something wrong with the product or the market. In the following case there were several things wrong with the prospective purchase: the price, the market, and the importance of knowhow possessed by the present owners.

♦   The company bought used cardboard cartons and rejects, which it reprocessed and sold at prices substantially below the cost of new ones but roughly three times what it paid. Following a year in which sales were $300,000 the owner was offering the company for sale at a price of "only" four times earnings. His wife, who worked full time in the business, and he, who also did, each had taken salaries of $25,000 after which there had been a profit of another $10,000. The owner added these three to show an earnings figure of $60,000, which he used to justify a price of $240,000. A quick checkout showed, however, that the company had paid no rent on the plant, which the owner planned to keep and lease to the buyer for $1,000 per month. It appeared that to hire a replacement for work done by the man's wife would cost at least $10,000 per year, and to replace the man would be very difficult, since it took experience to judge what used cartons to buy and at what prices to buy and sell them. When the prospective buyer asked to see income statements for prior years, the owner hedged considerably. It turned out that the business had been highly cyclical in the past, fluctuating with rather wide swings of the paperboard industry, and in no prior year had sales been close to the $300,000 figure. The "real" price-earnings ratio being asked by the owner, if these factors were taken into account, was more like twelve to one on the average. More importantly, the entrepreneur concluded that the company at this rate could not generate enough cash to pay itself off and thus was in fact an impossible situation as offered.

The owner of a business will have one or more reasons in mind for selling, but, as with those given by people for selling used cars, these will often not be the real reasons. A checklist of owners' reasons for selling, which the reader may find worthwhile to extend as his or her own search progresses, ranging from more to less attractive, appears in Table 9–2.

Even more worrisome at times can be problems that may lie beyond the present horizon of the company, some of which even present management may not be able to foresee, as illustrated by the following examples.

♦   A company was acquired that had developed a new process for bonding aircraft metals with organic adhesives. The resulting bond was lighter, produced a smoother surface without rivets or welds, and was cheaper to apply. Unfortunately, it was found after the acquisition that with time and exposure to varying temperatures and stresses the bond became increasingly brittle so that the joints

TABLE 9–2 Some Reasons that Prompt Company Owners to Sell

Reasons owners would be more likely to volunteer
1. Owner wants to retire.
2. Owner wants to collect his or her winnings and enjoy them.
3. Owner wants to live somewhere else.
4. Illness pressuring owner to leave the business.
5. To cope with estate and inheritance problems.
6. Owner discontent with line of business he or she is in.
7. Dispute between co-owners.

Reasons less likely to be volunteered by owners
8. Family pressures.
9. Marital problems.
10. Owner sees a better business opportunity.
11. Owner tired of coping with unions, regulations, taxes, consumer groups, stockholders, inflation, or insurance costs.
12. Company needs more financing than owner can raise.
13. Currently depressed market for what company offers.
14. Company losing money for reasons owner cannot diagnose.

Reasons still less likely to be volunteered by owners
15. Bigger companies squeezing ones like this out.
16. New zoning laws too restrictive.
17. Competitors moving in with more effective products or methods.
18. Union settlements cutting into profits.
19. Owner wants to start a competitive firm with greater potential.
20. Plant has become worn out or obsolete.
21. New government regulations too expensive to comply with.
22. Supply sources have become restricted or eliminated.
23. Location becoming obsolete.
24. Product or service company offers becoming obsolete.
25. Franchise being canceled.
26. Company needs more cash than operations can justify.
27. Key employees leaving (maybe as competitors).
28. Impending threat of major lawsuit.
29. Major customer returns likely from previous sales.
30. Company committed to backlog with major built-in losses.

became unacceptably weakened. With an additional six-figure investment and further research this failing was overcome, but the original acquisition in hindsight was no longer a good decision. It was further apparent that a relatively limited amount of professional laboratory testing of the product before acquisition would have revealed the shortcomings.

◆   A chemical company in the 1950s had developed a coating that helped "bleed off" static electricity, which built up an aircraft surfaces passing through clouds and interfered with radio and navigation electronics. The company was acquired for $600,000. Then market research turned up the fact that an electronic device cheaper than the chemical had been developed to do the same thing.

◆   A manufacturer of woven cloth fabric used in tarpaulins had a healthy record
when acquired, and continued to perform well for a while afterward. Then another
company introduced a new synthetic plastic material consisting of overlaid sheets
with a reinforcing grid of fibrous strands that under stress would slide together to
form a practially nontearable rim. It was more weather-resistant, lighter, and in
other ways superior at a potentially much lower cost.

◆   A manufacturing company had developed a milling machine that was unusually efficient in machining hard-to-work metals such as stainless steel, titanium,
and "super-alloy steels." Market surveys indicated substantial demand for such
capability, and control of the company was acquired. After two years of good sales
a new process, chemical milling, hit the market with significant advantages over
the milling machine for many purposes and set the company back seriously.

Failings like these, which lay in the future, would be highly difficult for
someone new to the business to foresee and would probably not be detected
during preliminary screening. The purpose of that screening, however, is simply
to narrow down the stream of leads to those that seem most promising and
worthy of a more thorough investigation. For some companies the preliminary
screening may be very cursory and for others deeper. Before closing a deal,
however, the entrepreneur should be prepared to check the company out in
depth.

DETAILED CHECKOUT

There is no way to be completely sure that a company does not have undetected
flaws. A search for companies will quickly reveal, in fact, that there are some
obvious things wrong in every acquisition situation and an unlimited number
of other things to worry about that *might* be wrong: inventories overstated,
backlogs with built-in losses, increasing future union commitments, impending
shortages among suppliers, built-in "bad will" in the form of customers who
have become unhappy or who have received things from the company that are
going to make them unhappy in the future, uncollectable receivables, understated payables, an unrenewable lease about to terminate on the shop, forthcoming loss of key personnel, major customers planning to change suppliers
shortly, or products, processes, or plans that are obsolescent.

All that can be done is to perform as thorough a search as seems reasonable in the particular case and then design terms in the deal, as will be
discussed in the next chapter, so as to hedge against things that might go
wrong after takeover. After a prospective acquisition has passed through the
preliminary screening process, it is helpful to formulate a list of questions for
more-detailed checkout of the company. The list should be tailored to the
particular company and circumstances under review, and no one list will fit all.
The objective must be not only to avoid pitfalls but to see ways for creating
and exploiting advantages in the situation.

Some factors to consider in detailed checkout are listed in Table 9–3.
However, lists can be boring and anesthetic to the vital process of penetrating
thought unless the reader recasts them in his or her own mind to "make sense."
It may be better to start with simple basic questions and trace the answers out

TABLE 9–3 Some Items to Consider in Checkout

1. *Receivables.* What has past collection experience been? Is it owner-dependent? How old are the receivables? Which are most uncollectable and why? Who owes them? A few large corporate customers may be easier to collect from than many small debtors. Can they be insured or guaranteed as being good collateral for obtaining financing for the buyout?

2. *Inventory.* What is really there? What may disappear during takeover? Which of it is worth how much for the future? What will it cost to get rid of what is worthless? Is it stored where it is safe and accessible? How much could it be liquidated for? (Lenders will want to know.)

3. *Physical equipment and plant.* Which of it will really be needed? Which would it be better to update or replace? How much would it cost to buy what is needed elsewhere? How much will it cost to get rid of what is useless?

4. *Lease or leases.* Will they transfer? What limiting covenants do they have? Are there options to sublet, renew, assign, resell?

5. *Records.* Are they complete and usable on such things as customer addresses and buying records, credit records, mailing lists, supplier lists and price performance, manufacturing drawings, user manuals, standard procedures, maintenance schedules, and records?

6. *Name, logo, trademarks, patents, copyrights.* Who owns them and how will they be transferred? Is there any litigation pending or likely over them? May the company be violating those of any other company?

7. *Customer and supplier relations.* Will any special arrangements leave when the former owner does? How will credibility be transferred to the new owner? Are there alternative sources?

8. *Key people.* Who are they at each organizational level? What will be needed to keep them and retain their performance?

9. *Liabilities.* Are there any pending or prospective lawsuits? Are there any debts not shown on the balance sheet? Have all lease commitments been listed? Are there back pay and vacation obligations? What assets are pledged? May the company be in violation of any laws or regulations, either now or later? Will any particular clearances, licenses, or permissions be needed by the new owner?

10. *Income performance.* What do the tax reports indicate performance, inventories, and the like to have been? How has performance on any income statement line items changed recently? Have maintenance or other routine expenditures been cut back to make profits look better? Are owners' salaries up to what would be required for hiring suitable people to replace them? Have there been windfalls that will not likely repeat? Can depressing factors on the horizon be foreseen?

---

wherever they lead, regardless of the lists. One question is simply, "What important things is the buyer buying?" Is it the machinery, the customer goodwill, the products, or knowhow on the part of certain key personnel? Is it a key location, brand identity, tooling, or simply inventory? Which of those things could be obtained elsewhere cheaper? If the buyer were starting a company fresh in that line of business, would he or she buy different things to do it better than the "used merchandise" that the going company represents? For instance, is the machinery in the shop the kind that should be bought starting fresh, or is it really obsolete?

Quantitative analysis of the profit potential is inescapably important. What is the upside potential of the operating profits, and of a resale of the business?

What is the downside risk? In other words, how much of the investment would have some sort of residual value in the event of failure, how much would have to be written off, and what is the likelihood of such an outcome? Breakeven, especially in terms of cash, but also in terms of profit, is extremely important if the business is being bought on time with payments coming from its own income. How far can sales slip (or in a turnaround how far must they rise) before the company will be able to cover the payments that must be made? Presumably, some sort of income for the purchaser must also be included in assumptions of the breakeven computation.

Questions concerning the gross margin can quickly get to the hearts of many enterprises. Out of each dollar of sales, how much is left after direct labor and materials are paid for? If the amount left is fairly large, say sixty cents out of the dollar in a manufacturing firm, it is usually a good sign, but not one without dangers. Large margins usually attract competition, often leading to industry "shakeouts" such as those that occurred in semiconductors during the early 1960s, computers during the mid-sixties, and franchises in the late sixties. How can the company protect its large margin?

Obviously, along with margin there must be a sufficient volume of sales to cover indirect expenses and pile up profit, and the slimmer the margin percentage, the higher the sales volume must be. Hence one line of questioning in a prospective acquisition is how the margin can be raised, and the other is how the sales volume can be increased. Does the entrepreneur have the ability to add higher-margin items to the product line or production knowhow that can cut direct cost per unit? Or does the entrepreneur rather know how to reach new potential customers and persuade them to buy from the firm? How is it that this company manages to sell what it offers against the competition anyway? Why do people decide to buy what it sells instead of spending their money elsewhere? What basically does the company do for the world, and how does that justify its existence? Can that justification be expected to continue, and how could a new owner capitalize on it?

If the new owner aims to raise profits and does not find ways of doing so by sales increase, then the only other hope is to cut expenses. Cost cutting is a limited approach to increasing profits, but perhaps it may be enough, particularly in a turnaround situation, to make the company more attractive to other potential buyers, and the entrepreneur may thereby profit through reselling the enterprise for substantially more than he or she paid for it. At the same time, however, this possibility raises a caveat for the would-be purchaser, which is to look for recent slashes of costs in the firm to be acquired. They may indicate a last squeeze (or even a failure to report actual costs) to increase profits by the former owner, possibly a squeeze that cannot realistically be maintained in the longer pull. A cut in R&D expenses, for example, may improve short-run profits but at the expense of longer-term success.

Some questions will be fairly easy to answer with confidence, such as when the company's lease will run out on the plant, and the main trick will be to think of those questions. Others will be easy to think of and less easy to answer with confidence. What the profits are, for instance, is answered by reference to financial statements, and clearly it is essential to ask that these be confirmed if possible. But that does not preclude the possibility of fraud, as recurring scandals demonstrate. Nor does it preclude the possibility of other unrevealed obligations, such as outstanding purchase orders that may essentially be firm commitments.

◆ After a small independent manufacturer of computer peripheral equipment had been bought out, an accountant was sent to set up a double-entry system to replace the checkbook that had previously been used to keep track of accounting information. He asked the inventor who ran the firm whether the company had any bills from suppliers and was shocked when the man replied, "Oh, sure," and pulled out a desk drawer full of requests for payment. Further checking with the suppliers revealed that the man had always sent a check immediately upon receipt of supplies, so that the bills had been taken care of. Until he learned with relief of this fact, the purchaser of this firm, who was counting on continued pleasant collaboration with the inventor to make it succeed, had some sleepless nights with visions of great negative net worth and acrimonious relations in his new acquisition.

In many small companies the financial statements may be ragged at best, nonexistent at worst. But the owner is bound to have copies of filed tax returns and these at least should be examined. A great advantage of working from the tax returns is that any distortions they contain will tend to be in the direction of stating earnings on the low side to minimize income taxes, and hence they usually present a conservative picture of the company that can work to the buyer's advantage in negotiating price and terms for a purchase. But a weakness shared by all financial statements, even tax returns and those that have been certified by audit, is that they tell only the "as was" of a firm while the "to be" is what most matters. They do not tell whether a competitor is about to file a patent infringement lawsuit, or whether some key salespeople will quit after the acquisition, taking with them major accounts, or whether a union is about to organize the shop and press for expensive new fringe benefits. To learn about these things as well as possibilities for improving the firm or reselling it at a profit, the acquiring entrepreneur must rely on resourceful personal inquiry and imagination.

Especially helpful in checking and cross-checking information about the firm and its prospects can be personal interviews with a variety of people. Officers of the different banks in a town frequently feed information to each other about companies and the people who run them, including such things as reputation for honest dealing, impending problems of various types, firms that may be for sale, relations between firms, and industrial trends of significance. It is clearly vital, however, to talk to the banker with the right connections and experience. Some handle mainly personal loans or internal administration and know very little about companies, though they may not readily admit it. Others who may be able to provide useful information or insights about a firm being considered for purchase include its accountant, attorneys, customers, suppliers, and employees. Obviously, there may be need for discretion in asking questions if the availability of the firm is a matter of confidence, but without violation it will still be possible to learn much if the purchasing entrepreneur will only take the initiative to do so.

Important to avoid is the possible temptation not to face negative evidence concerning the prospects of a firm that is in many respects appealing. The importance of this truism is underscored by the experiences of many who bought worthless franchises in spite of well-publicized franchise failures and some of those mentioned above, who failed to check out apparently promising products sufficiently before gambling on them and losing.

If the company is already profitable, the entrepreneur must beware the temptation to assume that he or she can quickly improve on performance of the existing management. The old owner may not have a facade of sophistication and may appear to be operating with little in the way of written information or formal controls. However, years of experience in a small and close-knit organization may have given him or her rules of thumb for making very effective decisions and a feel for operations that is highly accurate. Unless the company is clearly in trouble upon takeover, it is often advisable for the new owner to leave operations alone for several months before attempting to improve on how things work.

Somehow the entrepreneur must maintain, during checkout and the deal to follow it, a combination of attitudes including both critical pessimism and opportunistic optimism at the same time. Overlooking weaknesses can lead to purchase of a "lemon" or to very unsatisfactory price and term arrangements. But overlooking possible ways to make the most of a situation containing some negative aspects, as virtually every acquisition does, can result in missed opportunities. Both pessimism and optimism can work to the purchaser's advantage if the former is used in designing the price and terms to build in conservatism and safeguards and the latter is used to sustain enthusiasm for following through the deal and subsequent development of the company.

SUMMARY

Acquisition of a going concern is generally the best way for a would-be entrepreneur to enter a new line of work, and many successfully do so. There are some kinds of sellout situations that are more attractive, as, for example, if the owner has died or wants to retire although the business is healthy, and others that are less attractive, as when the company is riding high on the crest of a cycle or is basically doomed to fail because of changes in the market or makeup of the company. An entrepreneur can either wait and hope that a promising opportunity will arise, as it sometimes does, or can go looking, using such lead sources as the twenty listed in this chapter. Generally, it will not take long to turn up leads, and a major part of the search procedure will simply be to screen those that have been discovered. In this screening it is important to be aware that the seller is less likely to tell about some of the reasons for selling than others, and it is up to the buyer to look for the "bad news" as well as the good concerning the opportunity.

chapter 10

Acquisition Dealing

The three basic components in an acquisition deal—once the company has been checked out—are what is to be acquired from the company or from its owners, the price, and the terms. Each of these components in turn may involve a large number of variables, so that in structuring a deal the variety of possibilities is enormous. This chapter will identify the main variables, suggest some ways of working with them, and illustrate their application in putting deals together.

WHAT IS BOUGHT

"Buying a company" may sound like acquisition of an enterprise in total. Sometimes it is, but many times it is not. Often the buyer will have a considerable range of choice about what to acquire. On the stock exchanges, of course, people buy shares of stock in companies, but almost never all the shares of any given company. Similarly, in a company acquisition it may be possible to buy shares. However, usually the acquiring entrepreneur wants to buy a controlling interest at least, or possibly all the shares. Depending on how many present shareholders there are and the extent to which they favor the takeover, this may be an easy or a difficult task.

For instance, through buying a corporation intact the entrepreneur may be able to continue the benefits held by the corporation of leases or contracts it has that cannot be assigned to others. The corporation may also have loss carryforwards that the entrepreneur can use to reduce tax liabilities. Such aspects may favor buying a corporation rather than selected assets, as may the fact that trying to buy only some assets might cause trouble from some shareholders.

291

However, there may also be reasons to favor the purchase of assets rather than the corporation. One is that the value of assets can be stepped up to reflect the purchase price, thereby allowing greater depreciation than retaining them in the corporation would allow. Also, through buying only assets, the entrepreneur may be able to escape the union contracts and other obligations to employees, customers, and shareholders that would go with the corporation.

The following case illustrates some difficulties an entrepreneur might encounter.

◆   After six years in sales with IBM, a young business graduate had become restless. By starting his own company, he reasoned, he might be able to avoid what he regarded as the distasteful politics and confinement of working for a big company and also be able to amass greater wealth. He began talking to selected business acquaintances about the possibility of starting a computer software company. He worked up a written business plan and obtained verbal commitments from key staff people, a tentative major account, and prospective venture capital. When he was finally ready to sign a lease for office space, he told his boss of his plan and intended resignation. There it all stopped. "Basically, I was talked out of it by my boss at IBM," he recalled. "He was really a nice guy whom I enjoyed working with." Also, he was given a large raise and a promotion.

Four years later things were going well. His salary had reached $48,000 and his promotions had continued, but some uneasiness had persisted and now a new problem arose. His next promotion would require moving from the West Coast, which he loved, to the East, which he did not. Unmarried and with $50,000 in savings, he decided to go independent.

He gave IBM sixty days' notice in October 1963 and began looking for a company to acquire. His main criterion was that it should have the potential to reach sales of $30– to $40–million. He began by calling personal business contacts, business brokers, venture capitalists, and bank loan officers all along the West Coast. Leads from the brokers and bankers he found to be mostly companies with low technology, regional markets, and little growth potential. Those from venture capitalists he considered more promising. He spent extensive time analyzing and planning takeover of a Los Angeles tennis equipment distributor, only to conclude that it would take more capital than he could muster. He also considered a plastic prescription eyeglass company, which failed on the same grounds, and a winemaking kit company, which he decided was overpriced. Several other companies in the Palo Alto area had high-technology products, but insufficiently convincing markets.

After two months' searching, a friend told him about a banker he knew who held stock in a small collator manufacturing company and was dissatisfied with its performance. He was busy looking at other deals, so it was three more months before he began investigating this one in detail. In its six years of operation it had developed some products he considered promising, but at a net operating loss of nearly $1 million. Some of this he concluded had been due to overstaffing, and some due to premature release of new designs before "bugs" were eliminated. The net worth was minus $23,000, payments on an SBA–guaranteed loan were three months' delinquent, and some payables were over a year old. However, a $1 million order had come from 3M, and the company president was using optimistic sales projections in discussions with prospective investors to raise more capital.

The young entrepreneur made a proposal to the directors that he be made chairman and chief executive officer to turn the company around. He would loan $25,000 to the company to stave off creditors and would guarantee personally another $200,000 in return for an option to convert the loan after one year into 25 percent of the outstanding shares. His offer was refused by the board, apparently out of personal loyalty to the present founder and president. So the entrepreneur began contacting shareholders, pointing out that the company was on the verge of bankruptcy and he had a plan to rescue it while present management could offer no concrete solution. He approached ten of the shareholders personally, while some of them plus investment brokers who agreed with him talked to others. When he felt he had lined up support of a large enough number, he again approached the directors, telling them about the support he had enlisted. This time the board accepted his offer.

Upon taking control, his first move was to contact all creditors, requesting that they accept deferred repayment schedules. All but two of the forty agreed to do so. One was paid, and the other sued for payment but was defeated by a countersuit. On the basis of knowledge of the company gained during detailed checkout, he reduced the work force from thirty-one people to sixteen, telling managers how many people they could retain and letting them make the choices of whom to let go. He shifted salesmen from salaries to combination salary and commission plans. With these and other changes sales increased over the succeeding two years from $400,000 to $2 million, and net income rose from a negative $250,000 to a positive $190,000.

Here the entrepreneur, to obtain control of a company owned by a large number of stockholders, would have found it impractical to attempt to buy complete ownership. Had there only been a very small number of shareholders, say a half-dozen or less, he would have needed a majority of the shares. But with a large number, most of whom supported his moves anyway, it was sufficient to have a much smaller fraction to dominate.

In many other cases, it is preferable not to buy shares at all, but rather to acquire selected assets of the company. If the company is a proprietorship, for example, there are no shares, only assets and liabilities accumulated in the course of doing business which belong personally to the proprietor. So in acquiring the company, the entrepreneur and the owner must decide which of those assets and liabilities are to be transferred and which are to stay with the present owner. The buyer may feel that some of the assets are not essential to the business—extra-capacity machinery, for instance. The seller may desire to keep some things, often the real estate, which the buyer may pick up on a lease. Letting the seller retain assets can be a way of reducing what a buyer, who may be short on capital to buy with, must pay. Leaving assets out of the transaction can also remove disputes over value of such things as inventory, receivables, and even the plant. The following example illustrates a fairly clean purchase of selected assets:

◆　　In the first example of the preceding chapter, the owner decided to accept a price of $40,000 for the equipment (the plant was leased from another owner) and the inventory, but with an inventory assumed to be worth $10,000, this amount to be corrected by physical count and pricing at cost after acquisition. When the new owner took over, it was found that the inventory was actually worth $24,000, so the price then became $54,000. The previous proprietor personally owed the accounts payable, which he paid off by using some of the down payment, which the buyer borrowed from the bank against fixed assets of the business. The seller also retained title to the accounts receivable. These the new owner collected and forwarded to the former owner as they came in.

By leaving parts of the company with the prior owner the deal can often be simplified. Here the need to evaluate receivables was eliminated by letting the owner keep them. By leaving final evaluation of inventory until after takeover, no time had to be invested in that aspect while working out the deal. Letting the owner pay off the accounts payable lifted this chore and any arguments about what was due from the shoulders of the buyer, and also allowed the owner to take care of what he owed once and for all and therefore not to have any bills hanging over his head waiting for the new owner to pay them off. Another possibility not used in this case, but sometimes very helpful, is to leave some of the equipment with the prior owner, especially if not all the equipment is needed to run the company at present. One owner who sold a machine shop, for instance, kept a lathe, mill, drill press, and some hand tools, which he wanted in his garage for personal use. They buyer did not really need these particular machines to keep the shop running, and by leaving them with the owner, he was able to arrange a lower price for the company. Taking the inventory on consignment and paying the owner for it as it is sold or used can also sometimes simplify the deal and ease the price.

DETERMINING PRICE

Deciding what price to pay for a company can be quite simple, extremely complex, or anything in between. The best way in many cases is simply to accept the seller's price and work on the terms to design a deal satisfactory to the acquiring entrepreneur. But first the buyer should satisfy himself or herself that the seller's price is reasonably appropriate. The buyer should also get a feel for how relatively high or low the price is as a basis for negotiating the terms. It may be to the buyer's advantage to be able to apply price-determining methods that generate prices lower than the seller wants as a basis for negotiating either price or terms or both. Finally, whatever method is used for setting the price, the buyer will want to be sure that there was not a better way that would have given him or her a more attractive price.

For all these reasons it is desirable to approach pricing from many perspectives, and to use both complex and simple methods to make sure that nothing important has been overlooked. A list of seventeen methods for pricing companies appears in Table 10–1. These are grouped into six categories, and although not all the methods may apply to any given company, it will probably be to the acquiring entrepreneur's interest to apply several before finalizing terms in any substantial acquisition.

If the company has a balance sheet, the quickest method for looking up a valuation figure is simply to look at its net worth as indicated by the book. This is the *book value,* and if the company does not have a balance sheet, as many smaller firms do not, it can be calculated simply by adding up the value of the assets as reflected by whatever records there are and subtracting what the company owes to its creditors and lenders. An advantageous feature of book value in many closely held companies from the buyer's point of view is that the assets may be understated by having been written off as rapidly as possible by the former owners to minimize taxes. Whereas large, publicly traded companies like to show high earnings to please stockholders, small ones th

TABLE 10–1 PRICING METHODS

Net Worth Methods
1. Book value
2. Adjusted book value (goodwill added)

Asset Methods
3. Liquidation value (auctioneer estimates)
4. Fair market value (professional appraisal)
5. Replacement cost (go shopping for the best)

Income Methods
6. Historical earnings (maybe weighted) times a multiple
7. Future earnings, present owner, times a multiple
8. Future earnings, new owner, times a multiple

Cash Flow Methods (New Owner)
9. Payment servicing capacity (or payback on cash deal)
10. Discounted cash flow (assume eventual resale)
11. Adjusted cash flow (include salary, perquisites, fringes)

Market Methods
12. Last trading price (if there was one)
13. Competitive current bids (or what they would likely be)
14. Comparable company prices (whatever there may be)
15. Special formulas in some industries

Heuristic Methods
16. Intuitive value to buyer (including job, independence, learning, and other personal satisfactions versus sacrifices and risks)
17. Seller's preconception of price (buyer can yield on this and still recover on the terms)

to minimize them by such methods as taking depreciation as rapidly as possible and minimizing the valuation of inventory. In many small manufacturing companies, for instance, there is operating machinery in perfectly good condition that may have been nearly or completely written down to zero on the books through depreciation.

To correct these distortions of reality the seller in particular will want to make some modifications to create an *adjusted book value.* Most often the figure that is added to produce the adjustment is called goodwill. It is also usually a quite arbitrary amount expressing a judgment about the value not shown on the books to reflect such things as reputation with customers, working habits of employees, established methods of operating, and all the other things that it takes to transform the inanimate objects of a company into a living, going concern. The rationale is that since these things cost time, effort, and money to create, they should have a value that is reflected in the company's price. A rule of thumb for determining goodwill is sometimes to say that it should equal three times the "extra earning power" of the business. This extra earning power is equal to the amount that historical earnings per year of the business exceed the sum of the salary that the entrepreneur could obtain working for someone else plus the earnings that would come from investing the book value elsewhere rather than in the business.

Additional perspectives on the book value can be obtained by going beyond the books of the company to get more-detailed valuation of specific assets. Generally most advantageous from the buyer's point of view is the *liquidation value,* or the amount that could be obtained by selling off the assets as quickly as possible through professionals. The accounts receivable can be sold to a factoring company. The inventory may be sold to a scrap dealer, and the plant and fixtures may be sold by an auctioneer, who will run an advertisement in the newspaper, inviting buyers to come to the plant at a specific time when he will appear and conduct the bidding. These amounts can be determined quite accurately by talking to the various professionals involved and giving them lists of the items to be priced. Even the auction results can be predicted. Most auctioneers will not only give estimates but also be willing to state an amount they will guarantee to obtain with the understanding that however much the actual bids go above that price the auctioneer will be allowed to keep half.

Higher values for the assets, hence values more favored by the seller, can be obtained through estimating the *fair market value* and, usually still higher, the *replacement cost* of the assets. The first of these can be obtained either by looking at prices charged by others who are selling similar assets of similar age and condition or by hiring a professional appraiser to come in and estimate the fair market value. Replacement cost may be regarded in some cases as the same thing or in other cases as the cost of obtaining similar assets new rather than used because there are no used ones on the market at the time. Custom tooling to make parts, for example, generally has to be bought new; it usually has no fair market value beyond its liquidation value, which is usually the same as its value for scrap. Although consideration of replacement cost may work to the advantage of the seller in arguing for a higher price, it can also work to the advantage of the buyer when he or she is able to point out that if the assets were bought new they would be in better condition, or more modern, or, often most important of all, better suited to the company's needs. In fact, a question that should always be considered by the acquiring entrepreneur is, "Could I do better by starting fresh than by buying this company?"

Turning from the balance sheet to the income statement, the bottom line becomes earnings, and this can be looked at three ways for determining a price for the company. The first way is to look at *historical earnings.* It presumes that the future performance of the company is indicated best by its past, and this may not be a bad assumption in a company where past earnings have been fairly stable over a period of five or more years. The second way is to consider likely future earnings *under the present owner.* This can be important for appreciating the seller's point of view. Some sellers have urgent reasons—failing health, other pressing obligations, or important conflicting opportunities—that may pull them away from the company and leave it adrift to decline if they cannot sell. It can also be important in a situation where the company itself is already declining and extrapolation of the trend leads to low earnings. On the other hand, other sellers may hold companies whose future earnings picture is relatively unclouded or even rosy, and there may be very little pressure for them to sell. In such a case, there is footing for them to hold out for a higher price.

What the acquiring entrepreneur cares more about, of course, is *future earnings after acquisition,* so these prospective earnings too need to be con sidered in thinking through the price, especially if the buyer sees ways in which he or she believes earnings can be substantially increased by new management. As a word of caution, however, present management should not be underestimated. Many entrepreneurs have assumed that they could quickly introduce great improvements in a company whose "uneducated" former owner had obviously been using "seat of the pants" rather than new and sophisticated management techniques, only to find out that they were replacing an intelligent person whose many years in the business had taught him or her many clever tricks unknown to the newcomer that made the company run well without overhaul. Although spectacular improvements do sometimes occur, as in the first example of this chapter, many acquiring entrepreneurs do well to hold their own in the first one or two years after takeover.

The conventional way to translate these earnings figures into a price for the company is to multiply them by a price/earnings ratio. The reason for doing it is both to cross-check the price as determined in other methods and to see whether it generates a point of argument for the buyer in negotiating the price and terms. Price/earnings ratios can be obtained for listed stocks by referring to the financial pages of any major metropolitan newspaper or to the financial newspapers. Usually there are some very low ones, from which the buyer can reason, "If a company large and strong enough to be listed on the New York Stock Exchange can sell for a P/E ratio of only three (or so), how can I justify paying more for a company much too small to make the exchange and whose stock cannot even be sold in any market, let alone be listed on a major exchange?" Of course, the seller can look at some of the higher P/E ratios in the same paper and argue that the growth potential of the small company may be substantially greater than theirs. Looking from both points of view can help sharpen the price.

Notwithstanding the possibly helpful perspective from earnings analysis, a more important figure will be how much net cash the company can generate. This approach begins by noting several very important factors in the acquisition. One is the amount of money that the entrepreneur must be able to provide for down payment to the owner, and any additional working capital or other investment needed by the company to operate successfully after takeover. (This latter amount can be altogether too easy to overlook, and yet it is absolutely vital.) A second is the inflows and outflows of cash that will occur in operating the business. In these there may be many important special effects, such as seasonal impacts on inventories or tax implications of loss carry-forwards or write-offs that might accrue after takeover. A third factor is the crucial question of how much cash the company can generate to service the debt used to buy the company—its *payment servicing capacity*. The price must not only be one that the company can pay off, but must be one that it can pay off even if a few things go wrong after takeover. A theoretical maximum that this consideration imposes on the price is that it must be less than the net cash the company can generate divided by the entrepreneur's cost of capital (such as the interest rate at which he or she could borrow money). In reality the feasible price will be smaller than this amount, because the company will have to generate not only interest on the outstanding principal of the price but also the principal payments. Thus the price-determining question here becomes, "How big a price can the company generate enough cash to pay off?" In performing this calculation, an important decision can be whether to include real estate in the deal. Doing so can substantially enlarge the payments required and therefore can strengthen the buyer's argument for a lower price or easier terms. But it also increases the investment and obligations on which the buyer is gambling.

Another perspective on cash flow comes from exploring the question of how much cash the entrepreneur gets to keep. This can come from two sources, cash generated by operations of the company and cash received if later the entrepreneur sells the company. Cash generated by the business can be received in the form of salary to the entrepreneur, which is tax deductible to the business, although not to the entrepreneur, and dividends, which are deductible to the business if it is a regular corporation. Computation of these payments should already have been performed as part of determining the above payment servicing capacity. Cash received from selling the business at some future time has to be a speculative guess. Even if the entrepreneur does not plan to sell or know when, it can be useful to estimate how much cash the company should be worth at some future point, say five years hence. Then this amount plus the operating cash receipts minus what the entrepreneur would receive in salary elsewhere in each of the future years should be multiplied by the appropriate present value factor (with a business pocket calculator or discount table) for each future year to obtain a *discounted cash flow* representing the present value of the cash to come from the purchase, which represents another estimate of the appropriate price. Performance of this calculation will require plugging in some interest rate. Different numbers can be tried on this, such as the amount that the entrepreneur could earn in a bank account or elsewhere on the cash, and the amount for which the entrepreneur could borrow money at the bank or elsewhere. The higher he or she estimates the risk of the venture to be, the higher the interest figure to be plugged and the lower will be the price.

Further transformation of this figure to take note of fringe benefits in lieu of straight cash, which come with the company and can have cash values imputed to them, can provide an *adjusted cash value.* Things to take note of can be the cash value of savings the entrepreneur may get on personal goods bought through the company at discount and other fringe benefits, such as a company car, travel, and entertainment, on which cash may be saved by tax deductions through the company.

Regardless of what these calculations show, another perspective that the acquiring entrepreneur cannot afford to ignore is what, if anything, the market may say about the price of the company. If the company has been sold before, then the *last trading price* shows what the market valued the company at, something very likely to influence the sellers' opinion of its worth. For listed stocks, of course, the last trading prices of each day appear in the financial news. On closely held companies the information may also be available if shares were recently traded, although it may take more personal diplomacy to learn. If there is someone else trying to buy the company (most small companies that offer high payoffs repeatedly receive buyer inquiries), then the price that person is willing to pay becomes a *competitive current bid,* which any other buyer will have to muster strong arguments to underbid and win. If other companies somewhat like the one being acquired have recently been sold, then the prices at which they were sold can provide a reference point in judging its value. These *comparable company prices* can generally be learned by inquiring through a good banking connection.

Finally, for companies in certain industries there are *special formulas* determining prices. Insurance companies, for example, can be priced quite accurately on the basis of the number of dollars of insurance of different types on the books, using actuarial tables and assumed earnings rates on invested reserves. Formulas that have been used for pricing asset buyouts for a variety of small firms in the experience of one business broker are listed in Table 10–2. Here the common approach in firms where there are substantial assets is to add up the fair market value of fixed assets plus the owner's cost on currently good inventory plus around 90 percent of what appear to be good accounts receivable plus a percentage of the company's net income before taxes, as indicated in the table. In companies such as service firms, where there are relatively few assets, the approach is to calculate price as a percentage (also indicated in the table) of gross annual receipts of the business. A further refinement in looking at the historical earnings or receipts can be to use an average of two or three prior years or to form a weighted average through multiplying the most recent year by a factor of five, the preceding year by four, and so on back for five years, adding up the total and dividing by fifteen to get a weighted annual average.

For pricing a stock buyout rather than an asset buyout, the rule of thumb advocated by the same broker is to pay book value plus 75 percent of net earnings after corporate taxes averaged over the preceding three years. Clearly, many factors can influence adjustment of these figures, such as how the owner handled the accounting, what he or she took in salary or fringe benefits, and economic conditions. But the rules of thumb can provide a starting point.

Stock analysts who specialize in small and growing firms, many of which have not yet reached any stability—or possibly even positive numbers—in earnings, have suggested still other formulas.[1] One suggests, for instance, using a multiple of 1.5 times revenues for service companies and 2.0 times revenues for high-technology firms. Another proposes adding to 2.0 times revenues the amount of "net present value of excess cash." The excess cash number is computed by taking a three-year average of the sum of net income plus depreciation minus investments in working capital, new plants, and equipment, and dividing that sum by the cost of capital or rate of return that could be earned by equally risky investments.

Ultimately there is no escape in most cases from some sort of heuristic methods of applying judgment and negotiating. The *judged value of the buyer* must take into account such intangibles as the satisfaction of owning a company, the risk of failure in the enterprise versus the possible gain of succeeding, and the value of opportunities that may be foregone versus the life-style that the company may make possible. For many buyers the purchase of a company represents purchase of permanent employment, and this itself has a value that can be difficult to quantify. (Taxicab licenses illustrate this type of value. A taxi license in New York City can now cost as much as $140,000.) This value alone

Mark Mehler, "A Calculator or Perhaps a Ouija Board?" *Venture,* July 1986, p. 26.

TABLE 10–2 SOME RULES OF THUMB FOR PRICING ASSET BUYOUTS OF VARIOUS SMALL BUSINESSES*

A. Goodwill Basis

Price equals fair market value of fixed assets, plus inventory at company cost plus 90% on good receivables plus the following percentages of net income before owner's salary and taxes as goodwill

Goodwill Percentage of Net	Types of Businesses to Which This Percentage Applies
0	Small grocery and meat markets, used car lot, coin-operated car wash, oil distributorship
10	Small camera store, records shop, hi-fi store, nursery, feed store, paint store
15	Arts and crafts shop, new car dealership, small clothing store, small equipment rental
25	Auto parts store, hardware and appliance store, hobby shop, clothing store
33	Concrete mix plant, music store, pet shop
50	Construction equipment sales and rental, photo studio, printer
75	Building materials and lumber yard, drugstore, taxi company
100	Wholesale bakery, boat dealer, funeral parlor, good restaurant and lounge
125	Computer service bureau
150	Beer distributorship, dental practice, casket manufacturing, medical practice

B. Gross Sales Basis

Price Percentage of Gross	Types of Businesses to Which This Percentage Applies
30	Beauty shop (25%–35%), drive-in or cafe (25%–35%)
35	Travel agency
40	Franchised fast food (35%–50%)
50	Bookkeeping service, employment agency (average over two years)
70	Small coin-op laundry (60%–90%)
75	Small advertising agency
80	Small answering service
100	Baby sitting service, full service car wash, large coin-op laundry (80%–110%), weekly newspaper (100%–150%)
125	Accounting practice (90%–150%), larger answering service, insurance agency (up to $100,000 gross)
150	Rural garbage route, small radio station
200	Larger insurance agency (gross $100,000+)
250	Urban garbage route, hotel
350	Motel, restaurant and lounge
600	Large radio station

*Abstracted from James M. Hansen, *Guide to Buying or Selling a Business* (Englewood Cliffs, N.J.: Prentice Hall, Inc. 1975), Chap. 17. *Used with permission of author.*

tends to put a floor price on any company which may override all the calculations about present values of cash flow, especially in very small companies. One entrepreneur who bought out a partner negotiated a price based on estimated market value of the assets plus a certain percentage of the man's earnings for the most recent year. In contrast, Dave Ederer applied several approaches to triangulate on a price, as follows:

◆   In pricing the first deal, I looked at it from a fair market value of the assets approach and from a price earnings approach, but the one that meant the most to me was a cash approach. How many dollars was I going to be able to put in my pocket and how many could I use to finance the company? I made income projections and cash flow projections, looked at how much income my life-style required and what was left to do a deal. The owner's objective was retirement income, and he wanted $3,000 a month for fifteen years. He didn't care what the interest rates were or what the values were. He just wanted that much each month until he was eighty-three, which was an expected life span. We picked a low interest rate for discounting, because he would pay a lower tax as capital gains on principal than he would on income from interest. So we took $3,000 per month for fifteen years at 4 percent, which gave a purchase price of somewhere around $400,000 plus a down payment which could be borrowed from the bank against the assets of the business. The question then was simply whether the company could generate the $3,000 cash for him and still meet its other obligations with some margin for error while giving me what I needed to live on. It turned out the company could, so that is the basis we went ahead on.

Finally, the *seller's preconception* about what the price should be—and most small businessowners have on many occasions considered what their companies should be worth—may also override all the other calculations. Victor Kiam, who bought the Remington Razor Company, recalled a failed attempt almost twenty years earlier in 1960 to buy Jantzen, Inc., a Portland, Oregon, clothing maker:

◆   He heard about the acquisition opportunity from clothing retailers with whom he had been acquainted as a sales executive for Playtex. Apparently the existing shareholders of Jantzen had decided that selling out was the most constructive way to avoid disputes they had about how the company should be run. Kiam obtained financial information on the company and developed some forecasts.
        "Putting the word out in the financial community" that he wanted one, Kiam recalls finding a backer who "would bankroll the acquisition; I would receive equity in the enterprise and also run the company after it had been bought." Based on the financial data and forecasts, however, the backer stipulated that the price not exceed $21 per share.
        Kiam flew to Portland where he told the company president that a price of $23 per share was "a tad higher than we wanted to pay." Kiam recalls the reply he received from the president: "Perhaps it is, but that's the price.... If you can agree to our terms, you just bought yourself a company. If not, we'll just wait for another buyer."
        The financial backer, however, would not budge above $21 and the deal fell through. Four months later the company did sell, for $28 per share.[2]

Another illustration of the psychological importance of price to a seller

Victor Kiam, *Going for It* (New York: Morrow, 1986), p. 157.

can be seen in the following comment by an entrepreneur who had acquired several companies successfully:

♦   For small manufacturing companies, there is a standard rule of thumb for what the owner thinks it is worth. It is one million dollars. I recently negotiated the purchase of a company, and when we got around to price, there was the magic figure, one million. It seems the owner's neighbor had recently sold *his* company for a million dollars, and there was no way the owner was going to settle for less than the same. So we priced at a million, or at least it looked that way to him, although by the terms we gave him it was really a lot less.

Embodied in this comment is an operating rule that many acquisitions entrepreneurs have found to be effective. This rule is based on the observation that a company owner may be quickly alienated if told that the price the owner thought his or her company was worth is too high, and this alienation can put the buyer at a severe disadvantage relative to other buyers. Consequently, they look for a way to make it worthwhile through arranging terms favorable to the buyer. In short, the buyer's philosophy becomes, "The owner can set the price if I can set the terms." Before setting up the terms, however, the acquiring entrepreneur can obtain solider footing by cross-checking the price with as many of the seventeen methods listed in Table 10–1 as possible.

TERMS OF THE DEAL

Beyond determination of what is to be bought and at what price, variables that can be manipulated to structure an acquisition include the following:

1 Cash down payment
2 Installment payments over time
3 Guarantees of payment
4 Payment with stock
5 Use of options

These are not all the variables to be tied down in the purchase agreement as will be developed in later sections, but are the main ones available for structuring creative deals with sellers. By developing a familiarity and capability to deal with them, a would-be acquisition entrepreneur should be able to design attractive terms for most acquisition opportunities that may arise.

Except for some dire situations where the company to be acquired is on the verge of bankruptcy, virtually all acquisitions require the buyer to generate some sort of *cash down payment* to the seller. Rarely is this amount more than 30 percent of the full price, for tax reasons to be discussed later. Common sources of the down payment include the entrepreneur's personal savings, borrowings from family or friends, and recruiting partners who draw from similar sources. A most attractive type of deal, when it can be done, is the use of a "bootstrap" or "noncash" buyout in which the down payment is raised from assets of the business itself with the entrepreneur contributing virtually no cash at all. The first example in the preceding chapter involved a noncash buyout. There the entrepreneur borrowed $30,000 from the bank on a chattel mortgage against the plant machinery and used $20,000 of it for down payment while the rest was set aside for working capital. Dave Ederer, whose pricing method was just described in the preceding section, performed noncash buyouts on several companies, which he described as follows:

♦ "In the first acquisition, the heat-treating company, I formed a new corporation, which then bought the stock of the heat-treating company from the owner. I then argued that if the owner claimed his company was worth $475,000, which was the purchase price, and I was going to give him $60,000 down, then the amount he would want security on would be $415,000. To provide that security I offered to pledge the stock of the company he said was worth $475,000, plus the stock of the new corporation that bought the new stock, plus my personal guarantee on the note, which had significance to him because he had some faith in my personal integrity even though my personal assets to back up the guarantee were small. This left the assets of the company I was buying—the plant, land, equipment, inventory, and receivables—free of encumbrance, except for about $10,000 of accounts payable, so I could borrow against them at the bank. It turned out that these were worth about $800,000. There was cash of about $30,000. I persuaded the old owner to accept half the down payment at closing and the other half a couple months later in the next fiscal year to spread out his taxes. Then I went to the bank and told them I wanted to borrow $30,000, which I would pay back the next day. I gave the $30,000 to the old owner and closed the deal. The next day I filled out the signature cards for the company account to pay off the loan. Then to get working capital as needed and later to meet the other half of the down payment I simply borrowed against the assets of the company." This process began in June 1974. The deal closed with the first down payment five months later, in October, and the second half of the down payment was made in January 1975.

Meanwhile, Dave Ederer had already been working on his second acquisition—a metal-stamping company with a forty-year profit record whose seventy-seven-year-old owner wanted to sell out and retire—since February 1974, nearly five months before he encountered the heat-treating company. The metal-stamping company presented a different problem, because the owner wanted to keep his corporation and the substantial cash it contained while selling off other assets. Again Ederer, this time with a 50 percent partner, formed a new corporation, borrowed a down payment plus working capital from the bank against the fixed assets and receivables, and cosigned a note from the new corporation to the old owner to pay off the balance in five years at 8 percent. This deal took twenty months to close in October 1975.

His third acquisition began in February 1976, this time a tool supply company with an aging absentee owner who, although the company had a good record, was taking no salary. The owner wanted $400,000 cash down on an $875,000 price for the company, which included land, buildings, equipment, and operating assets with very small liabilities and no bank debt. Again Dave's problem was how to structure a deal that he could handle with no cash of his own. This time he set up two corporations, one to hold the land and buildings and the other the rest of the company. On the first corporation the real estate was listed at its value of $325,000 on the asset side of the balance sheet, while a note to the former owner was listed on the liabilities side for the same amount, leaving a book value of zero. Next he found an investor who was interested in buying real estate and offered him a 50 percent interest in this corporation if he would loan $100,000 to the other corporation formed to hold the operating company. Then he went to the bank and borrowed another $300,000 against assets of the operating company to complete the $400,000 down payment. This deal closed after eight months in October 1976.

When this deal closed Dave received a phone call from a man who had heard about it and was interested in selling the 57 percent interest he held in an aerospace subcontract manufacturing company. This time Dave's target was to acquire at least 80 percent of the stock so that the company could be consolidated for tax purposes with a new corporation which would pay off the purchase price. Negotiating with the major shareholders, he managed to find two who would accept notes for their stock with no money down and a third who wanted $100,000. Forming another new corporation with two partners, Dave arranged to borrow the $100,000 from the bank against stock holdings of the new company plus personal guarantees of the partners, plus another $150,000 for working capital in the operating company against its assets. After taking over, they had the operating company make tender offers to buy stock back from its shareholders until the new corporation's holdings would represent 80 percent of the stock outstanding. This deal closed in February 1977; and within three months the holdings were up to 77.1 percent, leaving only 2.9 percent to go.

Through this creative dealing Dave Ederer had managed over three years to acquire four companies, all with essentially no money down on his part and without sacrificing his personal life and many community activities. "No more eighteen-hour workdays for me," he said. "I did that for ten years at Price Waterhouse and that was enough. Now I go home at five o'clock whether there is more work to do or not." So far, all the acquisitions have remained in the black and the outstanding debt is being paid down ahead of schedule.

The *installment payments over time* used by Dave Ederer were straightforward, fixed amounts over a specified time to reach a fixed price and paid out of earnings of the companies. Each payment would represent a certain portion of the principal due plus a certain amount of interest. The principal could not be deducted as an expense by the company but would be taxable only on a capital gains basis by the seller. The interest would have to be taxed as income to the seller but could be deducted as an expense by the company. Yet another approach can be to cast the installment payments in the form of contractual payments to the former owner as a consultant, in which case they are taxable as ordinary income to him or her but can be fully deducted as expenses by the company.

Another variation on use of installment payments which deserves special note as a marvelous variation is to cast them in the form of a royalty based on sales. Doing so can be a deft way of handling the sometimes difficult issue of how much goodwill is worth. The entrepreneur described in the preceding chapter's section on preliminary screening, who discovered valuable assets in a money-losing company that had been on the market for three years, made highly effective use of a royalty arrangement to perform a noncash buyout as follows:

♦   The book value of the company was $300,000, and although the family who had inherited it knew it included assets written below their real value, they did not know how much. The entrepreneur hired professional appraisers and found that the true value was closer to $750,000, with $180,000 worth of machinery and equipment, $350,000 worth of real estate, and the remainder in receivables and inventory less liabilities. In the most recent year the company had lost $79,000 on sales of $150,000. Nevertheless, there were three other buyers competing for the company who had the entrepreneur worried. One was an out-of-state company, which was annoying the family by moving very slowly. The other two were individuals, both offering down payments of under $20,000, which the family considered too little.

To beat these competitors the entrepreneur decided to move faster with a bigger down payment. He offered the family book value of $360,000 with $75,000 down plus a royalty of 5 percent on all future sales over $150,000 of products currently in the company's line for thirteen years or up to $500,000, whichever came first. On the unpaid balance of principal, interest would accrue at the current prime rate of each year. There would be no payments beyond the down payment in the first year, interest only the second year, and twenty-six equal principal payments in the ensuing thirteen years.

To secure the principal owed ($360,000 minus $75,000 down equaled $285,000), he pledged the real estate and persuaded a wealthy acquaintance to become a partner and take 20 percent of the stock (which the company later repurchased) in exchange for cosigning the remaining principal. Pointing out to the owners that the real estate alone was worth more than enough to secure the debt, he asked for and received free title to the equipment and other assets. On these the bank readily loaned him $100,000, which covered the $75,000 down payment and left $25,000 for working capital. The owners saw a potential price of $360,000 plus $500,000 in royalties and took the deal. The entrepreneur became owner of the $750,000 company for essentially no investment on his own part beyond the $1,000 spent in legal fees to write up the transaction.

There are a number of factors worth noticing in this deal. A main one is the use of a *royalty* to sweeten the offer. From the seller's point of view, it offered hope of a substantially increased sales price; but from the entrepreneur's point of view—although it would cut into profits if the company succeeded—it was a risk-free gamble. In the first place, it did not cut into income until the company was above a sales volume that he estimated would allow, after trimming of expenses, breakeven. Second, if he could not turn the company around, he could put a stop to the royalty by liquidating the company, which would still net him more than he had paid. Finally, it applied only to present products, so that if the company prospered and expanded its line, there would be no penalty on new products. As it turned out, the sellers got the $500,000, but the entrepreneur made vastly more.

Another important component, which cropped up in some of the earlier examples as well, was use of a *cosigner* to facilitate obtaining debt. Here the cosigner was rewarded with 20 percent of the stock for putting up no money and actually taking little or no risk. But it was critical to making the deal go through, and it put a wealthy backer in the entrepreneur's corner, so that if other financing were needed there was someone to turn to. There are many ways in which cosigning can be worked. The following example will briefly illustrate another.

◆ An entrepreneur who was just beginning to get his small wooden novelty products company up to breakeven ran into a cash bind. The inventory and accounts receivable were such that banks would not lend on them, and there was not enough time to work through an SBA loan. Consequently, he approached a consultant with a proposal that the consultant cosign a loan at the bank for $25,000. In return, he offered to give the consultant 30 percent of the company's stock, plus a guarantee that the company would buy back the stock within two years for $25,000. Thus he would get the loan he needed plus the interest of a consultant who, to preserve his stake, might be willing to help the company out with counsel. The consultant would, if the company survived, get a profit of $25,000 on an investment of zero for assuming the risk of cosigning the note.

This example also illustrates another technique seen before, which is the use of *stock as payment* to buy assistance. Once the venture is going, this particular form of payment tends to take on progressively more power, reflecting the increasing worth of the company. Two young entrepreneurs, for instance, bought a restaurant and incorporated it. Then they bought a second restaurant by offering some stock from the first as part of the payment. The second restaurant they absorbed into the corporation, giving the stock still more value and enabling them to use it to buy a third restaurant. Within a couple of years they had built an entire chain of restaurants, all through purchase with stock in their expanding corporation. As a note of caution, however, there are many entrepreneurs who gave away stock too early in their companies' experience and later regretted it. This might happen, for instance, in attempting to save money on incorporation by offering the attorney a share of the company, perhaps 5 percent, in lieu of a fee. By the time the company reached a value of $100,000 that 5 percent would already represent $5,000, or roughly five to ten times the typical incorporation fee.

Options constitute a highly versatile ingredient for putting together acquisition deals. These can work to expand the choices of either party in the transaction. In the wood novelty products example above, the cosigner was to receive a choice between payment of $25,000 after two years or retaining 30 percent of the company's stock. In an example mentioned earlier, an entrepreneur proposed to work for a year at no pay for a tour company he wanted to buy in return for a percentage of the stock plus an option to buy the rest at a stated price. In yet another case, an entrepreneur offered to work for a manufacturing company for three months at no pay, doing any jobs management proposed, in return for an option to buy the company at whatever terms were mutually acceptable. The objective of the option was to give him time to become familiar with the company, to size up both its potential and his ability to operate it, as well as to line up the wherewithal to finance the deal. All that was required of the sellers was that they allow the entrepreneur three months to make up his mind about the mutually satisfactory deal. If he took it, they had what they wanted, plus the assurance that he was more likely to make a success of it and be able to pay them off. If he did not, they lost the three months but received several thousand dollars' worth of his efforts at the company for compensation.

Leveraged Buyouts

Recent years have seen numerous "leveraged buyouts" wherein an entrepreneur or small group borrows against assets for a down payment plus working capital and then pays off the loan through earnings of the business. Some of these have been buyouts of small independent companies, but many have been buyouts of divisions of larger companies that for some strategic reasons want to divest. Reasons for selling include lack of fit between the division and the corporation, desire to trim an organization that has become somewhat unwieldy and diverse down to a more manageable size, desire to get rid of a division that may be losing market share or money or both, and desire to convert more corporate assets to cash.

All of these reasons can create a situation where the division to be sold is valued substantially below what it is really worth. Often assets will be old enough that the purchase price shown on the books is, because of inflation, far below what they could currently be sold for. Other assets may, for reasons of tax advantage, have been written down or written off or may have depreciated to far below their value. If the entrepreneur can then buy these assets for the value shown on the books or something close to it, the purchase will be a great bargain.

Mitton has illustrated such a case wherein a division manager acquired his division from a corporation that was headquartered far away and had lost interest in it.[3] Essentially, he agreed to buy inventory for cash and pay book value for the fixed assets over time. The seller would keep receivables and take care of payables on the books.

Thus the balance sheet (simplified) at acquisition was as follows (amounts in thousands):

Assets		*Liabilities*	
Inventory	$100	Loan	$400
Fixed assets	400	Equity	100
Total	500	Total	500

However, since the fixed assets were worth more than had been paid for them, $1 million versus $400,000, a restatement of the balance sheet after the transaction looked quite different:

Assets		*Liabilities*	
Inventory	$100	Loan	$400
Fixed assets	1,000	Paid in equity	100
		"Added" equity	600
Total	1,100	Total	1,100

This increase in the equity amount from $100,000 to $700,000 reveals why an entrepreneur can often buy a business with no personal money down on a leveraged buyout. He or she simply borrows in effect against the equity for a down payment, usually from a bank. The former owner is fully secured by the fixed assets, but at their original book value amount rather than their actual value. Beyond the down payment the entrepreneur can borrow still more to cover working capital. Suppliers will then be willing to extend trade credit against the highly solvent business, and the entrepreneur is off and running with a conventional-looking balance sheet like the following:

[3] Daryl G. Mitton, "The Anatomy of a Leverage Buyout," in Karl H. Vesper, *Frontiers of Entrepreneurship Research, 1984* (Wellesley, Mass.: Babson Center for Entrepreneurial Studies, 1982), p. 414.

Assets		Liabilities	
Cash, prepaid interest and inventories	.200	Accounts payable	$400
Accounts receivable	400	Notes payable	100
Fixed assets	1,000	Loan	350
		Paid-in equity	100
		"Added" equity	600
		Retained earnings	50
Total	1,600	Total	1,600

What made this possible was essentially that the entrepreneur was able to value the division much more highly than the company selling it. This was due to (1) accounting conventions that prevented the parent company from valuing the division up on its books, (2) the parent company's disinterest in the division, and (3) the entrepreneur's ability to manage the division better through closer attention, different strategy, and higher dedication.

The kind of company most eligible for an LBO may be, as Kelly, Pitts, and Shin have suggested, one in a relatively stagnant industry, with cash-rich resources and operational slack.[4] But to date there has been relatively little systematic study of the subject despite substantial attention in magazine articles and despite the fortunes that have been made through this approach.

The spectacular profit potential of a leveraged buyout can be illustrated by the acquisition of Gibson Greeting Cards from C.I.T. Financial, a money-losing subsidiary of RCA, by William E. Simon in 1982, as related by Mitton:[5]

♦ The price was $81 million, substantially below Gibson's book value. Simon and his associates put up $1 million, but it was largely a token payment. They had persuaded RCA to lend them the rights to the real estate, which they could sell during the transaction to a tax shelter firm, W. P. Carey, who in turn leased it back to them. This gave them $35.4 million. They borrowed $13 million against machinery from Barclay American Business Credit and another $100 million against inventories from G. E. Credit to cover the remainder of the purchase price and provide working capital.

To reflect the new asset value and take advantage of the 1981 Tax Act depreciable property carried on the books at $18.7 million with a 50-year depreciation schedule was written up to $35 million on a 15-year schedule. This reduced the tax liability in such a way as to free up nearly $2 million in additional cash flow. Removal of the overhead charges Gibson had been paying RCA yield another $10 million per year.

Simon became chairman, but the existing management team was given 11% of the stock to stay on, including president Thomas M. Cooney with 5.4%. The first year after takeover revenues increased by $20 million and earnings by $2.4 million. The company crossed over into the black in early 1983 and the

---

[4] James M. Kelly, Robert A. Pitts, and Bong Shin, "Entrepreneurship by Leveraged Buyout," in Robert Ronstadt, John A. Hornaday, Rein Peterson, and Karl H. Vesper, *Frontiers of Entrepreneurship Research, 1986* (Wellesley, Mass.: Babson Center for Entrepreneurial Studies, 1986) p. 281.

[5] Daryl G. Mitton, "No Money, No How, No Who," in John A. Hornaday, Fred Tarpley, Jr., Jeffry A. Timmons, and Karl H. Vesper, *Frontiers of Entrepreneurship Research, 1984* (Wellesley, Mass.: Babson Center for Entrepreneurial Studies, 1984), p. 424

company went public at a valuation over $280 million. Simon's 28% had become worth $78 million. By mid-1986 *Fortune* reported that Wesray, the partnership formed by Simon and Ray Chambers, had made 20 leveraged buyout acquisitions and so far cashed out on six, including Gibson's, for a profit of $245 million against $14 million cash invested.[6]

"The largest leveraged buyout in recent years has been that of RJR Nabisco, whole board of directors approved a $24 billion buyout by Kohlberg, Kravis, Roberts & Company."

Notwithstanding the glamour stories of leveraged buyouts, not all are successful, as illustrated by the following:

◆   Duncan Soldner, Vaughn Paul, and Siddarth Shah with financing from Citicorp bought Mushroom King, a subsidiary of Castle & Cooke, for $13.8 million in 1985. At the urging of Citicorp, they later claimed, they promptly fired 100 people, cut research, and slowed payments to creditors. Production fell 27%, and soon the company had trouble making its payments to the bank, which foreclosed, locked the plant, and left $3.5 million worth of mushrooms to rot. Eventually, another company bought the enterprise at auction for $4.1 million and the three entrepreneurs sued Citicorp. Soldner said, "I don't believe our problems came from the business we were entering into or from our plan. We could have made a lot of money for a lot of people. What wasn't sound was the way the bank interfered with our management."[7]

Dealing with Financing Sources

Typically, financing will be needed for two things, to buy the business and to provide working capital. The seller will probably be the main source of financing by being willing to accept some sort of down payment and the remainder as a debt to pay off the remainder of the purchase price. Thus other sources will have to provide cash for the down payment plus working capital. Possibly some of this cash may come from savings of the entrepreneur(s) buying the business. But typically most of it will come from lenders.

The main lenders will most likely be

- Banks, which may loan against personal guarantees of the entrepreneur or others, receivables, inventory, plant, equipment, and land
- Individuals, who either may make loans to the entrepreneur or the company or may provide cash through purchasing selected assets and leasing them back to the company
- Finance companies, which may factor receivables or loan against other assets, typically at higher rates than banks, such as 4 percent over prime (the banks may charge about 2 percent over prime)

In dealing with such lenders, the entrepreneur will need to be alert to many factors, including the following:

[6] Ford S. Worthy, "Wes Threatens to Pull Out of Wesray," *Fortune,* July 21, 1986, p. 50.
[7] David Weber, "Will LBO'S Rise Again?" *California Business,* February 1988, p. 40.

- Having a firm deal on the purchase price and terms with the seller lined up and preferably signed before negotiating terms with the lender(s)
- Having a backup source in case the one hoped for backs down at some point
- Handling timing to make sure the financing is concluded before the seller backs out
- Having a written plan that shows how much will be needed when under different scenarios of performance and how the money will be repaid
- Having a verifiable list of assets with data such as aging that indicates how much each asset could be liquidated for
- Noticing any special costs such as service charges, prepayment penalties, up-front "points," prepayment charges, holdbacks on payments by lender, deposits to be forfeited if the entrepreneur switches lenders, and required reserves or compensating balances
- Being prepared to put up "earnest money" that may be forfeited if the buying entrepreneur backs out of the deal

There are of course many fine points in these financing arrangements not only where things can go seriously wrong but also where the entrepreneur can make costly, although perhaps not fatal, mistakes. Seeking professional advice on legal, contractual, and tax aspects can therefore be crucial.

TAX CONSIDERATIONS

In the above acquisition examples it will be noted that never did the entrepreneur pay the full price in cash. There are two reasons for this, one of which is that none of them had that much cash. But even if they could have raised it, there would have been a second reason not to, which is that if the initial payment exceeds 30 percent the seller has to take his or her profit on the sale all in one year for tax purposes rather than being able to spread it out. Hence the typical down payment in buyouts is 29 percent or less.

Another common feature of the examples is that each of the entrepreneurs first formed a new corporation and then had it pay the old owner, rather than paying the owner personally. This too was to reduce taxes. If the entrepreneur bought the company from his personal account, it would have been money that he had previously paid personal taxes on, and to replenish his personal account with money from the company he was buying, he would have had to pay personal taxes on that money, as it flowed from the company to his account. But by forming a new corporation with minimal paid-in capital (in these examples $500 each) almost no personally taxed money would have been used. The new corporation, owned by the entrepreneur from inception, could then buy the stock from the owner of the company being purchased, giving him a note for what was owed—still no taxes. Provided that the new corporation owned at least 80 percent of the purchased company's stock, the tax returns of the two companies could, in effect, be consolidated or merged to look like one company. Then as the company generated money, that money could be passed directly along to the old owner without flowing to the entrepreneur and getting taxed along the way. The corporation would pay its income tax, which it would have to pay anyway, but the entrepreneur would not. Moreover, any interest that was being charged on the note due the old owner for his stock could be charged against taxes as an expense.

A similar result could be achieved by another approach referred to as "seed purchase" in which the entrepreneur would buy a small amount of the stock from the owner and have the company buy back the rest of the stock from the old owner by giving him a note in exchange for it. Dave Ederer used a combination of this approach with the above approach in his fourth acquisition described earlier. An advantage of forming a new corporation to acquire the stock, however, is that the acquiring company can liquidate its newly acquired business any time within a two-year period and assign the cost it paid for the shares to property received in the liquidation and thereby obtain a higher basis for depreciation or for computing gain or loss on property later sold.

Better still in many cases is the approach used by Dave Ederer in his second acquisition, the metal-stamping company, which is to buy assets rather than stock. A corporation may not have the precise form the new owner might prefer. It can have hidden or undisclosed liabilities. There can be problems with recapture of depreciation if it is liquidated, or other tax complications that may come back to haunt it. Prior to the 1976 tax reform act there was sometimes a good reason to take a corporation that had losses from prior years which could be carried forward against later profits, but that law changed the rules in 1978 to take that advantage away. By purchasing only assets, the buyer can be more certain of what he or she is getting, and the transaction can sometimes be simpler.

A complicating exception, however, can be when buyer and seller argue over how much of the purchase price should be allocated to which of the assets. The seller's tax position is served best by allocating the price to assets that cannot be written off, such as goodwill, since there can then be no recapture of value on them and the seller can claim any difference between book value and sales price as a capital gain. But the buyer would prefer to attribute the value as much as possible to things that can be charged as expenses directly against income in the new company and thereby reduce its income for tax purposes. Inventory, for instance, would be such an item. After takeover the buyer can ship this highly valued inventory out and write it off against taxes. One tax accountant recalled the following episode, in which a nice solution was found.

◆   My client was buying a company in which the former owner had written his inventory way down to a low value to minimize his taxes. We were going through the assets and assigning the purchase price in the negotiations, and when we came to the inventory figure you could see his accountant start to get all tense and defensive. He said, "Well, we just can't show a high value on this or the tax man will come back and kill us." Well, we let him go on about it for about five minutes, and then I said to him, "I see your problem. Let's look at it this way. What will you be willing to give us if we let you drop the inventory price down to where you want it? Will you let us have half of what you save on taxes?" At that point their mouths both dropped open and they looked at each other. Then they said, "Sure, why not?" So we picked up half of their savings right there. Then we turned around and set things up in the new corporation to give us a LIFO inventory system, which meant we could keep that low value buried in the inventory and we didn't have to pay the taxes on it either.

When the individual values assigned to items in an asset buyout add up to less than the purchase price, the difference is what might be regarded as "goodwill." But for tax purposes it is generally best not to do so. Rather, it is better to price the company at the total value of the tangible assets for tax purposes and pay the owner in a different form than as part of the book price. One way to do this is to employ the former owner as consultant over a fixed period of years and at amounts that add up to the appropriate value. That way the former owner must report the amount as ordinary income and pay tax on it, but at least it will be spread over a period of years, and the corporation can deduct it as an expense and thereby justify paying him or her enough extra to make up for the taxes. If the buyer does not want the former owner as a consultant or on an employment contract, another alternative is to pay the former compensation in return for a convenant not to compete, again spread over a period of years.

As the tax accountant's deft handling of the inventory valuation negotiation above illustrates, working out the tax angles of an acquisition is an area in which virtuosity can yield substantial benefits. The complexities are limitless. For instance, it was noted at the start of this section that sellers generally prefer not to receive over 30 percent of the purchase price down, or their taxes go up. So suppose a buyer is going to pay 30 percent down and the remainder over time in payments that ignore interest. The Internal Revenue Service may then impute an interest amount to the payments, which thereby shrinks the amount of principal they represent and consequently shrinks them relative to the down payment, making it in effect expand to something greater than 30 percent, and the tax advantage is lost. Only a person with substantial experience in tax matters is going to be familiar with such subtleties. Other complexities can arise when an acquired corporation is consolidated into the acquiring one, or when an acquiring corporation uses its stock to buy the stock of an acquisition or to buy assets rather than stock of an acquisition. More importantly, the tax laws constantly change, and only a person continually and currently working with them will be up to date. Consequently, an acquisition entrepreneur should make it a point to obtain advice from an experienced tax accounting specialist and also from an appropriately specialized lawyer in finalizing the terms of any acquisition.

LEGAL ASPECTS

Purchase of selected assets is the simplest procedure from a legal point of view in many cases. The acquiring entrepreneur needs a bill of sale for the assets being bought and a certification by the former owner that the assets are free and clear, and this should be verified by contacting the appropriate state agency where any liens would have had to be filed to be binding. There needs to be a list of the assets that states the value of each for tax purposes. If a corporation is being bought instead of selected assets, the buyer should also obtain financial statements and warranties from the seller that they disclose the whole picture, including all liabilities that the company faces and whether such things as leases, patent rights, and other contracts are assignable. There should also be a statement to the effect that the company will be maintained "as is" between signing of the agreement and closing, that there will be no issues of stock, declaration of dividends, or other complications that would make the company worth less.

Many of these sorts of provisions may be included on a standard form, which can be obtained from a forms book in any law library. The entrepreneur should then take this to his or her attorney for revision and refinement. It should not be left to the seller's attorney. There can be substantial advantage in being the first one to have the agreement drafted and to have it checked by an attorney, and then let the other side and its attorney respond.

The attorney should also be consulted about laws to be complied with in closing the sale. There are "bulk sales acts" that require, for instance, that notice be posted by the buyer at least ten days before closing. The attorney knows how to make sure that assets are free of claims and liens and how to obtain certificates of assurance that appropriate taxes have been paid up to date by the seller. It is important to get the services of an attorney who is current in acquisition work for these and many other fine points, depending on the deal. For instance, there is a "doctrine of merger" in the law whereby representations and warranties by the old owner to the entrepreneur cease at the time the deal is closed. So the acquiring entrepreneur should probably have a phrase added to provide that they will continue long enough beyond closing for him or her to make sure that they are not violated, perhaps a year or two. Maybe an audit should be performed to verify them, in which case they should continue until an audit can be completed. Or if there are suits or claims pending on the company, the representations and warranties should be extended long enough to see those satisfactorily settled. It may be that an escrow account should be used for holding the down payment until the warranties can be checked out, as a way of protecting the buyer, and if so then the exact handling of this money needs also to be spelled out in the purchase agreement.

The following case involved purchase of a company based on incomplete information with use of special features in the purchase agreement to provide safety for the buyers.

◆   Two entrepreneurs, who had made substantial profits from a restaurant venture which they had built into a chain and later sold out, began looking for another venture. This time they used acquisition as an entry mode. After searching for three years and rejecting many companies as unsuitable, they found one that appeared highly promising. It manufactured a proprietary line of commercial products, had been in business for many years, had a good reputation in the trade, a healthy cash balance, no debt beyond current payables, and an aging owner who wanted to sell out and retire. Preliminary negotiations proceeded favorably, and the partners decided to perform a detailed checkout. Auditors were engaged to check the books, and quickly some serious problems surfaced. The company's inventory accounting practices were found to be so slipshod that no sense could be made of prior performance figures.

It was the impression of the partners that the company owner was not trying to hide anything from them. A check with other members of the business community through the bank turned up the fact that he was regarded as an honest man with whom to deal. His own best interest would have been to understate the inventory so that income would also have been on the low side for tax purposes, and messy records would have worked more to his advantage than that of the tax collector. The partners decided to press on with the deal. Because they knew the costs of further auditing and legal work would be high, they told the owner that they did not want to chance the expense only to lose the deal to a competitive buyer, and consequently that if any other buyer were brought into the picture they would break off their checkout and negotiations immediately. (They later learned that the owner did in fact turn away other buyers while they were negotiating).

While the accountants were establishing current values for the books, terms of the purchase agreement were worked out with an experienced attorney. The owner was to guarantee that he did not know any information detrimental to the company, such as impending lawsuits, or new competitive products or techniques that would threaten sales. The purchasers were guaranteed that the former owner would assume liability for any breaches of product warranties or tax liabilities of the company that had occurred prior to title transfer. The prior owner also agreed to guarantee the net worth as being at least as large as that reported on the books and to sign an agreement not to enter competition with the company after sale. Finally, it was arranged that 20 percent of the purchase price would be placed in an escrow account for three years to cover any receivables that proved uncollectable, unanticipated prior liabilities that arose or breaches of representations and warranties. A new corporation was then formed, which bought the stock from the old owner, after which the companies were consolidated and depreciable assets were stepped up to reflect the full purchase price and afford maximal tax write-offs. No hitches developed and the company proceeded very profitably under the new owners.

To economize the attorney's time and also help him or her shape the eventual terms as closely as possible to the entrepreneur's preference, it can be helpful to write a draft agreement first and then present it to the attorney for refinement. A checklist of some possible things to include in such an agreement appears in Table 10–3. Not that attorneys necessarily do better. One attorney for a company purchaser recalled poor workmanship on an acquisition agreement that had been prepared by the seller's attorney:

◆   It was simply an incompetent application of the forms book, leaving crucial points so vague that they could be interpreted to mean almost anything. For the price of the deal it said "approximately $250,000." I asked why and they said because they couldn't give an exact valuation yet. The company was a warehouse distributor, and they had to wait for a computer run to get the inventory. So I had them put in a clear formula for exactly how the price would be determined. They had completely left out the covenant not to compete. So we made them add that. There was another place where the wording was garbled and I asked what they meant by that. The other man's attorney said, "I don't know; Let's take it out."

The importance of having an attorney who both knows the specialty of writing acquisition agreements and is aggressively alert to the best interests of his client was stressed by another entrepreneur, who concluded a couple of years after the acquisition that the seller had attempted to take advantage of him, where-

TABLE 10–3 POINTS TO INCLUDE IN A COMPANY ASSET PURCHASE AGREEMENT

1. Names of parties.
2. Description of what is being purchased, list of items with prices of each added to total sale price, machinery, equipment, fixtures, furnishings, tools, supplies, drawings, charts, models, patents, licenses, process rights, orders in process or on hand, inventory, files of customers, manufacturing information, catalogs, procedures, lease, and rights to company names and trademarks.
3. Payment terms, how much cash down, time payments, interest rate and dates due, plus formula for determining any contingent payments or performance payments (such as royalties on sales).
4. Adjustments to be made at closing, such as those based on inventory count, rent, contracts, deposits, and insurance premiums.
5. Contracts and liabilities to be assumed by purchaser.
6. Seller's warranties as to legal ownership of things being sold, clear titles without encumbrances or liens, valid financial statements, no undisclosed liabilities, pending litigation or government actions, other threats to business known to seller, fullness of disclosure by seller, authority of seller to perform the transaction and hold harmless of buyer. (Stock sales can impose other rules.)
7. Duration of warranties and representation, whether they will end at closing or continue and if so, for how long.
8. Conduct of business up to closing by seller to maintain it in good shape, keep records up to date, allow access by buyer, comply with bulk sales act, and turn over title, records, and business at closing.
9. In case of deterioration of business, what are the seller's responsibilities and the buyer's rights, such as cancellation of the deal? What are the remedies or adjustments to be made?
10. Noncompetition agreement by seller for what line of work, in what capacity, for how long, within what geographical region. What amounts buyer is to pay for this and when. (This item needs to be given a specific dollar value and capitalized on the balance sheet, so that straight line depreciation can be charged against it to reduce taxes.)
11. Terms of any employment agreement or consultancy contract for engaging the seller—times, services, and amounts to be paid.
12. Closing—when, where, who is to deliver what in the form of agreements, bill of sale, and under what conditions. Who is responsible for what share of taxes, vacation pay, shipments, utility bills, rent and other liabilities?
13. Indemnification—for what things must the seller reimburse the buyer, such as liabilities beyond those agreed to, damage of company prior to closing, breach of warranty by seller, or nonfulfillment of any terms by seller?
14. Brokers—whether there is a broker involved who is eligible for commission, and if so who, how much is due, and who should pay?
15. Arbitration of disputes—how disputes will be settled, such as by using a panel of three arbitrators, one from each party and a third chosen by the first two.
16. Approvals—who has to approve the contract to make it valid?

upon the entrepreneur utilized a feature that his attorney had written into the purchase agreement to retaliate. The entrepreneur recalled:

◆   A year and a half after I got into the business, sales took a nosedive. It turned out that the market in our main line of work went in two-year major cyclical swings. It hadn't been possible to see that in the books, because they weren't very clear and the business had gone through a bunch of complicated transactions before I got it that obscured that bit of history. I would clearly have been unable to make payments to the former owner at that point if it had not been for the fact that by a stroke of good luck, I had moved us into some new lines that just happened to help balance out the swing. The owner got very tough about the payments when that dip hit us, and I was scrambling like crazy to make his payments, and somehow we made it, although just barely.

Then by chance I heard from someone I knew who knew a friend of the owner that he had been bragging in private about how he had figured all along that the cycle would hit and I wouldn't be able to make payments and he would get the business back along with everything I had paid out. That really made me mad, so I hit him back with a little weapon my lawyer, who was smarter than his lawyer, had written into the agreement. The way it was set up, control shifted from him to me when my payments added up to a certain amount. As soon as that point came, I kicked him off the board of directors. He also had an employment contract, but it contained four words that let me save about $12,000 at his expense. They were "or as a consultant." When I took control I switched him from employee, which meant full time, to consultant, which meant it could be interpreted as less than half time. That let me cancel the health insurance contract the company was carrying on him and also his FICA, which saved the company $2,000 a year over the next six years.

Both legal and accounting skills must work together, whether possessed by one person or by more than one on the acquisition team. Another attorney recalled the advantage his client had enjoyed over a seller whose attorney lacked understanding of financial statements:

◆   He had tried to write in some things to protect his client by tying the hands of my client who was buying the business. At one point he stuck in a phrase to the effect that the buyer would not increase his salary or sell off assets. I managed to add to it a phrase that said "except for bonuses based upon performance," which nullified the whole thing completely. Then at another point he had some reference to maintenance of book value. I persuaded him that it would make more sense to substitute maintenance of an appropriate current ratio. We were talking in front of his client, and I guess he didn't want it to show that he didn't know what the term "current ratio" meant, so he didn't fight it. He also accepted it when I said a current ratio of one to one should be sufficient, and since for that line of business a current ratio of about twenty to one was common and this particular company had one much higher than that, we were home free.

Entrepreneurs sometimes differ regarding who was the most important aid in an acquisition. The accountant, the lawyer, the banker, and many times the partners or other key backers are nominated. Clearly, it can depend on both the talents of the particular entrepreneur and the acquisition situation. The safest bet probably is to recruit a team that includes at least an accountant, a lawyer, and a banker who have prior acquisition experience and are willing to take an interest in the project and to have them informed and ready to help either before or as soon as serious negotiations with a seller begin.

NEGOTIATION

The lore of negotiation is virtually endless, and there is no tight set of rules for how to perform it with respect to company acquisitions in particular. Each entrepreneur develops his or her own preferred style, strategies, and tactics. There are books and articles that advocate particular rules of operating: Try to arrange the meeting on your "territory," because you will exhibit greater confidence there. Take the initiative by writing out a proposed agreement before the other side does, so that the points for negotiation begin from where you are standing rather than where he is. Bring a team to the negotiation to intimidate the other side. Arrange the seating so that you dominate, by sitting at the head of the table. Project an image of success by being well groomed, well organized, fast moving, and appearing confident of what you want. Try tactics like those used by police interrogators wherein one member of the team is antagonistic and the other one is friendly. Assume that phrases like "to tell the truth" really mean the opposite and that the stated reason for telling is not the real one. Try to win over your opponent as a friend. Always ask initially for more than you expect to get. Meet ridiculous requests by talking around them or else by countering with equally ridiculous counterrequests. Ask questions that draw a pattern of "yes" answers from your opponent; then, when it is established, slip in what you really want to request. Once an agreement is reached, leave the scene quickly; don't keep it open by further discussing.

Concerning many of the rules, people experienced in negotiating express contrasting opinions. One will advise to yield on small issues early in the negotiation to set a congenial tone, whereas another will advocate taking a small issue and holding firm on it, "just to show your opponent that you can hold your ground and be obnoxious if you have to." Some have emphasized the importance of not procrastinating: "Follow through as directly as you can, because it is all too easy for the other side to change its mind if you wait," while another well-seasoned rule of thumb is "Be sure to sleep on the deal before you sign," and "If it doesn't work out today, don't give up, try again another day, maybe through an agent."

There are at least two good reasons for seeking to learn about rules like these, most of which have been demonstrated by somebody's successful experiences. The first is that by being aware of them the entrepreneur may be better able to choose those that can best serve him or her. They can be learned by reading books and articles on negotiation and by discussing them with people who have been through business negotiations. A second reason is that by being aware of such deliberate tactics, an entrepreneur can detect whether he or she is being subjected to them by the other party in the transaction. Often when people attempt to apply such rules, particularly without practice, it shows.

Some rules are particularly hard to dispute. One is that the more a negotiator knows about what he or she is attempting to buy, the better the negotiating position. This puts emphasis on prior careful checkout of the company and consideration of what kind of deal would make most sense to both parties for exchanging it. It is also hard to argue with the notion that the better a negotiator understands the desires of the other side, the better. It is all too easy, for instance, to assume that the other side cares most about price when in fact the more influential factors may be security of the deal, assurance that the company will be continued successfully, or that the pride of the other side will not be somehow threatened by the outcome of the transaction. Sensitivity to the other person is a point stressed often by experienced negotiators. An entrepreneur may be able to learn things about the other party prior to negotiating through inquiry, and there are signs, including direct statements, "body language," and reactions of the other person in discussion that may reveal more about what the other party wants. The general rule seems to be to attempt to find this out and to look for ways during the negotiation to give the other party what he or she wants most. The skills involved in doing this are ones that can be practiced a great deal in everyday life if any entrepreneur wants to do so. Opportunities can be found for small negotiating matches, scheduling of meetings, committee discussions, agreements with superiors, subordinates, family members, and friends. Even games like poker are advocated by some as ways to build up negotiating skills for later situations such as company acquisition, where they may be important.

Some other less-disputed rules for negotiating are fairly mechanical, and although they may seem like common sense, may be easy to slip on: Verify material facts upon which key decisions hinge. Don't accept evasive answers that may obscure important points. Make sure that each point is clear to the other party and then write it down so that it will not get lost. Deal with principals if at all possible, rather than agents. (The other side of this rule can be for the entrepreneur to use an agent to deal with the other principal. The agent can attempt to draw out the strategy of the other side so that the entrepreneur can know it before entering personally. Also, the agent can take strong positions on major issues and then back down by being overruled, whereas it may be more difficult for the entrepreneur to do so personally.) Keep looking for the sticking points of the deal, asking such questions as "What are you afraid of?" and then looking for ways to write in phrases to take care of them.

How best to use attorneys is a question on which viewpoints differ. There are some entrepreneurs who regard attorneys as generally "deal killers" because they are so skilled in finding things to worry about, and in raising objections. Others counter with the view that the right attorneys are ones who do not do that and who have demonstrated experience in successfully concluding deals that protect their clients. There is some agreement that generally it is better for principals to negotiate first without attorneys present, both to avoid the discussion's becoming too formal or complex and to save money on attorney's fees. The two parties can draft up their mutual understanding, and each can take a copy back to an attorney for review and advice. Then after meeting more times and reaching successively more final agreements, the principals can bring in attorneys to tie up the final details and to make sure that the written agreement is appropriately certified.

In Victor Kiam's acquisition of Remington the price was set by Sperry, which owned Remington, at $25 million, approximately book value. After checking the books and making inquiries in the shaver marketplace, Kiam decided to move ahead. His negotiation activity was heavily mixed with making contacts, obtaining information, and exploring possible ways of making the deal work out. Sperry gave him seven weeks to do it:

◆   "I had to find an institution to arrange debt financing," he recalls. "I had several prospects. Prior to calling on them, I wanted to get advice from someone who was an expert on lending institutions."

Through his lawyer, Kiam met a bank vice-president, who in turn introduced him to an executive in the bank's finance department. Kiam asked how much could be borrowed on the company's various assets. The banker estimated that about $6 million in equity capital would be needed to raise the purchase price.

Rejecting $2 million from an investor who wanted two-thirds of the equity for it, Kiam next hired the bank to help seek equity. The bank's customary fee for this service was $50,000 down plus another $50,000 upon delivery. Kiam negotiated instead to pay the bank $5,000 down plus another $195,000 if the bank found the equity.

A sequence followed in which (1) that bank itself declined to make the loan, (2) other banks either were working with other prospective buyers of the company or were too small for the size of the deal, (3) a combination of federal and state agencies appeared willing to lend $19 million against the company assets, which would leave a gap of $6 million, (4) Sperry refused a request to drop the price $3 million, (5) Sperry agreed to take a $4 million mortgage plus $3.5 million in notes, with $250,000 cash upon signing and another such amount thirty days later.

Selling his painting collection to raise the cash, Kiam signed. Now he still needed the bank loan. A report of the sale in the *Wall Street Journal* brought forth contact with one of the banks that had been working with one of the rejected bidders. The consultant who had set up financing for that deal wondered if it could be applied to Kiam's deal instead and asked, "How does this stack up against what you have?"

Kiam replied, "I don't know. In some ways it's better, in some ways it's worse." He recalls thinking, "This was the truth. His financing was better because it existed; it was worse because it wasn't mine!" On that basis the deal went together. Kiam became the man who "like the razor so much he bought the company" for a price of $25 million. The total cash outlay was $200,000 to the bank he began with, $500,000 to Sperry, and $50,000 to the consultant.[8]

As a final viewpoint on negotiating, that of Dave Ederer might be noted after he had successfully performed his four acquisitions within five years:

◆   Frankly, I don't negotiate. I just look carefully at the company and estimate what it's worth. Then I ask the owner what he wants, and if he gives me something too high I tell him I can't make it and thank him for his time. On one of my deals, it went this way and the owner came back to me a few weeks later and told me he wanted to accept my position and look for a way to work it out.

I don't try to hide anything from the other side. In fact, just the opposite. I lay out the deal, my plans and my pro forma projections for the company to show him just exactly what I am going to try to do. I want him to know it all, so that he will be on my side later after we sign the deal when he may be able to help me. That way, if problems come up in the company his advice may show how to solve them. He may also help me find other deals. This is how I found one of them.

[8] Kiam, *Going for It,* p. 188.

And when I am talking to another deal, it helps to be able to send the person to someone else I bought a company from and let that person vouch for me as a person to do business with.

BANKRUPTCY TAKEOVER

Bankrupt companies represent a somewhat special kind of acquisition dealing, in that they involve working things out not so much with the former owner(s) as with other parties, principally creditors. Usually the entrepreneur in these cases will first have to line up some capital to inject into the failing company, either from savings or from other investors, and the next step is to approach creditors to negotiate some sort of payout terms with them. If the company has successfully petitioned through the courts for bankruptcy under Chapter XI, then it is in the hands of the existing management to work these things out, but if that fails, then the company typically proceeds to liquidation, at which time the entrepreneur still has a chance to take over by acquiring key assets of the company and starting it up again. This may, in fact, be the preferred sequence, because then the restarted company begins again with a clean slate and nothing owed to anyone, whereas if deals are worked out with creditors to stave off liquidation, then those deals hang over the company until they are paid out. In picking up the pieces from liquidation, the problem is to obtain all those necessary, and this generally takes more advance planning than simply showing up at the auction, as illustrated in the following example.

◆   The company manufactured travel trailers, and as of August 1976 was operating with an unknown, but clearly not very positive, net worth. It had been formed over a decade earlier by a gas station operator who began making trailers on the side. The company grew, but when an opportunity to sell it arose, he sold out. The buyers failed in their efforts to carry the company on, and when they defaulted on their payments, the former owner and his wife reclaimed it. While building the company back up, the owner died, leaving the company to his wife, who attempted to carry it on.

But then the Arab oil embargo of 1974 struck, and sales throughout the recreational vehicle industry dropped to virtually zero. In response, many large companies dissolved their trailer-making divisions and many small companies failed. This one went into Chapter IX bankruptcy, under which it was allowed to continue operating with debts to creditors to be paid off at a negotiated figure of ten cents on the dollar. But when the company's lease came due for renewal, the landlord decided to rent to another company, and the trailer enterprise had to move. During the move plant security became difficult to enforce, and much of the plant machinery was stolen. Soon the company was operating in another building, but at the expense of long hours at no salary to the woman who owned the company and her two sons. Replacing, repairing, and installing equipment used up the meager cash reserves and the company operated hand-to-mouth. Most suppliers required cash on delivery, and because the cash was so short, the company could pay for only small orders, which meant forgoing quantity discounts. Some supplies were even being bought at retail from local hardware stores on the owner's credit card. To reduce the heating bill, the central heating system of the plant was shut down and home electric space heaters scattered at only certain locations. Because the daytime temperature outside was warmer than the mean temperature of the plant, most employees at coffee breaks went outdoors to warm up. Several assemblers in the plant worked with gloves on to keep their hands warm. Wages were economized by hiring several workers on a prison work release arrangement which involved very low rates.

The owner attempted to interest a business professor who had looked at the company in becoming an investor and manager. Looking at the office, where the owner served as her own secretary, receptionist, and manager, he asked where the accounts payable file was. She pointed to a cardboard box against the wall, but when he looked in, it was empty. "Oh, that's right, I've been working with them," she said, and began shuffling among the various piles of papers on several vacant desks. During this shuffling he noticed one letter from someone who had received from the company a bad check and was threatening suit, and another letter from the Internal Revenue Service. Upon inquiring how much was owed to the government, he was told around $30,000 to the Internal Revenue Service for unpaid tax withholding plus over $100,000 to the Small Business Administration, which had guaranteed a loan at the company's bank. The professor decided that he was not interested in the company in that condition.

A month later he was somewhat surprised to receive a phone call from an entrepreneur who was interested in buying the trailer company. "Did you know," the entrepreneur asked, "that the company has gone bankrupt and closed shop?" The professor said he did not. "Did you know," the entrepreneur asked, "that the SBA has foreclosed and plans to auction off the assets?" The professor said he did not. "The auction will be held in two weeks," the entrepreneur went on, "and I thought it would be nice if you and I could have a meeting to discuss possible common interests."

The professor later recalled, "At that point it came together in my mind what this entrepreneur was trying to do. He wanted to pick up the company as cheaply as possible at the auction and would prefer that I not bid against him. I admired his clever foresight, but it turned out that that was not the half of it.

"We discussed where and when and decided to meet in front of the trailer plant, from where I assumed we would go to a nearby coffee shop and get a table. But instead when I got to the darkened plant, he pulled out a key and let us both in. I asked how he got it, and he told me he had purchased the lease that the trailer company was operating under and had thereby become the landlord of the plant. All the company's equipment was now effectively sitting in *his* plant.

"Then he told me he intended to buy the equipment at the auction and asked if I'd be interested in possibly teaming up. I asked which equipment he planned to buy, and he said all of it. It turned out that he had made a deal with the SBA to the effect that the auctioneer would start off by announcing that the equipment and inventory of the company would be auctioned off piecemeal, but that then the total would be added up, and if anyone was willing to bid ten percent above that total, the bidding would begin again on the lot as a whole. If nobody went ten percent above, then it would go piecemeal as previously bid.

"That impressed me too. That this man had set up an arrangement where he could bid on the lot if he wanted to in an auction where most people would be coming expecting to buy piecemeal. That could give him the plant intact.

"Then he pulled out two more high cards. First, he told me he'd had a meeting with the employees before the plant shut down and wanted them back. He said that those hired back would be paid the difference between what they would have made at their regular pay rates and the amount paid them as unemployment compensation while they were laid off. So he had his work force all lined up.

"He pulled a business card out of his pocket and asked if I recognized it. It was the trailer company's logo, and I asked so what. He said he had learned that the trademark was not owned by the company itself, but rather by the owner personally, and that she had sold it to him. So that gave him the market name recognition already in his pocket before the bidding began. That guy really knew how to pick a company up out of auction before the other players thought the game was beginning."

Here, even though he had never worked in trailer manufacturing, the entrepreneur did a beautiful job of anticipating his needs for resurrecting the company and of lining them up in advance. But there was still much more to be done. Auction buying in itself is something of an art form, and in this particular case some shady dealing by the auctioneer made the problem of acquiring the plant equipment particularly interesting:

◆   The entrepreneur sent a consultant early to the plant on the day of the auction to keep an eye on things. When the auctioneer came, the consultant heard him instruct one of the auction crew to load a roll of wire from the inventory into the auctioneer's car "to use in my attic," apparently thinking he was not observed or that nobody would care. Then during the auction the consultant noticed that the auctioneer sometimes announced nonexistent bids. "One hundred, who'll give one twenty-five, one twenty-five and one twenty-five and one fifty, now who'll go one fifty and one fifty, one fifty do I hear one seventy-five. One seventy-five. One seventy-five. Come on now fellas, who'll start it with a bid of one hundred?"
        After all the items had been auctioned off, bidding was begun on the lot as a whole. This procedure, prearranged by the entrepreneur and the Small Business Administration, had been announced at the beginning of the auction. Minimum starting bid for the lot as a whole had been set at 10 percent above the sum of the individual bids. As the bidding began, the entrepreneur took a position behind the auctioneer facing the audience, while the consultant stood in the audience facing the auctioneer. The bidding began and as each new bid was made the entrepreneur would nod his head, indicating to the consultant to keep bidding above each one announced. Finally, the auctioneer proclaimed him the winner at $20,000.
        Two weeks later the entrepreneur discussed the auction with the professor. "I accused the auctioneer of stealing the wire," he said. "The guy argued about it for a while and then backed down when I was going to go to the SBA with my witness and charge him. He promised to pay me for it. I also made him tell me who the person was who bid highest next to me, and then I checked with that person and he confirmed that he had done no such thing. Then I went to the SBA and told them the lot bids had been phony and I could prove it. They checked into it and told me I could have the lot for $13,000. So it didn't turn out too badly."

After obtaining the assets in this fashion, the entrepreneur went on to line up the other things he needed. He sought out and negotiated working arrangements with two key partners. One was a former plant manager in one of the trailer companies that had folded during the recent industry decline. The other owned and operated a large recreational vehicle dealership in the area. The entrepreneur persuaded each of them to invest a third of the estimated capital required in return for a third of the ownership, with the understanding that it would be the former plant manager's job to get production rolling and the dealer's responsibility to take charge of selling it. As the industry recovered from its depression, the company rose with it. Within a year the entrepreneur was negotiating for a larger building in which to expand operations.

SUMMARY

In contrast to the process of seeking out a company to buy, which is often tedious and discouraging, the process of negotiation once a company is found is usually intriguing, exciting, and enjoyable. The entrepreneur may seek only to obtain control, or to buy only selected assets, or to buy the whole company. There are many alternative ways of determining price, and the entrepreneur should probably consider all of them as a prelude to negotiating price and also terms, which can be an even more important part of the deal. Usually price is based largely on an appraised fair market value of assets plus some figure for goodwill as a percentage of historical gross or net, and usually terms consist of a down payment plus payout over time, but within these general patterns there are an enormous number of possible variations. In working these out it is often desirable for the negotiating parties to draft up some sort of purchase agreement of their own, and then to consult with specialists in both tax and legal aspects to make sure that nothing important has been overlooked.

appendix A

Corporate Ventures

Corporate venturing means doing new things, departing from what is customary to pursue opportunities that might otherwise (1) not be detected, (2) not be appreciated, or (3) not be effectively prosecuted even though appreciated. The departures may take many forms, may be more or less radical, may be initiated at different organizational levels, and may emerge at different stages in a given project. Historically, departures have at times played a crucial role in the development of companies, but there are relatively few studies. Generally, they occur "naturally," without programs or organizational contrivances designed to produce them. In recent years there have been some corporate experiments aimed at "cultivating" ventures. No record of consistent success from these has yet been reported.

The extent to which it should be possible for a venture to be created, develop, and operate inside a large organization, as opposed to simply inside the overall economy, is a question that has repeatedly been subject to academic discussion and corporate experimentation over the years.[1] The argument advanced to support concepts of "corporate entrepreneurship," "internal entrepreneurship," or "intrapreneurship" is that it should help make corporations more innovative and more responsive to new market opportunities while motivating employees through a greater sense of "ownership" in their intracorporate ventures.[2]

---

[1] For instance, Donald I. Orenbuch, "The New Entrepreneur or Venture Manager," *Chemical Technology*, October 1971, p. 584; K. H. Vesper and T. G. Holmdahl, "Venture Management in More Innovative Large Industrial Firms," *Research Management*, May 1963; Mack Hanan, *Venture Management* (New York: McGraw-Hill, 1976); Dennis R. Costello, *New Venture Analysis* (Homewood, Ill.: Dow Jones-Irwin, 1985).

[2] Gifford Pinchot III, *Intrapreneuring* (New York: Harper & Row, 1985).

Venture Forms

Corporate venturing can take a variety of forms, such as the following:

- *Strategically bold moves* wherein top management provides the venturing initiative. These may include not only internal startups but also acquisitions, joint ventures where two companies form and co-own a third, and strategic partnering where a large company and a smaller one team up to exploit a market or technology.
- *Venture division operation* wherein the corporation sets up an organizational subunit whose job is to encourage, spawn, nurture, and protect innovative projects that do not fit elsewhere in the organization. They may take the form of separate "skunk works" where ventures can develop their ideas, and/or "internal venture capital" offices that provide funding or grants for employees to pursue projects outside their accustomed jobs. The sponsoring entity may simply be one executive or a separate group or venture division.
- *External venturing* may also be undertaken through a venture office or venture division. In this activity, the venture is started somewhere outside the corporation, and the venture office becomes involved in it by either helping to fund it or acquiring it. The funding may take the form of research contracts to university researchers, for instance, or venture capital investment, possibly in collaboration with other venture capital firms.
- *Employee innovation programs,* often operated in conjunction with outside consultants, are activities undertaken to stimulate more venturing-type activities by more employees. Training sequences, incentive schemes, recognition awards, retreats, task forces, newsletters, and various kinds of hoopla may be undertaken to stimulate more innovative thinking by more employees.
- *Initiative from below,* where an employee goes beyond normal expectations of a job to pioneer a product or service, often beginning sub rosa and "bootlegging" resources informally that were assigned to other purposes, is another form of venturing. If successful, the project may eventually pick up a sponsor and move forward. If it does not pick up a sponsor, the employee will probably have to choose between dropping the venture and pursuing it outside the company.

Exceptional autonomy plus a dedicated champion seem to be necessary if new and different projects or ventures are to succeed. If the venture is to become substantial relative to the company's other activities, then higher executive support or sponsorship is also necessary.

Venturing Variables

From these different forms it can be seen that a host of variables can enter into the corporate venturing process. An alternative listing of venture types and significant variables was used by Ellis and Taylor for surveying corporate ventures.[3] Some dimensions along which ventures and their corporate circumstances can vary include the following:

1 Spontaneous ventures. These occur in the normal course of business without precalculation versus cultivated ventures that emerge from special programs designed to foster them.

2 Organizational setting and rules. What elements of the organizational setting foster ventures? Corporate culture and history are claimed to be important.

3 Objectives of the venture activity. They may include only "bottom line" results of the venturing or they may include the overall impact of the venturing on the organization. How accomplishments are to be measured in the latter case can be a problem.

4 Organizational level of the prime mover. Particularly in small companies, it usually seems to be the CEO. In large corporations, it may be subordinate employees.[4] Sometimes teams are involved. Sometimes ventures shift from one champion to another.

5 Other players and their positions. Who else besides the prime mover is crucial to the process? Sponsors who provide support and protection, and gatekeepers who provide needed information, as well as team members have been seen as important.[5]

6 Strategy and tactics used by the players. Some books have offered rules for both corporations[6] and individuals. Pinchot, for instance, has suggested "ten commandments" for entrepreneurs operating inside corporations.[7]

7 Major departures versus small innovations. Lee Iacocca's turnaround of Chrysler was hailed by some as a major entrepreneurial feat, while Kanter has characterized as entrepreneurial much smaller developments inside General Motors and other companies.[8]

8 Risk and commitment levels are dimensions of these major and minor ventures that have been given almost no treatment in the literature. It has concentrated mainly on organizational processes.

9 Venture outcome and its impact have also been given little analysis. The Strategic Planning Institute has published some data on variables correlating with corporate venture performance. For instance, Hobson and

[3] Jeffrey R. Ellis and Natalie T. Taylor, "Specifying Entrepreneurship," in Neil C. Churchill, John A. Hornaday, Bruce A. Kirchhoff, O. J. Krasner, and Karl H. Vesper, Frontiers of Entrepreneurship Research, 1987, p. 527.

[4] D. A. Schon, "Champions for Radical New Inventions," Harvard Business Review, March–April 1963, p. 84.

[5] E. D. Roberts and Alan B. Frohman, "Internal Entrepreneurship: Strategy for Growth," Business Quarterly, Spring 1972, pp. 71–78.

[6] Steven C. Brandt, Entrepreneurship in Established Companies (Homewood, Ill.: Dow Jones-Irwin, 1986).

[7] Pinchot, Intrapreneuring.

[8] Rosabeth Moss Kanter, The Change Masters (New York: Simon & Schuster, 1983).

Morrison reported on correlates with success, as were mentioned in Chapter 2[9] and in a study by Miller, Wilson, and Gartner[10] and in another by MacMillan and Day.[11] But these have all been limited to statistics based on ratios due to the nature of the PIMS database, and hence are abstract from other dimensions of the venture processes and limited.

Beyond these are two more general perspectives from which corporate venturing can be considered: the venture participant and the corporation. These two will mainly be used here, touching on the others as they may be involved.

Individual Perspective

The prime mover of a venture may be either the chief executive officer of the corporation or someone subordinate. Examples of the former would include the following:

- William Hewlett of the Hewlett-Packard company, who initiated the development of the company's pocket calculator because he wanted one, against recommendations of the company's market researchers, who predicted few would be sold.
- Kazuo Inamori, founder and CEO of Kyocera, a leading Japanese electronics company, who directed his researchers to undertake the development of artificial emeralds after he learned from a jeweler that such gems were in short and shrinking supply. When the established marketing channels would not accept his new gems, he had his company enter the retail jewelry business by establishing a store in Beverly Hills.

A venture leader can also occur lower in the organization and may be either appointed or a volunteer, or even a renegade. An appointed leader may be similar to simply a project manager except for other aspects that set venturing apart from typical projects. Kidder, for instance, describes a project team, working on a project it is not supposed to, inside a computer company where the project leader can be seen as a venturer with his own sub rosa enterprise.[12] Or it can involve an individual employee pursuing a venture solo, as illustrated by Don French at Tandy Corporation, who developed a prototype for the TRS–80

[9] Edwin L. Hobson and Richard M. Morrison, "How Do Corporate Start-Up Ventures Fare?" in John A. Hornaday, Jeffry A. Timmons, and Karl H. Vesper, *Frontiers of Entrepreneurship Research, 1983* (Wellesley, Mass.: Babson Center for Entrepreneurial Studies, 1983), p. 390.
[10] Alex Miller, Robert Wilson, and William B. Gartner, "Entry Strategies of Corporate Ventures in Emerging and Mature Industries," in Churchill et al., *Frontiers of Entrepreneurship Research, 1987,* p. 481.
[11] Ian C. MacMillan and Diana L. Day, "Corporate Ventures into Industrial Markets: Dynamics of Aggressive Entry," *Journal of Business Venturing,* Vol. 2, No. 1 (Winter 1987), 29.
[12] Tracy Kidder, *Soul of a New Machine* (Boston: Little Brown, 1981). Also see "Computer Engineers Memorialized Seek New Challenges," *Wall Street Journal,* September 20, 1985, p. 1, col. 7.

after management told him the company had no interest in computer products and he should not pursue them on work time.[13]

Aspects that may distinguish a venture from a conventional research or engineering project can include the following:

- A venture connotes a more complete business, including such elements as not only technical development but also profit responsibility, overall business planning, followthrough to market, production, selling, and servicing. In contrast, a project typically is more limited to particular functional specialties and lacks profit-and-loss responsibility.
- A venture usually involves a new direction for the firm or a more radical change in the way it does business, whereas a project connotes a more-limited innovation, usually in line with the accustomed strategy and direction of the company.
- A venture needs greater autonomy than a project because it fits less well with the company's customary procedures. This autonomy may come about by "hiding" the venture, by separating it geographically, or by housing it in a special organizational unit capable of shielding it from the normal company activities.

Corporate versus Independent Venturing

Autonomy can in some ways make the venture similar to an independent startup, but from the prospective internal entrepreneur's point of view, some major contrasts between venturing inside a corporation and venturing independently may be the following:

Internal Entrepreneurship	Independent Entrepreneurship
The person in charge of the venture still reports to a boss who has power of dismissal and can overrule decisions.	The one in charge of the venture has no superior officer, although subject to desires of customers, financers, and possibly directors and colleagues.
Financial risk is all carried by the parent company.	Financial risk is shared by the entrepreneur in charge, other shareholders, suppliers, and lenders.
Financial capacity is determined by parent company; outside sources may not be used without parental consent.	Financial capacity determined by venture itself; any sources can be used.

---

[13] Michael Swaine, "How the TRS–80 Was Born," *Infoworld,* August 31, 1981, p. 40.

Internal Entrepreneurship	*Independent Entrepreneurship*
Administrative formalities are decreed by the parent in such areas as accounting, personnel, contracts, public relations, advertising, and customer servicing.	Administrative formalities are at management's discretion and very minimal.
Success will not make a great amount of money for those in the venture. Can mean promotion.	The entrepreneur and founding investors may make millions. Can mean financial independence.
Failure will not put managers of the venture out of jobs. They can return to the parent.	Failure will mean that everyone in the venture, including managers, will have to find new employers.
Having managed an internal venture is likely to enhance career advancement if the venture succeeded and to retard career advancement if it failed.	Having managed an independent company is likely to enhance career advancement whether the venture succeeds or not.

Corporate Perspective

Almost all the discussion in the academic literature of corporate venturing is from the perspective of the corporation and corporate management, as opposed to that of the subordinate who carries out the venture. Some of it has been academic description of alternative venture forms. Schollhammer, for instance, suggested as alternative modes administrative, opportunistic, initiative, acquisitive, and incubative.[14] Much of it extols venturing as a kind of corporate elixir for rejuvenating the company and shifting its growth trajectory upward. The argument is generally based on one or more anecdotes of dramatic success in which a major product innovation occurred. The inference drawn is that if it happened in such an instance, then *it can be made to happen elsewhere by calculated management action.*

Circumstances under which corporations typically tend to go into one form of venturing or another are when (1) they are afraid they will not grow enough from "business as usual," (2) they have been losing creative employees and promising ventures to outside backers, (3) profits are up and cash is available, (4) takeover is a threat and management wants to "show some action," and (5) management develops enthusiasm because the concept of venturing is new or it has read and heard "wonder stories" of venture exploits at such companies as 3M.

A crucial distinction may be that of "natural" versus "cultivated" corporate ventures. The former refers to ventures that emerge in a corporation as exceptional events in the normal course of business. The corporation may be either traditionally innovative and supportive of ventures or not. In either case a "nat-

---

[14] Hans Schollhammer, "Internal Corporate Entrepreneurship," in Calvin A. Kent, Donald L. Sexton, and Karl H. Vesper, *Encyclopedia of Entrepreneurship* (Englewood Cliffs, N.J.: Prentice-Hall, 1982), p. 209.

ural" venture is an innovative episode that goes beyond whatever level of initiative and innovativeness the company is accustomed to. Virtually all the success stories about corporate venturing, such as those described by authors like Peters and Pinchot, have been of the "natural" variety. They have not been products of corporate venture cultivation programs per se.

A "cultivated" venture is one resulting from corporate policies introduced to stimulate ventures systematically. There are to date no published dramatic success stores in the literature from deliberate corporate venture cultivation programs. In fact, the current argument against corporate cultivation of ventures is that corporations that have tried cultivating them have often written such efforts off as expensive and unsuccessful.[15]

To this the proponents respond that the efforts either were not properly applied or were not pursued long enough to succeed. Fast observed from his study of corporate venture divisions that typically they were set up when old products were maturing, and profits and cash availability were high.[16] When later cash became short, profits turned down, new products began to catch on, or some combination of such events, management would decide the new ventures were costing a lot of money and could be dispensed with. The cycle of this phase-out might run for three or four years, which unfortunately is less than the time needed for the ventures to mature and begin to prove their worth. Hence they would be written off and venturing would appear in hindsight to have been a waste of time and money.

What both boosters and skeptics might agree on is that innovations can in hindsight be viewed as ventures but that they have not been produced consistently and profitably by formal corporate venturing programs. The experimentation nevertheless continues at companies like AT&T[17] and Eastman Kodak[18] and may yield discoveries in the future about how to perform corporate venturing more effectively.

Possibly such programs will, with more experimentation, become more effective in the future. The academic literature to date has not been massive enough to explore the possible relationships between management controllable variables (independent variables) such as those mentioned above and variables of management concern (dependent variables) such as innovation rate, sales growth, profits, or return on investment from venturing. Most academic literature so far has been confined mainly to articles like those of MacMillan, Block, and Narashima[19] or of Hisrich and Peters[20] describing how venturing seems to

[15] Robert K. Mueller, "Venture Vogue: Boneyard or Bonanza?" *Columbia Journal of World Business*, Spring 1973, p. 78.

[16] Norman Fast, "A Visit to the New Venture Graveyard," *Research Management*, Vol. 22, No. 2 (March 1979), 18–22.

[17] Dennis J. Cohen, Robert J. Graham, and Edwards Shils, "La Brea Tar Pits Revisited: Corporate Entrepreneurship and the AT&T Dinosaur," in John A. Hornaday, Edward B. Shils, Jeffry A. Timmons, and Karl H. Vesper, *Frontiers of Entrepreneurship Research, 1985*, p. 621.

[18] Colby Chandler, "Eastman Kodak Opens Windows of Opportunity," *Journal of Business Strategy*, Vol. 7, No. 1 (Summer 1986), 5.

[19] Ian C. MacMillan, Zenas Block, and P. N. Subba Narashima, "Corporate Venturing: Alternatives, Obstacles Encountered, and Experience Effects," *Journal of Business Venturing*, Vol. 1, No. 2 (Spring 1986), 177.

[20] Robert D. Hisrich and Michael P. Peters, "Internal Venturing in Large Corporations: The New Business Venture Unit," in John A. Hornaday, Fred Tarpley, Jr., Jeffry A. Timmons, and Karl H. Vesper, *Frontiers of Entrepreneurship Research, 1984*, p. 321.

happen "naturally," or describing dilemmas like freedom versus control identified by Sathe[21], or offering conceptual schemes such as those of Burgelman[22], or expostulating ideas of how it ought to happen. Fast, for instance, recommends corporate participation in venture capital partnerships.[23] There has been a trickle of reporting on outcomes of experiments in trying to cultivate it deliberately.[24] This last stream, if it becomes able to report consistent and significant results, could have powerful future implications.

[21] Vijay Sathe, "Managing an Entrepreneurial Dilemma," in Hornaday et al., *Frontiers of Entrepreneurship Research, 1985*, p. 636.

[22] Robert A. Burgelman, "Designs for Corporate Entrepreneurship in Established Firms," *California Management Review*, Vol. 26, No. 3 (Spring 1984), 154.

[23] Norman D. Fast, "Pitfalls of Corporate Venturing and Lessons to Be Learned from Venture Capitalists," working paper, Wellesley, Mass., *Venture Economics*, May 1, 1980.

[24] John E. Bailey, "Developing Corporate Entrepreneurs—Three Australian Case Studies," in Churchill et al., *Frontiers of Entrepreneurship Research, 1987*, p. 553.

Chemistry and Cultivation of Entrepreneurship

The purpose of this brief discussion is to introduce a framework and present a limited selection of facts as a basis for examining the chemistry and cultivation of entrepreneurship. A more extensive discussion appears in an earlier document by the author entitled *Entrepreneurship and National Policy*.[1]

Reasons for Interest

The chemistry of entrepreneurship—what makes it go and how—may not be of great interest or utility to a would-be entrepreneur who is more interested in finding his or her own venture and making it succeed than in learning how to stimulate more ventures by others. Governmental and institutional policy makers, however, may have more reason to be interested. The circumstances they manage will undoubtedly influence the rate and nature of new venture formation whether they intend it or not, and new venture formation is important to all economies, including the following.

Industrialized Economies

Jobs According to David Birch, large companies are a shrinking market for employment, and it is the rate of formation of new companies that governs

[1] Karl H. Vesper, *Entrepreneurship and National Policy* (Chicago: Heller Institute for Small Business, Walter E. Heller International Corporation, 1983).

the level of unemployment, not only in the United States but in Japan and the countries of Western Europe as well.[2]

Innovations Studies also indicate that numerous important innovations have come from new companies. For instance, the microcomputer industry was initiated by startup firms, both in hardware and in software.

Pursuit of Happiness Surveys repeatedly indicate that the idea of owning a business appeals to many people. Anecdotally, it is easy to find examples of people who left jobs to start companies, but not to find people who left their own companies to seek jobs.

Spur to Competition The extent to which startups prod established companies to perform better has not been systematically studied. Anecdotally, it can be observed that when airlines were deregulated, startups entered, some established firms failed, and then the established firms rebounded and absorbed or killed off startups, suggesting the possibility that the entry of startups made the established firms become tougher. *Business Week,* for instance, observed that "when deregulation opened up the industry, competitors such as People Express Airlines, Inc., popped up to grab market share from the older carriers, which fought back by cutting costs and merging with each other to create giant networks."[3]

Industrial Flexibility Established firms have great difficulty changing what they do. Consequently, when their markets are threatened they typically either seek government protection or turn to acquisitions or both. Startups undertake the new by their very nature and are therefore effective in helping an economy adapt. They are consequently expected to play a significant role in Europe if trade barriers within the common market are dropped as planned in 1992.

Underdeveloped Economies

A logical application of entrepreneurship is to help raise industrial output and resultant standards of living in subindustrialized countries. The question then becomes how to stimulate it. Should economic controls, incentives, and sanctions be altered, and if so, which ones and how? Should propaganda be promulgated to change social mores in favor of entrepreneurial activity? Should training programs be given to inculcate psychological qualities more akin to those that correlate with entrepreneurial success, perhaps further enhanced by technical training? Affirmative answers to such questions have been proposed by numerous academicians and bureaucrats, leading to governmental programs of various types, particularly in Latin America and India.[4]

A currently favored approach is that of the Peace Corps, which is seeking to develop "microenterprises," that is, profit-making startups as a way of helping economies advance. A Dominican Republic project claimed, for instance, to

[2] David L. Birch, lecture given to the National Federation of Independent Business, Colorado Springs, June 19, 1988; and Birch, *Job Creation in America* (New York: Macmillan, 1987).
[3] "It Wasn't Supposed to Be This Good for the Airlines," *Business Week,* August 8, 1988, p. 24.
[4] James W. Schreier et al., *Entrepreneurship and Enterprise Development: A Worldwide Perspective* (Milwaukee: Center for Venture Management, 1975).

have created six thousand jobs by loaning $1.2 million to 4,674 such enterprises with less than 2 percent of the loans being nonperforming.[5]

Communist Economies

In recent years the Communist countries have increasingly experimented with the relaxation of curbs against entrepreneurship to accelerate economic progress. Thus *Business Week* observed that in Poland, for instance, "entrepreneurs are springing up everywhere—and may be the key to reform."[6] And from outside the Soviet bloc as well have come reports of entrepreneurial developments in the People's Republic of China.[7]

Each of these environments differs significantly from the others. The implications of these differences have not been thoroughly studied and will not be explored here. The framework that will be developed below is based mainly on U.S. experience, although it may also apply to other situations.

Requisites for Entrepreneurship

There are four requisites for creating a venture: a practical business opportunity, technical knowhow, business knowhow, and resources. As depicted in Figure B-1, it is the job of the entrepreneur or entrepreneurial team to bring these four elements together in such a way as to make a venture viable. It may be possible for a policy maker to influence the availability of these elements and thereby the venture results.

Opportunity

Venture opportunities are continually cropping up—witness the fact that new ventures are formed in the thousands every week in the U.S., and many of them succeed. At the same time, other business opportunities are disappearing; hence there are always businesses failing at a rate close to, although usually slightly less than, the rate of startups. To some degree it could be said that the startups succeed at the expense of the other businesses that fail, usually by doing a better job. However, the failures exact a price in human disappointment, job displacement, and money. The argument in favor of entrepreneurship is that the benefits are more than worth this price. That can, however, be a hard argument to win politically. Consequently, in many industries there are governmentally imposed barriers to entry, such as import duties, licensing requirements, zoning ordinances, and favored supplier arrangements in purchasing.

Degrees of opportunity vary not only with time and locality but also with industry, as evidenced by the fact that the types of ventures that occur and where they occur will shift over time. Instead of auto companies, airplane companies, and microcomputer companies, the emphasis has recently been on

[5] "The Peace Corps' New Frontier," *Business Week,* August 22, 1988, p. 62.
[6] "For a Jump-Start, Poland Tries a Jolt of Capitalism," *Business Week,* August 8, 1988, p. 38.
[7] "Entrepreneurial Development in the People's Republic of China," *International Small Business Journal,* Vol. 5, No. 2 (Winter 1986/87), 37.

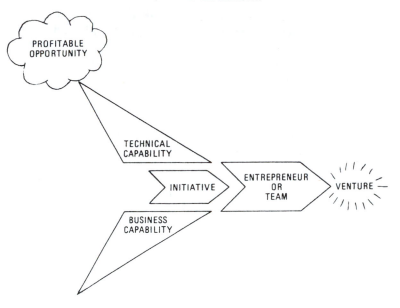

FIGURE B–1 ELEMENTS IN VENTURE CREATION.

biotechnology companies.[8] However, because of a cash shortage, the biotechnology industry has had a setback and prospects are not as bright as they once were. When the population of an area grows, possibly due to governmental action, plant relocation, or discovery of resources that people value, opportunities immediately arise for new firms in that area to provide construction, supply, and other services. Thus venture opportunities rise, fall, and shift over time and place.

Finally, it can be argued that when an opportunity occurs there is more than one company or person who could take advantage of it. Sometimes many do, and a new industry results. That industry may later "shake out." When it does, hindsight will usually reveal that those startups that failed might have survived had they operated differently. Presumably, then, others would have failed instead. Thus the processes of venture formation include degrees of freedom within which individuals can choose whether to attempt ventures or not and can influence their odds of success by actions they take.

Competence

To take advantage of a venture opportunity, the new business must possess both technical and business knowhow, as discussed in Chapter 2. *Technical knowhow* refers to the ability to make and sell what the venture will offer, and this knowhow must be professionally competitive. That is, the venture must be

Lawrence M. Fisher, "Biotech Plight: A Cash Shortage," The *New York Times,* Dec. 3, 1988.

able to match or outperform other companies offering the same thing or suitable substitutes for it. A low level of technical competence may be sufficient in the short term if there are no competitors. But in the longer term competitors will undoubtedly enter, producing "shakeout" in the industry, at which time a weak startup is likely to be eliminated.

Business knowhow, to control costs and quality, allocate appropriate resources to marketing and product development, and the like, will also be needed. Without a discipline directing the company to produce a positive bottom line, technical performance alone may not be enough to survive in the short term. And even if it does, it will probably not be enough to survive in the long term.

How effective the business knowhow must be depends on the kind of opportunity the company happens to be exploiting and the strength of such factors as technical competence, patent protection, and contracts. If they are very strong, then the venture may be able to survive considerable bungling of business aspects, at least in the short term. If those other factors are not strong, then the business aspects will have to be correspondingly stronger. Either way, weakness in the business side will detract from the company's performance.

Resources, possibly in the form of venture capital but more often not, are also a key ingredient, as discussed in Chapter 3. Again, it is possible to compensate for weaknesses in other requisites by trading off with greater resources. Or if the opportunity and other elements are strong enough, the outside resources may not be as important and/or will be easier to acquire.

Initiative

To put the startup process into motion, initiative is required on the part of the entrepreneur or entrepreneurial team. The extent to which this will occur is determined by personal "pushes" and "pulls" that act on the individual, as suggested schematically in Figure B–2. They are not mutually exclusive, and to some extent the absence of one factor may be caused by or may even constitute the presence of another.

Pushes

"Pushes" refer to the negative aspects of a potential entrepreneur's present employment that cause him or her to look for something else, either another job or a startup. For instance, a poll of *Venture* magazine readers who had their own companies found that the predominant reason for starting them was job discontent.[9] A study of displaced professionals along Boston's Route 128, for instance, found that 15 percent had moved away but 5 percent had stayed and started their own companies. It seems unlikely that all or even a majority of the 5 percent would have started these companies if they had not been laid off.

As another example, one of the laboratories at M.I.T. from which a substantial number of spinoff companies got their start was said to have had a policy of informing professionals when hired that their tenure would probably

---

[9] "Venture Survey," *Venture,* October 1985, p. 24.

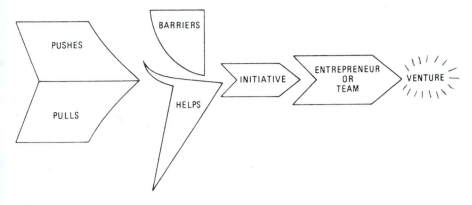

FIGURE B–2 Iimpetus and Drag in Venture Creation.

be limited to five years, thus giving them cause to think about forming their own companies as ex-employment alternatives. When Harvard, observing the rise of IBM in computers during the late forties, decided that computer research was vulnerable to too much commercialism and consequently held back on its own computer research laboratory, An Wang, an employee of the laboratory and inventor of the magnetic core memory, began (in his garage) to work on an enterprise of his own, which he formally started in 1951. By 1982 Wang Laboratories had annual sales of $1 billion and profits of $90 million.[10]

There are other patterns of "push"-inspired startups. Employees who find that their employer is uninterested in an idea may decide to pursue it on their own. Jobs and Wozniak went ahead with Apple only after proposing it to their employers, Atari and Hewlett-Packard, respectively, and having it rejected. Another employee may be frustrated by a career plateau at work. Donna Harrigan quit as Regional Administrator of the SBA in Chicago to start her own labor relations firm because, as she recalled, "I wasn't getting anywhere with the government and my salary was fixed. Why should you be tied to a fixed income when your income can be the result of your own initiative?"[11]

Numerous examples of employees who went out on their own because they believed themselves more competent than their employers have been noted by Collins and Moore, who focused on non-high-technology manufacturing startups.[12] Still other examples of various push factors in high-technology firms

---

[10] *Forbes,* February 15, 1982, p. 36.
[11] *Seattle Times,* February 14, 1982, p. H8.
[12] Orvis Collins, and David Moore, *The Enterprising Man* (East Lansing: Michigan State University Bureau of Business Research, 1964).

have been cited by Draheim,[13] and Susbauer.[14] From interviews with 250 high-technology founders, Cooper reported that 30 percent had quit their prior jobs with no specific plans for the future, 13 percent had to leave because of layoffs, and another 40 percent said they would have quit even if they had not become entrepreneurs.[15]

The need for a job when a person is unemployed is also among the push factors noted by these studies. Its prominence appeared to be highest, however, in a study of four hundred firms, of which 95 percent were in retailing, whole-saling, and services.[16]. Overall the research data show that individuals are more likely to be influenced by negative action rather than positive, and the data on company formations support that conclusion. Negative displacements are found to precipitate far more company formations than do positive possibilities, but, adhering to our notion of vector summation, it is the combination of both positive and negative forces that accounts for most major changes in life paths.[17] A summary of these "push" factors is displayed diagrammatically on the left side of Figure B–2.

Pulls

"Pulls" also come in different forms, as indicated on the right side of Figure B–2. Some pulls are simply the opposite of pushes. For instance, the push of not being able to pursue an idea with a present employer, "idea rejected," corresponds to the pull of being able to pursue it through a startup.

No systematic study of the relative importance of various pulls has been reported, but it appears from individual cases that they depend to some degree on type of venture. The opportunity to pursue a new idea that an employer has turned down seems to be a major factor in the startup of many technologically innovative companies. So too does the extension of financial support from prospective investors, who sometimes offer to set a person up in business, based on their perception of a given business opportunity in combination with their judgment of the particular individual as being capable of forming a com-pany to make the most of that opportunity. (Just who the entrepreneur is in that case, whether the individual selected to set up the company or the capitalist who seeks out and offers backing to that individual, is a moot point.) In contrast, the lure of "sideline" or "moonlight" income usually seems to be the pull that produces startups in such fields as handicraft manufacturing and small services. On the other hand, the pull that produces startups in machine shops

---

[13] Kirk Draheim, "Factors Influencing the Rate of Formation of Technical Companies," in Arnold C. Cooper and John L. Komives, *Technical Entrepreneurship* (Milwaukee, Center for Venture Management, 1972), p. 55.

[14] Jeffrey C. Susbauer, "The Technical Entrepreneurship Process in Austin, Texas," in Cooper and Komives, *Technical Entrepreneurship.*

[15] Arnold C. Cooper, "Incubator Organizations and Technical Entrepreneurship," in Cooper and Komives, *Technical Entrepreneurship.*

[16] Myles S. Delano, Dudley W. Johnson, and Robert T. Woodworth, *The Entrepreneurial Process* (Seattle: University of Washington School of Business, 1966).

[17] Albert Shapero and Lisa Sokol, "The Social Dimensions of Entrepreneurship," in Calvin A. Kent, Donald L. Sexton, and Karl H. Vesper, *Encyclopedia of Entrepreneurship* (Englewood Cliffs, N.J.: Prentice-Hall, 1982), p. 79.

usually seems to be the desire on the part of one of the more competent workers to reap the full rewards of his performance rather than having to share them with his employer.[18] Interestingly enough, the lure of wealth and luxury, although emphasized in magazines and achievements beamed at would-be entrepreneurs (such as *Entrepreneur* magazine), does not seem to be a major factor in the studies of those who examine the more successful entrepreneurs.[19,20]

In all cases there has to be a genuine market opportunity or need if the startup is to succeed. Sometimes it is an important pull for the entrepreneur, even though it may not have been apparent in advance of the startup. Apple's founders had not planned to start a company when they "liberated" parts from their employers to make their first home computer. It was the friends who admired the computer and requested duplicates who got the two founders to start making additional units and selling them.

Personality factors can also play a role in determining which people are impelled to undertake startups ahead of other people similarly situated to accomplish them. As noted in Chapter 1, among the concepts advanced to explain entrepreneurial drive are (1) the need to prove success to an authoritarian father (Collins and Moore[21]), (2) the need to achieve (McClelland[22]), (3) the individual's tendency to operate from an "inner locus of control" (Rotter[23]), (4) the motivation by ego drive and empathy (Swayne and Tucker[24]), and (5) the propensity for taking risks (Brockhaus[25]), as well as other personal values (Brockhaus[26]). There have also been attempts to reshape the psychological makeup of individuals into greater conformity with at least one of these traits—achievement motivation—so as to make them more entrepreneurial, attempts that the experimenters McClelland and Winter claimed were successful.[27] Such experiments have generally been confined to low-income individuals with relatively low educational levels in low-profit types of small firms.

Barriers and Helps

Policy makers interested in enhancing startup performance may be able to introduce or remove a variety of factors that can influence the operation of the entrepreneurial process. These potential barriers and helps have been added

---

[18] Collins and Moore, *The Enterprising Man.*

[19,20] Jane Adams, *Making Good* (New York: Morrow, 1981); and Gene Bylinsky, *The Innovation Millionaires* (New York: Scribner's, 1976).

[21] Collins and Moore, *The Enterprising Man.*

[22] David C. McClelland, *The Achieving Society* (Princeton, N.J.: Van Nostrand, 1961).

[23] J. B. Rotter, "Generalized Expectancies for Internal versus External Control of Reinforcement," *Psychological Monographs,* 1966.

[24] Charles Swayne and William Tucker, *The Effective Entrepreneur* (Morristown, N.J.: General Learning Press, 1973).

[25] Robert H. Brockhaus, Sr., "Risk Taking Propensity of Entrepreneurs," *Academy of Management Journal,* Vol. 23, No. 509, 1980.

[26] Robert H. Brockhaus, Sr., "The Psychology of the Entrepreneur," in Kent et al., *Encyclopedia of Entrepreneurship,* p. 39.

[27] David C. McClelland and David G. Winter, *Motivating Economic Achievement* (New York: Free Press, 1969).

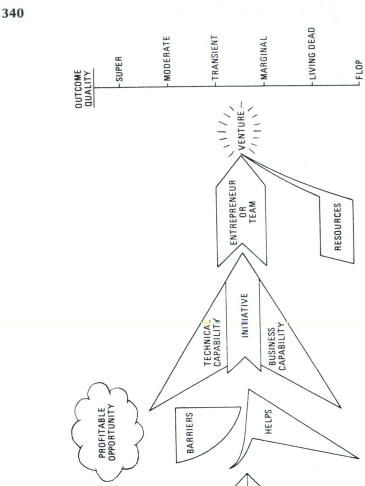

FIGURE B–3

schematically to a combination of Figures B–1 and B–2 to provide an overall depiction of the "chemistry" of entrepreneurship as shown in Figure B–3.

Actions that policy makers can take to influence the barriers, helps, and other elements of the process include the following:

- Enhancing the opportunity for startups by targeting government purchases at new ventures, developing and sharing new technologies with entrepreneurs, allowing private companies to compete more with each other through deregulation, allowing them to compete with governmental services such as the post office, and shifting governmental activities to the private sector through "privatization."
- Removing or reducing barriers by reduction of paperwork and reporting requirements.
- Adding helps such as incubator facilities, training programs in both technologies and business skills.
- Promoting the availability of resources through tax incentives for venture capitalists.
- Encouraging entrepreneurs through recognition of their accomplishments.

Whether any of these actions should be taken must be determined by assessing the benefits of entrepreneurship versus the costs. The benefits will be influenced by how well the additional ventures perform. Different types of ventures, for instance, will presumably yield different types of benefits. A better understanding of venture processes and tracking of results may help not only in assessing this performance but also in improving it.

Costs will take the form not only of financial expenditures but also of other opportunities missed and of political reaction by those with whom the new ventures compete. Careful tracking, study, and analysis should also help with the assessment of these factors as a basis for continual improvement of decision making to encourage venture development.

Bibliography

ADAMS, JAMES L., Conceptual Blockbusting. San Francisco: W. H. Freeman & Company Publishers, 1974.

ADAMS, JANE, Making Good. New York: Morrow, 1981.

ANDERSON, GARY B., "Defining the Game Board," in Stephen C. Diamond, Leveraged Buyouts. Homewood, Ill.: Dow Jones-Irwin, 1985.

ARMOUR, LAWRENCE A., The Young Millionaires. New York: Playboy Press, 1973.

ARRINGTON, LEONARD, Great Basin Kingdom: An Economic History of the Latter Day Saints. Cambridge, Mass.: Harvard University, 1958.

BAILEY, JOHN E., "Developing Corporate Enterpreneurs—Three Australian Case Studies," in Churchill et al., Frontiers of Entrepreneurship Research, 1987.

———, "Learning Style of Successful Entrepreneurs," in Ronstadt et al., Frontiers of Entrepreneurship Research, 1986.

BAILLIE, ALLEN, Strategic Management of Small R & D Subcontractors, PhD dissertation. Seattle: University of Washington, 1978.

BATY, GORDON B., Entrepreneurship for the Eighties. Reston, Va.: Reston Publishing, 1981.

———, Entrepreneurship—Playing to Win. Reston, Va.: Reston, 1974.

BEALE, LEWIS, "Young Entrepreneurs," Venture, October 1983.

BEGLEY, THOMAS M., and DAVID P. BOYD, "Psychological Characteristics Associated with Entrepreneurial Performance," Journal of Business Venturing, Vol. 2, No. 1 (Winter 1987), 79.

BEKEY, MICHELLE, "The Big Bucks Insurance Game," Venture, September 1980, p. 94.

BENNER, SUSAN, "Next Stop Wall Street," Inc., March 1981, p. 37.

BERSHAD, L. D., "Smart Cookies, Handsome Profits," Venture, October 1979, p. 29.

BIRCH, DAVID L., Job Creation in America. New York: Macmillan, 1987.

———, "Live Fast, Die Young," Inc., May 1988.

BIRLEY, SUE, "New Ventures and Employment Growth," *Journal of Business Venturing,* Vol. 2, No. 2 (Spring 1987), 155.

———, "The Role of Networks in the Entrepreneurial Process," in Hornaday et al., *Frontiers of Entrepreneurship Research, 1985.*

BRANDT, STEVEN, *Entrepreneuring.* New York: New American Library, 1982.

———, *Entrepreneuring in Established Companies.* Homewood, Ill.: Dow Jones-Irwin, 1986.

BROCKHAUS, ROBERT H., Sr., "The Psychology of the Entrepreneur," in Kent et al., *Encyclopedia of Entrepreneurship.*

———, "Risk Taking Propensity of Entrepreneurs," *Academy of Management Journal,* Vol. 23, No. 509, 1980.

BRUNO, ALBERT V., JOEL K. LEIDECKER, and JOSEPH W. HARDER, "Patterns of Failure among Silicon Valley High Technology Firms," in Ronstadt et al., *Frontiers of Entrepreneurship Research, 1986.*

BUCHELE, ROBERT B., *Business Policy in Small and Growing Firms.* New York: Harper & Row, 1967.

BURGELMAN, ROBERT A., "Designs for Corporate Entrepreneurship in Established Firms," *California Management Review,* Vol. 26, No. 3 (Spring 1984), 154.

BUSKIRK, RICHARD H., and PERCY J. VAUGHN, JR., *Managing New Enterprises.* St. Paul, Minn.: West, 1976.

BYLINSKY, GENE, *The Innovation Millionaires.* New York: Scribner's, 1976.

BUZZELL, ROBERT D., and BRADLEY T. GALE, *The Pims Principles.* New York: Free Press, 1987.

CALKINS, LAUREL BRUBAKER, "The E.Z. Way," *Inc.,* May 1988, p. 52.

CARSRUD, ALAN L., CONNIE MARIE GAGLIO, and KENNETH W. OLM, "Entrepreneurs—Mentors, Networks and Successful New Venture Development," in Ronstadt et al., *Frontiers of Entrepreneurship Research, 1986.*

CHAMBERS, BRIAN R., STUART L. HART, and DANIEL R. DENISON, "Founding Team Experience and New Performance," Babson Entrepreneurship Research Conference, Calgary, 1988.

CHANDLER, COLBY, "Eastman Kodak Opens Windows of Opportunity," *Journal of Business Strategy,* Vol. 7, No. 1 (Summer 1986), 5.

CHURCHILL, NEIL C., JOHN A. HORNADAY, BRUCE A. KIRCHHOFF, O. J. KRASNER, and KARL H. VESPER, *Frontiers of Entrepreneurship Research, 1987.* Wellesley, Mass.: Babson Center for Entrepreneurial Studies, 1987.

COHEN, DANIEL, "Lore Harp Is Back on Her Feet," *Venture,* July 1988, p. 42.

COHEN, DENNIS J., ROBERT J. GRAHAM, and EDWARD SHILS, "La Brea Tar Pits Revisited: Corporate Entrepreneurship and the AT&T Dinosaur," in Hornaday et al., *Frontiers of Entrepreneurship Research, 1985.*

COLLINS, ORVIS, and DAVID MOORE, *The Enterprising Man.* East Lansing: Michigan State University Bureau of Business Research, 1984.

———, *The Organization Makers.* New York: Appleton-Century-Crofts, 1970.

Committee on Small Business, House of Representatives, *New Economic Realities: The Rise of Women Entrepreneurs,* Report 100–736, Union Calendar No. 448. Washington, D.C., June 28, 1988, p. 1.

COOPER, ARNOLD C., *The Founding of Technologically-Based Firms.* Milwaukee: Center for Venture Management, 1971.

———, "Incubator Organizations and Technical Entrepreneurship," in Cooper and Komives, *Technical Entrepreneurship.*

———, and ALBERT V. BRUNO, "Success among High Technology Firms," *Business Horizons,* Vol. 20 (April 1977), 16.

_____, and WILLIAM C. DUNKELBERG, "A New Look at Business Entry," in Vesper, *Frontiers of Entrepreneurship Research, 1981.*

_____, WILLIAM C. DUNKELBERG, and R. STANLEY FURUTA, "Incubator Organization Background and Founding Characteristics," in Hornaday et al., *Frontiers of Entrepreneurship Research, 1985.*

_____, WILLIAM C. DUNKELBERG, and CAROLYN Y. WOO, "Survival and Failure: A Longitudinal Study," Babson Entrepreneurship Research Conference, Calgary, 1988.

_____, and JOHN L. KOMIVES, *Technical Entrepreneurship: A Symposium.* Milwaukee: Center for Venture Management, 1972.

COSSMAN, E. JOSEPH, *How I Made a Million Dollars in Mail Order.* Englewood Cliffs, N.J.: Prentice-Hall, 1963.

_____, *Entrepreneurial Flow Charts.* Palm Springs, Calif: Cossman International, 1975.

DANDRIDGE, THOMAS C., "Encouraging Urban Entrepreneurship," in Vesper, *Frontiers of Entrepreneurship Research, 1982.*

DELANO, MYLES S., DUDLEY W. JOHNSON, and ROBERT T. WOODWORTH, *The Entrepreneurial Process.* Seattle: University of Washington, 1966.

DENNIS, WILLIAM J., JR., "Explained and Unexplained Differences in Comparative State Business Starts and Start Rates," in Ronstadt et al., *Frontiers of Entrepreneurship Research, 1986.*

DIBLE, DONALD M., *Up Your Own Organization.* Santa Clara, Calif.: Entrepreneur Press, 1971.

DOUTRIOUX, JEROME, and BRANKO F. PETERMAN, "Technology Transfer and Academic Entrepreneurship," in Vesper, *Frontiers of Entrepreneurship Research, 1982.*

DRAHEIM, KIRK, "Factors Influencing the Rate of Formation of Technical Companies," in *Technical Entrepreneurship, a Symposium.* Milwaukee: Center for Venture Management, 1972.

DRUCKER, PETER F., *Innovation and Entrepreneurship.* New York: Harper & Row, 1985.

DUCHESNEAU, DONALD A., and WILLIAM B. GARTNER, "A Profile of New Venture Success and Failure in an Emerging Industry," Babson Entrepreneurship Research Conference, Calgary, 1988.

ELLIS, JEFFREY R., and NATALIE T. TAYLOR, "Specifying Entrepreneurship," in Churchill et al., *Frontiers of Entrepreneurship Research, 1987.*

"Entrepreneurial Development in the People's Republic of China," *International Small Business Journal,* Vol. 5, No. 2 (Winter 1986/87), 37.

FAST, NORMAN D., "Pitfalls of Corporate Venturing and Lessons to Be Learned from Venture Capitalists," working paper. Wellesley, Mass., *Venture Economics,* May 1, 1980.

_____, "A Visit to the New Venture Graveyard," *Research Management,* Vol. 22, No. 2 (March 1979), 18–22.

FATJO, THOMAS J., JR., *With No Fear of Failure.* Waco, Tex.: Word Books, 1982.

Financial Ratios. Philadelphia: Robert Morris Associates, 1978.

"For a Jump-Start, Poland Tries a Jolt of Capitalism," *Business Week,* August 8, 1988, p. 38.

FREIBERGER, PAUL, and MICHAEL SWAINE, *Fire in the Valley.* Berkeley, Calif.: Osborne/McGraw-Hill, 1984.

FUCINI, JOSEPY, and SUZY FUCINI, *Entrepreneurs.* Boston: G. K. Hall, 1985.

GARTNER, WILLIAM B., "Problems in Business Startups," in Hornaday et al., *Frontiers of Entrepreneurship Research, 1984.*

GERTH, H. H., and C. WRIGHT MILLS, *From Max Weber: Essays in Sociology.* Oxford, England: Oxford University Press, 1946.

GOODRICH, DAVID L., *Horatio Alger Is Alive and Well and Living in America.* New York: Henry Regnery, 1971.

GORMAN, MICHAEL, and WILLIAM A. SAHLMAN, "What Do Venture Capitalists Do?" in Ronstadt et al., *Frontiers of Entrepreneurship Research, 1986.*

GOSLIN, L. N., and B. BARGE, "Entrepreneurial Qualities Considered in Venture Capital Support," in Ronstadt et al., *Frontiers of Entrepreneurship Research, 1986.*

GOULD, ALLAN, *The New Entrepreneurs.* Toronto: Seal Books, 1986.

GUPTA, UDAYAN, "Buyouts Go Public," *Venture,* May 1981, p. 18.

HANAN, MACK, *Venture Management.* New York: McGraw-Hill, 1976.

HANSEN, JAMES M., *Guide to Buying or Selling a Business.* Englewood Cliffs, N.J.: Prentice-Hall, 1975.

HARRIS, MARLYS, "Testing the Entrepreneurial You," *Money,* Vol. 7, No. 3 (March 1978).

HARTMAN, CURTIS, "The Cleanup Crew," *Inc.,* December 1984, p. 61.

————, "The Spirit of Independence," *Inc.,* July 1985, p. 64.

HARWOOD, TED, "A Venture Is Not a Game," *In Business,* November–December 1980, p. 42.

HERMANN, CYRIL C., "Ideas for New Business Firms," *Monthly Review.* Federal Reserve Bank of Boston, July 1953.

HILLS, GERALD E., "Market Analysis and Marketing in New Ventures: Venture Capitalists' Perceptions," in Hornaday et al., *Frontiers of Entrepreneurship Research, 1984.*

HISRICH, ROBERT D., and CANDIDA BRUSH, "Women and Minority Entrepreneurs: A Comparative Analysis," in Hornaday et al., *Frontiers of Entrepreneurship Research, 1985.*

HISRICH, ROBERT D., and BARRA O'CINNEIDE, "The Irish Entrepreneur: Characteristics, Problems and Future Success," in Hornaday et al., *Frontiers of Entrepreneurship Research, 1986.*

HISRICH, ROBERT D., and MICHAEL P. PETERS, "Internal Venturing in Large Corporations: The New Business Venture Unit," in Hornaday et al., *Frontiers of Entrepreneurship Research, 1984.*

HOAD, WILLIAM M., and PETER ROSKO, *Management Factors Contributing to the Success and Failure of New Small Manufacturers.* Ann Arbor: Bureau of Business Research, University of Michigan, 1964.

HOBSON, EDWIN L., and RICHARD M. MORRISON, "How Do Corporate Start-up Ventures Fare?" in Hornaday et al., *Frontiers of Entrepreneurship Research, 1983.*

HORNADAY, JOHN A., EDWARD B. SHILS, JEFFRY A. TIMMONS, and KARL H. VESPER, *Frontiers of Entrepreneurship Research, 1985.* Wellesley, Mass.: Babson Center for Entrepreneurial Studies, 1985.

HORNADAY, JOHN A., FRED TARPLEY, JR., JEFFRY A. TIMMONS, and KARL H. VESPER, *Frontiers of Entrepreneurship Research, 1984.* Wellesley, Mass.: Babson Center for Entrepreneurial Studies, 1984.

HORNADAY, JOHN A., JEFFRY A. TIMMONS, and KARL H. VESPER, *Frontiers of Entrepreneurship Research, 1983.* Wellesley, Mass.: Babson Center for Entrepreneurial Studies, 1983.

"I Can't Believe It's Yogurt," *Entrepreneur,* July 1984, p. 24.

Insider Reports. Santa Monica, Calif.: Chase Revel.

"It Wasn't Supposed to Be This Good for the Airlines," *Business Week,* August 8, 1988, p. 24.

JOHANNISON, BENGT, "Network Strategies: Management Technology for Entrepreneurship and Change," *International Small Business Journal,* Vol. 5, No. 1 (Autumn 1986), 19.

————, "New Venture Creation—A Network Approach," in Ronstadt et al., *Frontiers of Entrepreneurship Research, 1986.*

KANTER, ROSABETH MOSS, *The Change Masters.* New York: Simon & Schuster, 1983.

KAZANJIAN, ROBERT K., "Operationalizing Stage of Growth," in Hornaday et al., *Frontiers of Entrepreneurship Research, 1984.*

KELLY, JAMES M., ROBERT A. PITTS, and BONG SHIN, "Entrepreneurship by Leveraged Buyout," in Ronstadt et al., *Frontiers of Entrepreneurship Research, 1986.*

KENT, CALVIN A., DONALD, L. SEXTON, and KARL H. VESPER, *Encyclopedia of Entrepreneurship.* Englewood Cliffs, N.J.: Prentice-Hall, 1982.

KIAM, VICTOR, *Going for It.* New York: Morrow, 1986.

KIDDER, TRACY, *Soul of a New Machine.* Boston: Little, Brown, 1981.

346

KINGSTONE, Brett, *The Student Entrepreneur's Guide.* Berkeley, Calif.: Ten Speed Press, 1981.

KURSH, HARRY, *The Franchise Boom.* Englewood Cliffs, N.J.: Prentice-Hall, 1962.

LALLANDE, ANN, "No Time to Write a Business Plan," *Venture,* July 1983, p. 70.

LAMONT, LAWRENCE M., *Technology Transfer, Innovation and Marketing in Science Oriented Spinoff Firms,* PhD dissertation, University of Michigan, 1969.

———, "What Entrepreneurs Learn From Experience," *Journal of Small Business Management,* July 1972, p. 36.

LAWYER, KENNETH, et al., *Small Business Success: Operating Executive Characteristics.* Cleveland: Bureau of Business Research, Case Western Reserve University, 1963.

LEONARD-BARTON, DOROTHY, "Interpersonal Communication Patterns among Swedish and Boston-Area Entrepreneurs," in Hornaday et al., *Frontiers of Entrepreneurship Research, 1983.*

LEVERING, ROBERT, MICHAEL KATZ, and MILTON MOSKOWITZ, *The Computer Entrepreneurs.* New York: New American Library, 1984.

LEVINE, JOHN, "5,000 Entrepreneurs and Counting," *Venture,* January 1982, p. 75.

LIPPER, ARTHUR, III, "Chairman's Comment," *Venture,* March 1985, p. 4.

LITTMAN, JONATHAN, "The Karma of Jugi Tandon," *California Business,* June 1988, p. 29.

LIVESAY, HAROLD, "Entrepreneurial History," in Kent et al., *Encyclopedia of Entrepreneurship.*

LONG, WAYNE A., and W. ED. MCMULLAN, "Mapping the New Venture Opportunity Identification Process," in Hornaday et al., *Frontiers of Entrepreneurship Research, 1984.*

LONG, WAYNE A., and NOBUKI OHTANI, "Facilitating New Venture Development through Market and Design Feasibility Study," in Ronstadt et al., *Frontiers of Entrepreneurship Research, 1986.*

LOW, MURRAY, and IAN MACMILLAN, "Entrepreneurship: Past Research and Future Challenges," *Journal of Management,* Vol. 14, No. 2 (June 1988), 139.

MCCLELLAND, DAVID C., *The Achieving Society.* Princeton, N.J.: Van Nostrand, 1961.

———, and DAVID G. WINTER, *Motivating Economic Achievement.* New York: Free Press, 1969.

MCGARRY, EDMUND D., "Mortality in Retail Trade," in Godfrey M. Lebhar, *Chain Stores in America; 1959–1962.* New York: Chain Store Publishing, 1963.

MCGUIRE, JOSEPH W., *Factors Affecting the Growth of Manufacturing Firms.* Seattle: School of Business, University of Washington, March 1963.

MACMILLAN, IAN C., "The Politics of New Ventures," in Vesper, *Frontiers of Entrepreneurship Research, 1981.*

———, ZENAS BLOCK, and P. N. SUBBA NARASHIMA, "Corporate Venturing: Alternatives, Obstacles Encountered, and Experience Effects," *Journal of Business Venturing,* Vol. 1, No. 2 (Spring 1986), 177.

———, and DIANA L. DAY, "Corporate Ventures into Industrial Markets: Dynamics of Aggressive Entry," *Journal of Business Venturing,* Vol. 2, No. 1 (Winter 1987), 29.

MANCUSO, JOSEPH R., "The Entrepreneur's Quiz," *Executive,* Vol. 4, No. 1, 12.

———, *Fun & Guts, the Entrepreneur's Philosophy.* Reading, Mass.: Addison-Wesley, 1973.

———, "William C. Durant, the Forgotten Entrepreneur," *The Entrepreneurial Manager's Newsletter,* Vol. 9, No. 1 (October 1987), 1. New York: Center for Entrepreneurial Management.

MAYER, KURT B., and SIDNEY GOLDSTEIN, *The First Two Years: Problems of Small Firm Growth and Survival.* Washington, D.C.: Small Business Administration, Government Printing Office, 1961.

MEHLER, MARK, "A Calculator or Perhaps a Ouija Board?" *Venture,* July 1986, p. 26.

"Merger Lemons," *Mergers and Acquisition,* Vol. 1, No. 1 (Fall 1965), 36.

MILLER, ALEX, ROBERT WILSON, and WILLIAM B. GARTNER, "Entry Strategies of Corporate Ventures in Emerging and Mature Industries," in Churchill et al., *Frontiers of Entrepreneurship Research, 1987.*

MILLER, HARRY, *The Way of Enterprise*. London: Deutsch, 1963.

MITTON, DARYL G., "The Anatomy of a Leveraged Buyout," in Vesper, *Frontiers of Entrepreneurship Research, 1982*.

———, "No Money, Know How, Know Who," in Hornaday et al., *Frontiers of Entrepreneurship Research, 1984*.

MOORE, HARRISON, "You Can't Run a Company by the Numbers Alone," *Inc.*, September 1981, p. 74.

MORRISON, ROBERT S., *Handbook for Manufacturing Entrepreneurs*. Cleveland: Western Reserve Press, 1973.

MUELLER, ROBERT K., "Venture Vogue: Boneyard or Bonanza?" *Columbia Journal of World Business*, Spring 1973, p. 78.

MULLICH, JOE, "Club Mania," *California Business*, May 1988, p. 34.

MURPHY, THOMAS P., *A Business of Your Own*. New York: McGraw-Hill, 1956.

NEISWANDER, D. KIRK, and JOHN M. DROLLINGER, "Origins of Successful Start-up Ventures," in Ronstadt et al., *Frontiers of Entrepreneurship Research, 1986*.

"New High Technology Firms Post 80% Success Record," *Industrial Research*, November 1970, p. 26.

ORENBUCH, DONALD I., "The New Entrepreneur or Venture Manager," *Chemical Technology*, October 1971, p. 584.

OSBORNE, ADAM, and JOHN DVORAK, *Hypergrowth, The Rise and Fall* of Osborne Computer Corporation. New York: Avon Books, 1984.

OSGOOD, W. R., and W. E. WETZEL, "Systems Approach to Venture Initiation." Paper presented to Academy of Management Annual Meeting, Kansas City, Mo., August 1970.

PALMER, MICHAEL, "The Application of Psychological Testing to Entrepreneurial Potential," *California Management Review*, Vol. 13, No. 3, 32.

"The Peace Corps' New Frontier," *Business Week*, August 22, 1988, p. 62.

PHILLIPS, BRUCE D., and BRUCE A. KIRCHHOFF, "An Analysis of New Firm Survival and Growth," Babson Entrepreneurship Research Conference, Calgary, 1988.

PINCHOT, GIFFORD, III, *Intrapreneuring*. New York: Harper & Row, 1985.

———, "Intrapreneurship, Holding onto People with Ideas," *International Management*, March 1982.

PORTER, MICHAEL E., *Competitive Strategy*. New York: Macmillan, 1980.

Proceedings of the First Karl A. Bostrom Seminar in the Study of Enterprise, April 25, 1969. Milwaukee, Center for Venture Management.

REYNOLDS, PAUL D., "New Firms: Societal Contribution versus Potential," Journal of Business Venturing, Vol. 2, No. 3 (Summer 1987), 231.

———, "Predicting Contributions and Survival," in Ronstadt et al., *Frontiers of Entrepreneurship Research, 1986*.

RICHMAN, TOM, "Going Their Way," *Inc.*, December 1983, p. 70.

———, "A Tale of Two Companies," *Inc.*, July 1984, p. 38.

ROBERTS, EDWARD B., "How to Succeed in a New Technology Enterprise," *Technology Review*, Vol. 73, No. 2 (December 1970), 25.

———, in Cooper and Komives, *Technical Entrepreneurship*, p. 139.

ROBERTS, E. D., and ALAN B. FROHMAN, "Internal Entrepreneurship: Strategy for Growth," *Business Quarterly*, Spring 1972, pp. 71–78.

ROCKEY, EDWARD H., "Envisioning the New Business," in Ronstadt et al., *Frontiers of Entrepreneurship Research, 1986*.

RONSTADT, ROBERT, "The Corridor Principle," *Journal of Business Venturing*, Vol. 3, No. 1 (Winter 1988), 31.

———, "Does Entrepreneurial Career Path Really Matter?" in Vesper, *Frontiers of Entrepreneurship Research, 1982.*

———, "Every Entrepreneur's Nightmare: The Decision to Become an Ex-entrepreneur and Work for Someone Else," in Hornaday et al., *Frontiers of Entrepreneurship Research, 1985.*

———, JOHN A. HORNADAY, REIN PETERSON, and KARL H. VESPER, *Frontiers of Entrepreneurship Research, 1986.* Wellesley, Mass.: Babson College, 1986.

ROSCOE, JIM, "Can Entrepreneurship Be Taught?" *MBA Magazine,* June–July 1973, p. 12.

ROSENE, MARCELLA, "Building a Mini-Conglomerate," *Venture,* January 1980, p. 24.

ROTTER, J. B., "Generalized Expectancies for Internal versus External Control of Reinforcement," *Psychological Monographs,* 1966.

RUSSELL, SABIN, "Life After Memorex," *Venture,* August 1984, p. 44.

SAHLMAN, WILLIAM A., and HOWARD H. STEVENSON, "Capital Market Myopia," in Hornaday et al., *Frontiers of Entrepreneurship Research, 1985.*

SANDBERG, WILLIAM R., and CHARLES W. HOFER, "The Effects of Strategy and Industry Structure on New Venture Performance," in Ronstadt et al., *Frontiers of Entrepreneurship Research, 1986.*

SANDMAN, PETER, and DAN GOLDENSON, *How to Succeed in Business Before Graduating.* New York: Collier Books, 1968.

SATHE, VIJAY, "Managing an Entrepreneurial Dilemma," in Hornaday et al., *Frontiers of Entrepreneurship Research, 1985.*

SCHOLLHAMMER, HANS, "Internal Corporate Entrepreneurship," in Kent et al., *Encyclopedia of Entrepreneurship.*

SCHON, D. A., "Champions for Radical New Inventions," *Harvard Business Review,* March–April 1963, p. 84.

SCHUMPETER, JOSEPH A., *The Theory of Economic Development.* Cambridge, Mass.: Harward University Press, 1934.

SEXTON, DONALD L., and NANCY B. BOWMAN, "Validation of a Personality Index," in Ronstadt et al., *Frontiers of Entrepreneurship Research, 1986.*

SHAPERO, ALBERT, "The Process of Technical Supply Formation in a Local Area," in Cooper and Komives, *Technical Entrepreneurship.*

———, and LISA SOKOL, "The Social Dimensions of Entrepreneurship," in Kent et al., *Encyclopedia of Entrepreneurship.*

SHOEN, L. S., *You and Me.* Las Vegas: AMERCO, 1980.

SHUMAN, JEFFREY C., JOHN A. SEEGER, JUDITH B. KAMM, and NICHOLAS C. TEEBAGY, "An Empirical Test of Ten Entrepreneurial Propositions," in Ronstadt et al., *Frontiers of Entrepreneurship Research, 1986.*

SILVER, A. DAVID, *Entrepreneurial Megabucks.* New York: Wiley, 1985.

SLUTSKER, GARY, "The New Publishers in Computer Software," *Venture,* September 1980, p. 79.

Small Business Administration, *The State of Small Business.* Washington, D.C.: Government Printing Office, 1988.

SMALL, MARVIN, *How to Make More Money.* New York: Pocket Books, 1953.

SMITH, NORMAN R., *The Entrepreneur and His Firm.* East Lansing: Bureau of Business and Economic Research, Michigan State University, 1967.

———, and REIN PETERSON, "Entrepreneurship: A Culturally Appropriate Combination of Craft and Opportunity," in Ronstadt et al., *Frontiers of Entrepreneurship Research, 1986.*

STUART, ROBERT, and PIER A. ABETTI, "Field Study of Start-up Ventures," in Ronstadt et al., *Frontiers of Entrepreneurship Research, 1986.*

SUSBAUER, JEFFREY C., "The Technical Entrepreneurship Process in Austin, Texas," in Cooper and Komives, *Technical Entrepreneurship.*

SWAINE, MICHAEL, "How the TRS–80 Was Born," *Infoworld,* August 31, 1981, p. 40.

SWAYNE, CHARLES, and WILLIAM TUCKER, *The Effective Entrepreneur.* Morristown, N.J.: General Learning Press, 1973.

UTTAL, BRO, "Inside the Deal That Made Bill Gates $350,000,000," *Fortune,* July 21, 1986, p. 23.

VAN DE VEN, ANDREW H., ROGER HUDSON, and DEAN M. SCHROEDER, "Designing New Business Startups," *Journal of Management,* Vol. 10 (1984), 87.

VAN SLOOTEN, JOHN D., ROBERT LAYNE HILD, and H. KEITH HUNT, "Characteristics of Collegiate Entrepreneurs and Their Ventures," in Ronstadt et al., *Frontiers of Entrepreneurship Research, 1986.*

"Venture Survey," *Venture,* October 1985, p. 24.

"Venture Survivability," in Churchill et al., *Frontiers of Entrepreneurship Research, 1987.*

VERITY, JOHN W., "Startups Emulate IBM with PC's," *Venture,* June 1983, p. 86.

VESPER, KARL H., *Entrepreneurship and National Policy.* Chicago: Heller Institute for Small Business, Walter E. Heller International Corporation, 1983.

———, *Entrepreneurship Education, 1985.* Wellesley, Mass.: Babson Center for Entrepreneurial Studies, 1985.

———, *Frontiers of Entrepreneurship Research.* Wellesley, Mass.: Babson Center for Entrepreneurial Studies, 1981.

———, *Frontiers of Entrepreneurship Research, 1982.* Wellesley, Mass.: Babson College, 1982.

———, "Venture Idea Sources," *Proceedings, Annual Meeting of the American Institute for Decision Sciences.* St. Louis, 1978.

———, and DAVID R. HAGLUND, " Strategies and Barriers to Growth in Job Machine Shops," *Proceedings of the Academy of Management Annual Meeting,* 1978.

———, and THOMAS G. HOLMDAHL, "Venture Management in More Innovative Large Industrial Firms," *Research Management,* May 1973, pp. 16 and 30.

WANG, AN, *Lessons.* Reading, Mass.: Addison-Wesley, 1986.

WEAVER, PETER, *You, Inc.* Garden City, N.Y.: Doubleday, 1973.

WEBER, DAVID, "Will LBO's Rise Again?" *California Business,* February 1988, p. 40.

WEBSTER, F., "A Model for New Venture Initiation," *Academy of Management Review,* Vol. 1, No. 1 (January 1976), 26.

WETZEL, WILLIAM E., and IAN G. WILSON, "Seed Capital Gaps," in Hornaday et al., *Frontiers of Entrepreneurship Research, 1985.*

WHITE, JERRY, "The Rise of Female Capitalism—Women as Entrepreneurs," *Business Quarterly,* Spring 1984, p. 133.

WHITE, RICHARD, JR., *The Entrepreneur's Manual.* Radnor, Pa.: Chilton, 1977.

WITT, SCOTT, *Second Income Money Makers.* Englewood Cliffs, N.J.: Prentice-Hall, 1975.

WOODRUFF, A. M., and T. G. ALEXANDER, *Success and Failure in Small Manufacturing.* Pittsburgh: University of Pittsburgh Press, 1958.

WOODWORTH, ROBERT T., et al., *The Role of Accountants, Bankers, Lawyers and Government Agencies in the Entrepreneurial Process.* Seattle: University of Washington, 1974.

WORTHY, FORD S., "Wes Threatens to Pull Out of Wesray," *Fortune,* July 21, 1966, p. 50.

WORTMAN, MAX, "Entrepreneurship: An Integrating Typology and Evaluation of Empirical Work in the Field," *Journal of Management,* Vol. 13, No. 2 (Summer 1987), 259.

Index

SUBJECT INDEX

Absentee owner, 265
Acquirers, 7
Acquisition, 246
Acquisition sources, twenty, 273
Acquisition, detailed checkout, 286–290
Acquisition, legal aspects, 312
Acquisition, price, 294
Acquisition, tax considerations, 310
Acquisition, three components, 291
Adjusted book value, 295
Adjusted Cash value, 298
Advance Study, 25
Advisability, 19
Ambitious Ventures, 16
Apparent Value Manipulation, 8
Assets, purchase of, 266
Auction 44, 296
Auctioneer, 322
Autonomy of corporate ventures, 325, 328

Bankruptcy takeover, 319
Barriers, 339
Begat chart, 51
Blake and Mouton Grid, 11
Book value, 294, 304
Borrowing Capacity, 254
Breakeven, 97
Breakeven analysis, 169
Breakeven, time to, 119
Brokers, business, 275
Bugs, 260
Bulk sales act, 313
Business format franchising, 218

Capital Aggregators, 7
Capital, starting, 52
Capitalization and success, 52–55
Capitalization level, 15
Cash down payment, 302
Cash, shortage of, 254
Catastrophes, chain of, 254
Channel, wrong choice of, 123
Chapter XI, 320
Checkout questions, 287
Chemistry of entrepreneurship, 332
Coca Cola, 4
Cold–call, 273
Collaboration, 46–50
Combinations of Wedges, 251
Commercial lending officers, 275, 278
Competition, 250
Competitive advantage, 192

Competitive current bid, 198
Competitive patterns, 35
Competitive Shield, 185–188
Competition, 259
Confidentiality agreement, 133
Connections, 46, 145
Constraints, Legal, 132–136
Consultants, 275
Contacts, critical role of, 242
Contacts, personal, 109
Contacts, seeking, 154
Control, 108
Copyright, 135
Corporate Ventures, 15
Corporate versus independent ventures, 328
Corridor principle, 92
Craftsman entrepreneur, 5
Credit line, 97
Crowd caps, 68
Cultivated ventures:
   corporate, 330
   independent, 332
Cultivating ventures, 324
Curricular followons, 66, 71
Curricular startups, 66
Curtis–Toledo, 267
Customer beliefs, 194
Customer constraints, 194, 195
Customer Contract, 234–237
Customer habits, 194
Customer orders, 109

Deadly 2 percent syndrome, 163, 189
Deal to Dealers, 4
Deck Staking, 156
Degree of Advantage, 201
Degree of Innovation, 15
Delay line, 232
Delta Faucets, 4
Demographics, 227
Detailed checkout of venture idea, 165–167
Differentiation, Product, 251
Direct job outgrowth, 75
Direct postgraduate startups, 67, 75
Discontinuance, reasons, 20
Discounted cash flow, 298
Disposition, 269
Distinctive competence, 189
Distress situations, 281
Doctrine of merger, 313
Domestic breakup, 265

351

Downside risk, 170
Downstream development, 252
Dropout ventures, 66, 74

Economics of Entrepreneurship, 16
Economy–of–Scale Exploiters, 6
Education, importance of, 39
Elements in venture creation, 335
Entrepreneurial Work, 17
Entrepreneurship and Environment, 16
Entry Barriers, 35, 194–196
Environmental Sciences Corp., 271, 274
Established relationships market, 123
Experience, 257
Experience, how it works, 43
Experience, importance of, 39
Experience, not necessary, 108
External venturing, 325
Extracurricular followons, 66

Failure Causes, High Technology, 38
Failure Correlates, 37
Fair market value, 297
Family ventures, 86, 88, 89
Favored Purchasing, 249
Feasibility, apparent, 160
Female Entrepreneurship, 14
Financial Analysis, 168–171
Financing sources, dealing with, 309
Financing, operational, 124
Financing, operational, failure to obtain, 119
Fireside Lodge Corp, 70
Five key ingredients, 109
Foreseeing venture, 98
Formalization, 252
Fostering Entrepreneurship, 16
Founder, typical, 40
Franchise, 135
Franchise Entry, 194
Franchising, 217–224
Franchisor, becoming a, 221
Fraud, 8, 289
Future earnings, basis for acquisition, 296

Geographical Transfer, 226
Government Policy, 247
Government Sponsorship, 249
Growth level, 14
Guarantees of payment, 302, 305

Habits, 258
Happenstance versus planning, 22
Head start factors, 160
Helps, 341
High–growth ventures, 173, 183–185
High–pay, stably small ventures, 171, 179–183
High–profit Franchisee, 220
Historical earnings, basis for acquisition, 296
Hobby, choice of, 154

Home to venture, 86
Homemaker–Started, 86
Hours worked, 19
Hurdles, three main, 119

Idea checkout questions, 172
Idea, high margin, 124, 127
Idea, product or service, 109
Ideal Ventures, economically, 188
Ideas, from deliberate search, 147–151
Ideas, from hobbies, 143–145
Ideas, from self–employment, 140
Ideas, from social encounters, 145
Import Substitution, 250
Inception point, 97
Incubator, 36, 51, 341
Independence, 20, 21, 24
Independent Innovators, 5
Independent Ventures, 14
Individual makeup, 58
Industrial sector, 15
Industry choice, importance of, 32–34
Industry maturity, 35
Industry, structure, 35
Industry–Strategy Interaction, 34
Informal investors, 125
Initiative, 336
Initiative from below, 325
Inner locus of control, 339
Insider Reports, 180, 214, 226
Installment payments, 302, 304
Integration, degrees of, 252
Internal entrepreneurship, 324, 328
Intrapreneur, 3
Intrapreneurship, 324
Invention agreement, 134, 135
Inventors, teaming with, 138
Invitation, 127
IRS, 312

Job selection, 153
Job to venture, 76
Joint Ventures, 240

Kanter, Rosabeth Moss, 3
Knothole, 103
Knowhow, importance of, 284
Knowhow, technical and business, 335
Komives, John, 3

Lawyer, 136
Leads, locating, 269–278
Lease, 97
Leavitt, Harold J., 3
Legal aspects of acquisition, 312
Leverage, 252
Leveraged buyouts, 306
Levey, Morton and Fryer, Jerry, 209
License, 134–138

Licensing, 240, 241
Licensing Executives Society, 137
Life style, 155
Lipper, Arthur III, 3
Liquidation value, 295
Loan, guarantee of, 264
Long–term viability, 171
Low-pay Small Firms, 176
Low–pay, stably small ventures, 171

Management practices, 55–58
Margin, 288
Margin, profit, 120
Market Analysis, 167
Market hole, 207
Market Relinquishment, 244
Market Segments, 251
Market share, 189
Markets, long warmup, 123
MESBICS, 13
Message, choice of, 123
Milestones in venture creation, 96
Minority Enterprise, 13
Model, quest for general, 98
Moonlighting, 154

Natural versus cultivated ventures, 330
Need for Achievement, 10
Need Hierarchy, 11
Need to achieve, 339
Negotiation of acquisition, 316
New Product, 197
New Services, 203
Non–cash buyout, 304
Noncompetitive agreement, 135, 214

Occupational starting points, 65
Off–campus sidelines, 66, 70
On–campus sidelines, 66
Opportunity, identifying, 99
Opportunity, 229, 247, 260, 334, 335
Opportunity driven, 3
Opportunity, acquisition, 261
Opportunity, better, 265
Opportunity, discovery of, 64
Opportunity, waiting for, 270
Ownership, retention of, 46

Parallel Competition, 193, 207
Parallel Products, 213
Parallel Services, 209
Parent Company Sponsorship, 239
Partial Momentum, 225
Partners, 46
Patent, 135
Patent rights, 24, 244
Pattern Multipliers, 6
Payment servicing capacity, 297
Payment with stock, 302, 305
Payoffs of venturing, 161

Payroll, 97
Pedestrian observations, 146
Personal contacts, 50
Personal exposure, 153
Planned direct pots-job, startup, 75, 79
Planning and success, 56–57
Pre-venture stage, 99
Preliminary screening, 162–165
Price of venturing, 161
Price/earnings ratios, 297
Pricing methods for acquisition, 295
Prior choices, 50
Prior employment, as idea source, 129–136
Product Introduction, speed of, 252
Product Service Combinations, 216
Product warranties, 314
Product–Service Sequences, 205
Profitability correlates, 36
Projecting the enterprise, 103
Psychological characteristics, 58
Psychology of Entrepreneurs, 10
Pulls, 338
Purchase agreement terms, 315
Pushes, 336

Ratios of expenses, 163, 165
Reasons for selling company, 285
Recycling, 104
Relatedness, 266
Repeat order, 97
Replacement cost, 296
Requisites for Entrepreneurship, 334
Resignation to start, 82
Resources, 336, 341
Resources, physical, 109
Retirement to start, 85
Rights, 136
Rigidity, 255
Risk, 22
Risk taking propensity, 339
Road map for venture, 100
Role, deterioration of, 103
Royalty, 304, 305
Rule Changes, 250
Rules of thumb, pricing companies, 300

Sales scheme, failure to develop, 119, 122
Savings, personal, 124
SBA, 249, 258, 276, 278
School to venture, 66
Scope, 251
Screening of acquisitions, preliminary, 278–282
Second Sourcing, 237–239
Seed purchase, 311
Selection factors, 159
Seller's preconception, 301
Seller's warranties, 315
Selloff of Division, 245

Sequence, best, 112
Sequences, in conventional manufacturing, 102
Sequences, in high–tech manufacturing, 105
Sequences, in other fields, 106
Sequential Entrepreneurship, 89
Set asides, small business, 250
Shakeups, 255
Shareholders, number of, 293
Side street effects, 91, 141
Sideline startups, 75, 77
Similar venture sequences, 89
Small Business Management, 15
Sociology of Entrepreneurship, 12
Solo Self–employed, 3
Stably Small Firms, 173–176
Stages, six in venture formation, 99
Starters and runners, 90
Strategic Planning Institute, 36
Strategic position, 34–36
Strategically bold moves, 325
Strategies of size, 176–179
Study, 154
Success, measurement of, 31
Success, rules for, 29
Supply Shortage, 229
Survival rates, 31–34
Swayne-Tucker model, 101
Switching costs, 194, 195

Takeoff, 185
Tangential opportunities, 75, 77
Tax considerations in acquisition, 310
Tax liabilities, 314
Team size, 48
Team, external, 46, 48

Team, internal, 46, 47
Teams, 47–50
Technical Knowhow, 109, 195
Technology type, 15
Terms, 267
Terms of the deal, 302–309
Theory X, Y, 11
Time, for startup 118
Timing, 36
Trade secret, 133
Trademark, 135, 241
Trap situations 283–286
Trial and error, 189
Turbulent industries, 252
Turnaround, 185
Twain, Mark, 127, 200
Two-stage growth, 184
Tycoon History, 9
Types of Entrepreneurs, 2–7

Unemployment to venture, 80
Unsuccessful products, 200
Unutilized Resources, 232
Upside potential, 170
Use of options, 302, 308

Varied venture sequences, 89
Vector Graphic, 88
Venture alertness, 153
Venture Capitalists, view on failure, 37
Venture divisions, 325
Venture idea, failure to obtain, 119
Venture idea, high margin, 120, 121
Venture type, 14
Vision, 98

Working capital, 260

ENTREPRENEURS AND VENTURES INDEX

Abbott, James N. Jr., 263
Allen, Paul, 74
Advanced Micro Devices, 237
Alza, 105, 116
Amdahl, Gene, 215
Ampex, 5, 51
Analog Devices, 190, 241
Anderson, Reid, 8
Anderson, Vern, 156
Apple, 61, 199, 255, 337
Arcadia Metal Products, 214
Arden, Elizabeth, 93
Armstrong, Thomas, 93
Ash, Mary Kay, 216
AST Research, 143
Atari, 61
Avis, Warren, 188

Baldwin, Dwight, pianos, 93
Ball Jars, 93
Barish, Keith, 145
Bean, L.L., 147
Bean, Ron, 88
Berkeley, Bernard, 145
Bissell, Anna and Melville, 92
Blueberry Woolens, 6
Bowmar, 124, 161
Box, William and Kennedy, William, 213
Bradley, Milton, 93
Braunstein, Michael, 208
Bricklin, Dan, 62
Browning–Ferris, 193
Buchtal, Stan, 74
Buick, 242
Bushnell, Nolan, 61

Business Opportunities section, 260, 269, 274

Calina Industries, 215
Carpenter, Ken, 267
Carter, Carol, 6
Carver, Bob, 185
Citation Cards, 213
Clark, Chip and Lovin, Rusty, 214
College Marketing & Research Corp., 70
Colonel Sanders, 6, 222
Colt, Samuel, 10
Comdex, 7
Computerland, 6, 141
Cossman, E. Joseph, 100, 149, 214, 232, 233
Cowen, Joshua Lionel, 92
Cramer, Kirby and Opdyke Wally, 78, 271, 274
Crane, Richard, 4
Crazy Eddie's, 268

Deere, John, 4
Denny's, 6
Diefenbach, Otto, 146
Dr. Pepper, 4
Digital Equipment Corporation, 193
Digital Research, 193
Dimplex, Ltd., 263
Diners Club, 146
Dotts, Dick, 267
Durant, Billy, 241
Dussman, Peter, 267

Ebony, 77
Ederer, Dave, 258, 261, 262, 266, 267, 299, 302–304, 311, 319
Edgerton, Harold, 236
EG&G, 236
Ely, Carol, 89
Eveready Flashlight, 92
Evinrude, 146

Fairyland, 145
Farrell's Ice Cream, 210
Fatjo, Tom, 193
Fed Mart, 6
Federal Express, 6, 193
Fields, Debbie, 216
Fly Cake, 233
Ford, Henry, 5, 9

Gates, Bill and Allen, Paul, 74
General Motors, 241
Gerstenzang, Leo, 146
Gibson Greeting Cards, 308
Gillette, King C., 146
Gofette, Patricia, 87
Graham, Florence Nightingale, 93
Greenberg, Sanford D., 128

H&R Block, 4
Harp, Bob, 89

Harp, Lore, 89
Harwood, Ted, 36
Helm, Douglas, 7
Henderson and Johnson Paint Co., 262
Hernandez, E. Norman, 261
Hershey, Milton, 10
Hewlett, William, 327
Hewlett–Packard, 5, 76, 106, 255, 327
High-Voltage Engineering, 105
Hires Root Beer, 4
Hobson, John, 210
Holiday Inns, 230
Homesmith, 204
Hosmer, A.J., 139
Hot Rod Magazine, 203
Howard, Bob, 70, 166
Hubert, Conrad, 92

Ikeda, Masayoshi, 77, 117
IMSAI, 142, 199
Inamori, Kazuo, 327
Intel, 105
Intermec, 202
Ionics, 105

Jacobson, Ray, 8
Jenrette, Dick, 107
Jobs, Steve and Wozniak Steve, 61, 255, 337
Johnson, John H., 77
Jones, Jim and Wallace, Joe, 213

K-2 Ski, 52, 91
Kaiser–Fraser, 230
Kaman, Charles, 76
Kaye, David, 213
Kent, Calvin A., 3
Kessler, Carl, 60
Kiam, Victor, 259, 278, 301, 318
Kildall, Gary, 192
Kirschner, William, 82, 86, 90
Knight, Philip, 71
Kohlberg, Kravis and Roberts, 309
Korter, Lewis J., 147
Kresge, Sebastian, 6
Kroc, Ray, 188, 221
Kurtzig, Sandra, 87

Land, Edwin, 5, 141
Lasater, Dan, 107, 130
Lesney Products, 184
Lindsay, Robert, 202
Ling, James, 7, 83, 106, 254, 267
Litronix, 106
Little, James, 7
Liz Claiborne, 6
LTV, 264
Lufkin, Dan W., 107

Manoogian, Alex, 192
Manpower, Inc., 140

Masco, 4
McCarthy, Kenneth E. and Farrell, Robert E., 209
McDonald's, 6, 107, 130, 188, 219, 222
McGowan, William G., 60
McGuire, Sig, 242
MCI, 60
McNamara, Frank, 146
Mecca, Lorraine, 113
Memorex, 51
Meyer, Walter, 21, 166
Microsoft, 74
Millard, William, 6, 141
MITS, 61, 74, 142
Moog, William Jr., 136
Margolis, Robert, 75
Moore, George C., 132
Morss, T.C., 210
Mushroom King, 309

Next, 255
Nicolai, Bill, 143
Nicolai, Carl, 185
Nike, 72
North, Henry E., 214

Olds, Ransome, 9
Olsen, Ken, 193
Osborne Computer, 253
Osborne, Adam, 199, 253

Pedus International, 267
Penney, J.C., 6
Pennies, 117, 155
Perot, Ross, 130
Personal Software, 6
Peterson, Robert, 202
Phase Linear, 185
Pizza Hut, 4
Pizza Pete, 227
Polaroid, 5, 141
Ponderosa, 107
Ponsford, E.R. and Copestick, L.B., 236
Price, Sol, 6

Remington Razor, 259, 301, 318
Riklis, Meshulam, 108

RJR Nabisco, 308
Roberts, Ed, 61
Rudkin, Margaret, 87

Salton, Lewis, 146
Sanders, Jerry, 237
Scheinfeld, Aaron, 140
Schoen, Leonard, 188
Seadyne, 272
Simon, William E., 308
Singer, Isaac, 10
Small, Marvin, 123
Smith, Fred, 193
Smith, Norman R., 5
Smith, Richard and Dell, William, 234
Solartron, 236
Soldner, Duncan, 309
Stata, Raymond and Lorber, Matthew, 190
Steam–stir, 201
Spud gun, 233
Strite, Charles, 146

Tandem Computer, 24
Tandon, Jugi, 187
Tektronix, 5, 52
Teledyne, 264
Textron, 264
Thorssen, Bob, 4
Treybig, James, 24
TRW, 4
Tucker, 230

U–Haul, 188
Utter, Pete, 227

Verbatim, 8
Vidar Corporation, 156
Visicalc, 62

Wyly, Sam, 130

Xerox, 124

Yuen, K.D., 143

Zaffaroni, Alejandro, 116, 166
Zimmerman, William, 266, 267
Zinn, Elias, 268